Buffalo
and Nights

Buffalo Hunt near Red River

Courtesy Glenbow Archives,
Calgary, Canada / NA-1406-7

Buffalo Days and Nights

Peter Erasmus

As told to
Henry Thompson

FIFTH
HOUSE
PUBLISHERS

Front cover painting (detail), "The Prairies in Flower," by Clarence Tillenius, courtesy The Loch Mayberry Gallery, Winnipeg, MB

Cover design by John Luckhurst / GDL

The publisher gratefully acknowledges the support of The Canada Council for the Arts and the Department of Canadian Heritage.

THE CANADA COUNCIL | LE CONSEIL DES ARTS
FOR THE ARTS | DU CANADA
SINCE 1957 | DEPUIS 1957

We acknowledge the financial support of the Government of Canada through the Book Publishing Industry Development Program for our publishing activities.

Printed in Canada.

99 00 01 02 03 / 5 4 3 2 1

Canadian Cataloguing in Publication Data

Erasmus, Peter 1833-1931
    Buffalo days and nights

(Western Canadian classics)
Includes bibliographical references and index.
ISBN: 1-894004-27-2

1. Erasmus Peter, 1833–1931. 2. Northwest, Canadian—History. 3.
    Frontier and pioneer life—Northwest, Canadian. 4. Indians of North
    America—Northwest, Canadian. 5. Pioneers—Northwest, Canadian—
    Biography. I. Title. II. Series
FC3213.1.E73A3 1999   971.2'02'092   C99-910109-9 F1060.9.E73A3 1999

Fifth House Ltd.
#9 - 6125 11 St. SE
Calgary, AB, Canada
T2H 2L6

Contents

Foreword

P ETER ERASMUS LOOMS LARGE in the history of western Canada. He was a member of the Palliser expedition of 1857–60, an interpreter for Methodist missionaries, an eye witness to events during the Riel Rebellion, and—of particular interest to First Nations people—an interpreter at Treaty No. Six. What sets Erasmus's book apart from other more formal histories is the personal nature of his account. It is the story of Erasmus's life as recorded by Erasmus. It is filled with anecdotes, observations, and personal opinions that make readers feel as though they are part of the events.

Erasmus follows a Native practice in telling his story. When an Indian recounts an historical event, whether or not he was part of it, he describes it as though he was there, complete with conversations among the principal participants. Erasmus, raised with a strong tie to Indian ways, follows this practice, no doubt remembering each incident in detail and telling it just as an Indian would, conversations and all. The reader should not think that this is fictionalizing the account—not at all. It is following the ways of his mother's people.

Historians are fortunate that Irene Spry consented in the early 1970s to edit and prepare an introduction to this volume. A painstaking researcher with an eye for detail, she had earlier edited *The Palliser Papers* for publication by The Champlain Society and was already familiar with many aspects of Erasmus's career. She also took the opportunity to interview Henry Thompson, who had worked so closely with Erasmus in putting his reminiscences into order, and to discuss the manuscript with descendants and friends of the author. These included the Edward and Arnold Erasmus families, Peter Shirt, Jr., and Frank Mitchell. All were of great assistance in putting the manuscript into its final form for publication.

Irene Spry was aware that a new edition of *Buffalo Days and Nights* was scheduled for publication, and warmly welcomed its reappearance. Sadly, she did not live to see this occasion. She passed away in Ottawa on December 16, 1998, just as the manuscript was being readied for the printer.

Peter Erasmus was a highly literate and well-educated man for his time. Ralph Steinhauer, Alberta's lieutenant governor, recalled as a boy seeing Erasmus with his manuscript tucked under his arm. The work had obviously been a labour of love and occupied much of his thoughts in later life. His earlier writings and reminiscences may have become the basis for his manuscript, which he and Henry Thompson later prepared, and which is produced here. Too much credit cannot be given to Thompson for the countless hours he spent with the author, filling in details, expanding on information, and producing something that is essentially Erasmus's but which would never have been brought to fruition without Thompson's guidance and direction.

The first and only edition of *Buffalo Days and Nights*, published by the Glenbow Museum in 1976, was extremely well received. Not only was it of interest to historians, but Native people were fascinated by the detailed information it contained about the lives of their ancestors. It also gave a far more detailed account of the signing of Treaty No. Six in 1876 than could ever be found in the official reports of the federal government. That account alone was a major contribution to western history. The original edition has been out of print for several years and has been in continual demand by historians, bibliophiles, and Native people.

From the time of his birth in 1833, Erasmus was not simply an observer of history—he was a part of it. Educated at Red River Settlement, then at Cumberland House by his uncle, the Rev. Henry Budd, Erasmus became a schoolmaster by the age of eighteen. He continued his own studies, including Greek, at the same time. But the urge to travel was irresistible to the young man, and when offered an opportunity in 1856 to act as interpreter for the Rev. Thomas Woolsey in the Fort Edmonton area, Erasmus jumped at the chance. From there he joined the Palliser expedition, thereby fulfilling his love of travel. With Dr. James Hector, Erasmus explored the plains, foothills, and mountains in his quest for knowledge. In the early 1860s, he settled at Whitefish Lake, an area that he called home for the rest of his life. There he was an interpreter, guide, trapper, hunter, and trader. After his assistance in negotiating Treaty No. Six, Erasmus was engaged by the Department of Indian Affairs and remained with them off and on until his retirement in 1912. Peter Erasmus—traveller, trader, and buffalo hunter—died in 1931 at the age of ninety-seven.

Hugh Dempsey
1999

Introduction

T HIS REMARKABLE STORY was told by one remarkable man to another remarkable man. It is a fascinating and revealing account of life on the unsettled prairies and parklands in the old days, vividly imprinted on the memory of one of the great men of the pre-settlement West.

Peter Erasmus lived from 1833 to 1931. His life spanned the critical period during which Rupert's Land became western Canada, the period in which the open buffalo plains were transformed into townsites and farmsteads—policed, surveyed, fenced, settled, and threaded with railroads and roads. That this change took place in the Canadian West without any major Indian war was at least in part due to the notable mixed-blood guides and interpreters who helped the missionaries, explorers, surveyors, police, and other precursors of the new way of life. Among these guides and interpreters Peter Erasmus was outstanding. His long career was remarkable both for his prowess in the old life and for his work as a forerunner of the new. A celebrated buffalo hunter and traveller, he also made a name for himself as a pioneer mission worker, teacher, and interpreter.

When he was 87 years old Erasmus told the story of the first half of his varied and eventful life to Mr. Henry Thompson, now of Lac La Biche. Henry Thompson, himself of mixed blood, describes the circumstances in which he met Erasmus, and wrote down his reminiscences:

I have always enjoyed writing but after receiving a number of rejection slips, sometimes accompanied with advice and a few complimentary, encouraging words, I decided or, rather, was forced to admit, that I must seek some more substantial means of gaining a living.

In August, 1920, I received an assignment to interview Peter Erasmus from an Edmonton newspaper. In spite of my recent decision to quit trying to write, I found myself more than delighted to be on my way to carry out this new work.

I had spent much time in Edmonton libraries and bookstores looking for anything written about past history. I found a variety of information, none of which gave the Native any credit in the building of western History—in fact very little mention at all. Most of what I found was contributed from the records of Hudson's Bay Factors' reports.

Peter Erasmus had been educated by the English Church with the idea of having him don the black robes of the Priesthood. I knew that he had worked among the Indians, first with Mr. Woolsey and then with the Rev. John McDougall for a number of years.

I was personally acquainted with two of his sons, who were men of their word, rated as men of honesty and integrity. I looked forward with much anticipation to this assignment as a wonderful opportunity to learn something of the character and ways of the early Indian people.

Peter Erasmus, being an educated man, would be able to tell if the biased opinions I had gleaned from my reading would be justified from the long, intimate experiences of a man who had married a native woman and had raised two outstanding six foot examples of [the results of] a native marriage.

Erasmus was retired on a small pension from the Dominion Government for his work as an interpreter for the Indians in their negotiations with the Government for the transfer of their rights to the lands occupied by the western Indians.

I learned that Peter Erasmus was staying with his son David Erasmus at Goodfish Lake. I found them camped on a hay field at the flats at Goodfish Lake. When I advised him of the purpose of the trip he did not express any enthusiasm over the idea of my getting some stories of his travels.

"Yes," he answered, "I will consider your proposition tonight and will give you my answer tomorrow morning."

I was rather disappointed that he did not show more interest but realized that I was in no position to demand his co-oper-

x

ation. I spent the rest of that long evening hunting ducks, in order to curb my impatience.

The next morning he called me to his tent. "Yes," he said, "I will give you my story, from my early school days to the last of the Buffalo on the western plains; that is the only way to keep the dates in my memories clear without making some stupid statements, as has happened in stories that I have read in other writings."

This was far more than I had bargained for, and covered far more territory than I had planned for. I knew that Mr. Erasmus would consider no other plan, so I accepted his ideas, as I knew he would consider no other way of telling his story.

It took me the better part of twelve days to write his memories in long hand as I had no typewriter with me. At that time he was approaching an age of ninety years.

When I brought my notes and volume of words to Edmonton, the paper was under new management and refused to honour my first assignment as to days and hours previously agreed of five dollars a day and expenses. I did not put in any bill for any expenses as I had used my own driving team for the trip.

I believe some hot words were exchanged and, as a consequence, I gathered up my papers and departed without any further comment. That is how I came to have the story of "Buffalo Days and Nights".[1]

After operating a ferry across the Saskatchewan from 1910 to 1919, Henry Thompson had become a real estate salesman, but still found time to submit news stories to Edmonton papers during the next few years. In 1928 he moved to a homestead at McRae, a short distance northeast of Goodfish Lake. He found that Peter Erasmus, by then ninety-five years old, was a near neighbour. He "jumped on a saddle horse" and went over to see him to verify uncertain points in his manuscript. Despite the seven years' gap and the fact that the old man had become still older, Henry Thompson was amazed by the unwavering consistency of Erasmus's statements about what he remembered. He decided to complete and type the document instead of throwing it away in disgust, as he had very nearly done. He began to take Erasmus out on fishing trips, thereby making opportunities to discuss with him points in the record about which he was not sure, checking and rechecking and rechecking apparent discrepancies, and being continually astonished at the accuracy of Erasmus's memory.

This book is the result of that painstaking work. It is a

document of substantial importance in the gradually growing record of western Canadian history. Already it has been used in typescript by research workers.[2] Published in this volume, it becomes available to a wider range of readers, having escaped destruction a second time when Henry Thompson's home at McRae, with everything in it, was destroyed by a prairie fire. Luckily the document was at the time in the hands of a publisher and so was saved from the blaze.

The substance of Erasmus's reminiscences are here printed as they were received from Mr. Thompson, but some changes have been made with his approval. The document which he typed from his original manuscript posed a number of difficult editorial problems. Henry Thompson wrote down what Peter Erasmus remembered as he talked of the first half of his life. He worked on the script over a period of time, himself making some changes. Since Erasmus cannot be consulted about problematical points, it has been necessary to steer a middle course between reproducing Mr. Thompson's record exactly as it stands, word for word, and making the normal editorial revisions that a contemporary document would receive. Substantial alterations are explained by a reference note at the appropriate point in the text; minor changes are indicated by an asterisk.

The first essential has been to attempt to preserve the meaning and character of Peter Erasmus's recollections in their full integrity. To achieve this, some modifications have been made in the original typescript in the possession of Glenbow-Alberta Institute, where the document is available in the Archives for consultation. Evident typing errors in spelling (especially in names), syntax, and punctuation have been corrected. Obscure passages have been clarified and revisions made to increase the readability of the finished product. Duplications have been eliminated, and, in an effort to reduce the volume to a manageable length, a few peripheral matters, such as other people's stories, have been left out, but only where the omissions do not affect the significance or substance of Erasmus's recollections.

It is extraordinary how clearly Erasmus, at his great age, remembered events that took place half a century or more before he described them to Henry Thompson. It is not to be expected, however, for all his care and remarkable memory, and for all Mr. Thompson's cross-checking, that Peter Erasmus could, at eighty-seven and ninety-five years of age, looking back on a full and eventful life, remember with perfect precision all the specific particulars and exact sequence of each happening in which he had taken part. In spite of his insistence on accuracy and his and Henry Thompson's efforts to ensure it, there are still, inevitably, a few discrepancies as to places, dates, and persons. Such of these as have been identified are noted in the Introduction or in footnotes, in which, also, references are given to other first-hand accounts that have been found of events about which some disagreement is known to exist. When, in some cases, Erasmus's memory transposed the times at which well known Hudson's Bay Company officers were at specific places, an effort has been made to sort out the date of postings. Similar transpositions of the sequence in which the activities of the Palliser expedition are recounted which do not coincide with the record in the official blue books containing the reports of the expedition, or in Dr. Hector's field notes, or in extant contemporary correspondence, have been noted or, if necessarv, rearranged.[3]

A few passages in the original document have been left out: for example, inadvertent references to trouble at Fort Garry at the time of the second Riel Rising. Historical and geographical impossibilities that seem to have slipped in through misunderstanding have been omitted, and the order of related events adjusted accordingly. Among these are an account of a journey with the geologist of the Palliser expedition, Dr. James Hector, to Fort Chipewyan, Great Bear Lake, and Lac La Biche[4] in 1860, when Hector was already on the Pacific Coast on his way back to England; a journey on horseback to the Pacific Ocean, also in 1860; and a visit to York Factory en route from Red River to Fort Pitt in 1856.

Erasmus's lively impressions of the character and attitudes of Palliser, Hector, and Bourgeau are of great interest, but his memories of their observations seem to have been coloured by later events. His report of their concern about the future of the Indians of the Plains and the problems that would arise as the buffalo grew progressively scarcer is fully borne out by other sources. No evidence has come to light, however, in the papers of the expedition (or elsewhere) that its members believed, as Erasmus states [on page 71 below], that in the United States "a policy of buffalo extermination had been adopted as the quickest way to break down Indian resistance to American authority." The expedition hoped that in British North America the "inevitable extermination" of the "wild Plain Indians" would "not be hastened, as on the eastern frontiers of the United States, by ruthless warfare." Such warfare would be unavoidable if settlers were allowed to push their way into the country before any form of government had been established which would consider the interests of the Indian subjects of the Queen as well as those of the settlers.[5] The dangers foreseen in 1858 and 1859 did not, however, include the wholesale massacre of

xiii

the buffalo by hide hunters that took place between 1867 and 1883, let alone any policy of deliberate extermination; both of these developments were still in the future.

All this suggests that some blurring of time sequences had taken place in Erasmus's memory. Moreover, there are a few instances in which a question arises whether a good story may, perhaps, have grown in retrospect into a better one still. In one or two cases it seems that a fondly regretted "might have been" is described in place of what in sad fact happened, for instance in the account of Charlotte Erasmus's death.

Buffalo Days and Nights cannot, therefore, be taken word for word as a source of precise, factual information. It is none-the-less a record of considerable importance. It gives a vivid picture of the old way of life on the untamed plains and of the traumatic process of change under the pressures of encroaching white "civilization". It gives equally vivid pictures of the character and preoccupations of a number of notable historical figures, and of important happenings such as the inception of missionary enterprises, the smallpox epidemic of 1870, the Carlton Treaty negotiations of 1876, and the Rising of 1885. These are the pictures that had imprinted themselves on the mind of this man who was a descendant of two officers of the Hudson's Bay Company, the son of a European settler in Red River, and also a grandson of a Swampy Cree Indian and a mixed-blood woman. Erasmus had worked on his father's farm and had been profoundly influenced by the ideas of missionaries, as well as by an education designed for a future clergyman. The other side of his heritage gave him a deep sympathy with the Indians' attitudes to wild-life and to nature, to each other, and to unseen spiritual powers. His was the viewpoint of a highly intelligent mixed-blood poised between two cultures and two ways of life. What he remembered, as he looked back over a long life spent between the Red River and the Columbia, and how he interpreted his memories, is, therefore, of more than ordinary interest.

As Henry Thompson points out, in the letter quoted above, the history of the West has been written largely from material in the rich archives of the Hudson's Bay Company. Other sources have been journals, correspondence, and reports of explorers, missionaries, big game hunters, tourists, and government officials—all men who saw the changing life of the plains and mountains of the West from an outsider's point of view. We have not many records left by native observers of the great change from a wandering to a settled life. Edward Ahenakew, of the Plains Cree, and Chief Dan Kennedy, of the Plains Assiniboine, have published reminiscences; Samuel Bull has left a sketch of "100 Years at Whitefish Lake", and Joseph François Dion a "History of the Cree Indian of Western Canada"; while Alexander Sandison, of Red River Settlement, dictated an account of his life in the good old days. Erasmus's memories are a notable addition to this scanty total.

Erasmus personally not only experienced but played an active part in the transition from a free, roving life of hunting, travel, and adventure to a sedentary life subject to the constraints of organized government, property rights, and market prices. He saw the buffalo disappear; he helped in the negotiation of one of the treaties by which the Plains Indians gave up their tribal lands and traditional hunting grounds to the Crown; he worked to get them settled on reserves, as well as to contain the spread of trouble in 1885, when the suppression of the second Riel Rising finally constrained roaming Indian bands and mixed-blood hunters to accept a settled life. He both witnessed and took a hand in the establishment of centralized authority where, formerly, scattered groups of wanderers had been accustomed to living in independence according to their own ideas and concerns—subject only to the decisions of band councils, tribal custom, and the discipline of the buffalo hunt —and the influence of the Hudson's Bay Company. Erasmus himself traded for a time for the Honourable Company, but he played a part in eroding its supremacy, both when he set up as an independent trader and in his restless probing of new economic opportunities that offered some prospect of getting a living outside the fur trade in the service of the Company. As mission worker, interpreter and translator, explorer and mapper's assistant, miner, farmer, trader, government employee, and teacher, he contributed to the diversification and transformation of life in the West.

Born in the Red River Settlement on June 27, 1833, Peter Erasmus was the second son and fifth child of another Peter Erasmus, a Dane who fought in the Battle of Waterloo and came to Rupert's Land in the service of the Hudson's Bay Company, which he left to become a river-lot farmer. His mixed-blood wife, à la façon du pays, was formally married on the day she was baptized, more than a year after her first two children had been baptized. She seems to have cherished her people's folklore, telling the young Peter Indian stories when he was a child. Years later, between 1909 and 1912, when he was living on the Blackfoot Reserve, Erasmus wrote these stories down. Unhappily the record has been lost.

Peter Erasmus, Senior, died when he was 55 years of age, and was buried at St. Andrew's on October 23, 1849. Peter, Junior, was then still in the early stages of his education. He wrote to his uncle by marriage, Horatio Nelson Calder, on June 27, 1850, as follows:

My Dear uncle As the express is about to pass here I would gladly embrace the opportunity of Dropping you a few lines I think it due to our long acquaintanship to write you a few lines in order to let you know that we are all in good helth at presnt time thank the allmighty for all his bllessngs to wards us and I hope that these few lines will find you the same with tears droopping down my cheeks write I to you we have lost our parrent our father the 17th of september 1849 I have no news to inform you of at present time onley that henry has hade a wife a few weeks ago henry has left me alone with my mother and at present we ar all still in the same way of lifing yet so far my father died on a sundy murning on sunday befre he fell sick of the graval he was sick 8 days since you left [??] he cept it to his deth by my assistance thank god for it we are just geting our money the same as befor by selling wheat to the company and our lifing the same thanks be to him that is alls good to us we have got our granny besids us to the care of me she is still in the hand of the living god always unwell since she came here we have hade a very good crop the last seson this year it is coming on very well your sister-in-law sends her complanentss to your wife and famely and you also Your mother in law sends her complainents to you and her daughter he grand childrey also give my complaiments to my brother John Also to charles Michel and nancy by writeing If you plese sir an also to your famely to my mother sister the tears drooping I can not write you good hand writ her I cluse dear uncle your Dear and Affectionate nephew young Peter Rasmus

Peter Rasmus
it is to the care of geor[g]e your brother and I hope it will reach you safe

Henry sends his complaints to all his brothers to the whole of you and I hope that you will try to write me again th first opportunity

Your Dear and affectionate

Peter Rasmus Rasmus[6]

Henry, the older brother, had gone elsewhere to work, and Peter, at the age of sixteen, took over the responsibility for running the farm. By then the farmstead boasted a house, two stables and a barn, one horse, four oxen, two cows, four calves, four pigs and three sheep, one plough, two harrows, and two carts. Nine acres were under cultivation out of a total property of seventy-six acres on the west of Red River and forty-two acres on the east side.[7]

Seemingly, young Peter did not take kindly to farming. He went off on June 3, 1851, to work with his uncle, Henry Budd, at Christ Church Mission, Cumberland (The Pas) in accordance with a three-year engagement made with Bishop Anderson.[8] Under his uncle's supervision he became the schoolmaster, at the same time pursuing his own studies, including Greek, with the Rev. James Hunter as his instructor.[9] Another letter, written in 1852 to Horatio N. Calder, gives an idea of his educational progress and also of the curious mixture of dutiful earnestness and rebelliousness that characterized the young man's attitude to life:

Cumberland Station
August 10th 1852

Mr. Horatia N. Calder
  My Dear Uncle,
          As opportunity offer only once a year to your quarter, I cannot allow such a favourable one as this to pass without writing you these few lines; whereby you may learn that I had the pleasure of receiving your kind, and interesting favours, one of whom is dated 10th March 1851 from the which I had the pleasure of receiving a piece of Gold in its natural state, and another of this year dated 10th March 1852. So I suppose you expect a long letter from me because, I have two of yours to answer.

  I cannot adequately express the joy I had when, I received the piece of Gold. It brought to my remembrance your person, I could not help sheding tears for joy, and gratitude to Almighty God, for having preserved us to thus far of our lives, and in permitting us (poor dust and ashes as we are) to hear how we, and all our friendship's fare though at a distance from each other. But, I hope though we are absent from each other in the flesh, yet, we may be present in Spirit. Yea, believe me that when ever I prostrate myself before the throne of Grace, I remember you, and all the family, to God in my imperect prayers, and I hope you do the same. For it is only by prayer and supplication to God, that we are able to assist each other in this sinful world

  In both of your letters you was wishing that I should go, and see you. I hope your wish will not be in vain; for I am intending by the help of God, that when my time is out, to try and go to see that good Country you live in, that is if the Church Missionary Society will tell me go; for let me tell you, I have a

xvii

great iron Chain to break off of my neck before, I can say, I will go; however I will try to go in a year or two after this one

---

The last accounts I heard from Red River, was on June Last and I am happy to say they were all well in health, and doing well. Henry, and William my brothers are both with my mother, and am happy to say they are errecting fine buildings about the place. As for me I am put to one side by them, I am the poorest among them in the way of lands and houses and Cattle, but not so in money—I was the only one of the family that got nothing after the death of my father, all the rest got except me. I did not get even so much as one hair of an animal, and I was the only one that had brought up those animals they now claim, you know that my father was unable to do anything, and my brother Henry was always in service, and my brother William too young to do anything. I was the only one then left to do any thing, I had to provide hay, and wood, and farm all the crop alone by the help of my poor brother William and all the other hardships that you know that a man is exposed to in Red River. But as I knew it was my duty to obey my poor father, I found it a pleasure to do so. And now, I am no more with them but for myself. And may God assist me in the same. I am now nineteen years of age and when my time is out, I will be twentyone
    This summer the Red River was all in a flood similar to the deluge that was in 1826, and I am informed that many a one lost their houses, biers, barns, and all the buildings they had. I did not see your brother George for he did not come down this way. He went by the Road they went, when they went off. But I am informed that he reached Red River in good health, and strength. According to my aunt's request I have written to my Mother, and granny and told them that you and all the family were well, and they would be happy to receive a few lines from you_____ With regard to myself I am quite well in health, inasmuch that I am able, by the help of God to persue my daily duty_____ I am very happy here, and am glad to say that my name has gone far and near, as a good teacher, and interpreter to the Clergy. May God make a continuance of the same untill the end. I am still living with My Uncle the Rev Hy Budd and am happy to say all is well with him. I think he is writing to you, and will probably be telling you of himself Peter Erasmus[10]

    Peter Erasmus did, indeed, do well as a teacher; the number of children attending school was good and their improvement satisfactory. He also helped his uncle with the translation of the Bible and parts of the Prayer Book into Cree, and surprised the devout missionary by his "improvement" when he addressed the Indians on the subject of confirmation.[11] In 1854 he was sent off to an out-station of the mission which his uncle had established at Upper Nepowewin, just downstream from Fort à la Corne, on the south bank of the Saskatchewan River. There the Indians lived among the buffalo, clothed themselves with their skins, and were "truly heathen and truly barbarian." Peter's main responsibility here too was the school, but he spared no effort in attempting to Christianize these Indians. Shortages of food, however, compelled him to interrupt his work at the mission to go hunting and fishing to procure supplies.[12] Curiously, there is no mention in his reminiscences of this experience.

Erasmus's work as teacher, translator, and evangelist had been so promising that his uncle and the bishop decided that the young man should be sent back to Red River to study at St. John's School with the ministry in view.[13] Peter's story of how he came to abandon his studies is told in the text: after two terms (not years, as stated in the original),[14] he was feeling an increasing lack of both inclination and suitability for the life of a minister. When the Chief Factor[15] of the Hudson's Bay Company offered him a job on the upper Saskatchewan, he jumped at the chance to give up his studies. The Rev. Thomas Woolsey had arrived in the West the year before to take up the work started in the 1840's by the Rev. Robert Rundle, but abandoned when ill health forced him to leave the country. He was looking for an interpreter. Peter Erasmus accepted the job and set off on an exciting journey into the far western wilderness.

The missionary met him at Fort Pitt on September 5, 1856. For the best part of the next two years Erasmus worked with Woolsey as interpreter, voyageur, hunter, builder, freighter, and general assistant in his travels and missionary work. He became a fine horseman and a redoubtable buffalo hunter and traveller. He learned how to make the most of local materials in building, greatly improving the parsonage at Pigeon Lake. He took advantage of contacts with the Blackfoot at Fort Edmonton to learn their tongue, so widening his already impressive command of languages. Woolsey reported that "the people say he gives my words as direct as possible."[16] Erasmus's unusual combination of educated intelligence and his physical hardihood, in which he gloried, fitted him especially well for his work as Woolsey's assistant.

While he was at Fort Edmonton, Dr. James Hector, geologist, naturalist, and medical man to the Palliser expedition, arrived in search of the men who would be needed for the next season's work out on the southern prairies and in the Rocky Mountains. Erasmus took Hector to look for the buffalo hunters from Lac Ste. Anne, who were out on a hunt to the south of the Fort, and who might provide suitable employees for the expedition. With the help of Chief Factor Swanston, Hector engaged Erasmus and a number of other men, and arranged that they should join the expedition at Carlton House in the spring of 1858.

From this time until August 3, 1859, Erasmus travelled and worked with Dr. Hector, who instructed him "in the use of those instruments which rendered him very useful as a surveyor's assistant. . . ."[17] His "qualities as a traveller" Hector had "well ascertained in several hard trips"[18]—a tribute from one legendary traveller to another. The partnership came to a sad end that was later to be a cause of regret to Erasmus. In August, 1859, Hector proposed to travel from the Cypress Hills to the headwaters of the North Saskatchewan with a view to crossing the Rocky Mountains by way of Howse Pass, which Hector called Blaeberry Pass. Erasmus, with good reason, as a letter from W.R. Mitchell establishes, declared the "journey too desperate to undertake, considering the condition of the horses, the rivers that would have to be crossed, and the prospects of food on such a journey."[19] As it turned out, Hector achieved the hazardous venture successfully, but only with great difficulty and danger. He was forced "to curtail his plans" once he was over the Rockies by giving up the project of trying to find a way through or around the Purcell and Selkirk ranges. Instead he had to go directly to Fort Colvile to rejoin Palliser there. Forty-one years later, on June 27, 1900, Erasmus wrote to Hector, when he had become the first Director of the Geological Survey of New Zealand, and Sir James:

Dear Sir:

In the first place I must apologize for presuming to write to you, but I have so often thought of you I cannot resist from troubling you with these few lines which will show you that it was with a proud heart that I came across your name mentioned with great distinction in connection with the Geol: Survey in New Zealand. Many changes have taken place since we parted. The iron horse climbs the R. mountains on to the Pacific through the Kicking horse pass. The cars pass within 10 yards from the spot where the Blonde horse kicked you— little did I think then, when I was so much afraid you was killed, that I would at a future day ride on a different horse from the Sorrel through the same grounds. Wonders never cease!

You and I are the only two living of the party that explored the Kicking horse pass. Sutherland, Brown, and our great Nimrod are dead. The Buffalo are a thing of the past. The last living and dead one I saw and killed was in —'82, near the Cypress Mountain. The country is getting settled up very fast; all from Fort a la Corne away beyond Edmonton is so settled up that there is no need of camping out doors in the open air. There is a town on each side of the River at Edmonton. Another on the Bow R. about 20 miles below the Ghost River, and all along the foot hills from the Red Deer River to Montana, there are Ranchers some with thousands of cattle and horses. There is also another town where we camped at the foot of the Cypress Mountain when the hunters killed the Red Deer if you remember Oh I wish I could fly and go to you for an hour or two then I could tell you all what has happened, and what is going on. A year ago I saw Nimrod at Morley Mission on the Bow R. across the Ghost. R. at the foot of the Mountains—we had a long talk about you and our wanderings through the Mountains. He was then still able to kill Moose, but poor old fellow he died that winter. There are Gold Mines all through the country we travelled through; on the Tobacco Plains and the Kooteny Lake as well. All the old timers that you knew are gone the way of all flesh. Mr. Moberly left the H.B.C. and is living at a place called Prince Albert below Carlton near the junction of the Rivers where there is a large settlement and a big town. When I think of the past there is one thing I am ashamed of and which I cannot forgive myself, that is, when I left you at the foot of the Mountains. If I had not been induced by some fair promise, which I did not realize, I would not this day regret having done the like. From Colville[20] I went to the gold Mines and made a snug little sum of money, and from —76—to 86 I was with the Canadian Gov. in the Indian Department at a Salary of $1000.00 per Annum. I retired after investing all my earnings only to loose it all by the failure of the Commercial Bank.[21] I now find myself a poor man at this my 67th birthday. I would not find it so hard if I was not a victim of Sciatica in both my hips. I know you could help me if I was near enough. Months I am laid up in bed. If it was not for this misfortune I would go to the Gold fields and make another stake.[22] I must close with many good wishes for your welfare and prosperity. I am dear Sir,

You obedient servt

Peter Erasmus.[23]

xxi

How Erasmus got to the gold diggings from the Cypress Hills is not clear, but on October 31, 1859, he was at Fort Colvile, the Hudson's Bay Company post west of the Rocky Mountains in the Columbia River valley, as on that day he drew a wage payment due to him by the expedition, of £46.14.8d.[24] Perhaps he went across the mountains with Palliser, but it seems more likely that he went with Palliser's friends Captain Brisco and W.R. Mitchell, when they left the Cypress Hills for Fort Benton on the Missouri River. Instead of crossing the mountains, as they had intended, they went down river to hunt, hearing that game was plentiful downstream. They sent the two men they had with them and some horses across the Rockies to rejoin Palliser.[25]

Somewhere en route Erasmus encountered two hopeful miners, "Butcheesh Annas"—probably Baptiste Anasse—and Peter Whitford, with whom he set out for the "Pandara" gold diggings.[26]

Erasmus returned to Edmonton the following year, in the company of the "man in charge of the supply station," though by what route is not known. He was fortunate in finding someone to travel with as the Hudson's Bay Company no longer organized regular trips across the mountains[27] and independent travel over the Rockies was still an infrequent adventure.

However he got there, Erasmus was back in Edmonton in time to help establish a new mission at Smoking (now Smoky) Lake, north of the North Saskatchewan River. Here he worked on the construction of a "log shack", the first building at the mission station. He sawed lumber, he travelled with the missionary when he made his rounds of Indian camps, and he freighted for him and for the Rev. Henry Steinhauer.[28]

It was while he was bringing supplies from Fort Garry for Woolsey and for his colleague at Whitefish Lake that Erasmus encountered the Rev. George McDougall and his son John. The missionary engaged him as guide and interpreter, a role for which Erasmus was well fitted. His superb hunting and travelling skills and his knowledge of the people and ways of the West played a crucial part in equipping the McDougalls for the work they were to do in pioneering the transformation of the western wilderness into the settled farmlands and cities of the Twentieth Century. They learnt from Erasmus the rudiments of how to travel and hunt on the plains, and how to look after themselves and their stock. As "an 'A1' interpreter", Erasmus provided the essential link between the newcomers and the native Indians and mixed-bloods, introducing and explaining them to one another. For example, John McDougall wrote of Ka-Kake, the Hawk, "From Peter I learned that he was brave and kind, and full of resource, tact, strategy and pluck;. . ." Erasmus "proved himself to be an earnest friend of this people (the Cree) and a prince of interpreters."[29]

He was, indeed, a remarkable linguist, speaking Swampy and Plains Cree, Ojibway, English, Blackfoot, and Stoney (Assiniboine)—six[30] living languages, besides reading Greek. Of this last accomplishment, George Gooderham tells a tale: "A commercial traveller was stumped when a friend who was driving with him on the road to St. Paul de Métis asked him to interpret a notice in funny characters nailed on a telegraph pole." Just then Peter Erasmus appeared, seemingly an old Indian. In signs and Pigeon English the drummers asked him about the notice. Coming forward with a smile, he "stated it was no foreign language though the characters were not unlike Greek; they were actually Cree syllabic characters and the notice said it was unlawful to buy intoxicating liquor and the supplier would be penalized by fine or imprisonment, or both."[31]

Erasmus's contribution to the work of the McDougalls seems to have gone even beyond initiating them into prairie skills and interpreting for them. John McDougall wrote, for example, that Peter Erasmus had "joined our party as father's interpreter and general assistant and was well to the front in all matters pertaining to the organization in the new mission" at Victoria (Pakan) in 1863.[32]

Among the many references to Erasmus in John McDougall's books there are accounts of three journeys that are not described in *Buffalo Days and Nights*. The first of these was made in the fall of 1863 with Erasmus as guide to look for the Mountain Stoneys with whom both the Rev. Robert Rundle and Woolsey had worked. The following summer, while John McDougall was away on the annual journey to Red River to freight in supplies for the missions, Erasmus and the Rev. George McDougall went again to visit the Mountain Stoneys, travelling as far as the present site of Morley on the Bow River. The third journey was a peace mission to the Blackfoot on which both McDougalls and Erasmus accompanied the great Cree chief Maskepetoon.[33]

Peter Erasmus's association with the McDougalls lasted for three years, but in 1865, rather than accept a drastic reduction in pay, he left the service of the missionaries. He had been married the year before to a Whitefish Lake girl, Charlotte Jackson. Now the couple came to Whitefish Lake to live. So began, for Erasmus, a new phase of life—one which was symptomatic of the change that was to spread across the western plains. Erasmus and his wife established a settled home for themselves, building a house on a piece of land allotted to them, at the Rev. Henry Steinhauer's request, by Chief James Seenum (also known as Pakan) on a lovely spot on the shore of Whitefish Lake.

While this was his home, Erasmus signed a petition, dated January 9, 1871, which the inhabitants of Victoria and Whitefish Lake sent to the Lieutenant-Governor, expressing concern about the urgent need for law and order. They were "deeply anxious that British authority should be established without a conflict of races"; they were alarmed that there was no protection for life or property; they recognized that the prohibition of the importation of ardent spirits was a boon, but said that the newly appointed magistrates had no power to enforce the law; they feared that the plains tribes believed that their hunting grounds would be destroyed and their lands taken from them without compensation; and they warned that if regular communication with Manitoba was not immediately opened up, part of the country would shortly form a connection with Fort Benton. Among the other signatories were Henry Erasmus, Peter's brother, and John and David McDougall, as well as a number with Indian and French names.

Meanwhile, Chief Seenum had also allocated the Erasmuses a trapping ground. Charlotte taught her husband how to trap, and successful trapping led to trips to Red River Settlement to trade the pelts. Erasmus brought back trade goods with which to set up as an independent trader—a second important change in his way of life, though for the time being the Erasmuses continued to make journeys from their home base out on to the plains for the buffalo hunt, which was still the basic source of food supply.

But buffalo were becoming scarce. The big organized hunt of 1876 turned out to be the last one in which Peter Erasmus was to take part. It was cut short for him by the arrival of messengers who summoned him to the Treaty-making at Fort Carlton. Two leading chiefs of the Plains Cree had asked him if he would act for them as interpreter in the forthcoming negotiations for the surrender of their lands. He had agreed to do so and now he made a quick journey to Carlton. Here he was to begin still another phase of his career, this time as a Government interpreter.

At the Carlton House negotiations, however, Erasmus acted for the Indians, taking part in their own council meetings at which they discussed the Treaty terms they had been offered and reached a decision as to what to do. Erasmus's account of the Indians' deliberations among themselves, and especially of the speeches made by Mista-wa-sis and Ah-tuk-a-kup adds new insight into the considerations that persuaded the Indians to accept the Treaty. He reports Poundmaker's desperate cry: "This is our land. It isn't a piece of pemmican to be cut off and given in little pieces back to us. It is ours and we will take what we want." This does not appear in either Lieutenant-Governor Morris's summary or in the record kept by the Secretary of the Commission, Dr. Jackes, that was published by Morris in his book on the seven treaties between Canada and the Indians in the West.[34] In general, however, Erasmus's account of the proceedings is very similar to that given by Morris and Jackes; indeed, some passages in *Buffalo Days and Nights* are almost identical with passages in Morris's book. For example, Erasmus quotes Mista-wa-sis as saying, "When a thing is thought out quietly, that is the best way. I ask this of him [Morris] today, that we go and think over his words." Morris has ". . .when a thing was thought of quietly it was the best way," and he asked "this much that we go and think of his words."[35]

Did Erasmus keep a written record of the proceedings? Or is the similarity to be attributed to the "remarkable degree of accuracy" in the spoken record which Hugh Dempsey notes in his biography of Crowfoot, citing modern informants about the Blackfoot Treaty of 1877 who "have been able to pass on conversations which are not unlike those recorded in Morris's *Treaties of Canada*," though they spoke only in their native tongue?[36]

Summing up the treaty negotiations, the Lieutenant-Governor remarked: "We also had the advantage of good interpreters, having secured the services of Messrs. Peter Ballenden and the Rev. John McKay, while the Indians had engaged Mr. Peter Erasmus to discharge the same duty. The latter acted as chief interpreter, being assisted by the others, and is a most efficient interpreter."[37]

This is in interesting contrast to a later comment made in connection with Chief James Seenum's "very exaggerated idea of the quantity of land to which his band was entitled," an idea attributed by the Department of Indian Affairs to "inaccurate translating when the Treaty was made."[38] Erasmus's interesting account of the affair suggests that it was not the interpretation that was at fault. In any case, he helped to secure a settlement in the end by going with the chief to Regina in 1884, when it was arranged that the band should take up land in the

Saddle Lake area that was better suited for agricultural purposes than the area bordering Whitefish and Goodfish Lakes. The issue seems to have been essentially one of the number of Indians that would have to be provided for on the reserve. By 1884, when the difficulty was finally adjusted, the number listed as belonging to the band had apparently increased as Chief Seenum had expected it would.

Whatever the rights of the Seenum case may have been, Erasmus did so well at the Carlton negotiations that he went on to act as interpreter in the negotiations leading to subsequent adhesions to Treaty No. 6 of Indian bands that were not represented at Carlton.

That Erasmus's work as interpreter at the treaty negotiations still has significance today is suggested by the fact that he was quoted by the Indian Chiefs of Alberta in their presentation *Citizens Plus* to the Prime Minister in June, 1970.[39]

Erasmus's old friend John McDougall, now himself a Methodist Minister, was present at Fort Pitt for the second round of negotiations for Treaty No. 6. Oddly enough, neither he nor Erasmus mention each other in their respective accounts of what happened there, though Morris mentions both of them.[40]

Another interesting point that emerges from Erasmus's account of the Treaty proceedings is the disquieting impression of the Hon. James McKay as arrogant and hostile to the Indians, a contrast to the more usual idea that he was their sympathetic friend.[41]

Following the Treaty negotiations, Erasmus was taken on as an official interpreter by the Department of Indian Affairs, working in the Saddle Lake Agency and later in the Edmonton Agency. His name appears in the *Reports* of the Department for 1881, 1883, 1886, 1887, and 1888 as "interpreter" or "storeman and interpreter", with a salary rising to $660 in 1887. As well, various payments are reported for miscellaneous jobs, such as distributing seed, notifying Indians of payments, and making improvements on the Seenum Reserve. In addition Erasmus was paid for small quantities of barley, wheat, and potatoes. The Edmonton *Bulletin* for February 14, 1881, reports that he took four bushels of wheat to be ground at the new mill, getting 198 pounds of good flour in all. By 1887 he had ten acres of land at Whitefish Lake "cleared of timber and fenced, of which six acres" were "under cultivation," with a house, storehouse, and stable. In that year he surrendered the holding to the Department of Indian Affairs, as an indenture between Peter Erasmus, "Gentleman" and the Superintendent General.[42]

He was not, however, wholly engrossed in administrative and agricultural activity in this period. To one especially interesting assignment, Erasmus unfortunately gives only a few lines (p. 268, below). This was a trip to the Cypress Hills and the border country made in an attempt to persuade Indians camping there to come north, and settle on reserves. The *Report* of the Department of Indian Affairs for 1881 refers to the anxiety created by the large number of "defiant" Indians in the vicinity of Fort Walsh who had been trading and hunting across the Line. Their numbers were swelled by the arrival of disaffected Indians from the North to a total of between four thousand and five thousand Crees, Assiniboines and half-breeds. The next year's *Report* mentions the return of the "malcontents" from the southern plains. Though Peter Erasmus is not named in connection with the work of persuading them to go home,[43] the Edmonton *Bulletin* for September 9, 1882, states that "Peter Erasmus, government interpreter, got home on the 21st last. He reports that he has induced 3,000 Crees to return to their homes on the North Saskatchewan from the Missouri River and the Canadian frontier...." It must have been while he was on this trip that Erasmus killed the last buffalo he ever saw, as recounted in his letter to Hector.

Whether or not Erasmus continued to trade on his own account while he was working for the Government is not clear, but in the early 1880's he was trading for the Hudson's Bay Company. Already in 1873 he had written hopefully to Chief Factor Richard Hardisty:

Victoria Saskatchewan
Octr 21st 1873

Richard Hardisty Esqr
Sir

Allow me to trouble you with these few lines on a matter which undoubtedly you may think I have no business, that is, the Whitefish Lake indians at one time objected to the Company having a Post or a claim at Whitefish Lake,—they now repent and see they stood in their own light and interest. Before my coming to here they convened together and the Chief and his staff delegated me to make the thing known to you,—He says it is impossible for him to resist, or restrain his people from giving whatever fur or produce they may have to dispose of to the free traders so long as the Company does not have a Post there. He now in this instance asks you if the thing could not be done. He says it was the fault of

*the Missionaries that he was influenced to speak against any
thing of the kind being done by the Coy.*

*I would also ask you one favour if it can meet your views. I
am now on my way to winter at the Beaver Hill. Could you not
in any way whatever give me something to do in the way of
having a few articles of trade, and giving me a chance to do
something by allowing a certain per centage as pay, if so, I
should stand under great obligation to you. I would also remind you that a few years ago you told me that when Mr.
Christie was out of the Saskatchewan you would see what you
could do for me. It is well known that I have been wild, and so
have a many an one, but it is not what I have been, or what
another has been. It is the present and not the past, and that
will speak for itself. I hope you will take these items into consideration, and then send an answer as soon as you can for I
shall be here for some time.*

Hoping you are well, as also yours
I am
Sir
Your obt servt
P. Erasmus[44]

Erasmus's name has not been found in any of the Company's lists of personnel, but official depositions concerning
losses incurred during the Riel Rising, made on August 1,
1885, by Erasmus and Harrison Stevens Young, the Company
clerk at Lac La Biche, establish that, although by then he was
no longer in the service of the Company, Erasmus had been
trading at Whitefish Lake for Young and so, indirectly, for the
Company.[45]

Erasmus's account of the Rising (p. 275 *et seq.*) gives a vivid
impression of the anxiety it caused and the uncertainty that
was felt as to how far the trouble might spread. Also it brings
into sharp relief the conflict between Indian mysticism and
Protestant rationalism in the matter of a dream that foretold to
his adopted son, Peter Shirt, what would happen in the Rising,
a dream that was fully borne out in the event.[46]

This was not the only instance in Peter Erasmus's experience in which it seemed to him impossible to explain powers
not recognized by the Church and unknown to civilized processes of thought. Another such case is described in a story
attributed to Erasmus by Mr. Pete Tompkins of Prince Albert:
A medicine man undertook to trace some lost horses. He
carried out the ritual of being tied up and breaking free of his
bonds to the accompaniment of eerie sounds in the medicine
lodge. His spirit soared away to look for the missing beasts.

When he came back to earth he described the place where the horses were, saying he had marked the route to them. Full of doubt, the travellers set off to the spot indicated—and there, precisely, were the horses.[47]

A more mundane aspect of the start of the trouble in 1885 at Lac La Biche, that Erasmus does not mention among his memories, was stressed in his and Young's depositions afterwards. The Indians had not received from the Government the supplies of seed and provisions they usually got in the spring. They promised to remain quiet if Young and Erasmus would get the supplies for them, but it was already too late. The freighters, alarmed by news of the Frog Lake massacre, refused to leave Edmonton.

Meanwhile, some of Big Bear's Indians had visited both Lac La Biche and Whitefish Lake, inciting the local Indians to pillage the stores. Nonetheless, neither the Indians of Chief Seenum's band nor most of the Lac La Biche Indians joined the Rising. Peter Erasmus's influence and his adopted son's dream seem to have played a considerable part in their decision not to go to war, as is suggested by Mrs. Annie Gaetz, who, in recounting Youman's reminiscences in 1958, gave a good deal of weight to the effect of the speech in favour of peace in which Peter Erasmus told the story of Peter Shirt's dream.

Erasmus himself gives much of the credit for heading off trouble to William Stamp, afterwards called "Cootsoo" (i.e., "Man Slayer"), for his prompt action in shooting Louis Cardinal to silence his urgings to join Big Bear.

Peter Erasmus chose to end his reminiscences with his account of the Riel Rising. After that Rising, as George Gooderham points out, an intelligent mixed-blood like Erasmus was bound to resent the attitude of the Government. Even men who had not supported Riel "were hurt by the manner" in which they were treated. "After the rebellion virtually all half breed[s] were treated as outcasts and never again could they hold up their heads with pride for their earlier accomplishments."[48]

Further, the suppression of the Rising effectively marked the end of the old, independent, wandering life when the gifts of nature had been free to all comers within the wide range of territory claimed by tribal custom or military prowess as hunting grounds. When resources of space and wildlife, of timber and water, were open to any passer-by who could find them and cared to use them, a man's well-being and the esteem in which he was held depended on his personal qualities of courage, endurance, resourcefulness, and skill as a hunter, traveller, and warrior. Now it was becoming necessary to have specific property rights to a piece of land before you might use it or its produce. The buffalo had disappeared; other wild game and fish were growing scarce. Production for a market, property, employment, favourable prices, and commercial success were coming to assume decisive importance, bringing with them the need for different human qualities than those that had been valued in the old days. As well, new hazards outside the control of the individual were becoming important, as Erasmus found when a bank failure cost him his savings.

His life in this new world was to go on for another forty-six years. He continued to work for the Government, but left the Whitefish Lake Reserve, relinquishing to the Department of Indian Affairs his home and land, along with all the improvements on it, and receiving in return a payment of four hundred dollars.[49] For a time he lived at Saddle Lake but soon went back to Victoria, today named Pakan in honour of Chief Seenum, who was sometimes known as "Pakan" (Erasmus says the name was given because the chief liked nuts, but in another version, he was "the nut who had been too hard for Big Bear to crack.")[50]

While he was at Victoria, Erasmus lived in a house he had "hired built" on a homestead taken up in 1880 when the importance of property rights had become unmistakable. His oldest son, James, completed the ownership requirements for him. This is the house that is now in Fort Edmonton Park.

At Victoria, Erasmus returned to his early avocation as a school teacher, working at the local school,[51] but in 1890 he was back at the Whitefish Lake Reserve, teaching at the Reserve's second school, established at Goodfish Lake. The *Report* of the Department of Indian Affairs for 1890 commented: "The other school at Goodfish Lake has Mr. P. Erasmus for its teacher, and I am glad to be able to report on the state of efficiency to which he has brought his school and pupils," who numbered 31, as compared with 25 the preceding year when circumstances had limited progress.[52] By 1893 the number on the roll was 43 children, though average attendance was only 17, sickness being the reason given. The building was cold and uncomfortable. Examination results were not encouraging, and materials were somewhat short. "More energy on the part of the teacher might be given with advantage." The building, for example, should have been banked; being a strong man, why had not the teacher done this?[53] Evidently the days of "do-it-yourself" were not yet quite at an end. The report for 1894 was still less favourable. There were 28 children on the roll—all the children on the reserve—but attendance had dropped to an average of 10. The examinations did not show that much care had been bestowed on the children though the teacher was getting a government grant of $300 and $350 from the Mission.[54] Next year there was a different teacher at the school.[55]

Peter Erasmus was no longer young. He had lost his first wife suddenly and tragically, and had married again in 1882. His second wife was another Whitefish Lake girl, Mary Stanley.[56] This marriage too was cut short by death, on March 31, 1891.[57] Erasmus was left with three small daughters and with mounting economic anxieties. As he had explained to Hector, he had lost his savings.

He still had friends, however, and his name re-appears in the *Report* of the Department of Indian Affairs for the year ending June 30, 1906, as "Assistant Farmer", at a salary of $420 a year.[58] The record indicates that he lived on at Whitefish Lake in this capacity until 1909[59] when he moved to the Blackfoot Reserve at Gleichen. There he is listed in the Departmental *Reports* as "Labourer",[60] but George Gooderham, who got to know Erasmus at this period when he came home at intervals from the University, says that he filled "a newly created position—that of assistant rationer," the pay remaining the same as it had been on the Whitefish Reserve. The new appointment is attributed to Frank Oliver, then Minister of the Interior, who had a long-standing interest in the mixed-blood population. An "old party heeler" said "Peter was rewarded for faithful service with a 'Government Sit!' "[61] Erasmus had also been involved as an interpreter in at least one election.[62]

Mr. Gooderham described Erasmus's life on the Reserve:

His demands were very simple. He lived in a room over the office and the furnishings comprised a cook stove, bed, table and chairs with a few utensils and a lamp. He wore only pants and dark cotton shirts, except when it was very cold then he donned an old black coat. Around his waist, however, was tied the traditional half-breed sash. Peter had the spirit and dash of a young man, but kept mostly to himself when off duty. He did not mix with the Blackfoot, though he spoke their tongue very well. The children of the Indian Agent were his real pals; he was gentle and kind and told such wonderful tales. . . . . The clerk who had supervised the rationing before Peter's appointment did not take kindly to the change; he could not order Erasmus about like the poor hungry Blackfeet. . . . . .He'd square off to old Peter in the ration house when he was crossed but Peter would merely look down at him and smile."[63]

The position on the Blackfoot Reserve lasted until June 30, 1912.[64] Thereafter his name does not appear in the *Reports* of the Department of Indian Affairs; there had been a change in Government. When the Hon. Charles Stewart, a former Premier of Alberta, became Minister of the Interior in the Federal Cabinet in 1921, he included a pension of $500 a year for Peter Erasmus in his estimates; this was supplemented at the end of his life by the Old Age Pension of $165 a year which the Province of Alberta paid.[65]

Erasmus was in his seventy-ninth year when he left Gleichen, but he was still "as straight as a mountain pine."[66] He spent his last years with one or another of his children. For a time he lived with his eldest son, James, at Victoria, and for a time with a younger child, Mrs. C.M. Williams. Eventually he went back to Whitefish Lake, to the home of his son David, where Henry Thompson had an opportunity to verify and amplify his record of a remarkable life.

Peter Erasmus died on May 28, 1931, when he was almost 98 years old. His unmarked grave is in the cemetery beside the little church at Whitefish Lake on a hill overlooking the lake and the site of his first home.[67]

In his own lifetime he had become a legend. No less than eight mini-biographies of Erasmus have come to light. He was featured as an "old timer", guide, explorer, and pioneer in a variety of newspaper articles. These are listed in the Bibliography at the end of the book. It is good to have his own account of the first half of his life, an account that not only provides useful historical material, but is also a fascinating and revealing personal story, told by a master story teller. Mr. Henry Thompson has earned lively gratitude for preserving this record of a career that was as significant as it was extraordinary.

Irene M. Spry
Ottawa.

CHAPTER ONE

Early Days in the Red River
Settlement

I WAS BORN on the 27th of June, 1833, and was named Peter
Erasmus after my dad, whose first name was Peter. I had two
older sisters and an older brother. Another boy and a girl were
born later. Mary Anne was born nearly ten years after my
younger brother and became the favourite for that very reason.

Father came from Denmark. He had volunteered with the
British army, was wounded at the Battle of Waterloo and
received a pension of twenty-five cents a day. Discharged from
the army he had taken service with the Hudson's Bay Company
until his retirement, when he took up land at Fort Garry. Dad
was a big man, weighed over 220 pounds, stood six feet tall, but
was not fleshy. A non-drinker and careful with his money, he
was well respected in the community. We were considered
fairly well off as we had two carts and oxen, a flock of sheep,
and a saddle horse that was always kept in the barn, besides a
couple of mares on the range.

I remember some of the first cows that were brought to the
settlement. Father and three other men went to the States where
they bought several head of cattle. Two of the neighbours also
commissioned them to buy one cow each for them. It was a
great moment in the lives of us children when we took visiting
playmates to see our cows, and it was a never-ending source of

1

wonder to the little ones that our black cow gave such creamy white milk. Their expression of delight when they tasted milk for the first time was truly astonishing, although there were a few who couldn't be persuaded to touch it again.

Milk added a greater variety to our usual food supplies. Wheat browned in a hot pan over a fire was ground in a handmill that Father made specially for the children. The coarse flour mixed with milk or cream was delicious. The dish became a popular favourite to visiting children. They brought wheat to our mill to be ground, and many happy afternoons were spent in feasting on this wonderful new dish. Father and Mother offered no objections and encouraged us to share with our less fortunate neighbours. Buffalo meat, game birds, and fish were the main foods. Flour was considered a luxury and not the essential part of a meal that it is today.

A dour Scotsman, whose name I only remember as Scottie, lived on our west side. He was a small figure of a man who never joined in the social life of the settlement or went to church. He worked from daylight to dark in his small fields and rather extensive garden — Sundays or weekdays were all the same to him. He had an ox and a handplow but in spite of the long hours, never seemed to accomplish very much. His noisy outcries to the ox could be heard quite plainly from our house.

"Peter," said Mother, "you'd better see about our neighbour, he hasn't been out of the house these last two days. He may be sick as he worked all through the rain Saturday and Sunday."

"Perhaps I'd better do that," replied Dad, "though he'll not thank me and probably dress me down for my curiosity, but I must take that chance."

Father found the old Scot a very sick man in bed. Inquiries about his condition only aroused the old chap's abuse, that he needed no help and wanted no interference. Dad without further words simply rolled the old chap in his blankets and packed him over to our house. Spluttering with anger and cussing all the way availed him not at all, and with Dad's size and strength, his efforts to get away were useless. We had a big house and a spare room where Dad deposited his burden, stripping him for bed.

"Be quiet you little beggar! You are going to stay here till you are better. There's no use for you to make a fuss, you're a very sick man."

Shortly after that Father had his unwilling guest ready and called my mother. She came into the room with some hot potion for the patient to drink as well as other remedies to apply to his chest. The old gentleman objected to the exposure

2

of his chest but with Dad's forcible assistance, the medicine was applied.

Father stood waiting in the other room and when he caught him trying to dress himself, he took away his clothes, leaving only a woman's dress that happened to be in the room. Mother mentioned this but Father knew his neighbour would never consider this a suitable wardrobe to brave a chance settler's sight.

Scottie became more amenable by evening under the soothing effect and patient ministrations of Mother and, realizing the hopelessness of any escape, became resigned to his position. However, the moment Dad came into the room he glared with venomous hatred. The next morning he was too weak and helpless to offer resistance but both our parents seemed terribly worried about the man. They hardly left the house and banished the children to the neighbours to have absolute quiet.

Two weeks went by. His recovery was slow, but he finally asked to see Dad and begged him for his clothes. The request was granted, but not before he had promised not to leave the house without permission. He reluctantly gave his promise and after seemed to have lost his resentment for Dad's forcible treatment. They became friends and the evenings were spent in exchange of their travels and other things of mutual interest.

Neighbours often commented on Father's peculiar hold on the old Scotsman's friendship, which none of the others shared in the slightest manner, but no one ever received a satisfactory answer or surmised the truth. The old gent's admiration for Father and loyalty to the family became the wonder and curiosity of the neighbourhood

Land in the district was not settled in quarter sections, but by common consent was apportioned in narrow frontage lots that were worked for a considerable distance back from the river. The reason for this in the early days was in case of Indian trouble; later, with the men being away on hunting trips so much, the families at home were within easy reach of each other in case of sickness or other needs.

Later the system became a source of grievance in that no recognition of the lines of occupation was considered by the government surveyors, but the land was divided into quarter sections. Frequently, these river-lot parcels, owned by the residents for as long as fifty years in some cases, were crossed by survey lines. The people feared the loss of their land; little wonder that those involved in this controversy were aroused to the apparent injustice of the system.[1]

Our nearest neighbour was a Scotsman, Murdoch Spence,

who had been in service with the North West Company during its roughest period of opposition to the Hudson's Bay Company. He was a huge man with strength and agility that belied his great age. When I was yet a mere boy I remember his long beard and hair were touched with grey. Mrs. Spence was a small woman, the very opposite to her burly man. She was a kindly sociable person and a frequent visitor to our home, and always carried some rare tid-bits for the younger children. Her reddish-blonde hair was an outstanding feature where black was the rule. For all her small size she ruled her husband with an authority quite unusual for the time where women were treated as mere drudges or servants at best, a practice the white men were not slow to adopt from the Indians.[2]

Murdoch was a wonderful gardener; his luscious produce was always more delicious than our own and an open temptation for our adventurous spirits. Being the youngest at that time, I received the greatest benefit from the old gent's cane, since I was the slowest escaping over the high rail fence. I now realize he was most generous with his crop, giving away to less capable gardeners many sacks of vegetables. Each fall he made us carry sacks according to our size over the high rail fence to the house when the gate was just as handy. Apparently he had a practical sense of humour.

Fences enclosed only cultivated land, and it was one of our duties to herd a flock of sheep on the open range. The first money I ever earned was from Mr. Spence, for taking his animals along while herding our flock, a task I assumed with considerable misgiving. I was paid every cent promised and after that I refused to join any raid on his garden patch. I thereby discovered that my slowness in getting over the fence was the chief reason for the game, and the sport was abandoned for more exciting diversions.

When I reached my seventh year, I was ready for school. Our clothes were leather pants with a soft deerskin coat, cotton shirts, Indian moccasins with blanket duffels for our feet. The girls wore print dresses with, I believe, homemade knitted underwear. The boys wore nothing else, winter or summer. The moccasins were either moose hide or buffalo skin, as they were considered warmer and more durable.

I do not remember being really cold with these meagre clothes. Perhaps it was the strong foods we ate that helped us resist the cold. Meat was always our main diet. Buffalo was plentiful and few men of that day ever thought they would be completely killed out.

We had nearly four miles to go to school, but on stormy days or cold weather the neighbours with children took alternate trips with the children going and coming from school. We rode in the sleighs with good buffalo robes to keep us warm. My older brother and sisters seldom rode in the sleigh but wrestled and played tag with other children going our way.

There were twenty children going to school. James Settee, a Swampy Cree Indian, was our first teacher. He was one of four boys educated with the help of an English gentleman named Mr. Budd,[3] who contributed to their education. The boys had been chosen by an English clergyman, Rev. Mr. West, and all received their education at Fort Garry. Mr. Budd's only condition was that one of the boys take his name. The Rev. Mr. West considered my Uncle Henry the most receptive to education, and chose him to carry his benefactor's name. The others were James Settee, James Hope, and a fourth[4] whose name I cannot recall.

Our next teacher was James Garrett,[5] a half-breed son of a Hudson's Bay factor. The man was very strict and had a keen sense of his own importance. The slightest error was sufficient to bring down his wrath — the rod plied with vigour. However, our parents seemed to think that our progress at school depended on the strictest discipline, for certainly there was no playing in school. It was all serious business; even the little ones were forced to cover their lessons with diligence and were never spared the use of the rod.

I had to quit school because of the death of my father. This was a serious blow to our happy carefree life. I do not know the cause of his death, but I realize now that it must have been very sudden, for I do not remember him being sick in bed for any length of time.[6] He was not a trapper, but joined in buffalo hunts on all the regular trips after meat.

He was always active on his farm work, and frequently lectured us boys on the fertility of the soil and the great future in farm life for those who would develop its wonderful resources. He was among the very few of his day who realized that the free life of the prairies and the vast herds of buffalo would someday be replaced with domestic animals and other agricultural pursuits.

My Uncle Budd was named guardian of our family, and as soon as word reached him he came to the settlement to arrange our affairs. He considered it necessary for my older brother Henry and me to quit school — Henry to work out to earn money for the family support, and I to take care of the stock and cultivate the land.

Our neighbours were all very good to us; our old enemy Murdoch Spence proved to be a real friend in spite of all the

5

trouble we had caused him. His advice and actual supervision in the farm's management was most helpful. I am afraid our father's lectures in regard to the land were never seriously taken. I found I knew very little, but under Mr. Spence's direction we made out very well.

Farming in those days was not the big grain-growing operation it is today. Only sufficient grain, mostly wheat and barley for table use was grown. We now had five cows and some young stock. Haying was the biggest job, but during that first year neighbours helped me to put up enough hay for our animals. Under Mr. Spence's direction our oxen were put to use in exchange for manual labour.

My brother Henry accompanied the buffalo hunters on trips to the prairies after meat, and although he had no part in the actual killing, our carts were returned with our full share of the hunt. It was the general practice in the event of the death or sickness of the head of a family that all members of the party shared their portion of the hunt. Henry was given other useful work in camp, and tended stock to repay the assistance given in filling our carts.

During the early part of the second winter after I left school, my uncle arrived from The Pas. He had been recalled by the Bishop for consultations and reports in regard to opening another mission further north, and he was instructed to hire an assistant to take over his school work. He came by dog team direct to our home before reporting to the Bishop. He had a talk with my mother before leaving for the mission.

The second day after his visit to the mission, he came to our house again. I was busy at the barns looking after the stock when I was called to the house.

"My boy, I've been instructed by the Bishop to start a new mission and to hire an assistant to help in the school work. We have prepared some tests and if you can pass these, I'm authorized to hire you for the work, provided of course that you're willing to accept. You must make your own decision as I cannot advise you in the matter, but I believe that it's a good opportunity to advance your education, and the pay is adequate; however, your decision must be of your own free will."

I was past fifteen years, big and husky for my years, and in fact I considered myself grown up. I used to play the fiddle at the dances, and of course had an instrument of my own and practised every spare moment away from my regular work, probably not because I was fond of music but because I wanted to be accepted as one of the regular fellows who contributed their music at the parties. There were many French Metis people who were wonderful violinists.

Learning to play the fiddle and attending dances occupied more of my time than the matter of improving my education. However, James Garrett had not allowed me to neglect my studies completely; he had, after I left school, continued to send lessons with my brother, and compelled me to attend written examinations. I was therefore not afraid of the test, but it was the good times at parties and dances that held the best reasons for a refusal. Finally the urge for adventure and travel, unrecognized as such at the time, won out, and I advised my uncle that I was prepared to take his examinations and that if I passed I would accept his offer.

The tests set by the bishop and supervised by my uncle were not too hard and fortunately were along the lines of instruction my teacher had given. The bishop and my uncle were well satisfied with the results, and I was accepted for the position. I was to continue a course of study set by the bishop and my teacher to better fit me for employment in the following school term.

I was to take passage with the boats on their return, freighting goods upriver with their yearly supplies after delivering the annual spring furs down the river from the various forts along the North Saskatchewan and the forts further in the wilderness to the north. There was little idle time for me that winter for dancing and parties, although I managed to squeeze in a few. I had to submit weekly reports to the teacher, and this occupied a lot of my time. However, I experienced a growing interest in the work, and found myself with an increased anticipation for my prospective employment. When I received notice from the bishop to make ready for the trip, I was quite elated over the news.

I found myself growing impatient for the early breakup of ice on the river that presaged the arrival of spring and passage for the boats. The open admiration of teenage companions, tinged with envy for the importance of my new position as a teacher, swelled my ego and dulled the thoughts of leaving all my friends and my mother's home. Finally I got word from the bishop to go to Norway House and await the boats. It was early in May when I arrived at Norway House and presented my letter from the bishop.

The bishop had given me five pounds sterling with which to buy extra clothes, camp bedding, and anything that I might need for the journey. It was not easy to bid my family goodbye and leave my friends. This would be the first time in my life to be away from the family, and the realization of what it meant did not strike me until it was time to say goodbye. The saddle horses were waiting at our front gate and brother Henry's impatient call to hurry probably saved me from breaking into tears, like the big baby that I was at that moment.

Arriving at Norway House, I was assigned a room and rations which consisted of a bag of pemmican, sugar, and tea. These rations were to do me until the arrival of the boats. There was no word as yet of when they would come but I kept a continual watch every day I was at the fort. I borrowed a gun from one of the inmates at the fort and scoured the surrounding country and lakes for game, which made a welcome addition to our rations.

I was first to see the boats when they came in sight, and I rushed back to tell the man and wife in whose house I had a room. The man notified the others and all went down to the landing to make them welcome.

There was a great deal of handshaking as every person at the post shook hands with the men on the boats. They had a fine load of furs and the factor was most cordial to the boatmen. I was to note later that the factors kept themselves aloof from the more genial manifestations of friendship with the workmen. In fact, the factors occupied a high plain of social distinction that they, with few exceptions, were zealous in preserving. The workmen seemed to accept the situation without visible complaint.

There was a great deal of activity as the boats were unloaded and again reloaded with bales of goods for the western posts. This was all a new and exciting experience for me. There was no rest or delay except for meals as they hurried with their work, acting as if they were fighting against time. In truth they were, as they had been delayed almost three weeks by the late spring break-up of ice at Edmonton.

I was again issued rations: a loaf of sugar of about ten pounds, a sack of pemmican, a packet of tea, a small block of buffalo tongue, and also a packet of hard biscuit. This latter I found quite edible if soaked in water. It was called hard tack by the boatsmen and described as a favourite resort for worms and grubs if allowed to become damp at anytime. As children we had never been allowed to drink tea at home, milk or water being our only beverage, so I gave my tea to Steersman Short, who made a great show of gratitude for the gift. Up to that time I had no taste for tea drinking.

My recollections of that trip from Norway House are not too clear. I know I was awful sick and lost interest in all that went on around me. After we reached the mouth of the Saskatchewan

River I began to recover. No one seemed to worry in the slightest about my condition. Only Mr. Short paid any heed to my misery but when I saw him wink at one of the men while appearing very solicitous in his inquiry about my health did I begin to realize my sickness was not fatal. My recovery was rapid after that.

When we reached the Grand Rapids every bale had to be transported overland to the quiet waters beyond the falls. It was a tremendous task but there was no complaint; each man assumed his work without orders or delay. It was all in a day's work to them. Some of the men could carry three packs at a time with hardly a rest in between.[7] My own efforts to pack a single bale made me dizzy with perspiration, and my muscles proved too weak for any prolonged walk without frequent rests. The men were amused at my efforts at helping, and some of them stopped to show me the best way to pack one of the bales as I persisted in my determination to help.

Always afterwards I held these men in high esteem when I realized the tremendous work and endurance required in one of these trips. They kept their happy good humour in the worst conditions of their labour, through rain or shine, from daylight till dark, tracking their heavily loaded boats upstream.

My own slumbers had to be adjusted to these hours but I soon enjoyed the early sunny mornings and learned not to grumble at the rain or discomforts of wet clothes on a bad day. These men, tough and hardened to their work, had no respect for weakness and certainly no sympathy for complaint. I accepted their attitude to these things as my own and was thereafter treated with consideration and kindness.

Tremendous amounts of food were consumed by the men as they slowly pushed and pulled the cargoes upstream. The boats were pulled by manpower, each man harnessed to a central towline that was fastened to each boat in such a way that the front pointed out from shore. A man stood in the boat with a pole to keep it from bumping the shoreline. There was a crew for each boat, a steersman in control of each crew.

There were always two hours of tracking before breakfast and only short periods of rest between meals. The only diversion from the monotony was when some unfortunate chap slipped on the rocks or was pulled up to his waist in water around a sharp bend and received a ducking. Everyone laughed and passed some witty suggestion for his benefit. They rotated position on the towline. I noticed that the last fellow to receive a ducking laughed the hardest next day when the chap in his previous position caught the same medicine. A few cuss words by the victim and the incident passed over.

I often walked the shore but was never allowed to get out of sight unless we were in camp. Mr. Short had a voice like a foghorn and lost no opportunity of trying its timbre. My curiosity was insatiable; whenever I delayed to examine something of interest, Mr. Short yelled with a ferocity that chilled my blood and killed any desire for future investigation. This of course was for my protection, but I felt a keen resentment for the man who had accepted my gift of tea with such profuse thanks and now showed so little remembrance.

At last I arrived at The Pas. My uncle was waiting for me and we were soon on our way to his home. My aunt was waiting to welcome us at the door. I was greatly impressed with her kindness; when she showed me to my room I could see that she had gone to a lot of trouble to make it comfortable. The chair, though homemade, was covered with deer hair with leather fittings. The table had a well tanned caribou skin, white as paper and velvety to the touch. There were bookcases and shelves for my things and a peg with a red ribbon for hanging my violin. A big bear skin with the head and claws lay next to the bed for a mat. I was to spend a number of years in that room and I will never forget the kindness and consideration that they both gave me during all my stay in their home.

There were thirty Indian children attending school, mostly all in the lower grades. They were attentive, obedient, well disciplined boys and girls; for the first week my uncle helped me, and I was thus able to begin teaching with very little difficulty. In my first year of teaching I used all my spare time in improving my education by the use of books and material from the Rev. James Hunter, who was the Anglican minister at The Pas. Uncle Henry was at this time called a catechist, and was preparing to take his examination for the ministry.

During my second year of teaching, the work became much easier, and I began to find more time on my hands. Experience develops confidence, and my own studies were making me better fitted to impart the knowledge to my students. It was at this time that I began translating the books of the Bible into the Swampy Cree language. There was then no syllabic for the Cree language as in later years,[8] but I used English letters for the Swampy Cree pronunciation of the meaning contained in the word and text.

I was in the third winter of teaching; study had become a habit for recreation. I still practised on my violin and continued further interpretations of other books in the Bible. I sometimes made weekend trips with my uncle's dogs but these were all of short duration. Sunday travel for anything but services was strictly prohibited in my uncle's household. I did not get to see much of the country around The Pas; only in extreme cases of sickness or food needs for the Indians were we allowed to break this rule.

Uncle Budd left in the early part of the winter for Fort Garry with a dog team. He was to complete his studies for the ministry. He was successful in his examinations and returned in the spring a fully ordained minister of the English Church. He had instructions to start a new mission at Fort à la Corne which was on the border between the Wood Cree and the Swampy Cree Indians.

Uncle Budd left for Fort à la Corne as soon as the waters were free from ice, accompanied by a helper to paddle the canoe and help in the building. He left his family at The Pas till he prepared a habitation for them at the new place.

Before he left for the trip my uncle and I were invited to the home of the Rev. Mr. Hunter, where both endeavoured to persuade me to prepare myself to enter the ministry. They were anxious that I should immediately begin my studies for that purpose. The fact that I had made interpretations of several books of the Bible they considered as strong proof of my inclination towards their objectives and my fitness to become a member of their profession.

After considerable enthusiastic argument by both these worthy gentlemen, I was forced to make a definite refusal, stating that I had no inclination or desire to such a course as I felt myself totally unfitted for service with the church. Although I could see my uncle was deeply disappointed with my answer, he dropped the argument.

Speaking to Mr. Hunter, he said, "Peter must make up his mind with his own free will; any other attitude but an inspired desire for the work of the Lord would be useless and barren of effective results."

"Yes," said Rev. Hunter, "I must agree with your uncle but I think we should all pray for your conversion and that you should honestly ask God for guidance in this great work for the Lord."

I remember the years at The Pas by the month of my arrival, in June of 1851, and by my birthday a few days after I reached there. My aunt did not let a single birthday pass without some preparation for that event. She would save some flour for the occasion and bread was served that day, and a specially choice meat or game was arranged for through her many friends among the Indians of the mission. Even my uncle endeavoured to be on hand for birthdays.

I was tempted to leave after my third year at The Pas but my uncle was away so much of the time that I decided to stay with

11

the family and help, in part for the many things they had done for my comfort and pleasure, by teaching another year and doing chores after school hours. It was in the spring of the fourth winter that the bishop notified Mr. Hunter that he would be at The Pas to preach the ordination service for my uncle. The Rev. Mr. Hunter asked me to interpret the sermon. This was the first time I would have to interpret before a crowd of over one hundred Indians and others who would attend the service. I was pretty nervous and got stuck in one place, but Bishop Anderson helped me out and from there on I got my nerve back and had no more difficulty.

I interpreted hundreds of services after that date but Bishop Anderson's sermon among an almost pure native congregation was one of the finest I ever listened to for co-ordinated, eloquent adaptation of scripture to native understanding. Bishop Anderson's quiet expression of appreciation after the service gave me keen pleasure.

We were assembled at my uncle's home when a messenger came to the door, informing us that the bishop had sent word that he wanted to see my uncle and me as soon as convenient for us. My uncle's eagerness to comply with the bishop's request far exceeded my own. I was filled with a strange reluctance to attend this interview. I feared that my uncle and the Rev. Mr. Hunter had enlisted the bishop in a renewal of their appeal for me to join the ministry. I dreaded renewal of the arguments under the weighty influence of the bishop.

My suspicions were quickly realized a few minutes after entering the Rev. Mr. Hunter's study. The bishop went into an enthusiastic appraisal of my work on the scriptures which Mr. Hunter had in his possession for reviewing and correcting. The great man fairly beamed with the pleasure of his discovery. Bishop Anderson looked upon those interpretations as if they were a sign from heaven pointing to me as a worthy servant of the Lord's will, and both the Reverends Hunter and Budd renewed their arguments and pleas for a reconsideration of my former refusal. Bishop Anderson without any thought for my past refusal or present objections went on with his plans for my further education at the college at Fort Garry.

"You have a considerable sum of money due you for your work in the last four years; other than the money you have sent to your mother you have saved nearly every cent. This I consider a most commendable support for my opinion of your character. You made an excellent interpretation of my sermon, Mr. Hunter advises me. Your work as a teacher has been very good, considering your youth. If the money you have saved is insufficient to complete your course, I will personally guarantee the balance and ask no return of the money except your service to the Lord's work among these native people.''

In vain I tried to explain that I did not feel fit, and had no inspiration for the course. My own unworthiness was heavy on my conscience but no argument on my part affected them in any way. Uncle Budd flushed with the high approval expressed by the bishop for his nephew, and pleaded with me to consent to the bishop's offer. Mr. Hunter joined in the pressure. At last wearied with the prolonged argument, I heard myself agree. My voice appeared detached from my body. It was an empty victory for them. It was only because I wished to avoid Uncle Henry's deep disappointment that I had finally given in to their wishes. While I had great respect for the inspired work of men of the cloth such as Rev. Mr. Hunter and my uncle and others of the church, I could not imagine myself as one of their number. Their sincerity and devotion to duty, their all-consuming force for the good of their people, the religious fervour that carried them through hardship in happiness and personal satisfaction was something I realized I could never attain. Although I was raised under the influence of a Christian home, I felt no happiness in my consent. All their praise and argument left me cold and resentful.

Young people were expected to follow the wishes of their elders, guardians, or parents. I knew the bishop considered that it was unthinkable that I should refuse my guardian's wishes or turn down his magnanimous offer of paying to finish the whole course. They all dropped to their knees as the bishop led them in thankfulness to God in giving them a new servant to broaden their work of Christianization. Each man in turn prayed for my continued efforts to realize their objective. I had no feeling other than wonder that they placed so much importance on the step that I had just consented to, but I was faced with a deep sense of the seriousness of the situation and a profound knowledge of my own unworthiness.

It was arranged for me to go down with the boats when they arrived with their annual fur brigade. My uncle would finish the remaining period of the school term. It would be a few days before we could expect the boats, perhaps a week or more. My aunt was busy making my clothes ready for the trip. I had looked forward to the time when I would be returning to the family and my friends, but somehow the fact of my entry into the collegiate dimmed the pleasure of anticipation.

Up to my departure from The Pas the strict code of my uncle's household and the work and studies left little time to enlarge my acquaintance outside our own family, even had I wished to do so. In the last winter my uncle had allowed me the use of his dogs in taking him to his various appointments to the Indian trappers. He had suffered an ailment to his foot that made it difficult to trail behind dogs. I was now twenty years old, stood six feet tall, and weighed two hundred pounds. The trips with the dogs had hardened me considerably and I enjoyed every minute of these snowshoe excursions which taught me the exhilaration of physical accomplishment.

The feeling of being forced to do something that was not of my own choice faded, however, and I determined to take advantage of the schooling to advance my education. As the day drew nearer to my departure, I grew excited at returning to the family and my former friends. I left The Pas in the middle of May 1855 and arrived at home some time in June.

My old acquaintances and even my brother Henry and older sisters failed me in renewing the happy carefree comradeship that I had hated to leave four years previously. The prestige in which teachers of that day were held and the fact of my coming entry into the Collegiate school to study for the ministry may have been the reason, or perhaps I had somehow failed to meet their expectations; whatever the reason, it created an invisible barrier that I found impossible to break down. I was sadly disappointed and discouraged; the happiness that I had joyfully looked forward to did not materialize. Even my pup, who had been my inseparable companion, did not recognize his master and refused to make friends — a small matter in itself, but in my present state of mind it made me very sad and restless.

Bishop Anderson on his return to the settlement had made a personal visit to my mother and advised my folks of my plans for entry into the ministry. He was quite profuse in his praise of my achievements and most discreet in regard to my un-willingness to accept the position, disclosing nothing about the pressure used to bring this about. The wisdom of His Eminence in thus placing me on a pedestal for the church was certainly effective in separating me from my old associates. True, my friends treated me with kindness and the fatted calf took many forms, but it struck me that it was always shadowed by the eminence and weight of the bishop's mantle. The custom of the times held teachers, ministers, factors, and other officials in very high esteem; and I realized the futility of my efforts to renew old comradeships. As an elect of the church and a student of the cloth my destiny was set and my course unalterable. I stayed a week at home, then took up residence at the collegiate, determined to make the best use of its facilities for a better education.

I found younger men far in advance in academic studies, but

my tutors set up a course of study to make up this handicap and I was kept too busy to grieve over disappointments. In less than half the term I was able to meet competition on equal terms. I worked very hard that first term but soon began to enjoy the life at the collegiate and make friends among the student body.

Going into my second term the courses were still largely academic but the work became easier and I had more time on my hands; I was able to take part in things that were not strictly within collegiate rules. Ability to evade restrictions has always been a fine art among students. The closer the surveillance, the more pleasure in their evasion. My chum and I were successful in getting away to a few dances and in spite of the long neglect I found that the enticements of the dance had lost nothing in the time elapsed. Practice with the fiddle, though long restricted to church music on account of my respect for my aunt and uncle, quite easily adjusted itself to reels and square dances. Now for the first time since that long interview with the bishop at The Pas life became tinged with a rosier hue, not shadowed by the drab black robes of the Church. Many of my companions in the student classes were fun-loving friends, who looked upon the work of the church as a great opportunity, and were happy and contented. My own dim views of the strict obligations required of a minister were not shared by these young men. They all, with few exceptions, had made their own choice and were inspired to carry out its principles.

As my second term at the college drew to a close, I gradually grew more dissatisfied at my failure to develop any enthusiasm for the purpose of my training. I was filled with doubts, and I feared I would fail in my examinations. I knew none of the spiritual devotion that most of my fellow students had in their preparation for the church. My prayers had no substance. Even after two terms I had no convictions to bolster my doubts. The inspired messages of our tutors who drilled us in the great purpose of our training had no effect on me whatever. If it touched me at all it merely raised resentment against the men who had placed me in this position. I was greatly relieved and surprised when I found out I had passed the examinations with good credits. Perhaps it was a subconscious wish that I might fail and have an excuse to quit. Whatever the reason, the report gave me encouragement and I was delighted to find my name high among those with the best marks.*

We were well on our third term when I received a letter from the chief factor of the Hudson's Bay Company. It was very brief, simply stating that he requested my presence at his office and said he had a matter of some importance to communicate. Badly worried that something had happened to bring the man's

15

attention to me for a personal interview, I felt certain that he had learned of our escapades from the college. Although we had done no harm, our attendance at the dance was a flagrant breach of the rules. Determined to face the worst at once, I obtained permission to be absent from classes. I knew that the chief factor took considerable interest in the affairs of the students and occasionally lectured the classes on interesting subjects concerned with our future status in the affairs of the country. My walk to face the man was of doubtful pleasure. Stepping into the building, I enquired of the clerk where I could find the chief factor. The man informed me that he was instructed to show me into his office as soon as I arrived. I was worried more than ever now that my immediate response to his letter was apparently anticipated. After a formal greeting I was asked to be seated.

"Your name is Peter Erasmus," the factor said. "I knew your father. He was an honourable gentleman to the Company." I took this as a prelude to something more serious but his friendliness and offer of a seat were reassuring. "I have a letter from a man at Fort Edmonton requesting my services in finding a young man to act as guide and interpreter. The salary offered is fifty pounds sterling per year and, of course, board and transportation paid. I will recommend you for the work if you decide to accept the position. I do not wish you to be hasty in making a decision. In view of your good standing in your last examinations and the circumstances concerned with your entrance to the college, I have no hesitation in offering you the first chance." I was amazed at the man's knowledge and wondered how he had obtained the information; for I was positive I had never expressed any opinion that I was not there of my own choice. "However," he continued, "this offer cannot be held for an indefinite period. Take a turn around the grounds, give the matter your serious thought and bring your answer back, say, in half an hour, more if you require it. The man you will work for is a Methodist minister by the name of Rev. Mr. Woolsey."

Turning, I walked out of the building without uttering another word. Here made to order was the solution to my difficulties. I would still be in church work although of another denomination. The hypocrisy of continuing a course of study to be a minister when I was spiritually and otherwise totally unfitted for such a career would be gross folly — worse than folly because I would be a weak influence. Lacking in convictions of my own, how could I hope to fulfill the great expectations of my tutors and those two good men, Hunter and

Uncle Budd, both of whom had, I was sure, my best interests at heart.

I was now past twenty-two years of age and master of my own destiny. I would be better to take this way out than be a disappointment to my friends and a cause of sorrow to those two good people who were so determined to shape my life for me. Once I assumed the cloth, there would be no honourable way of turning back. The strict code of the English Church would condone no weakness in its servants. Their high purpose, the "saving of men's souls", would exclude all personal inclinations and desires. Truly a wonderful concept but one that revealed itself as impossible for me ever to achieve. I was under no obligation to any man for financial help, being fully paid up for my board and tuition fees. It would be my own money I was wasting if I quit before I had finished the whole course. However, my education would not be lost and the divinity studies would be useful to me as an interpreter to a minister of the gospel, although of another denomination. With these thoughts and others racing through my mind, I laughed out loud, for it came to me that I had made up my mind to accept the first moment that I learned of the position. All the arguments in my mind were to justify myself to those men who held such high hopes for my future.

Walking back to the factor's office, I told him of my decision. "Peter, I hope you realize that the bishop won't approve of your change of plan and may be very difficult in the matter, especially when he knows that you'll be working for another denomination of the church. However, if you find the task too difficult, call on me again. I believe I can be of some assistance to you in overcoming his objections." The latter remark was accompanied by something of a smile.

The chief factor had put the bishop's attitude quite mildly; he was in a towering rage. I explained to the best of my ability my doubts, contradictions of spirit, even the breach of college rules. I made a clean breast of everything, hoping thereby to receive his understanding, even his forgiveness, but when I told him that I had accepted a position as an interpreter for a Methodist minister, the bishop became very violent in his abuse of my prospective employer and me personally for easily dropping the mantle of the English Church for what he described as a blind adventure about which I knew nothing. I was amazed at the bitterness and rancour displayed in his speech.

I lost patience and heard myself defending my position with an eloquence and determination that I had previously been unaware of. "Sir, this man Woolsey is worshipping the same God as we are. I'm surprised that the English Church considers itself the sole custodian of the keys to Heaven. I don't share your views, and the money and time that I have spent is my own. I'm of age, no longer required to follow the dictates of a guardian against my own wishes." I had started to leave the room without further conversation, but feeling guilty of disrespect and unrestrained anger I turned back. I could not leave this great man in my present state of mind. Holding out my hand I said, "Bishop, can you find it in your heart to forgive a poor sinner?" I saw the old gentleman's face light up with a smile that had something of sadness and disappointment at the edges. Taking my hand he said, "Young man, we can both profit by this experience. You have been more truthful than you realize. At least you have been honest in your convictions. I am afraid that I have been rather selfish in my viewpoint." The bishop then gave me his blessing and we knelt for a word of prayer together. I was saddened and dispirited by the experience, for I knew in my heart that these men were almost fanatical in their work. There was no hardship or sacrifice too severe for them. Their strong devotion to the spreading of God's word were qualities that I could never hope to attain.

CHAPTER TWO

Off to the West

T HERE WAS LITTLE TIME left to catch the boats on their return upriver, so after a hurried visit to the family I made my way to Norway House[1] where I was to embark. I would visit my aunt and uncle at The Pas where they were again in residence. Steersman Stark advised me that there would be a stopover at The Pas for repairs and a brief rest, possibly two days, and that would give me lots of time for a visit. Arriving at The Pas I set out for my uncle's home with a heavy heart. I did not feel happy at advising him of my change of plan as I knew that his disappointment would be keen. The nearer I approached the place, the more reluctant I became. Somehow I felt a sense of guilt as if I had committed a dreadful sin. Perhaps it was my long association with the place and my earlier subservience to its influence that had this effect. My uncle's home was a half mile from the river and I wished it to be much further. My aunt met me at the door and welcomed me into the home. "Have you finished your studies already?" she asked. "Your uncle's not at home."

"No," I somewhat angrily replied, "I've decided that I cannot study to be a minister."

"My goodness gracious! Your uncle will go crazy when he hears that."

"My uncle is no longer my guardian, I'm over twenty-one years old and I will make my own decisions from now on."

"Goodness! Don't be angry with me. I never thought you'd make much of a preacher. I always thought you were too fond of playing your fiddle."

I had to laugh at her naive remark and thereby lost the tension building up for this visit. Her remark so honestly spoken was just the thing to put me at ease.

"Your uncle has gone to Moose Lake but I expect him home at any time now; but you never can tell till he arrives as he has many calls to make."

He did not arrive that night nor the next day at noon when the boats were ready to leave, so I wrote a long letter telling him about the reasons that led up to my decision and about the new work I was going to do. I received an answer to this letter the next year, though he had written it the following week. He accepted my decision without any resentment, unlike the bishop, and commended me in choosing a position with one of his brothers in God's work. I never saw him again, as he met his death by drowning four years afterward while travelling among the northern Indians.[2]

The boats were waiting and immediately started on their long and arduous trip upriver, but this time I had more freedom of action. I scouted along the banks of the river for game and birds which were quite plentiful. The crews appreciated it as it relieved the monotony of their regular diet.

I found a letter waiting for me at one of the Company posts advising me that my employer would be at Fort Pitt with the horses. Mr. Woolsey was waiting for me when we arrived there. He was greeted with respect as he shook hands with each man and talked for a moment before going on to the next. I learned later that he had a word for them all about the health and well-being of their families they had left early in the spring. He must have gone to some trouble to have news for each man.

Ours was among the last boats to land, as I was assigned to Mr. Stark's crew and he usually kept to the rear of the others. "Mr. Woolsey," said Stark, "this is your man, Peter Erasmus. I hope you have a horse big enough to pack him back to Edmonton. My men will be glad to be relieved of his weight in the boats." After walking practically the whole distance up river I was slightly peeved till he burst out laughing.

The Rev. Woolsey joined him in a hearty but more reserved laugh and his eyes twinkled as he replied, "Oh, yes! I've a horse capable of carrying a little extra weight. A tireless animal on the road but with a disposition and will of his own, quite unusual in a horse. I'm sure Peter won't care to drag along with

20

the boats once he is mounted on a good horse." He had greeted me with a firm handshake and a grip that surprised me from a man so slight in build. Woolsey was not really small but he had the appearance of a man of delicate physical development. He was openly pleasant of manner, smiling and affable as he greeted the rest of Stark's crew by their first names. He had some news of each of their families in Edmonton, Lac Ste. Anne, and St. Albert—a name later given to a new settlement.

The men, a long way from their families on the annual summer trips, crowded around him with eagerness and pleasure for the first knowledge they had of their people since early in the spring. His thoughtfulness in this kindly act was typical of the man, as I was to learn in my association with him later. I was pleasantly impressed at this first meeting. I liked the man; his spontaneous laugh at Stark's joke indicated a happy, easy disposition. A well balanced sense of humour was a delightful contrast to some of my recent experiences.

"Peter, I suppose you're anxious to get acquainted with the horses. You can go see to their hobbles, and also repicket the roan which will be your saddle horse."

I was eager to see the horses, and started up the bank as soon as good manners would allow, but snubbed back at Stark, "I'm through travelling at a snail's pace and providing feed for your whole crew! Hereafter I'll stay clear of such a miserable means of travel." There was a big laugh from the crew and Stark removed his hat and scratched his head in a gesture of disgust for such a thankless expression of appreciation after all he had done for my comfort on behalf of the Hudson's Bay transport system.

Mr. Woolsey had described the horses and I wondered how I would be able to recognize them among a hundred ponies or more feeding on the plain near the fort. I saw a young man walking out to the horses with a rope in hand so I inquired of him and he walked along with me and pointed out Woolsey's horses. The roan horse was picketed with a long line made of partly tanned leather cleverly braided into a strong pliable rope, commonly called a shaganapee, which is raw leather with the hair removed and worked until it becomes soft and pliable. The roan snorted and backed away at my approach. It took a lot of coaxing and patience before I could lay my hand on him without him flinching and trying to get away. Not being a good horseman at the time, as most of my experience in the last six years had been with dogs and boats, I wondered if I had the ability to handle such a wild horse. The few times that I had ridden saddle as a boy, the horses were well trained, gentle animals.

Mr. Woolsey held a service among the Indians that evening but I did not have to interpret as he had arranged for a man by the name of Ballenden[3] to attend him at the service, not knowing when to expect the boats.

The next morning I was out before daylight getting breakfast ready, as Mr. Woolsey had expressed a wish to get an early start in the morning. It promised to be a beautiful September day, and as soon as it was daylight I woke my employer and told him that his breakfast was ready and I was going after the horses. I was already on my way when I heard him answering my call. Returning with the horses, I learned then that no morning or evening would pass without a period for devotions, regardless of time, conditions of the weather, or any other circumstances, or whether we were with a crowd or by ourselves. I watched Woolsey approach the roan and was surprised to find how docile he was under the minister's handling. The saddle was placed and the cinches tightened without a move by the horses. I did not offer to help him with the roan and confined my efforts to the other animals, a pack horse and saddler for Woolsey.

I waited as long as I could before climbing into the saddle; Mr. Woolsey's friends had gathered around to see him away and in spite of the early hour there must have been twenty Indians present. I approached the horse in hopes that his good behavior would be transferred to myself, but not so: the minute I approached closer he drew back, snorted, and tried to back away. Fortunately my friend of the day before was present and took the horse by the bridle and held him for me to climb to the saddle. Mr. Woolsey was already mounted and on his way with the pack horse on a lead rope. My roan showed no inclination to follow his mates; and in spite of my digs in his sides refused to go ahead, but backed and turned in every direction except towards Woolsey's receding figure.

My young Indian friend again came to my rescue. In a low voice, he told me to slacken my lines, at the same time grasping the lead line and starting the horse forward. Freed, the roan now struck out at a fast pace as if he had suddenly discovered what was required of him; however, the laughing voices behind me did not help my dignity. I soon caught up with my employer, who did not appear to have noticed my delay — at least he did not remark on the cause of the amusement and laughs that must have been quite within his hearing when I was stranded at the start.

My first day in the saddle was delightful after the slow movement of the boats upstream, but my second was a different matter entirely. My legs had become chafed from rubbing the

22

saddle straps. The roan was a big animal and rough-gaited and I felt as if I were being pounded to pieces. The horse seemed to find every gopher hole on the road and failing those, reached for any small obstruction in his path, striking his toes and stumbling.

Only the presence of the minister saved me from using some of the boatsmen's rather colourful language to relieve my agony. Finally in desperation I turned to my employer.

"Sir, is there some method of riding a horse with less agony or is this choice of a saddle horse your method of testing a man's endurance?"

He chuckled with delight at my assumed humility of speech and replied, "I have been waiting for just such a question since yesterday noon." Then he went on to explain my mistakes, demonstrating on his own horse at the same time. I gathered from his remarks that a person should match the sway of his own body to that of the horse. Putting his advice into practice, I was able to avoid some of the shocks that I had endured for the last fifteen miles. I still shudder when I remember that trip from Fort Pitt to Saddle Lake Crossing.

About the fourth day of riding, that roman-nosed monster became resigned to his burden and avoided a few of the holes, even becoming more careful with his feet. I learned the rudiments of controlling my steed by the use of the lines, and by the diligent use of buffalo fat reduced the chafing on my legs. The few times I hit the ground had done no real harm except to my pride. Of this latter commodity I was soon to learn that I could lose a considerable amount without any visible effect.

When we caught up with the boats Mr. Woolsey decided to ride with them as the trail made a wide detour around what is called Moose Hills, just east of where Elk Point is now situated. A passenger on the boats, a Mr. Mitchell, volunteered to ride with me. I suspect that Mr. Woolsey had little faith in my ability with the horses and had suggested the idea to him.

The distance from Moose Hills to Saddle Lake Crossing would be about forty miles. I was instructed to make my way directly to the crossing and wait for Mr. Woolsey there without coming back to the river to follow the boats.

I was very glad to have Mitchell's company as he was an experienced western traveller and had been over the trail we were to follow. Being new to the country I didn't have too much faith in my ability to keep my direction on the prairie, as I learned to do in later years. The cart trail we were following was used very little, as most of the travel was on the south side of the river. The country was slightly rolling land with some large clumps of brush along the creek beds. Grass and vegetation were luxuriant; slough hay was past our stirrups. We had camped the first night at what was called Dog Rump Creek, and getting an early start were well on our way to make Saddle Lake Crossing by night. I enjoyed the sight of these fine meadows and the beautiful level land through which we were passing. There were just enough young trees and brush to vary the view. Mitchell paid very little attention to the scenery — it was an old story to him — but to a man who had done most of his travelling in the bush country at The Pas and further north, it was a sight to take one's breath away.

We spent a lazy noon hour resting the horses, as Mitchell said it would be an easy ride to the crossing. He suggested that we were too far north and would have to angle southwest to get a sight of the river banks. We had been warned that a division of the trail might lead us to the old Lac La Biche pack trail through Whitefish Lake. We had been riding all morning without seeing the mark of any trail.

Again we were riding through level land that stretched out for miles in each direction, its parklike appearance without a single mark of human habitation. The thick prairie grass made our horses' hoofs soundless. Often we stirred up prairie chickens which flew just a short distance before lighting again. Mitchell leading the way seemed somewhat doubtful of the direction we should take and turned to me for advice.

"Let's go to that high hill to our left and ahead of us. We might be able to see the high river banks from there."

"That is a good idea," he replied. "From the time we have travelled, we should be very close to the river by now."

We reached the hill, and there before us lay the broad ribbon of the river less than two miles to the south.

"We'd better stay within sight of the banks so we will not get astray again. We shouldn't be too far from the crossing and should be able to make there before nightfall. In this territory they'll have scouts out and I'd rather we arrived at the camp in daylight hours."

All my attention was taken up with observing the country when suddenly my horse took fright and leaped wickedly, almost knocking the pack horse down. Finally I got him under control and rode back to where I saw Mitchell slowly circling the area where my horse had fled. I had some difficulty getting the horse back to Mitchell as he motioned me to come closer. I was horrified to see the naked bodies of seven Indians exposed to the elements, scattered where they had fallen, all with arrows piercing their bodies and most with fearful knife cuts. Their heads were a bloody mash where their scalps had been removed; some of them must have been still alive judging from the blood clots where their heads lay. I felt sick at the sight and rode off before Mitchell had completed his observations.

Mitchell soon caught up with me and observed, "This raid must have taken place early yesterday forenoon. The Blackfoot massacred those poor fellows. The victims are all Crees who were caught on the open prairie by mounted riders. At least twenty mounted men took part in the killing. They must have followed these Crees a long way to get their horses back. The Blackfoot are a long way from their own hunting grounds. This is the first time I ever heard of them this far away."[4]

I was somewhat nervous as we rode away from that grisly sight but my companion seemed quite indifferent. However, I noticed that he looked to the priming of his gun and kept it in front of his saddle on the ready from there on. I had no gun of my own at the time but I made up my mind to get one the first opportunity, regardless of my employer's objections if he had any. I was proud of my hair and always took good care to keep it trimmed in the latest collegiate style. I had no wish to contribute any of it to a Blackfoot's grimy glory.

Mitchell related tales of Indian fights that did not help my peace of mind. The sun was getting low in the west when we spotted a rider some distance away. Shortly after two more riders appeared; they seemed to be openly trying to intercept our trail. Mitchell cautioned me about taking any action before we were sure what they wanted.

"I think they're scouts for the camp we are seeking. Our horses are too tired to make a run for it if they are hostile. They must be Crees; none of the Blackfoot would hang around after the mass killing back there."

"Go ahead," said I. "You take the lead but the next time I get caught in a jam like this I'll have a gun. Believe me I feel like I'm attending a dance without my clothes."

"Cheer up, my friend. If you stay in the West, you'll find your head is worth more than a gun in lots of cases."

The riders had spread out in a V, one man being in advance of the others. We boldly rode up within fifty yards of them when Mitchell stopped, holding up his hand in a peace sign. The leader responded with a like sign and came closer to meet us. "These men are Crees without a doubt. Ask them what they want," whispered Mitchell.

"We are peaceful travellers, going to Saddle Lake Crossing to meet the boats," I said.

"We're scouts for a party from Lac La Biche and Steinhauer's mission at White Fish Lake. We're also waiting for the boats."

The other men rode up and shook hands with us. I think

25

they were just as relieved as we had been, that we were friends. The leader climbed back on his horse and motioned for us to precede him. I didn't like the idea of those three guns behind me but as Mitchell did not hesitate, I had no choice. We were escorted into camp without further conversation. After riding about three miles, we came in sight of the teepees pitched on the lower flat next to the river. I learned later there were more horses than were required to carry the goods assigned to the post and the mission, but a buffalo hunt was planned and the extra pack animals would carry the meat back. A horse would carry two bundles each weighing about ninety pounds. There were a number of saddle horses, and some riders were still out on scout duty. It was an impressive sight as we stopped above the flat to take in the scene.

Mitchell rode up to within twenty-five feet of a group of men standing in front of the teepees, got off his horse, and strode forward to greet a man who detached himself from the others and came to meet him. I copied my companion's actions and was standing beside him when he met the man. "Mr. Steinhauer, this is Peter Erasmus, who has been engaged as an interpreter for your colleague, Rev. Mr. Woolsey, who is with the boats." Mr. Mitchell added, "I'm afraid he has been slightly upset by the welcome your people gave him before we got to your camp."

"I am sorry," said the minister, "if we have given you any concern, but it is rather difficult to distinguish between friends and foes at a distance of three miles." Here he gave a hearty laugh, out of keeping with the serious tone he used while explaining our escort.

"Turn your horses out with the herd. You will share my teepee; there is plenty of room for you both with your duffel."

Though we turned Woolsey's mare and the pack horse loose, I took the precaution to hobble the roan as it would be hard work to catch him otherwise.

The boats arrived shortly after sundown and there was the usual round of handshakes and greetings after the boats were tied up at the shore. Campfires lit up the area as each group gathered with their acquaintances for an exchange of news and stories of their experiences.

There was a mixture of Cree, English, and French among the various groups. The boatsmen, apparently tired of their own company, were intermixed with many groups, glad of the chance to speak of other things with the French half-breed packers from Lac La Biche. There was much laughter and storytelling that night and the campfires burned long after the usual time for bed.

I was a little annoyed at the casual way our news of the massacre was received by the men. They seemed to view the matter as lightly as a game of chance in which someone had to be the loser. I could detect little real sympathy for the poor chaps whose bodies lay exposed to the elements or any prowling beast. I heard more than one statement that the beggars knew what chances they were taking when they raided Blackfoot territory.

The story of the fight had been brought back by a party of Saddle Lake Indians who were out tracking the Blackfoot across the river in the hopes of rescuing their friends. There were eight men in the party who had gone out on foot to steal horses from the Blackfoot. Not satisfied with one horse each they had attempted to take a herd of about twenty horses. Delayed by the slower animals in the bunch, they had the misfortune to run into a large party of Blackfoot buffalo hunters who were all riding good fast horses. The Crees were still hidden in a ravine when one of the men spotted the hunters. They hoped the riders would miss their tracks, as they were still three miles away. The Blackfoot crossed the tracks, got suspicious, and took up the chase. Quickly changing horses for the best of the unridden animals, the Crees tried to outrun pursuit, leaving the rest of the horses where they had them hobbled. The Crees then tried to mislead their enemies by taking a direction east instead of the more direct route to the river only five miles away.

The Blackfoot pretended to abandon the pursuit, but guessing that these men were from Saddle Lake, went straight to the river crossing and forded the river, leaving two men to watch the crossing from the south. The leader posted men over a wide range of the prairies on the north side. The Crees, jubilant over their apparent escape, made their way back to the ford, but an overconfident Blackfoot scout set to watch the Crees opened fire on them and gave the ambush away. The Crees raced their played-out animals down stream, abandoned them, and swam the river to the north side where there was good cover. There they killed the Blackfoot who had fired the shot.

The Crees stayed under cover for two days, hoping the Blackfoot would try to hunt them out or give up the chase after they recovered all the animals. One man argued that they should split up, each man for himself; the others did not agree but offered no objections to his own attempt to get away. He was the only man that escaped.

The Crees had no food, and after hiding two days decided that the Blackfoot would not stay so close to the main camp for that length of time. They were wrong, for as soon as they walked out in the open they were outnumbered, surrounded, and killed to the last man.

The Rev. H. B. Steinhauer picked volunteers to go out and give the men a Christian burial the next morning. I wondered how the task would be handled without digging tools but I found that the minister had tools to do the job. He not only taught Christian burial but had the means to carry it out.

Early the next morning, the boatsmen were busy unloading the packs for the Lac La Biche post as well as those for the Whitefish Mission, reloading and equalizing the loads among the boats again. They were away before the sun was much above the horizon, anxious to be back with their families, now just a few days away. The only news they had about the welfare of their families had been brought by the kindly inquiries made by Mr. Woolsey, who had again decided to ride with the boats.

The scouts had reported a large herd of buffalo about ten miles south of the river, so I asked and received permission from Mr. Woolsey to join the hunters; but he cautioned me against getting into trouble: "The distance is not great and I think you will be safe among Steinhauer's Christian Indians. It will be a fine adventure for you but you must be careful. Remember, you're in a country where war among the unchristian and pagan Blackfoot is still considered an honourable occupation. You must not under any circumstance take part in any of that horrible business. Your recent experiences should make this clear to you."

"I'll confine my efforts to only the buffalo, rest assured, sir. I have no desire to risk my scalp for the doubtful glory of any skulking Blackfoot."

The boats would likely take five days to reach Fort Edmonton, and I was advised it would be an easy three-day ride on horseback. Mitchell again offered to accompany me on the trip; meanwhile he would rest up and enjoy the hospitality of the camp.

There were five of us in the hunting party. Each had a saddle horse, three pack animals with packsaddles, and three buffalo runners led by their owners. The pack horses trailed loose and followed the lead horses without much trouble. Sam Jackson and I brought up the rear, and it was our duty to keep the pack animals following the others.

We went upriver some distance to reach the ford where we could swim the horses across. I was considered a good swimmer, but crossing a wide stream with a horse was something I knew nothing about. Too proud to ask advice, I thought by watching the others I would get by.

28

When we were near the crossing, one of the pack horses took fright and broke away to turn homeward. Handing my gun to Jackson, I took after the brute. My roan, though a slouchy-gaited beast, had plenty of speed and had to extend himself to turn the truant back. Sam was waiting at the edge of the stream and waded his animal into the water as soon as the pack horse caught up. The others were already halfway across the river; the pack horse obediently followed Jackson's horse as he got to deeper water.

The water was shallow some distance from shore and my horse followed eagerly. I felt confident that swimming was no new experience for him. Suddenly we struck deep water and I was in trouble. My weight sank the horse and he started to plunge. I thought I was drowning the beast and slid off his back, but of course on the wrong side, as I learned later. I felt a terrific blow against my leg. I thought to myself, this is the end if it is broken.

Sam, about four lengths of a horse ahead, yelled in Cree, "Grab a tail! Hurry up, grab a tail!"

I was lucky with the first grab and I really hung on, but my right leg felt quite numb. I floated behind my steed, using one hand and one foot to keep my head above water. An elaborately trimmed leather jacket and the best-grade Hudson's Bay pants can soak up a lot of water. Besides, my good hat floated downstream to make some Indian or boatman happy when he found it. Not encumbered with my weight and stupid handling, the horse kept pace with the others, and I soon hobbled ashore, the last man to land.

The horse hung his head down, shaking it from side to side, his ears flat, the very picture of dejection. He had taken in a lot of water before I had the sense to leave his back. As he continued to shake his head as if nodding, peals of laughter came from my unsympathetic companions.

Knowing that ridicule was best stopped by joining in the fun, I asked, "What kind of medicine do you use to keep your clothes dry when I see that it doesn't work on the horses?" This brought fresh peals of laughter while they all got busy building a big fire to dry my clothes.

The Indians of those days were not greatly encumbered with clothes, and thus they considered my outfit just a bit too elaborate for a mere interpreter, even if it was for a minister of the gospel. The whole business of the horse being frightened was planned for my benefit, for they suspected I would react as I did.

After I had become better acquainted with the people I found they dearly loved a good joke. Having no choice in the matter, I took it all with good humour and realized they intended no offense, that it was all for a good laugh.

I had borrowed a good muzzleloading shotgun from one of the men on the boat, but after my experience the day I entered camp, I bought it off the man.

I found the gun very accurate and killed a deer with it the first time I took it hunting on the way upriver. The gun was in excellent condition and the owner didn't want to sell it, but when I offered him its original price in sterling, he accepted. Being the first gun I had ever owned, I was naturally proud of my marksmanship and challenged my companions to a contest while my clothes were drying. I beat their best shot and thereby regained some of the prestige I had lost over the river crossing.

Two of the men started out ahead; this, I was told, was a precaution against surprise by the enemy in case there were still Blackfoot lurking in the area. We had been riding for several hours when we met one of the men who had gone ahead. He told us there was a large herd of buffalo less than a mile ahead, browsing on a hill at the head of the ravine, in a fine position to approach without being seen.

Saddle horses and pack animals were hobbled at once in the deep ravine we had been skirting for some time. Hurried preparations were made as the saddles were stripped and changed to the buffalo-running horses that had been led all the way. I left my own horse saddled while I helped with the animals, as I was determined to try my luck with the others. Returning, I was surprised to find my saddle off my horse and placed on a white buffalo runner. I was about to protest when Samuel motioned for me to take the horse. "You'll use that horse; your own might carry you clean into Blackfoot country when he catches sight of the buffalo."

My excitement and joy were unbounded; apparently I had been accepted into their company. To be given the use of this fine animal while its owner watched camp was most gratifying. It was more than satisfactory recompense for the rather severe teasing at the river.

After proceeding under cover of the ravine as far as possible, Samuel stopped to give me last-minute instructions on just what procedures to take in the chase. Sheltered by the ravine, we would approach the herd as near as we could get; then, at a given signal, every man for himself, we would race the horses straight for the buffalo. We all had muzzleloading single-shot shotguns and lead bullets, a powder horn, and a bag of extra bullets.

Again we stopped to examine the priming of our guns and

were cautioned against getting jammed among the herd once they started to stampede. I was told that the trained horse would swing close to the animal I wanted to kill and that I should aim my shot close behind the shoulder.

I could hear the buffalo as they made a kind of low grunting sound. I was last in line as we rode single file and picked our way along the ravine that seemed to be getting shallower. Samuel stopped and motioned us to draw up beside him. He told us that we would climb out to the top level about fifty yards ahead. We would now travel abreast and as soon as we sighted the animals, we would charge towards the herd at top speed.

The horse I was riding responded to prods of the heel or a lash of the lines with lazy indifference, and I doubted if the lazy beggar would keep up with the others. The other two horses were chucking their heads and tugging at the lines in their eagerness to be on with the chase.

Taking advantage of a heavy willow clump at the top of the ravine, we climbed to the level above. A single buffalo feeding close to the rim whirled and raced towards the others. The moment my horse caught sight of the lone animal he took a tremendous leap ahead, almost unseating me. It was just pure luck that I was able to hold onto the gun. The lazy brute in a twinkling turned into a fiery meteor that swept forward with such terrific speed that we soon outdistanced the others.

I was so excited and exhilarated that it was some time before I noticed my horse was keeping pace with one particular animal at a distance of about four yards. I took aim and fired. For a minute I thought I had missed as the beast kept on running, but suddenly it turned head over heels. I knew then I had scored a fatal shot. My companions were swallowed up in a cloud of dust stirred up by the herd.

My horse immediately increased his speed, drawing up beside another buffalo that seemed to be converging from my left side. I found that I had lost my ramrod so I tried to pull away from the herd to avoid being caught, as I had been warned. My horse had other ideas about this. When I tried to slow down his speed and draw away from the herd, he reared, jerked his head, and tried to grip the bit in his mouth; and did his best to keep on running. I lost a stirrup but finally got him checked.

In a few moments the herd had disappeared over another hill, but it took some time before the dust settled and I could take stock of the situation. I was surprised at the distance we had travelled in such a short time.

I could see my friends around an animal almost a mile

31

away. My horse had again settled down to a nice leisurely pace, for which I was thankful, although I was still glowing with excitement and pride at my first buffalo kill.

"Well," said Samuel, "we were just debating whether you had gone to visit the Blackfoot and if we should follow up to see what happened or start skinning your fat cow. What were you doing all that time?"

Deciding to have some fun of my own I replied, "Oh! I was trying to spot another fat cow, but I couldn't find one, so I turned back."

I offered to skin my own animal to gain time to find my ramrod before they noticed I had lost it, but they knew that I had never skinned a buffalo and told me it would take me too long.

"You're our guest — we couldn't allow you to do the killing and also do all the work."

The best I could do was throw my coat over the gun as I laid it in the grass. It wasn't long before they had the animal skinned and quartered, ready for the pack horses that were being brought up by the other two men. Samuel had killed two cows and the other chap a young bull, so the horses would be loaded to capacity on the way home.

The others had gone back to prepare the other buffalo, leaving Samuel and me to complete the last of the work. Then Samuel walked away from the meat and came back with my ramrod. Grinning broadly he remarked, "Never use a ramrod for a marker; you never know when you might need it again." A ramrod in a muzzleloading gun is used to pack the charge down for greater velocity. It is usually a saskatoon willow, dried and whittled to the exact size of the barrel to hold the stick. I have known some experts in the hunt who carried the lead balls in their mouths, poured the powder into the palm of the hand, then tilted the barrel to receive the powder. They simply tapped the gun butt against their leg or saddle for the powder to settle in the nipple, then put the ball down the barrel, and the gun was ready to shoot. I never tried that method, but I have known others to do effective shooting in this manner.

All I could do at Sam's remark was to grin. I learned then and had it proved many times later that it was almost impossible to hide anything from the eyes of these trained observers.

The rod must have come loose from its holder in those few desperate moments when I was fighting to hold my seat at the start of the chase. Nothing further was mentioned about my loss but it must have cost Samuel a great deal in self-restraint to withhold the information when they told of my other misfortunes later that night at the camp.

It was still early in the day, so it was decided to load lightly and get across the river before dark. They would send others back for the balance of the meat in the morning.

We reached the river with daylight to spare. This time they showed me how to keep my clothes dry by tying them to the mane on the highest part of the withers just ahead of the saddle. I had no trouble and by watching the others, I got off on the downstream side of the horse. An animal swims with his legs slightly up against the current. That is how I had been hit in the leg at my last crossing.

It was dark when we reached camp but kettles were waiting and ready for the meat. A big central fire was blazing and soon everyone in camp was preparing supper. There were roasts and boiled meat and a huge cauldron of tea. This would be my first time to eat buffalo meat from an animal I had killed myself; and consequently twice as sweet for that reason. There were some pretty husky men in that camp but I doubt if there were any to equal my capacity.

We were treated to an excellent account of my misfortunes at the river, with the near-drowning of the horse and his dejected appearance afterwards. Also the loss of my good hat was suitably bemoaned by the listeners. Many of them offered their own head gear, all in various stages of dilapidation — the more disreputable the hat or cap, the more insistent they were. All this created a great deal of harmless fun.

The whole episode lost nothing in the telling, but my answer after returning from the chase, about looking for another fat cow, brought the loudest reception of all. I thought it out of all proportion to so mild a joke. Long afterwards, from later experiences, I learned that it was almost impossible to pick out a choice animal from a large herd because of the heavy dust cloud raised by a stampeding herd. The hunters estimated the animals we had chased numbered around three hundred head.

We were late getting to bed that night but at daylight in the morning everyone was astir. Most had stayed up all night taking care of the fires to dry the meat. The men had gone before daylight to fetch the rest of the meat back to the camp. Morning service at daylight in the open prairie air was most impressive. I wondered what the bishop would say, if he were there to see the assembly gathered to hear Mr. Steinhauer's short service and prayers. Adherents to the Catholic denomination were quite as reverent as any in other churches. We were one people, with one purpose, to give thanks for our bountiful gifts and acknowledge God's creations.

Many stages had been erected during our absence on the hunt; they were now loaded with meat cut in fairly thin slices and hung over drying fires. Drying stages were being put up in preparation for the balance of the meat to be brought into camp. I marvelled at the minister who was quite as busy as any of the men, cutting meat or hanging it to dry, and removing that already finished and replacing it with fresh supplies. Nothing was wasted — the bones were boiled for immediate consumption and later burned on the fires, broken, and the marrow fat extracted and placed in containers to be cooked and poured into pemmican sacks with the pounded dry meat.

Mr. Steinhauer, a fully ordained minister of the church, had shed the dignity of his position and joined in the laughter and stories at the evening fires with the freedom of companionship that would have set my Bishop back staggering in scornful disgust and disapproval. Yet I noticed there were none of the borderline stories associated with indecency, so often the theme in many campfire stories.

After a big breakfast we delayed our departure, watching the men busily preparing the meat for their return north to their homes. We had fetched less than half the meat back with us, and it was surprising how quickly it dried under the slow fire treatment and the hot September sun. Samuel officiated in the distribution of the meat. I noticed his decisions were accepted without question. Those on other duties away from camp would receive their share from the prepared meat.

We were getting ready to leave but they insisted that we have an early dinner, besides packing a hamper of the choicest parts for the trip. The whole camp came to bid us goodbye. I was glad of Mitchell's company as he knew the trail and the best places to cross several creeks on our route.

There was not a single bridge in the country at that time. The earliest bridge that I can remember was built on the Sturgeon River, just below the present Catholic buildings. Father Lacombe engineered the work and it contained a way to block any undesirable warrior from crossing over without permission. A well marked cart trail, fifteen miles south of the Saskatchewan River, was used by buffalo hunters who supplied meat to the Hudson's Bay post at Edmonton. Many retired servants of the Company added to their living by selling pemmican and also fresh meat to the post for winter supply. In fact, the Hudson's Bay Company was the only source of employment in all the West.

The old trail passed through what was later called Hairy Hill, Whitford, Andrew, Star, Bruderheim, and thence to Fort Saskatchewan, where there was a good crossing, and then it followed the north side of the river to Edmonton; none of these places were in existence then except Fort Edmonton. There were no settlers in any part of the area until a number of years later, and nothing to spoil the natural beauty of the land in its primitive state. We saw herds of buffalo every day in bunches of twenty-five or so, but no large herd like the one we had stampeded on my first hunt. Hairy Hill was an old name for a high hill where the buffalo gathered and shed their hair in the spring time, no doubt to get the cool breezes and escape the insect pests. It was also a favourite range for them in the earliest heavy migration from the south, being well watered and having a heavy growth of buffalo grass.

The trail we were following passed through open land with islands of poplar and willow clumps, where creeks meandered their way to the Saskatchewan ten or twenty miles north of us. It was a beautiful country. Wild game birds took flight from our approach but only flew a short distance to light and start feeding again. The lakes were black with every species of duck, and a large flock of geese and waveys flew over our heads, low enough to have been shot down, to light on what was later called Whitford Lake.

It was truly a land of plenty, with nothing to spoil its magnificence or the abundance that nature had provided so profusely. I was destined to pass over this trail many times but never again to witness the plenty that met my vision on every hand that year of 1856.

The trail finally ended at the ford. I now had more confidence in myself and had lost my nervousness after the near-accident at Saddle Lake Crossing. My leg was still black and blue and became very stiff after riding any distance. I realized I could easily have been drowned if I had missed Samuel's suggestion of grabbing a tail. I found out later that few of the northern Indians could swim a stroke; they had no need to as they were all expert canoemen.

The moment we struck out into deep water my horse took over with a sagacity completely opposite to his general conduct on land. There were times when I almost became fond of the beggar but just about then he would indulge in some capricious act that would test my patience to the limit. I have ridden many horses since that roman-nosed roan but none with the all-day tireless stamina and few to equal his individual contrariness.

CHAPTER THREE

Fort Edmonton

W E CAMPED TWICE on the road and reached Fort Edmonton late in the afternoon of the third day. I reported to Mr. Woolsey who had arrived the previous evening.

"Hobble my mare and the pack horse," he said. "Picket the roan as usual till morning, then you can turn them out with the Hudson's Bay horses herded around the Horse Hills. They're always brought back to the fort and put in a horse stockade at night. There's still danger from horse thieves here, but I think our horses will be safe for one night; they need the feed after the long trip."

There were quite a few white men employed at the fort, which had the largest staff of any of the posts I had visited. Fort Edmonton was the supply station for many of the northern stations, and bought considerable buffalo meat supplies from the Indians as well as from retired Metis servants who hunted and fished for the fort. There was a well established settlement at Lac Ste. Anne and the beginning of another at St. Albert.

The chief factor had a three-storey building, and another building connected for the exclusive use of Indian trade. All the buildings were on the second bench of the river flat and enclosed by a huge stockade probably one hundred and fifty yards each way.

The stockade was built of large spruce logs, some whip-sawed and others hewn, set upright eleven feet above ground, the ends sunk to a depth of four feet in the ground. The earth from the trench dug to set the timbers was tamped solid around the uprights so that there was no moving them in any direction. The shoulders of the logs were hewn to fit tightly against each other. This made an impregnable barrier against any guns of the time.[1] The single entrance was fitted to swing inwards, the hinges being of solid wood, and a hung bar was built to withstand a tremendous battering against any attempt to break in the gate. A walk, seven feet high, was built around the inside of the whole stockade. Each corner of the stockade had what was called a bastion, which was constructed in the same way as the stockade but with longer legs, and was sufficiently higher to allow a man to stand and work the brass cannon erected on two sides of the enclosure. The guns covered the south and west approaches.

Most of the forts were of similar construction, but the one at Edmonton was built with more elaborate care for strength and security than any of the others. There was little danger from the Crees, but the Blackfoot, Peigan, and Blood Indians were an excitable lot, easily aroused and dangerous when excited.

There were a number of tents on the flat below the fort, so I decided to take a walk that evening after supper. While there I heard the people singing hymns and praying. I thought it strange and asked Mr. Woolsey for an explanation when I returned.

"Yes, it would be strange to a newcomer to this area. Those people are Christian Indians from Pigeon Lake. A man by the name of Rundle was a minister among them and had some mission buildings there that I hope to make habitable for ourselves in the spring. We'll stay here for the winter and go there in the spring. The Rev. Mr. Rundle met with a bad accident when he was thrown from a horse and a layman by the name of Sinclair carried on the work for a time after Rundle was gone. The Pigeon Lake Indians are a friendly, peaceful people; it is through their request that I have been sent here." The Pigeon Lake Indians continued to camp in the vicinity of the fort all winter, hunting and trapping.[2] They were staying within the protection of the fort, as the Blackfoot and Peigan Indians were active in their wars that winter.

Mr. Woolsey was not a severe taskmaster. Although he insisted that I be familiar with the text of his sermon, the reading took up little time, but I was thankful for the tuition that I had received at the Collegiate School.

His sermons were easily interpreted; they were adjusted to

the understanding of the native people in a language that was stripped of all high-sounding terms and delivered with a sincerity and convicion that kept his audience attentive. The Rev. Mr. Woolsey had a natural understanding of the Indian viewpoint, and his adaptation of scripture to their way of life was natural and easily understood.

Mr. Woolsey did not confine my labours to himself entirely but allowed me to join in the activities of the fort, going out several times with the company men after fish at Lac Ste. Anne or after fresh buffalo meat near what is known as Beaver Hills. I enjoyed these trips as they relieved the monotony that would otherwise have been a hardship. Later when the factor learned that I was an efficient dogdriver, he sent me on trips alone.

My employer only required me to make a good interpretation of his sermons that were at that time confined to the Pigeon Lake Indians and the fort people. He did no travelling that winter but considered it only right that I should help in keeping the post supplied with food. Meat, fish, and game were the only food, and it required the steady work of a number of people to keep a supply ahead.

The factor assigned me a room with one of his workmen, William Borwick, a man of approximately my own age but who had been in service with the Company for several years, mostly at Edmonton.

We were approaching the Christmas holidays and there was a growing excitement noticeable among the inmates of the fort. Bill and others spent their spare time making ready their best clothes. The preparations the week before Christmas took on a new tempo of activity. Every dog driver and team was rushing supplies of fish to the fort for the dog trains of the expected visitors. The factor engaged two of the Indians who had buffalo-running horses to go with me after fresh meat, with orders to bring nothing but the best. We returned in four days with our pack horses loaded with two fine cows.

It was the custom of Hudson's Bay officials to meet at Fort Edmonton during Christmas week, staying for New Year's Day. They discussed business concerned with the trade, and prepared their orders for the following year. The conference had developed into a week of social activities commemorating the Christmas period.

Fort Pitt, Slave Lake, Chipewyan, Fort Assiniboine, Jasper House, Rocky Mountain House, and Lac La Biche were all represented. The two days before Christmas was a bedlam of noise as each new dog team arrived. Every arrival was a signal for all the dogs of the fort and those of the Crees camped nearby to raise their voices in a deafening uproar of welcome or defiance as their tempers dictated.

The noise was terrific, yet none of the regular inmates paid any attention or made any effort to silence any dog within reach. The drivers of the dog teams and the factors were assigned quarters as quickly as they arrived; the arrangements for the guests was a wonderful example of organized planning.

On Christmas Eve, Father Lacombe drove in to conduct Midnight Mass. I was somewhat surprised that the priest and my employer were on such friendly and cordial terms. Woolsey went out to meet him and immediately invited him to his room, where they spent several hours of congenial conversation. Of course I was on hand to take care of his dogs, as the man drove his own team.[3]

Knowing the Rev. Woolsey's strong views against dancing, I was reluctant to ask permission to attend the celebrations, but I was burning to go. It was getting late when the priest finally departed for his duties with Catholic members of his church, and I finally screwed up enough courage to face the man.

Mr. Woolsey was seated reading his Bible when I entered his small room. I was in such a hurry to have his verdict that I had prepared no opening speech, although he looked slightly surprised at my late visit. He asked me to be seated, then as if reading my mind or perhaps noticing my flustered condition, said, "So you are fond of dancing."

It was my turn to look surprised as I answered too quickly in a tone of voice much too loud for that small room, "Yes I am, and that is what I came to see you about. I want your permission to attend."

Slightly smiling, he answered, "I surmised as much from this late visit. I have given the matter some thought, for you know my principles over dancing. However, you're a young man and need some recreation; your own conscience must be your guide. I have no objections, provided you conduct yourself as a gentleman. Drinking will be quite conspicuous in tomorrow's festivities and as my associate I will not permit your indulgence in this miserable business."

"I can promise you that I'll do no drinking whatever as I've cultivated no taste for liquor. You have my promise on both counts."

"Thank you, I accept both promises," and in an amused tone he added, "I hope you don't find them too heavy an obligation."

Wishing him the Season's Greetings, I bade him goodnight. Delighted with the interview I ran back to our room to tell Bill

39

the happy news. I was greatly relieved. Had he refused, I would have been in a difficult position. Bill was still up awaiting my return and I asked him what would be the order of the day.

"Well, many will be quite jolly as it is the custom for each of the employees to receive a ration of rum the day before Christmas, but by a rule of the Company no-one is to touch it before the next day. There will also be a dance at night; most of the women will come from the two settlements, Lac Ste. Anne and St. Albert. Let me assure you that some of the best-looking women in the West, and for that matter anywhere else, will be at that dance tomorrow night."

Then I told him of the wonderful news of receiving Woolsey's permission to attend. I danced a few steps for his benefit. Of course I did not tell him about the promise to abstain from drinking. I wanted all the credit to myself about being a gentleman. That always comes natural to a sober man for I have noticed that some of the most polished gentlemen lose some of their colour under the influence of drink.

It was some time before I was able to get to sleep, then suddenly it was morning. I was aroused from a deep sleep by a tremendous bloodcurdling noise that actually seemed to vibrate the room. For a moment I was shocked motionless, then the notes of music sounded into my senses. I was out of bed and scrambled for my clothes. Bill was already half dressed.

John Graham, a Scottish employee, burst into the room, almost incoherent with excitement and fairly dancing in his joy. Finally he shouted at the top of his voice, "The Pibroch! The Pibroch!" Tears coursed down his cheeks as he motioned for Bill and me to come. We dressed in seconds that morning and followed him out as he turned and dashed for the door.

Striding back and forth on the walk that surrounded three sides of the factor's three-storied building was a man by the name of Colin Fraser playing a set of bagpipes. The long droning notes that precede the actual music were what awakened me so suddenly. He made a striking figure, dressed in all the gay regalia of tartan and kilt, his knees exposed to the elements. He seemed quite indifferent to the weather that was at least thirty degrees below zero. The deep notes of his instrument echoed back from the high hills of the ice-covered Saskatchewan River. It was beautiful even to my unfamiliar ear; never till then had I heard the bagpipes played.

I turned to watch the face of our old friend and felt some of the deep loneliness that marked the features of this old man, whose life ambition had been to return to his native land; he now realized he was too late ever to attain it. He stood with his hand on Borwick's shoulder; unashamed tears flowed down his

40

cheeks. That night Bill and I carried him to his room, too inebriated to manage his own way.

Shortly after breakfast a horn was sounded, a sign that the factor was ready to receive the salutations of the men at the fort. I accompanied Borwick in this customary courtesy. After greeting each man in turn the chief clerk, who stood at the factor's elbow for this purpose, handed each man a drink of rum. I watched Bill out of the corner of my eyes as I took my turn to shake hands and offer the factor the happy returns of the day. When I refused my offer of a drink, I could see consternation and anger on Bill's face. We were scarcely out of the room when he gave me a sound going over for refusing the drink.

"Look here, Peter! You have been guilty of a grave discourtesy in refusing a drink. This has been the custom of the Company since the memory of the oldest man in the service.".

"My dear sir, I'm not an employee of your grand Company; my first duty is to my employer. The matter of the minister's man refusing a drink of rum will, I hope, not create a revolution in the service. Perhaps you'd better interview Mr. Woolsey before the situation gets too serious."

He gave me a disgusted look but said no more. However, I noticed that he made a great fuss and ceremony when it came time to open his own ration in our room and never offered me a courtesy drink that he had so strongly advocated early that morning. Up to this time and for several years afterwards, I had no desire for strong drink nor had occasion to test its possibilities, but regret to say that at this late date, I'm afraid I could not claim that boast.

Christmas day was spent in visiting among those gathered at the fort. Woolsey held a service in English which everybody attended, regardless of affiliation. I was not called up to interpret but sat with his audience.

I had heard stories of unrestricted convivial times at these Christmas gatherings but there was no evidence of excess that day, other than our friend Graham who appeared to be under no obligation to share his portion with any other of the workmen. He gave Bill a drink but when I refused mine, he took an extra for himself, first holding the glass high in the air in my direction, smacking his lips in anticipation, then sipping with evident relish, nodding his head towards me with an air of admiring approval as if my refusal was a personal act of kindness to himself.

The dance that night I thought upheld Bill's claims; in fact he had slightly underrated it. Borwick, being an old-timer in the area, seemed to know every person there and soon made me

41

acquainted with a number of his friends. They were friendly and cordial and called me by my first name without the formal use of surname. When Bill introduced me as Peter, I drew him aside and pointed out his omission.

"Heck, every one around here knows you as Erasmus, the minister's man, so why waste time? It's the custom around here to use first names or nicknames. They would think you were trying to put on airs if I called you Mr. Erasmus. Only factors, ministers of the church, and priests have a handle to their names."

Colours in clothes were quite in evidence but nothing so startling as in later years. The Hudson's Bay stores at that time were more conservative in their choices of colours and they were the only source of supply. Therefore dress in those days gave more attention to utility than fashion. Neatness of apparel was of primary importance and the winsome maids of the prairie were quite as adept at adjusting the means at hand as their sisters a quarter of a century later.

A big lunch was served at midnight in the homes of the married couples, where the guests had previously left their contributions of food at the homes of their friends and acquaintances. Young bachelor residents of the post were pressed into service as chore boys, regardless of their wishes in the matter. I presumed that usage had established a precedent; at any rate I found that single men were mere appendages of the wives' organization for entertaining their guests; we were errand boys. Bill's apparent enjoyment of my hesitant and clumsy handling of the job was plain to see. Wherever there was a shortage of any particular food, we were sent to a neighbouring house for supplies and we were both too busy to share in the talk and pleasantry going on wherever we went.

I was getting quite rebellious and said so in a low tone to Bill, who just laughed and told me to have a little more patience. At last the guests were all served and started drifting back to the dance floor. Most of the crowd had taken their food standing up around the tables. Not us; we were seated at a table with our hostess and the husband who from some hidden secret place brought out a sadly depleted bottle. Bill's malicious grin and wink was a determining factor in stiffening my weakened resistance.

Three attractive young ladies kept us supplied with food and talk; I refused the drink but needed no second invitation to start on the food. Under these circumstances I regained my good humour and for revenge on Bill, entered into a gay conversation with our attentive and pretty waitresses. Bill's

42

devotion to the bottle left him badly handicapped in that competition.

There was very little rest for the musicians between dances, and there were plenty of fiddlers among the French Metis people from Lac Ste. Anne. Having too good a time dancing I did not offer my services that night, but later on I happened to mention to Bill that I liked playing the fiddle, and thereafter on Borwick's insistence I had to do my share.

The settlement guests all left for their homes at broad daylight. After dancing all night they had to run behind dogs for another forty miles before they would have any rest or sleep. The men were tough athletes to stand a grind like that and I did not envy their trip under those conditions.

The more serious business of the post leaders was of course not neglected for any of the social events at the fort or at the settlements. The conference was brought to a final grand finish with New Year's Day sports. There were foot races, toboggan slides on the North Saskatchewan River hill, some competitions for the women, and the big dog-train race of three miles on the river. Every team from each post competed in this race. Each factor contributed a share to this prize; the winner took all, which was a choice of any clothes in stock to the amount of approximately twenty-five dollars.

The employed dog drivers for the Company at Edmonton asked the factor if they could allow me to drive one of their two dog teams. He consented, provided the other leaders agreed. They readily consented as they considered me poor competition against their own hardened and skillful drivers.

Bill heard about the arrangement and came to me with the intention of talking me out of it. "Man, you haven't a chance in the world against these men from Jasper House and Athabasca; fifty miles a day is a regular run for them. They would be ashamed if they were caught riding. They are tough, strong young men. Heck, man! That's all they know, just running behind dogs all winter."

"Bill, I'm going to beat every last one of them; I'll tell you how I aim to do it. Every driver has been idle, eating and drinking to the limit of his capacity all week. Their dogs are the same, and will be in no fit condition for a short fast race like this will be. Our dogs are in work shape. The team I drive has made a trip to Lac Ste. Anne this week; they are not overfed and they are rested enough to be keen in tomorrow's run. Bet your shirt, Bill; if you lose, I'll give you one of mine. Besides, I don't drink and that's my biggest lead over all the others."

This latter remark was just a dig for Bill's private opinions on drinking, but I had considerable faith in my ability as a runner, for I had won foot races against some pretty strong competition. My trips for the post after game and fish had kept me in good condition. Pierre, the driver of the second team, had urged me to enter the race and had been the one to approach the factor.

"Peter, you by gar, are de best runner in dese parts. You win de race for sure. You never drink de whisky, while dem men dey drink, dey eat an' feed de dogs like peegs. Dey lazy like Hell, all de week. For sure you win dat race, maybe."

The starting point was marked by stakes frozen in the ice far enough apart to accommodate the seven teams at the line. One mile and a half downriver was another set of stakes, three in number around which we must drive before returning to the starting line. Failure to pass around the far stake would disqualify any driver. There were judges at this end and watchers at the other to make sure the drivers complied with the rules. No man was allowed to foul up another driver or cut in unless he had a clear lead to the trail that would be well marked on our trip downriver.

We were off! Bill was my helper at the post. I had given him instructions to hold the dogs back until at least half of the others had started. They would be ploughing snow on an untravelled track. Bill, disgusted at that foolish way of starting, nevertheless obeyed. There were four teams in the lead, all abreast for the first two hundred yards or so. The Jasper man had the same idea as I had; he was holding his dogs to the track already made by the other four toboggans. One man was left at the post as his dogs in their eagerness had become fouled up in their harness. I could see that the man from Jasper would be my strong competitor.

What none of the other drivers knew about was a stretch of overflow ice on the last half mile of the course downriver where I hoped to pass the others without plowing deep snow. Pierre, our Edmonton driver, was now in second place behind the Fort Pitt man. We were all closely bunched when we made the turn but I got ahead of the fourth team as his dogs cut short instead of rounding the marker posts, and he had to turn his dogs.

I was now in third place, the Jasper man directly behind me. When I came opposite the overflow ice, I struck into the deep snow as if to pass the team ahead; he started to follow me but seeing the depth of snow turned back. The minute I reached the thin snow on the overflow ice, I cracked the whip over the dogs' backs and yelled. They almost threw me off the sleigh with their increased speed, as I had climbed on the sleigh to give it weight.

Now ahead of all the others, I allowed myself plenty of room before cutting back to the track. I had the race if I could stand the pace that I was being forced to travel to hold my lead. I had a brief breather while riding the overflow but jumped off when I came to the now well-marked trail.

The Fort Pitt man was close up behind me and I knew I had to outdistance him before we reached the last quarter mile, because then he would also have a broken trail to follow. Now for the second time since starting I cracked my whip over the dogs, yelling for more speed, not hitting them but my voice and whip urging more speed.

I did not dare to look behind me at the others but was content with side glances only. For truth to tell, I had no breath to spare nor energy to worry about opponents as long as I could see no driver ahead. We were only a hundred yards or so from the starting posts when another side glance showed the Fort Pitt man gaining beside me, his lead dog almost opposite my toboggan front. Only the short distance would save the race for me as I had the limit of speed out of my dogs. I hit the finish line with only a two dog advantage over my opponent.

Bill was like a crazy man, shouting and yelling his triumph for my win, but I found out later his delight was for himself as he had won a new shirt and pants by betting on my team to win. He even forgot to congratulate me as all the others did as soon as I could get my breath to acknowledge my thanks. Pierre and the Jasper man had fought for third place but the Jasper man beat him in a closer finish than my win. In fact the judges had some doubt about it but Pierre acknowledged his defeat. He told me afterwards, by gar, he didn't care as long as our Edmonton team won a first.

At daylight the next morning the far-distant post managers had pulled out for another long year of isolated wilderness where their duties held little of entertainment and no social life whatever, until the following gathering a year hence at Edmonton. No wonder the Chief Factor[4] had put so much effort and attention for their comfort and entertainment while they were in Edmonton. Their dogs still were dressed in all the ribbons, tassles, and bells of the previous day, but at noon the dogs would be stripped of the decorations which were carefully put away for the next year.

A week had passed since quiet had again settled on the fort. Then two Blackfoot arrived at the gate and were given admittance. They were envoys who had been sent ahead to notify the factor of the arrival of their band the next day. It was customary for any band of Indians to send word ahead and receive tobacco to smoke the peace pipe the night before their arrival. This was an indication of their intentions for a trade mission.

The next forenoon a big band arrived. The men were all mounted on good horses. The horsemen came in sight first as they were strung along a deep ravine that enters the Saskatchewan on the south side. They were followed by a long line of dogs and loaded pack horses. They followed the flat upriver until they were about opposite the fort, then crossed over the river. A number of other horsemen now appeared above the flat; these I presume were guards to protect their rear.

It was a picturesque sight to watch from the heights of the bastion where I had gone to get a better view. The Blackfoot took up a position west of the fort, on a flat up from the river. I was somewhat worried for the Pigeon Lake Crees who were stationed near the south stockade of the fort, but apparently they were to enjoy immunity because they were under protection of the fort.

The next morning I was again on the bastion where the men had been stationed in preparation for the reception of the Blackfoot. A horse was led up to a teepee where we could plainly see that he was being loaded with all kinds of tanned hides and furs. We could not see exactly what was placed on the horse but the men told me what the pack would probably contain.

The chief held the line as they made their way towards the fort, followed by a bodyguard and a troop of singers whose voices could be heard quite distinctly from where we stood. As they advanced towards the fort they continued what I thought was a weird but melodious tone, till they almost reached the gate. The chief and his bodyguard all held their guns towards the sky and discharged them. The first bastion gun was fired, and at a signal flashed back from the gate, a second volley was fired from the other cannon. Then the gate was swung open. The firing of Indian guns was an indication of peaceful purposes, as their guns were empty and could do no harm.

The factor was standing at the gate to welcome the visitors. The chief then handed the line to him and he passed the line to the chief clerk, who walked with the chief towards the trading house where the door opened at a signal from the factor.

The Indian house where the actual trading was done was a special building, extremely long, divided in the middle and containing two chimneys, one at each end. A door giving entrance for the traders was fastened with a heavy bar similar in construction to the outer gate, and opened inwards. Bill showed me where the guards would be stationed for the whole of the trading. This was a precautionary measure in case of

46

treachery. From where we lay above we could through portholes command a view of every part of the room.

The room was divided in such a manner that any goods handed out would pass through a small opening about breast high. A ledge on the inside wall allowed the display of any goods asked for. Too large a display at one time excited the Indians and made them difficult to handle.

A clerk appeared from behind the small door and handed out a black suit of clothes with brass buttons, a stove pipe hat that had a red feather attached to the band in front, and a special medal with the coat of arms of the Hudson's Bay Company. The medal was fastened to the chief's new coat with a great display of ceremony.

A ninety-pound roll of tobacco was shoved out of the window and also a ten-gallon keg of rum. This latter, of course, had been heavily diluted with about two-thirds water. A quantity of ammunition, shot, powder, and bullets — not a large amount but I thought a quite generous amount — made a fairly well-balanced exchange for the chief's horseload of skins and furs.

The Blackfoot chief then gave an oration which I presumed indicated his appreciation of the generosity of the factor and a promise of good fellowship for him and his people in their trade with the Company.

The factor made a return speech, translated back to Blackfoot language by his interpreter, in which he spoke of his high regard for the chief and his admiration for the fine braves accompanying him. On behalf of the great Hudson's Bay Company he hoped that these fine Blackfoot people would continue their trade in good fellowship and friendliness with the Company to their own mutual benefit. Referring to himself as but a poor servant, he expressed his personal feeling for the whole Blackfoot people as the finest examples of all the native people.

The singers, who had been patiently waiting outside the door while all this was going on, were now summoned by one of the chief's guards. They all came inside in an orderly manner, picked up the presents, and were ready to depart. The chief, who had stood waiting, now strode towards the door, followed by the two guards a pace behind, and the singers swung in behind, two abreast. When they passed the door they again started to sing. They had a weird rhythm and their voices blended together with a thrilling penetration that affected me with something of fear and dread. Perhaps my memory of the massacred Crees at Saddle Lake was still heavy on my mind. If this singing was intended for good will and friendliness then I wanted none of their war songs. The careful precautions in the loaded guns held in readiness for any eventuality were to my mind well justified.

None of the usual work was carried on during the Blackfoot visit as the men were all assigned to garrison duty and alerted to the necessity of extreme care. I was greatly impressed with the efficiency with which this was accomplished. Each man assumed his task and was relieved of duty without any apparent orders from any particular officer.

The exchange of goods for tanned hides, fur, pemmican, fresh meat, or any other article of Indian make was done by barter. Lead bullets were used to signify the value of approximately fifty cents. A pile of furs, skins, or other articles was valued by the trader and an equal number of bullets pushed towards the seller as an estimate of his valuation. From there on they bargained to an agreement, and the final sale completed. It was a cumbersome procedure and took up a great deal of time, but a system that had become a custom and was satisfactory to native understanding. In my opinion the quality of the goods offered for sale were good value when one considers the tremendous labour and cost entailed in the transportation, especially upriver by hand as the boats were towed against the current.

The Blackfoot departed as soon as they had traded all their products of the hunt. Five or more riders started out ahead. The chief led the main body with his personal bodyguard of a half-dozen mounted riders, the women and children following. I noticed that a number of riders took up positions at the rear and flanked the main body of the band on both sides.

The usual work was resumed after the Indians had left, but the men on the bastions continued their duties until the following day, or I presume until it was certain that there would be no unannounced return.

Early in the spring of 1857, as planned, Rev. Mr. Woolsey and I moved to Pigeon Lake. The Indians had gone a few weeks earlier. We were both on saddle and our pack horses were loaded heavily with our supplies. We found the buildings were in a bad state of repair, the roofs caved in and the doors hanging from rotten leather hinges. The chimney had to be torn down and re-built. We had a canvas tent along so we would be protected while this was being done. Early the first morning I started to work, tearing the roof off the house. I was just nicely started when a number of young men came with their tools and offered their help, but I told them the minister could not pay for help. They just laughed and said they had been ordered to help by the chief; pay was no concern of theirs. This kindly act was typical of their way with the minister. They were generous and careful to see that we had all the food we could use. In fact we had so many offers that we had to refuse for fear of wasting food.

I was invited on hunting, trapping, and fishing trips, and bird-game hunts. Mr. Woolsey made no objection to these excursions and said it was only right that I should help to provide provisions that they were giving so graciously. There were about two hundred souls in the band; such a large number required almost constant hunting to keep up supplies. It was no hardship for me as I enjoyed tramping through the woods hunting with these good-natured, unselfish bushmen. What I learned while travelling with the Pigeon Lake Indians was of vast help in later years.

For some reason or other the larger game, moose, elk, and deer upon which they depended for most of the meat supplies were getting scarce in the region. Greater distances had to be travelled to obtain game, which consequently was hard on the horses. At last fish were the only dependable diet. No food in my experience can get more monotonous or less nourishing than a straight diet of fish without any vegetables. The Indians thus decided to go out to the prairies after buffalo.

Woolsey advised me to round up our horses and make ready to follow them out to the plains. The roan had been the only horse I had kept up during our stay at the lake.

I had been sent to Lac Ste. Anne with two young Indian companions to buy potatoes, bringing them in by pack horses. The land was all spaded and ready when we returned, and Mr. Woolsey lost no time getting it seeded. I suspected Mr. Woolsey's haste in getting potatoes planted; he feared the seed might be placed on the tables instead of in the ground.

We left the lake in the latter part of May and I wondered how our garden would fare after an all summer neglect. Oddly enough the potatoes were a good size, and also the turnips were an enormous size in spite of their neglect. Scarcity of seed for the ground prepared had allowed us to use plenty of space between each plant and that probably accounted for their large growth.

We were all summer travelling with the Indians, frequently meeting with other bands. Mr. Woolsey was active in visiting and preaching among the travelling bands we met. On those occasions I had to be in constant attendance as his interpreter. He surprised me with the boundless energy he appeared to have. We sometimes rode long distances to these other camps, spending long days and sometimes staying late at night, then riding back to our own camp with the Pigeon Lake band.

We were continuously on the move as the band followed the buffalo. At one time we must have been almost three hundred miles east of Pigeon Lake and our range covered possibly one hundred miles south of the North Saskatchewan River. Our stay at one place was about a week, seldom more than twelve to fifteen days, then we moved the camp to some other location.

Contrary to the stories I had heard of idleness among Indian tribes, I found this band very industrious. They never killed more buffalo than they could use without waste. When we had no Cree camps to visit, Mr. Woolsey allowed me to go with the buffalo hunters, and I gained a great deal of experience as a result of my work as interpreter travelling with the Indians. I was always on call for Sunday services; the chief did not allow any hunting on the Sabbath day.

There was a definite assignment for each member of the tribe. The elder men acted as guards and buffalo hunters. The young men were given regular duties scouting or locating buffalo or enemy camps; they were being trained to be the eyes and ears for the camp. They travelled in a wide radius of the camping grounds and some of them would stay out several nights if there was any suspicion of strangers within reach of their people. The women were always busy tanning hides or making moccasins, leather clothing for the men, and their own clothes.

Even the young boys in camp had to go through a course in physical training which took the form of wrestling, jumping, and racing. High-jumping over hurdles was a favourite with the bigger boys. Their elders made them bows and arrows, and I was surprised at the proficiency which these young boys developed in their use.

The young men rotated in their scout duties, and there were days when only a few of them were out on the trail. They all appeared to be fond of trying their strength and agility against each other in friendly jousts. I was frequently challenged to join in the exercises, running, jumping, wrestling, and other more serious physical contests.

My stay at Edmonton, in comparative idleness except for dog-train driving, had left me a poor second in these competitions of strength and agility. My size made me fair game for repeated invitations to join in the sports. It took me half the summer to make a fair showing among those trained athletes.

Mr. Woolsey remonstrated with me over being a victim of their skill, but I just laughed and pointed out to him that as long as none of us lost our tempers there was no harm in it.

Certainly I was not hurting his Indians. I knew they would have no respect for a weakling and if I could equal or beat them in these games I would be accepted as one of themselves and have the benefit of all the knowledge that they were masters of in the bush, prairie, and trail.

Later that summer Mr. Woolsey was quite as exuberant as the rest when I won in a three-mile race against one of their best runners. I was doubtful of the attitude this man might have if I beat him but I was delighted when he gave me a fine pair of beadwork moccasins and deerskin gloves, saying, "My brother, you and I are the two best runners in all the prairie, and you are the first man to beat me in a fair race." He never guessed how many aches and pains I had endured or how much heart-breaking energy was spent to enable me to win in their games, and especially that race with him.

It was around the first of September when the Indians finally decided to make their way back to Pigeon Lake. They now had prepared quite a quantity of pemmican. The women had tanned the buffalo hides of the animals killed and made countless pairs of moccasins, gloves, leather coats, and other parts of their wardrobe. The making of teepees was a community affair in which a number of women took part under the direction of one of the older women. The pack horses would be well loaded when they got home. Woolsey, who was getting quite anxious to get back to see about his experiment with the vegetables, one morning told me to get ready as we were going back to the lake. We were pleasantly surprised when I started to dig potatoes. We had a good crop; although they were not large each hill contained a goodly number. I set to work digging a root cellar. It was a big job and I have never had a liking for the use of a shovel since that day.

We were very comfortable in our building as the weather in October and November got gradually colder. We had no fodder for the horses but they did very well on the range. There were always guards watching the horses, and they were usually penned close to the camp at night. The Crees were always on the alert against the danger of horse thieves, so they kept men patrolling a large range of territory within a radius of the home camp.

I was free during week days to go with the Indians hunting and trapping. I now enjoyed the confidence and trust of the men, who made every effort to teach me the secrets of their way of living, such as the best way to approach moose, deer, and elk, and the signs in the woods that different fur-bearing animals made. They were very patient with my mistakes. There were

51

two things that were hardest for me to learn: to make a good set for fur bearers, and to be as noiseless as they were in approaching game.

Big game were again very scarce in their usual haunts and we had to travel greater distances to obtain results. Horses, fed on the range sloughs, had no stamina to stand the long rides and packing necessary to keep us in supplies. We had to supplement the pemmican and dried buffalo if they were to be expected to last all winter.

The chief and his councillors decided they would go out on the plains, rather than ruin their horses under such bad conditions. Woolsey did not care for the hardships of the open prairie with a canvas tent and no stove. However, he finally decided that his duties were more important than his own comfort.

The weather had been quite pleasant the first week on the prairie, but during the second week it turned bitterly cold and I found it difficult to find fuel to keep our tent warm. A fire was built at the front of the tent, sheltered by a tanned buffalo-calf skin which was moved as the wind changed. The deeper we went out on the open prairie the more difficult it was to find wood.

Woolsey was offered shelter in the good buffalo teepees of several of the Indians as well as of the chief, but he had a stubborn and foolish notion of not imposing on the friendship of others. He was determined in his notion of preserving his independence from people's privacy in their own homes. He developed a hacking cough and was afflicted with alternate chills and fever. Finally, he had to admit that he could stand no more cold.

I knew he was very sick but I thought if I mentioned anything about it, he might have been more determined than ever. Believe me, I wasted no time getting ready to make an early start in the morning.

We left the Indians near Battle River at a place known then as Iron Creek, not far from Flag Hill. The weather had now eased from its severity of the last two weeks. Our horses were fresh, and being idle, had picked up in flesh. It is remarkable that horses on the range eating prairie wool, where it was plentiful, even in the cold weather, would quickly show increased vigour and stamina.

We made good time that first day, considering the sick man, but I stopped often — wherever I could find fuel — to make a fire and give him a good hot cup of tea and see that he got thoroughly warmed up before proceeding on our way again. I picked an early camp in a nice wooded spot before the sun went down. Pitching the tent and building a fire in front I had it comfortable in short order.

Returning to the tent after taking care of the horses, I found the man sound asleep. I had difficulty to get him awake to eat his supper, and that was one night when the reading of a Bible passage and his prayers were very brief. I did not undress that night but kept the fires going to keep the tent warm so he could get a good sleep for the next day's travel. I woke him for breakfast at daylight in the morning. He seemed more cheerful and declared he felt like a new man.

I knew that if we made twenty miles a day we would be doing all that could be expected. Each day saw him in better condition to face the ride and more impatient to be on his way. Finally he refused to allow more than a half-hour for the noon stop, scolding me soundly for trying to make a baby out of him. I knew then his recovery was assured and that I need not fear having a corpse on my hands.

We were about ten miles from Fort Edmonton when I looked back and saw ten riders following at a good fast pace. I recognized them as Blackfoot riders when they were yet some distance away. I knew it was useless to try and outdistance them with Woolsey again showing signs of much weariness.

We decided to continue at a leisurely gait, until they drew up closer. When we turned our horses around to face them, they stopped about fifty yards away. We eyed each other with suspicion, and I held my gun carelessly across my saddle for they were as hard a looking bunch as any I had ever looked upon. Holding their hands up in the peace sign, one man addressed us in good Cree.

"Where are you going? You are a small party to be alone on the plains."

"I am taking the man of God back to the fort," I answered. "He is a very sick man and needs protection from the cold."

"Good," said the spokesman. "We will leave two men with you. Our two envoys to the post will help you with the old man if he falls from his horse. He looks to be in a bad way."

Without further words they turned and rode away. The two men rode on each side of my employer, while I stayed behind leading the pack horse. They paid no attention to me, though I continued to hold my gun across my saddle till we were safely inside the fort stockade.

It was now late in January of 1858 and I had again been assigned rooms with Bill Borwick. Though I had missed out on the Christmas week festivities, Bill had given me a full account of the program, which was similar to that of the previous year. There were only three of the previous contestants of last year to appear in the big dog-team race, and the Fort Pitt man had won against all the others. Our Edmonton teams had not placed; Pierre had not been able to take part as he had met with a slight accident which had laid him up for a week before the race.

A few days after Woolsey's arrival at the fort, the eastern packets arrived. This yearly delivery of mail, held over from the last boats, was forwarded by dog team to the far post at Edmonton, and the outgoing packets returned by the same courier. This service of course was Hudson's Bay operated solely for their own convenience. However, the post managers allowed the missionaries and others the use of the service subject to restrictions as to amount and bulk.

The factor had informed me that he had a matter of some importance to discuss with me as soon as he was able to dispatch the outgoing packets, but the arrival of a big band of Blackfoot numbering around 250 counting women and children for a trade mission prevented any further talks with him.

The Blackfoot, to a man, were wonderful horsemen, a proud and arrogant people, even to the least, most diminutive man among them. Like all races there were a few who were not the best specimens of their tribe. One of these latter was riding a light-coloured sorrel horse. The animal was almost cream with a long flowing white mane and tail. The little beggar manoeuvered his horse in rapid motion to show off his horsemanship.

The western sun shone brightly against the movement of horses and riders who were putting on a performance for the spectators. I looked at that one animal to the exclusion of the others. I wanted that horse regardless of the cost. I forgot my prejudice against these fierce-looking rogues and held up my hand as a sign I wanted to talk to the man as he passed nearer where I stood.

He whirled his horse and with added speed rode the animal straight at me. For a moment I thought he intended to ride me down. He was fifty yards away when I first caught his attention. However, I held my ground, intending to grab his horse and throw him aside. He pulled his horse up within inches of my feet, and its hooves threw snow all over me as it was pulled to a sudden stop.

With a studied coolness to match his impetuous conduct, I made signs that I wanted to buy his horse. He beckoned to another man who was sitting on his horse and watching us with considerable interest. The man rode towards us and asked me in good Cree what I wanted.

"I want to buy this man's horse. Ask him what he will take in trade from the Hudson's Bay stores."

The arrogant little beggar made a motion with both arms indicating a roll of tobacco and a hunting knife and a shirt.

"All right," I said. "I will pay that much for your horse but you will have to wait here till I arrange for the things with my boss."

Woolsey refused to arrange for payment, saying, "We are not allowed to trade with the Indians in any way. This is a rule of the Company, and although I would be dealing indirectly, it would still be breaking an agreement with Company officials. Go to the factor and make your arrangements yourself. You can kill wolves and coyotes to pay quite easily."

I had not drawn my money for some time and I was very provoked at the man's determined refusal to honour my account for the goods but I wanted the horse too much to allow this to stop me. I went to the factor.

"I want to get a roll of tobacco, a hunting knife and a shirt on credit. Will you let me have them? I can pay you by shooting wolves or coyotes and bringing the skins in for payment."

"Certainly, you can have all you want at once if you wish. Woolsey did right in refusing to be a party to any deal in trade with the Indians. Our officials are very strict in matters of this kind, but it does not prevent you from trapping and killing your own fur."

The little Blackfoot was still waiting patiently for my return when I arrived with the articles of the deal. I placed the tobacco on the ground, the shirt and knife on top. He very reluctantly got off the horse and handed over the line. The horse was bareback and had a single line fastened to the neck. This hung loosely down to its mouth, where two half hitches around the jaw was all the bridle required to cut figure eights and other manoeuvers such as stopping the animal within inches of riding me down.

I climbed on the animal's back and rode him up to the fort, where the man at the gate swung it open for me to enter. I proudly displayed the horse to Borwick and the other men on the walk and the bastions. Borwick climbed down and came to where I was sitting on the horse.

"Peter, I advise you to place the horse under lock and key. It's considered a good joke to steal the animal back after a deal, and the Blackfoot don't consider it a dishonest act."

I was astonished at this statement but remembered how reluctant the man had been in getting off the horse. Acting on Bill's advice I kept the horse enclosed and did not turn him out with the Hudson's Bay horses until several days after the Blackfoot had gone.

CHAPTER FOUR

The Palliser Expedition

A SHORT TIME LATER I was summoned into the factor's presence.

"I have received instructions to hire men for a geological survey to be made some time this summer. They want an educated man to act as interpreter for Indian languages and to act as foreman to take a crew of men to Fort Pitt where they will join the expedition that will be coming by way of the States. Captain Palliser will take over at Fort Pitt; he is the man in charge. The salary will be seventy-five pounds sterling per year. Would you care to take the position?"

"Yes, I would, but I'm not too familiar with the Blackfoot tongue. I only started to learn it last summer and fall. I can speak Cree and the Swampy Cree language, but the latter would be useless on the prairie as these people do not leave the bush."

"That will not matter a great deal as I have a man in mind who is quite familiar with the Blackfoot tongue. He lived in the Blackfoot country for a number of years and is part Blackfoot himself, though now living in these northern parts."

"Well, in that case, I will accept, provided my present employer releases me for the work. The Rev. Woolsey is a grand old gentleman and I would hate to leave his services without first consulting him. I signed a one-year contract at Fort Garry last year which lapsed in June of this year. I have not been bound under contract since that date."

"Very well then, you let me know in the next few days. You are the only man in this area who has the qualifications specified in my instructions."

I spoke to Mr. Woolsey, and informed him of the offer and the wages. I could see that he was not pleased, but after a few moments of silence he searched in his desk and came up with a letter from which he read a portion. His superiors were asking him to lower the interpreter's wages or endeavour to get along without an interpreter.

"Peter," he said, "you've been a great help to me, not only as an interpreter, but through your knowledge of the scriptures and your personal conduct with the people with whom we've been working. I had some doubts in regard to your joining in their games but your attitude in respect to all their ways of living has gained you many friends among my Indian charges. What you have learned from them will be of enormous value in your travels. Yes, Peter, you have my blessings in your new work. I can't hope to retain your services at a still lower salary when you are offered much more than you are now earning. I hope you'll continue to be as fine an example of spiritual and physical well-being as you have been in my service."

"Mr. Woolsey, I greatly appreciate your words and I will try to bear them in mind. I shall continue my assistance in whatever capacity you require until April the first, when I presume I will have to prepare matters concerned with my new employer. I shall expect no salary from your church after the end of this present month."

"Oh, no!" exclaimed Woolsey, "that would not be fair. I will not have it. You will be paid until the end of March, regardless of official wishes in this regard. You have earned every cent you have been paid. Without your help as interpreter, we never would have accomplished what we have among the tribes we have contacted on the prairie and here among the Pigeon Lake Indians."

During the second week of February, 1858, while we were experiencing a most unusual period of warm weather, I heard that Dr. Hector had passed through Edmonton on his way to Rocky Mountain House, and had left word with the factor that he wished to see me on his return and that he wanted me to go with him to make certain we could obtain enough men for the trip to Carlton. I had been out with the hunters after fresh buffalo meat; we had difficulty in finding a herd and had to go a long way out before we had any luck.

Around the first of March Dr. Hector returned to Edmonton, and I had an opportunity to meet him. He was a man about my own age. I had expected to see a scholarly type, but his athletic appearance and brisk step impressed me very favourably. His handshake was firm and had a hint of strength that captured my interest immediately. He had an affable, easy manner of conversation with any person he was speaking to. A thoroughly pleasing personality that had nothing of that assumed superiority or condescending mannerism that I was beginning to associate with all Englishmen of my narrow acquaintance.[1] I liked the man at once and nothing in my experience on the expedition or elsewhere ever changed this good opinion.

The factor had given us an introduction saying, "This is Mr. Peter Erasmus, the man that I have recommended to Captain Palliser, as my instructions required. I believe you will verify my word after you two become better acquainted." Acknowledging the introduction in formal words, he laughed.

"Well, well! I hardly expected to find a minister's man of that size holding the easy duties of an interpreter. I think I can agree right now that your choice has been very well placed."

"Dr. Hector, you have nothing on me; I did not expect to meet or find such well rounded proportions in a medical doctor myself."

Without further preliminaries he said, "I'd like to get two saddle horses and pack animals to go out and secure contracts for the summer expedition from the list that the factor has been kind enough to prepare. These men are out on the plains. Perhaps you can find them without too much delay."

"I will have horses and outfit ready at daylight tomorrow morning, if that is suitable."

"That will be excellent," he replied, "but I hope it does not interfere with your present employer's time."

"My duties with Mr. Woolsey only require Sundays at present, and I think we can locate your men in less than three days."

We caught up with the hunters at Hay Lakes, and Dr. Hector was able to secure all the men he needed and sign contracts for their hire, as was customary in those times. The factor's list was a good one and the men he recommended were all experienced plainsmen, good with their guns. One man in particular on that list, hired for a hunter, was reputed to be the most accurate shot of any man in the area and always boasted of killing more game with fewer wasted shots than any of his companions.

The doctor went back to Carlton, leaving me with detailed instructions as to the things required for the trip, such as horses, carts, tents, food supplies, tools, and numerous other items. Apparently the outfitting was to be well financed, and enjoyed unlimited credit with the Hudson's Bay Company.

Dr. Hector wanted to start me on a pay roll immediately, but I replied that the first of April would be soon enough. As I was staying at the fort, I could attend to a number of things without interfering with Mr. Woolsey's work and had promised to stay with the minister until the end of March. Dr. Hector agreed that there would be plenty of time after the first day of April, as in any case we would have to wait for the spring break-up on the Saskatchewan River.

I had another talk with Mr. Woolsey and told him that I wanted two weeks' holiday after the fifteenth of March.

"Yes," he replied, "I think you deserve a holiday and I hope you are successful; the lady according to all reports is a very fine young woman."

That I was surprised is putting it mildly. In all the time that I had been with him, he had never, with that one exception about the Christmas dance, showed any interest in my private life. I managed to reply, "I was not aware that you had widened the scope of your labours. I do not mind admitting that you have come very close to the mark and that my intentions are honourable. As to my success, that is a matter that gives me some concern. Your own lack of success in matters of this kind makes me hesitate in asking your advice."

He had a hearty laugh and said, "Young man, you'll probably realize that the project you are about to embark on requires the agreement of two people. That is a lesson I learned when quite your own age; I will look forward with pleasure to the calling of the banns at the happy conclusion of your mission." He turned and went away chuckling to himself.

Undoubtedly he had given me an insight into another side of his character: intensely serious in his work, I had no idea that he had any interest outside the study of the Bible and its interpretation to his people. He had bested me in the little discussion and enjoyed a good laugh at my expense.

I caught up my saddle horse the day before I was to start on my holiday. The factor had asked me to lead a hunting crew after buffalo and I did not like to refuse as supplies were running low at the fort. We were over a week away on the trip before we met up with any success and returned homeward. I had now a little over one week left before I would have to start working for my new employers.

Bill handed me a note from Lac Ste. Anne that contained an invitation for us both to a dance the following day. I tried to persuade Bill to go with me.

"No, thanks," he said. "Do you want to kill me? Ride fifty miles, dance all night, then ride another fifty miles back again? No thanks."

No argument could induce him to go with me. I even offered to hire a Company dog team and let him ride all the way.

"No, Peter, you are going on a holiday and would have to change your plans, as I know you had intended to stay a week. I am a hard-working cog in the Hudson's Bay Company machine; they can't run the place properly without me for three days. Besides, I must save my money for my old age."

My spirits were at high peak when I started out bright and early next morning. This was the first real holiday of my life. Four years at The Pas, one and a half at the Winnipeg college, and now my nineteen months with Mr. Woolsey. For the first time my days were my own and not under the direction of other people. No wonder I was feeling gay.

My horse champed on the bit, chucked his head proudly and shied from every imaginary thing on the road. He was eager to run but I held him down to a quiet, easy, walking gait. He was a high-spirited, mettlesome animal with the springy gait of a deer, a pet whose intelligence demanded respect, a watchdog in a hidden campsite, and company on a lonely ride. No wonder Indians risked their lives with careless indifference if by so doing they could possess such a prize.

I was amused at Bill's actual horror of such a ride — to me it was a pleasure. There was just enough nip in the air to make me feel the comfort of warm clothes. The sun rose when we were already ten miles on the trail to light up a million glittering frost jewels that brightened the drab greys of leafless poplars or the deep green of the spruce. The willows on the flats had assumed their red-tinted glow, indicating an early thaw.

I reviewed the various incidents since that first Christmas dance in Edmonton where I had met the young lady, Florence, whom I was now on my way to see. She had shown a marked preference for my company but had consistently avoided any definite promise that I might consider binding. My half-serious teasing and reference to marriage were lightly parried with the matter-of-fact statement that she had no desire to become a traveller's widow before she was a properly married woman. She made it plain that my occupation was not of sufficient stability to warrant a serious answer to her ideals of a happy married life. In fact she had been very frank and said, "Peter,

60

when you give up travelling for a more respectable occupation as a farmer then I might consider your affections serious enough to deserve the sacrifice of a home and living with my parents for the serious responsibilities of marriage."

She had been quite definite and made me understand that she was perfectly happy with her parents. She invited me to share a week's holiday for the social events of her settlement; perhaps she might wean me from my passion for travel.

The claims of the church rested lightly on her shoulders. My education under the banner of the English Church and the strong views held by its adherents declared a mixed marriage as impossible of success. Though I had defended my position against the Bishop's arguments so eloquently, in that all different denominations of the various churches had the same objective except only that they disagreed in methods for salvation, I'm afraid I had imbibed more of church prejudices that I cared to admit, after an education under the banner of the English Church with its strong views on mixed marriages. The worthy and sincere Rev. Mr. Woolsey, in his kindly and unbiased mind, had, in that amused reference to my holidays, given his approval of a mixed marriage, but had made it plain that his church should bless the nuptials. The broadminded Father Lacombe, had, I felt certain, discussed the situation with his brother in God's work and they had decided in favour of the characters of the persons concerned and not on their divided church adherence.

This of course was purely presumptive reasoning but I felt convinced that it was the truth. Suddenly I realized that the real reason for doubt or hesitation in declaring my intentions was not actually the difference in religious adherence but in my own dislike for a settled existence and my love for travel. I had accepted the job in the Palliser expedition without any hesitation and without thought for the wishes of my girl.

Approaching my destination, I began to feel some doubt of my reception in view of the fact that it was common knowledge among the residents of Ste. Anne that I would be going out with many of the men of the settlement on a period of travel that might take a couple of years. My acceptance of this new work was hardly consistent with my declared intention to become a landowner in the St. Albert area.

Florence gave a poetic description of the pastoral beauty of a settled existence in some well sheltered spruce grove along the fresh waters of the Sturgeon River: horses and cattle contentedly grazing, a garden green with vegetables and fruit that would be her own special project. Of course for the first few years there would be annual trips after buffalo — that was a regular custom of the settlement — but in these times she would be along to help make pemmican and cure the hides.

I liked the idea of stock feeding on the luxuriant grasses, waist-high vetch, and pea vines, but cattle would never have any value as long as buffalo could be found at the cost of a leaden bullet and a little energy. Horses — well, that was a good thought, but when one remembered the constant vigil that was necessary to guard them from theft, a man by himself would get very little sleep if he had to hold his stock in these uncertain days. No, unless times changed within the next few years, one night's raid could clean out years of saving invested in horses.

I reminded myself that I was hired for the summer months only and was not under contract for any specified length of time. Thus fortified with this flimsy excuse, I felt a lot better, and dug my horse in the ribs so hard that he broke into a fast run from an ambling walk, probably surprised at my sudden change of mood.

Riding into the settlement, I had a number of invitations to stay for the night, but chose a place the nearest to my lady's home. Putting up my horse, I walked over to her house. Her father, finishing the evening chores, waved me on to the house. I wanted to be sure of taking her to the dance.

She was busy preparing the evening meal when I knocked on the door.

"I'm here to invite you to attend the dance with me."

"Why certainly, Peter, but come in and talk for a moment. Surely you're not that busy. I was hoping you would come but I was not planning on missing the dance if you had failed to arrive."

"Here, Here, young lady! That's not a very flattering remark. After a ride of fifty miles just to see you dance all night with somebody else."

"Shame on you, Peter, for starting an argument before I can get used to that welcoming smile that I have been practising all day just for your benefit."

"You'd better use a smile that will last all week, because I intend to wear it ragged before I leave. I have a week's holiday and the length of my stay will depend on how long your smiles last."

"Oh, Peter, how nice, but are you sure you can stay in one place that long?" Her affectionate clasp on my arm took the sting out of that one, but I do not think she realized how close to the truth she was.

The dance that night was the beginning of a whirlwind of social functions that kept me on the go for the rest of the week. There were sleigh rides, toboggan slides, dog-team rides with a dozen different sleighs, girls loaded two to a sleigh and the men trailing the dogs. Then a huge lunch served by the campfire and pots of tea served by the girls, all in the shelter of a fine spruce grove. They were all young people and their hospitality and friendliness was a memory to treasure for years afterward.

My stay lasted a day over the week; April the first was coming all too rapidly. Somehow or other, there was seldom any chance for private conversation with my lady friend and I was no further in advancing my claims than when I arrived. She showed me every preference in the company of others, and her welcoming smile never faded, but she parried every move that I made to any private conversation.

The very last day of my stay, I managed to catch her alone at her home. "Florence, this is the last day of my holiday. Tomorrow I must be back at the fort. I must insist that you give me a definite answer to my proposal."

"Peter, I was hoping that you wouldn't make me give you an answer until you were sure of your own feelings. I hope you will understand. Although this is the first time that you have seriously asked me to marry you, we have discussed marriage like two sensible people should but we could never agree about the way we should live after we were married. My father, who was a traveller all his life before meeting my mother, is a great admirer of yours. My mother likes you; even Father Lacombe, in spite of the tenets of his church, has intimated he would have no objection to our marriage. I like you better than any man I know, but I will not marry you. Our ideals are as far apart as the poles. When I leave my father's home it will be to a fixed abode of my own and not to be moved each day or week of our lives as do the Indians of the prairies."

"My goodness," I responded, "who could think that such cold-blooded reasoning and so much profound knowledge could be found in such a pretty head."

"Peter," she said, "marriage will not be a light matter with me and I know it will not be all pleasure and good times as we have enjoyed in your stay with us. I wish you would give more thought to the changing times, with what you call cold-blooded reasoning. There is no need to discuss my ideas of marriage further; they are as familiar to you as they are to me."

The parents both came into the room at that moment and no further conversation was possible. They insisted that I stay for supper, but Florence was not the gay, vivacious person of other times. Her father entertained us with a recital of some of his most hazardous experiences of the north country where he had served with the Hudson's Bay Company. Several times he had nearly lost his life by drowning or freezing to death. Then, watching Florence, I began to understand why she had such a hatred for my way of living, hearing these tales from her early infancy.

Finally I told them I would be riding back to the post that night and begged to be excused. I detected a tear drop on Florence's eye lashes. Her father never noticed, but I saw her mother look at us both with a doubtful, questioning expression on her kindly face. I bade them goodbye and took my leave.

Florence put on her outdoor clothes and came with me to get my horse.

"Peter," she said, after we had left the house, "I wish with all my heart that circumstances had been different; my answer would be yes, regardless of my people, the church, or anything else."

I could find nothing to say while I led my horse out of the barn, fixed the saddle, and prepared to mount.

"Peter, will you kiss me before you leave?"

"Goodbye, Florence. Do not forget me, for I will be back again before too long."

Riding through the warm moonlight night was comfortable, but my thoughts were not too pleasant. My stay had been the most enjoyable experience of home living since boyhood days. Yet I was feeling a deep sense of dissatisfaction, knowing that I was in the wrong.

Though I hated to acknowledge the ugly truth, the fact was that I loved the free life of the prairies, the excitement of adventure, of riding down buffalo, the tracking of game, the thrill of a well aimed shot, of reading signs with my Indian companions, the excitement of scouting a Blackfoot camp in which, unbeknown to Mr. Woolsey, I had joined with my Pigeon Lake friends during the summer. I was unwilling to sacrifice these other things for a settled existence. I was a product of the times that gave little consideration to the opinions of women, though I did not recognize this fact at the time.

"To heck with her," I said out loud. "I will not have a woman dictate terms to me."

Daylight was beginning to show in the east when I reached the fort. I had some trouble gaining entrance and received a good going over from the watchman for keeping such unreasonable hours, in spite of the fact that keeping watch was his main duty. Only for the tremendous barking of the dogs that might disturb his employer, he probably would have left me to cool my heels outside of the gate.

During the balance of April I was busy in preparation for

the trip to Carlton that would start as soon as the ice cleared in the river. One by one I was able to mark off the items listed in Hector's notations of things needed. When the ice started to drive on the river I sent word by one of the settlement trappers trading his furs at the post that we were about ready to start on our journey. We were thirty men, four carts, and four big canvas tents. Each man rode his own saddle horse and we had about ten Company horses.[2] I had carefully picked the best of their bunch for our use. The Company had quite a large herd of horses at this time.

We crossed the river at Fort Saskatchewan. The water was low but mighty cold at that time of year. The first men to cross over had a good fire going. Knowing the ford, they had crossed without swimming the horses, but the rest of us were not so lucky. The carts were dismantled and fastened to carry our bedding and other stuff, and these emergency rafts had to be towed behind horses. The cumbersome rafts could not follow the best crossing place of the shallow, sluggish river, but were pulled in the straightest line possible.

It took the balance of the day to get everything across but no one complained; it was a common task for these men and was accomplished without a hitch. I did not attempt to give orders to the men because at the time I knew nothing about how this crossing would be done.

The distance travelled each day was seldom more than twenty miles. The Company horses had rustled their feed all winter and were not in condition to stand a big day's travel. There were a number of creeks in our way swollen by the spring run off. These delayed our passage considerably and sometimes we had to make a wide detour to get by. We reached Carlton in a little over two weeks.[3] The rest of the party had not arrived then and Mr. Clarke, the post factor,[4] had not heard when they would arrive. We camped about ten miles from the fort, hunting buffalo to keep us in provisions.

Later, I rode to the fort again to see if word had been received from Captain Palliser, and was informed that he would be arriving in two days. I went back and advised the men we would move to the fort and wait his arrival there. We now had plenty of provisions, as Vitalle[5] had been successful in killing two buffalo during the previous week. The men had processed the meat which was now ready to be packed and stored for future use. Our outfit was in good shape as the men had used their idle time in making certain that everything would be ready for the captain's inspection. We had been told that we would be under military orders.

Captain Palliser was quite tall and always appeared to hold

himself erect so that he had a straight-backed military appearance. He had a pleasantly smooth voice and expressed each word with exact and clear pronunciation. He seldom raised his voice higher than ordinary conversational tone but when he spoke his voice carried further than any other speaking at the same time. His age must have been in the early sixties or less. I liked his manner of addressing the men. The first evening in camp he called us all together and explained our duties and the purpose of the expedition.

Bourgeau, the botanist, was an elderly man. Sullivan was about thirty-five, and two gentlemen who had come for sport, Captain Brisco and Mr. Mitchell, were about the age of Sullivan.[6] They looked and acted as though roughing it in camps was an old story for them and so it proved; both won the respect of the men of our group by being able to stand up to the roughest conditions with the best of them.

Our men were getting impatient with their long idleness and complained to me about the long delay. I intimated as much to the captain, who appeared pleased at the information. "We will be moving as soon as I can obtain two more carts; they will be ready today. Advise them to be in readiness for a start tomorrow."

We now numbered about forty men, including the men that were with the captain. All were armed with flintlock guns, except the sportsmen and officers of the expedition, who had better rifles of more recent manufacture.

Discipline was strict; we were advised that orders must be obeyed without question. Our duties would be the protection of the party and the care of the equipment and animals. We were to obtain food supplies from the country we would be travelling through. Our first permanent camp was near the junction of the Red Deer with the South Saskatchewan River.[7]

Captain Palliser assigned me duties with Dr. Hector, who made trips away from the main camp mapping and making observations. Hector was interested in Indian characteristics, their way of obtaining a living, their beliefs and superstitions. He had a remarkably retentive memory, a gift for shrewd observation, and a deep sense of humour. His description of what he called civilized living among the British, the habits and customs of its lesser people as well as those of the titled rich, told in that droll humourous way of his, was a constant source of delight to me. Having once made a slip of the tongue that revealed my poor opinion in regard to his countrymen in the West, he gave me an insight into the many good qualities of his race that made his country great and him proud to belong to it.

We were not allowed to work on Sunday, hunting was

prohibited, and no moving was allowed. The captain held a service on Sunday. He never preached, but read a portion of the scriptures and a word of prayer. I was never called upon to interpret these services, as all the men had an understanding of English and talked the language more or less fluently. Vitalle, our buffalo hunter, alone spoke very bad English, but he would have been deeply offended at any correction or suggestion that he did not understand every word. He succeeded in intermixing French, English and Cree to a degree unequalled by any person of my acquaintance. His special duty was to kill buffalo or game birds, which he did far better than any man I ever knew. His uncanny accuracy in picking off ducks, geese, and other birds on the wing was truly amazing. He became somewhat of a favourite with the men, who admired him for his skill with the gun.

Crossing big streams was never an easy operation, as each cart had to be dismantled along the shore and floated across. Experience in the management of this work seemed to be a natural attribute of the plainsmen employed, and each crossing was accomplished without mishap. Captain Palliser and the doctor as well as the two sportsmen appeared quickly to adapt themselves with as much enjoyment as if they were winning some big stake race, although the captain warned them against any foolish or needless risk.

Mr. Bourgeau expressed doubts of the safety of a contrivance like the raft for his use in crossing, but afterwards declared it to be a wonderful experience and that none of his friends in France [8] would believe that such a thing could be done.

We had made several camps and were again on the move. Wabaska and I were ahead of the party to pick up some game that Vitalle had killed the day before. Wabaska had no sense of direction on the prairie and I was along to guide him to the place Vitalle had described to me that morning. We were following the edge of a deep ravine that led to a creek bottom, when I spotted four bears.

I thought it would be a splendid opportunity to secure a grizzly for the captain's collection. The bears could be approached upwind from where the ravine entered the creek. I was able to get very close to them around a sharp bend of the creek bottom. Riding a well broken Company horse that was trained to allow his rider to shoot off his back, I was sure of getting a good shot. The bears were busily stripping an ant nest and never noticed me until I was within easy gun range. The nearest reared up on her hind legs, possibly alerted by some sound of the horse, but didn't seem to know from what direction it came as she was standing sideways for my shot. I took aim at the body just behind her front paws and fired. I felt myself being flung through the air and struck the ground with considerable force.

The fall knocked the wind out of me and partially stunned me before I realized what had happened. The horse I was riding was a lazy brute and probably never noticed the bears till I shot, took fright, and bolted back down the trail. Wabaska, losing sight of me, had driven to the brink of the ravine when he saw the bears and later noticed me lying on the ground motionless. The horse was racing with the empty saddle up the ravine near where he had stopped the cart. That was too much for his courage. He whirled his horse around, and with whip and yells urged the poor beast back to the party, shouting at the top of his voice all the way "Erasmus is killed! Erasmus is killed!"

Captain Brisco and Mr. Mitchell as usual were riding in the lead. Hearing the man's excitement and his furious whipping of the horse, and also seeing the loose saddle horse that was keeping pace with the frenzied antics of the cart, they raced their horses to find the cause of his excitement.

I was sitting up when they arrived and their sporting instincts were greater than their concern over my plight. They took after the bears. Brisco got one with two shots, and Mitchell got in a shot just before the bear jumped into the creek and another shot as he swam out on the other side. This time his bear dropped. Vitalle, hearing the shots, raced back to see what was the matter, saw the bear on the level above the creek banks, and cut off his escape. The bear turned and made for the carts. Most horses have a terrible fear of bears unless trained otherwise. The cart horses became unmanageable and their drivers created such an uproar that the bear turned back towards Vitalle who raced in to meet him and shot him in his tracks. Vitalle came in for a lot of highly descriptive language for driving the bear straight at the carts. This did not disturb the man at all; he merely looked surprised and remarked on their ingratitude for saving them the trouble of having to drive a long way to get the hide and meat.

The captain had ordered a cart to follow up to get my body while he and the doctor rode ahead to investigate. I was on my feet when they came in sight at the top of the creek bank. They were pleased to find me alive. After I had explained what had happened, the doctor made me strip off my shirt for an examination, in spite of my protests that I was only stunned from the fall and had my wind knocked out.

Though still feeling kind of shaky, I was thankful that my

68

shot had proved fatal. After dressing the beast we found that the bullet had penetrated the heart. I was lucky that she had been standing sideways when I shot, otherwise she might have been just wounded and could have killed me instantly. It was my first experience with a grizzly, and I only realized later how extremely lucky I had been.

"Are you bitten anywhere?" asked Sullivan. "You look pale."

"No," I replied, "just stunned and my wind knocked out in the fall."

"You may consider yourself lucky to be alive; these grizzlies are the most dangerous animals of all beasts in America, and a she-bear the worst of all the species. The others must be cubs, or they might have taken a hand in finishing you off. It amazes me that you would tackle a grizzly with a flintlock gun. Young man, you had better think twice before you try another venture of this kind."

I was in no shape to argue. I knew it was pure ignorance on my part and not bravery that had induced me to do what I now recognized as a foolhardy venture.

"What a monster," exclaimed the doctor. "Look at those claws."

"Yes," added the captain, "you can thank God, Peter, that she did not use them on you."

Meanwhile the rest of the party came up. The bear was skinned like a rabbit; an incision was made down the back legs and the hide rolled back down over the body as it was skinned right down to the nose. The claws were retained on the hide.

Moving again, this time our objective was the Cypress Hills, a wooded area where the sportsmen expected to do some deer hunting.[9] Bourgeau was joyfully anticipating some new forms of plant life, and was delighted over his discoveries when we got there. He could hardly wait to complete his meal before starting out on his search. The captain had assigned a man by the name of Bellcourt as his guide and, I suspect, as caretaker, for the old gentleman got so enthused over his work that he never took notice of time or direction.

The botanist's enthusiasm was almost as great as a gold miner in the discovery of a big nugget. It gave me a lot of amused satisfaction to watch his delight when he found a new species. I watched for new plants in my travels with Dr. Hector, and when I was fortunate enough to bring an addition to his collection, I was treated to a lesson that was most instructive.*

I knew that the Indians sought out plants that they used in their medicines with remarkable effect. I could never again

69

heedlessly trample plants without reminding myself of this man's gentle and almost reverent handling of a rarity in plant life.

Captain Palliser killed a fine buck, as did Brisco and the doctor. It takes a lot of food for forty men, especially when the main diet is meat, and no opportunity was lost to add to our supply.

All the officials were continuously occupied with their various duties concerned with the surveys, the doctor travelling in various directions from each camp, mapping and taking observations, and the captain recording data accumulated from the different members of his staff. Palliser apportioned the work among each man of his crew in such a way that everyone had a share in the work. Moving the camp became a simple matter, as teams were assigned that were the same in moving and again in camping. There never was any confusion after the first few days of travel and the Captain got his outfit organized.

The men all respected the captain's authority, not because he was their boss, but due to his sincere concern for their welfare.* The character of the man himself and his attitude of friendly equality aroused a loyalty that was greater than mere respect. Every man was stirred to give his best to any task assigned to him.

Our men were all of poor education, and a number had no schooling whatever, but they had been picked for their proficiency with guns, and were all experienced in travel on the prairies. Had the need arisen they would have handled themselves against attack with the same matter-of-fact efficiency and unconcern as that with which they met every obstacle crossing rivers and unmapped creeks. It was all part of their duty and as such had to be managed with the least fuss and delay.

Wabaska, whose cart contained most of the specimens chosen by the captain and the plants picked by Bourgeau, was one man who was disgusted by the work of the expedition. He could never understand the sense of preserving dry bones and hides that were not taken care of in the usual way. His complaints, directed to me in an undertone, were spaced with choice French swear words. Any effort on my part to explain the purpose of such things met with a fresh stream of epithets, till he choked and walked away talking to himself. He was a strange chap; no one dared touch any of the stuff in his cart unless strictly on the captain's own expressed wish.

After a camp had been established near the international border, Captain Palliser decided to make a trip to Fort Benton. Dr. Hector, Vitalle, and I were to accompany him.[10]

We were on saddle with two pack animals trailing on lea ropes. The captain expected to purchase some supplies at th fort. None of us knew the trail, but Dr. Hector, using hi compass and taking observations, led us straight to our destination without any trouble. Vitalle was amazed; he considered the compass as something approaching magic. A stream of mixed French, English, and Cree in praise of Dr. Hector's powers drew a smile from the captain's usually sober countenance.

We travelled through herds of buffalo nearly all the way. Deep ruts scored the prairie grass where the buffalo had travelled for centuries in their migrations back and forth across the plains. It is not surprising that few people in that day believed that they would ever be all killed.[11]

Our journey was frequently interrupted by the need to wait for the huge herds of buffalo that blocked our passage. These vast herds were the greatest I had ever witnessed. I only then realized that we had been in the extreme northern edges of the great herds that grazed along our borders and away south into American territory. It was then beyond my imagination to believe that the next fifteen years would see the last period of the buffalo's existence in our country.

Both the captain and Dr. Hector believed that a policy of buffalo extermination had been adopted as the quickest way to break down Indian resistance to American authority.[12] The Indians obtained all their needs in food, clothing, and shelter from the buffalo.

"The Indians of this territory will be the first to suffer from the scarcity of buffalo. The vast herds we have seen have, by natural increase, been forced to move northward for better feeding grounds. Their natural feeding and breeding area is south of our border," said the doctor. "Domestic cattle from the huge herds of cattle in Texas and the southern States will replace the buffalo. A great migration of people will follow the big herds. Cities and towns will stand where but a few native teepees now occupy big territories. Even now the fighting tribes across the line are being forced back into areas they never used before. These herds are the last means of maintaining their resistance. Buffalo are being slaughtered for their hides and the carcasses left to rot on the prairie."[13] I listened to the captain with disgust and amazement that there were people who could destroy one of God's most bountiful gifts by such abominable means.

"Peter," the doctor observed, "you must prepare yourself and your associates to adjust to a new order in this country. The progress of civilization renders this inevitable."

"Yes," added the captain, "your work with our expedition is but a phase of things to come. All the great territory now sparsely populated by a few wandering tribes will someday be the homes of thousands of prosperous people engaged in agricultural pursuits, stock raising, and other industries that always follow the settlement of vacant lands."

These statements were almost unbelievable when I looked and counted hundreds, yes thousands, of buffalo scattered over the plain as far as my eyes could see. Was it any wonder that I was doubtful? Only a few years later I was to be reminded so vividly of these predictions that I can recall almost their exact words today. Common sense indicated the truth of the prediction of the great changes that would take place when the buffalo were gone. I had only been in the country a little over two years and already there were fewer buffalo along the Saskatchewan valley.

There were only two houses at Benton. They were made of adobe mud and were situated on the north side of the Missouri River. There were ten men at the place and they lived in buffalo teepees pitched near the buildings during the summer; apparently they, like the river men of the Saskatchewan, enjoyed immunity from Indian raids because they were a source of supply to the tribes. Otherwise, their situation would have been precarious. The trading post was supplied by shallow draft-boats, and freight costs were a great deal lower than our own transport up the swift Saskatchewan River. There is no doubt that had it not been for the ferocity of the Blackfoot, Peigan, and Blood tribes against any encroachment in their territory, the American occupation of the southern parts of the territory would have been accomplished long before our own claims could have been established. The natural flow of cheaper transportation would have made this possible.

The authorities in England and later in Canada were slow to realize the potential value of these trackless prairies. The fur trade placed little value on the long-haired furs, and after some difficulties with their prairie forts, abandoned them for posts in the bush country where the most valuable skins were more plentiful and the Indians more peaceable.

CHAPTER FIVE

With Doctor Hector

P ALLISER NOW ORDERED a change of direction towards the West and the mountains. Although our rate of travel seemed very leisurely for those who remained to guard the camp, those of us who had to follow the officials in their various side excursions knew they were covering a wide range of territory to secure exact data about the terrain, soil, land contours, and sundry other information required in the survey.

Dr. Hector was a tireless worker. His capacity for endurance in any kind of weather was the talk of men around camp. He had four horses to his string and they were not too many for his demands. There was no let up in his persistence, as day after day, all except Sunday, he continued his unending labours to cover as wide a range of territory as possible.

Vitalle was possibly the busiest of the hired men. It kept him busy to provide meat for the camp; however, he was ably assisted by Mitchell and Brisco. Vitalle complained of their utter disregard for the finer points of stalking game, and deplored their terrible waste of ammunition, but they still got game. I believe he was a bit jealous of their superior guns and free use of shots, when one effective bullet could have done just as well.

It was well on in August when we reached the foot of the

mountains, and we travelled north from there until we came about opposite to where Morley is situated. Our progress was slow and our moves with the camp quite frequent.[1]

It must have been around the last of August when the party decided to split up into four groups. Dr. Hector was to travel up through the mountains as far as the North Saskatchewan River, establishing the location of the divide between the rivers flowing east and those going west; Bourgeau was to study plants in the mountains; Blakiston was to examine the two passes through the mountains; and Captain Palliser would continue with the carts and the balance of the men back to Edmonton where he would wait the arrival of the other parties.[2]

Dr. Hector as usual was the first to be on his way with Sam Ballentine, Brown, Sutherland, a Stony Indian nicknamed Nimrod, and myself. The Stony Indians were so called because of their preference for the mountainous country where they lived and did most of their hunting. Nimrod was happy to be back in an area with which he was familiar and in conditions more suited to his talents. He never liked the prairie, and had wistfully told me that he would be glad when we went into the mountains.

We were lucky in finding an old Stony Indian who drew a map for us on birch bark that proved to be an invaluable aid in our search for a pass. This later proved to be near where the doctor met the serious accident with his saddle horse. When we were through the pass he predicted that some day it would be the route of a railway.*

The Stony Indians were a peaceful people. Their policy was to avoid trouble unlike the Blackfoot, Peigan, or Bloods, their nearest neighbours. They raised good mountain horses that were greatly sought after by the plainsmen. They had great stamina, were sure-footed, and when properly trained were very reliable as buffalo runners. The Stonies were less inclined to migratory habits, and lived in selected parts of the mountain country more or less permanently for the greater portion of their lives. In my experience they were the best trackers of any of the Indian people, and they developed the use of medicines to a degree unsurpassed by any of the other tribes. It was largely through their knowledge of medicine plants that the Crees looked to them as friends and never bothered them when they went after buffalo in that area bordering the North Saskatchewan River which the Crees claimed as their own hunting grounds.

It was some years after my trip through the mountains with Dr. Hector that I had occasion to use some Stony medicine to stop a cancerous growth on my nose caused by a bruise in a trail accident and irritated by frequent freezing before it was properly healed. This nose defect caused more comment and attention by some thoughtless people than all the feats of physical endurance and strength, under all kinds of weather conditions or trail hardships. These latter qualities were, in my day, the yardstick of a man's true worth, the same qualities that won Dr. Hector the respect and admiration of the plainsmen far beyond those that knew him personally. A trip from forty to seventy miles by dog drivers on snowshoes, breaking trail or running behind the dogs, was no sinecure. The travelling fame credited to most white men ignored the fact that they were usually warmly wrapped in buffalo robes with a blazing fire ready and a carpet of spruce boughs laid for them to step on before they left the cozy warmth of the toboggan. Many of the early famous travellers would have been hopelessly lost, starved, or frozen to death without the guidance and advice of the Indians and half-breeds. Historians fail to note these factors in crediting their heroes and glorifying their characters in their stories. The Indians and half-breeds were paid servants and thus not entitled to any praise for their deeds, which were quite frequently at the risk of their own lives.

I was to learn later that Dr. Hector alone of all the men of my experience asked no quarter from any man among us, drivers or guides. He could walk, ride, or tramp snowshoes with the best of our men, and never fell back on his position to soften his share of the hardships, but in fact gloried in his physical ability after a hard day's run to share in the work of preparing camp for the night, building shelters from the wind, cutting spruce boughs, or even helping get up wood for an all-night fire. He was admired and talked about by every man that travelled with him, and his fame as traveller was a wonder and a byword among many a teepee that never saw the man.

We had been travelling through the mountains for about two weeks; our progress was very slow as sometimes we had to retrace our steps because of some impassable obstruction in our way. The doctor wanted to cross over to the Columbia River and to establish the latitude and longitude of the divide, going by compass as much as possible and only consulting the guide as a last resort.

Our food was getting low; Nimrod could find no game to replenish our dwindling supplies. Finally we were on short rations and gave up compass-reading for Nimrod's guidance north to where he promised better hunting.

We were following along a river bank as the easiest way in the direction we wanted to go when one of the horse's packs came loose. The horse lost his balance and tumbled backward into the river. The clumsy brute had been giving us trouble all the way. The river was quite deep and the banks steep. We all left our saddle-horses and rushed down to save the brute. Losing the pack would have been quite serious in our present situation as it contained most of our food supplies. Sutherland, an old cow puncher, roped the horse and we were able to finally get him on safe ground.

The doctor went to pick up his own horse which was feeding among some spruce with his lines trailing. The instant the doctor reached for the lines, the horse whirled and kicked him with both feet in the chest. The doctor was knocked unconscious.

We all leapt from our horses and rushed up to him, but all our attempts to help him recover his senses were of no avail. We then carried him to the shade of some big evergreens while we pitched camp. We were now in serious trouble, and unless Nimrod fetched in game our situation looked hopeless. One man stayed and watched the unconscious doctor. The rest of us took turns trying to catch trout that we could see in the clear mountain water of the river. Dr. Hector must have been unconscious for at least two hours when Sutherland yelled for us to come up; he was now conscious but in great pain.[3] He asked for his kit and directed me to prepare some medicine that would ease the pain. I had him sign a document stating the facts of the accident in case his illness might prove serious. He readily agreed that it would be the proper thing to do. I asked and got permission to try to find something to shoot. The accident happened in the early forenoon, and it was late in the afternoon before I got started.

I found some fresh deer tracks shortly after I left camp, but was too anxious, and startled them before I could get a good shot. Following them I had another running shot, drew blood, but did not knock the buck down. I kept after the wounded deer, and before I realized that I had gone so far, it was dark, and I had lost my directions. It was hopeless to try to find the way in the dark so I built a fire and tried to forget that I was hungry, cold, and worried over the doctor. Nights in the mountains get pretty cold and that one was the longest and most miserable of any time I ever spent on the trail.

Early next morning I climbed a high place and got my directions from the fog rising from the river. There were no rabbits or bird game of any kind and I decided the deer had not been hurt enough to be worthwhile chasing again. Although I watched for any moving object I could not find any sign of a squirrel. The area was totally barren of any game. Nimrod had gone on the hunt long before I got back empty-handed and tired to the party. The doctor was still in pain but feeling much better, for which I was thankful.

"Peter, you must rest up today to conserve your strength and make another try tomorrow. It'll be impossible for me to ride for a day or two. It'll be up to you and Nimrod to get us food, for we're nearly at the end of our rations."

Late that evening our hunter hobbled into camp, empty-handed. He had fallen when he missed his footing while stalking some sheep. The doctor said he had a badly sprained ankle. It was already swollen, and looked bad. The doctor gave me instructions to treat the man's ankle, and then said, "Now, Peter, it's entirely up to you; that man cannot walk for a few days."

Nimrod gave me directions to where he had last tracked the sheep. I had not yet reached the place when I spotted some of the animals across a deep ravine. They had not seen me or scented my presence. Taking advantage of every cover I could, crawling on my knees for the most part, I reached a point directly opposite. Trembling with excitement and weakness, I slowly raised my head above cover and looked. There in plain sight was a big sentinel sheep, his head raised watching something in the opposite direction. He was standing dead still. I slowly pushed my gun across a dead log and tried to take aim, but my eyes watered and the gun shook so I had to wait to calm my nerves.

Biting my lips in vexation at my foolish nerves, I finally got a grip on myself, took aim, and fired. He gave a tremendous leap and landed twenty feet below, tumbling and rolling to the bottom of the ravine. I knew the sheep would be dead. The others disappeared in a twinkling of an eye. I lay for a moment stunned at the effectiveness of my long shot, then with a yell that echoed back from the mountain, scrambled and slid down the slope after my kill.

It was hard to keep from dancing and holding my gun in triumph as I had seen some of my Indian friends do after some extraordinary shot. I quickly skinned the animal, cut off a thigh for my carrying sack and hit back for camp, anxious to carry the good news to the others. Nimrod got up and hobbled over to where I had placed the meat. After examining the meat he turned to me in disappointment, "No good, Peter. No good. Can't eat." Then I remembered: I had killed a buck, and at that time of year, during the rutting season, they were not fit for human consumption.

My disappointment was the keener because of my early exultation over the kill. In my eagerness to get food I had completely forgotten one of the first lessons I learned from the

Pigeon Lake Indians. This was the last straw, and I sat in silent misery. The others tried to cheer me up. "Never mind, Peter. If you can kill a buck, you can just as easily kill a doe. You try again tomorrow." But nothing the doctor said was any help in my misery.

Brown said, "Hell, you're the only man among us who would have the guts to try. The rest of us will give our rations to keep you on your feet. Nimrod sure can't travel with that ugly black ankle of his." The other men echoed their agreement to his suggestion.

The Stony did his best to prepare some of the meat but none of us could get it down. Sutherland kept on trying for trout; he gave a tremendous shout, finally landing one. One trout for six men was not a big meal but it helped a lot, especially with the Stony's herbs to add taste to the fish soup.

Nimrod, who knew of a salt lick only ten miles away where he felt sure he would get a moose, also wanted to try again next morning, but the doctor ordered him to stay in camp. "Erasmus will go out again today, and tomorrow I will try to ride; we will go together to where you think you might get a moose. We'll ride within a mile of the place; maybe you can walk that far."

That morning, fortified with the rations of all three men and I suspect the doctor's share as well, I felt like a new man. I didn't see a thing all day, but on my way back to camp shot a partridge. I ate the gizzard raw and felt much better. It was a temptation to eat the rest of that small bird, but the thought of the men's sacrifice that morning was enough to overcome my greed.

The Stony immediately took charge of the bird for cooking, taking elaborate care that not a morsel would be wasted; he added his own mountain ingredients and apportioned the meat with the same care as he used in its preparation. "Drink the soup," he said, "it will do you more good than tea." The doctor took his share that night, the first nourishment since his accident. There was more cheerful talk that night than any of the last five nights, as we prepared to make an early start next morning.

Nimrod had been busy the previous evening preparing some kind of contraption that, he said, he would use the next morning on his moose hunt. He was humming a little song as he prepared to leave. I could see the contraption was to be a foot strap to take some of the weight off his foot. I rigged up a back strap for him to carry his gun and leave his hands free. "You know," said Brown, "that little beggar might just do what he says, kill a big moose, and he still can sing while the rest of us hate to talk; it takes too much energy."

78

We put the doctor on the quietest horse we had and started for Nimrod's promised land of the moose. I was somewhat doubtful that such could be possible in an area barren of game prospects. However, he took the lead and we soon came to a well marked pack trail which took a northerly direction, and after travelling about eight or nine miles, Nimrod mentioned that we had reached the place to stop. We quickly stripped the animals of their gear, while the Stony made ready for the hunt. My companions lay down and were asleep almost at once. I helped our hunter get into his foot sling and gun carrier, slightly irritated at the monotonous little humming song of his. I watched him, curious to see how he managed that foot. Every time he put the lame foot forward, he pulled on the knee strap, giving him a kind of rolling motion. It worked, and he was still singing in a low tone hardly noticeable fifty yards away. Walking must have been painful, for his ankle was still black and swollen, yet he was cheerful and as determined as ever.

About four o'clock in the afternoon we heard a shot, then another.

"Nimrod has shot a moose," I yelled. "Come on, let's go and find him."

"Go ahead," said the doctor. "If he has had any luck, we can move the camp later."

It was tough going through the heavy brush and timber as we tried to go straight towards where we thought the sound came from. It sounded close but it was more than a mile before we got there. Brown followed close behind and when we saw our hunter, we both yelled together.

"What did you get, did you kill anything?"

"Moose, of course, moose," pointing with his pipe at the same time to where a big moose lay, close to the salt lick.[4]

Smiling happily between puffs, he explained how he had nearly lost the moose when his foot sling had caught a stick and almost threw him into a pile of dry brush. The noise would have scared the moose, and it would have been out of sight before he could have gotten a shot. He had to wait a long time before the moose quieted down and he could approach to gun range.

We were proud of him, the smallest but the most courageous of us all. Brown walked up to him where he was sitting on a rock and said, "From now on, Nimrod, you're my brother. If my name was White instead of Brown, I'd give you my name, for I think you are the whitest friend any man could have."

When I interpreted Brown's long speech, Nimrod laughed

and said, "I would rather be Red than White; it is closer to your colour than White, and tell him I am proud to be his friend, for he is more like my people than his own." Brown was a dark, swarthy man, with black hair and bristling black eyebrows. Brown got a big laugh out of my interpretation and shook the Stony's hand again.

Sutherland and the other man went back to move the doctor, while Brown under my direction rustled sticks for a drying stage.

However, they wouldn't leave till they had made a fire and started roasting some meat. Nimrod cautioned them against overeating: "No eat too much. This size first time; rest, then after while eat more," showing with the palm of his hand the size and thickness it was safe to eat.

One man failed to curb his appetite and was very sick later; the doctor had to treat him, and scolded me for not enforcing Nimrod's warning. The man could quite easily have killed himself by his own stupidity. I watched him at the fire but he had slipped an extra piece in his pocket and probably ate it on his way back to the camp. We had the stage nearly full of meat when the doctor and the others found their way to our new camp. There was a nice spring close by, and feed for the horses.

Buck moose are at their best in August, when they are fattest; this one had a heavy layer of fat three inches thick. On a straight meat diet the body craves fats. The carcass would provide a wonderful relish to our meals when it was safe for us to eat as much as we needed.

At sunrise the next morning we heard a shot. Nimrod said, "It is someone looking for us." The doctor ordered a reply. The answering signal used in the bush is a single shot, then two shots closely spaced. Some time later a Stony Indian arrived. He knew our hunter and they engaged in friendly conversation. Then the man turned to the doctor and invited him to move camp to where he was staying. The doctor agreed, if he would consider preparing our meat. This he readily agreed to and helped us to pack and load our outfit to move to his camp.

We stayed at the man's camp for five days, and we were treated like royalty. Nimrod was in his glory as he heard all the latest happenings of his own people and got word that his wife and family were all well and looking forward to his return in the fall.

After leaving the Stony camp, we continued our way in a northerly direction six or eight days until we struck the North Saskatchewan River near Kootenay Plains. We had passed the headwaters of the Bow River not long after leaving the Stony's camp. The Kootenay Plains was a small prairie about ten miles long and maybe four miles wide. This in my mind was a splendid change after travelling through heavy timber and mountain country for the last month, hardly finding a grassy place big enough to feed the stock.

We worked upriver from there. The first night we camped we heard dull sounds like the echo of distant guns; we all wondered what it was. Nimrod explained that it was rams fighting, as it was now the full rutting season for them.

Our progress upriver was slow, as the doctor was continuously mapping and taking observations. During these stops the Stony and I went ahead marking the best trail and trying for game if we got any chance. It was often necessary to cross the river several times in order to find a trail for the pack animals, to avoid heavy fallen timber and steep banks.

Dr. Hector had again set up camp, and told Nimrod and me to go after some meat. "I want a specimen of the biggest buck you can find. I want the skeleton of the biggest buck bighorn sheep for our collection."

We went together, stalking a dozen or more sheep in a flock, and we managed to kill one doe each before they got out of range. They are fast climbers and can descend steep slopes impassable for a man. I saw them jump a twenty-foot ledge and land with effortless ease, with hardly a break in their speed.

I believe that the mountain sheep are far keener-sighted than any of the other big game animals. A moose has good hearing and also depends a great deal on scenting any approach by the hunter, always circling back down wind. I have been with Indians when they have shot a moose from a distance of less than thirty yards. They had outguessed the animal waiting for them to follow his track, yet the animal never saw them till he lay kicking his death throes.

While I was dressing out the meat of the two does, the Stony said he was going to look for a good buck for the doctor's collection. I had finished the work and packed the meat where we could get at it with the pack animals. I was about to leave for camp, tired of waiting for our hunter, when I heard him coming. I heard him humming that little song of his that I had now began to accept as a sign of good luck.

"Peter, our luck is all good now. I shot a real big buck that fairly walked into my gun to be killed and I found a trail almost to where he is lying."

We stayed in the vicinity of that camp for another five days, then moved up river to the head of the waters. It was a tough task, with lots of fallen timber and places where the banks almost defied passage. We had to make wide detours, and that took us another five days before we reached the foot of the glacier at the source of the river.

Dr. Hector was up at daybreak and hurried the men with breakfast. He was always in a hurry to start the day, yet when he began his work, time seemed no object with him.

"Peter, you'll come with me today. We're going to climb the glacier. Take a tea pail along as I want a cup of tea made up from waters of both sides of the divide. The rest of the men remain in camp. Nimrod can go hunting if he wishes, otherwise he can rest in camp."

It took us all day to climb to the top and it was dark when we got back. After he got to the top and his observations had verified the position of the divide, we had our tea as he wanted, from both sides of the slopes.

"Here is the divide. Waters flowing to the west feed the Thompson and Fraser Rivers. Those on that side flow to the east — and now you know the source of your own Saskatchewan River."[5]

We took plenty of time going back, as the doctor was still feeling the effects of his accident. I was afraid it would be too dark to see our way down, but I didn't say anything. The high elevation affected my wind, and I was perspiring more than the work warranted.

The next morning the doctor advised us that we would now be on our return to Fort Edmonton. There would still be some work east of where we had touched the river, but that would not require too much time. We were of course all happy to know that at last we were turning our faces homeward. Although I actually had no home, my stay at the fort made me feel as if it was a home.

The weather had been unusually sunny and bright for the most of our time as we went up the Saskatchewan but now the nights got much colder and the days dull with little sunshine. The fact that we were on the return trip made these discomforts of little effect.

If was around the middle of October when we reached Rocky Mountain House, which was only a winter post for trade with Assiniboines and a few Blackfoot who made their way that far north. We had been around eight days since leaving the mountains. There was no-one at the fort yet. We were again getting out of grub, as our last bundle of dried meat had got loose from the pack and was lost. It was useless to go back to get it as it only contained a couple of meals and we had not followed the same track.

There was a light fall of snow that night, and I told Dr.

Hector I had hunted with the Pigeon Lake Indians in these parts and thought I knew where we could get rabbits. We crossed the river at a ford but found no rabbits. The Stony in the meantime was scouring the sloughs in hope of finding some late ducks but had no luck, as the small lakes had frozen over.

Again I suggested that I ride ahead to Gull Lake. The creek that entered the lake always had late ducks. When I reached the lake, I tied the horse out of sight and crawled on hands and knees as close to the water as I could get but I could see no ducks. Just as I was about to get to my feet, I heard mallards call on the near side of the creek close to where I was watching, behind a clump of bush.

I got four in the water and knocked two down when they flew over after I reloaded. The first four I reached with a stick, but the others were too far out in the stream to reach. Nothing for it but strip off and swim after them. The water was very cold but a hungry man will take risks for a full stomach. My teeth were dancing a jig when I dressed but I was happy to know that this time my guess about game was good and I had the proof. I lost no time in getting on the trail of our party, who would pass about a half mile from the lake.

When I caught up with them, they were a happy bunch of noisy men as they got busy plucking the ducks, making fires to singe the feathers, and a big one to cook them. I think that was one meal that was made in record time. Nimrod, with his usual forethought, made certain to save enough meat for breakfast, a precautionary measure that was well needed.

All next day we travelled hard, wanting to cross Blind Man River before dark. Breakfast had finished the last of our food and we didn't see a thing that we could kill for a meal. It was thoroughly dark when we reached the river, the water dark and uninviting to my partners. I knew the ford but did not say anything to the others, waited to hear their disgusted comments, especially when the Stony said he could smell smoke.

Brown rode with Nimrod to a high point on the hill and yelled back, "I see the light of a camp fire."

"I know the ford here, Doctor, and have crossed over several times. If you follow in a line behind me, I believe we can get over safely."

"All right," he replied. "Men, catch the pack horses and lead them across. We will follow Peter."

Brown had returned and said, "Drowning or starving, what's the difference; lead the way, Peter, I'll be right behind your tail."

We crossed over without mishap except that Sutherland's

long legs got wet. His horse slipped. To hear his roar at the cold water, I thought the man was being killed.

A lone Stony Indian was camped about a quarter of a mile upriver with his wife. They had a stage of red deer meat drying when Nimrod informed them of our plight. The man pointed to the stage and told us to help ourselves. We did not need any second invitation. Even the doctor, always so precise and particular about observing the strictest code of ethics among the Indian people, stood around the fire munching dry meat.

The lady was busy preparing cooked meat for our supper. We all agreed after several cups of tea and second helpings of the meat that it was the finest meal we had ever enjoyed.

Sutherland said, "I wouldn't trade that good meal for the best the Queen of England could produce."

"I agree with that statement a hundred percent," I said, "but I wouldn't care to be bound to that one course, like our host, for the rest of my lifetime."

The next morning those good people stripped the choicest pieces from the stage and Nimrod apportioned them in our saddle bags. The doctor asked me if I thought there was anything in our packs that the man could use.

I asked him. "No," he said, "ammunition is all that I need, if you have any to spare."

The family had only a poor canvas tent, so the doctor went for his own buffalo tent and gave it to them. He told us to give them the balance of our shot, sufficient powder to match the shot and the few bullets we had left, some flints, and tobacco. We left a happy and grateful Stony Indian behind us, but Dr. Hector considered it small service for feeding six starving men all they could eat as often as they could be induced to sit down to eat the food, besides giving us more than enough for the balance of our trip.

We camped overnight once more before reaching the fort. There were no people at the Pigeon Lake mission where we had our meal and rested the horses for a short time. The doctor now appeared in a tremendous hurry; he could hardly wait for the horses to feed but kept pacing back and forth the whole noon hour. Our horses were in fair shape and could stand a little fast travel; only the Stony complained. "The chief for the first time is in a hurry. He doesn't stop to say his prayers to the sun, like he always does. Surely the devil must be riding behind him."

This latter remark of Nimrod had no implication of pagan worship but was in reference to the belief among the Indians that the doctor's observations were based on some religious rite. I was often faced with the impossible task of explaining the purpose of the doctor's actions. The Stony was now fully

convinced of the mechanical use in the doctor's ability to k
directions and obtain locations with his instruments.

We were still some distance from the fort when we hear
big guns. We presumed it to mean another visit for trade l
tribe but we found out that it was a salute to the boats that had
only just arrived. This was unusually late as they generally
came in September and it was now well into October.

Captain Palliser on his return to Edmonton had retained
only two of the men of his summer expedition. The rest had
gone to their homes. These two men were to take care of the
horses for next year's work, in a camp north and west of the fort
where he had arranged for hay-making during the summer.

The predictions of Captain Palliser and Dr. Hector on the
trip back from Fort Benton, and Sutherland's eye-witness
description of the wholesale slaughter of buffalo across the line
by hide hunters who left the carcasses to rot on the prairie, had
made a tremendous impression on me. These hide hunters were
equipped with a long-range gun that did away with the former
method of running buffalo down with a fast horse like we did
on this side of the line. Sutherland said, "I have witnessed with
my own eyes one man killing ten animals within a radius of
one hundred yards with a gun they call a Sharps rifle. Hide
hunters think nothing of killing forty and fifty head in one
day's hunt, sometimes not even bothering to take the tongues.[6]
These men are doing more to stir up trouble among the Indians
across the line than any other single factor in the American-
Indian wars."

"Yes," he said, "there's a growing belief among all the
Indians who know about this terrible waste that the American
Government is authorizing these hide hunters to exterminate
buffalo to break up Indian resistance, because practically
everything that an Indian needs in shelter, clothing, and food is
contained in the live buffalo of the plains."

Recalling the words of Palliser and Hector had reminded
me that the location of a permanent home for ranching
domesticated animals was the inflexible condition of my lady's
good will. The mere fact that I made a decision to take up land
would remove all her previous objections, but I hated the
thought that it might be construed as a weakness in my
position as master in my own decisions. I had the means to start
my ranch in a small way. All I lacked was the determination to
make the choice. Common sense finally prevailed over my
indecision and so I decided to take up land while a good
location was available. I went to Captain Palliser and asked for
a few days leave following Christmas day.

"Certainly, Peter. I will arrange for a man to handle your

work till you return, but I would like to know if you will be available for the summer expedition."

"Thank you, sir! Yes, you can depend on me for the summer. I have decided to locate a ranch and stock it with horses for breeding purposes. It will have to be north of Edmonton as there is still danger from horse raids further south. I will need every dollar I can earn in the next year to get started."

Palliser replied, "I'm delighted to hear you say so, Peter. There will be a big market for horses once settlers start coming into the country. It may be a few years yet before this takes place but by then you will be in a fine position to take advantage of the market. I believe you are showing good judgement. Dr. Hector and I have been discussing a proposition that might be to your advantage but I will say no more for the present; there will be plenty of time as we still have a year's work ahead of us."

Bill Borwick again invited me to share a room with him when he found out that I would be stationed to Edmonton for the biggest part of the winter. "Peter," he said, "it is all very well and natural to seek the company of the opposite sex but you know you are too fiddle-footed to travel docilely in double harness. You persist in lavishing your time and affections on one single person and one of these days you'll find yourself chained to a hitching post, with no prospect of looking over the next hill."

"You watch your own step, old chap! I know of half a dozen mothers who have already picked you for their next son-in-law. I'm taking up land and going to start a horse ranch just as soon as I get enough money cached away for a beginning."

"That's a mighty good idea but I doubt if you'll get much sleep watching your brood mares against the Blackfoot and Cree horse thieves seeking glory and fame among their own people for the number of horses they can steal and scalps to hang on their belts. When I take up land, ten years from now, it will have to be in the shade of the fort's brass guns. However, I wish you luck in whatever you do."

He had hit exactly on the point that I knew I would have to face. No man could make a living on the land unless he trapped or hunted for the Hudson's Bay Company. This latter was something I hoped I never would have to do. I hated the servile attitude of most of their servants, and the almost autocratic power which some of the officials used to assert their authority, though in my day it had become more benevolent towards their people.

Our arguments and discussions in our room did more to

bolster my determination to carry out my decision to become a land owner than agreement could have done. The very fact that I had to advance arguments in support of my views helped me to overcome my own indecision in the matter.

The Christmas-night dance as usual was well attended from the settlements, and Borwick and I again assumed duties in regard to the entertainment of the guests. This time it was a pleasure when Florence and her dad put in an appearance. I considered myself an old hand, and required none of Bill's coaching to find the best method of making the best of my opportunities. I managed with the connivance of our lady director to secure the services of Florence to assist us in our duties. After our lunch was served I managed a private conversation that obtained an invitation for a visit at Florence's home.

Mr. Christie,[7] the chief factor, provided an opportunity for me to visit at Ste. Anne a few days after Christmas when he asked me if I would take a dog team to the lake for a load of fish. I agreed, provided I was allowed to stay a day or so visiting.

"There's no hurry for the load providing you do not charge your visiting days against the Company."

"No," I replied. "I have some private business of my own and was planning to ride saddle but I would much rather take your dogs."

"I have already got permission from Palliser and one of my men is to take over your duties while you are away. Go ahead, but try to be back in four days."

"Four days it is, Mr. Christie. Of course you will not count today as this day is already half spent."

"Get out," he said, "before you talk me out of another day. Your time will start from tomorrow morning."

I could hear him laugh as I made a hurried dash for the door. The team was already hooked up and ready but of course he did not know about that or he might not have been so generous with the allotted time.

Train dogs are a good deal like horses. Some teams are fast and eager to go while others are slow and have to be urged to keep up a fair speed. The five-dog team I had were matched crossbred huskies, eager as race horses when the gatekeeper opened to let me out. They had a well beaten toboggan track to follow. It kept me hustling to keep up with their steady untiring speed.

This time I went direct to Florence's home, as her dad had invited me to stay at his place when I came to visit. They had a big house and a spare room. They were about ready to go to bed but the mother insisted that they make me some supper, although I had stopped twice for a brief rest and a cup of tea, which in my case meant a full meal each stop.

I was never troubled with my stomach in spite of the fact that in those trail days it was either a feast or a famine. Even today at my age of eighty-seven years, I can eat a good meal and sleep like a dog all night. That evening the cup of tea turned out to be a full meal and I am afraid I flattered the cook in the amount I put away.

The next day was a round of visits in the settlement. Florence of course was with me, wrapped in good buffalo robes I had bought from the Pigeon Lake Indians and stored with the Company at Edmonton. These robes, which I seldom used except on these trips to Ste. Anne, were both of special silken hair, very rare among the hundreds of buffalo killed in a summer on the prairie.

My visit was very pleasant. Florence was tearfully happy at my arrival. Her mother was kindness personified, and her husband, as hospitable as any man could be, did everything possible to make my stay agreeable. He entertained us with stories of hunting and trapping, of the habits and beliefs of northern tribes: humor, tragedy and tribal customs.*

Florence did not mention marriage but listened to what I told her dad about the slaughter of buffalo in the States for their hides and the carcasses left to rot. Also what Dr. Hector and Captain Palliser had advised and my own decision towards locating some land. I presumed that she would accept my invitation, as this removed the last obstacle in her objections to my way of life.

I took my departure with some regret. In spite of myself, I felt an ominous feeling of uncertainty that was unaccountable. I could only come to the conclusion that she had no faith in my sincerity; yet there was nothing missing in her affectionate acceptance of my attentions and her response was all that any man could desire.

CHAPTER SIX

To the Athabasca and the Southern Prairies

DURING THE SECOND WEEK in 1859 Dr. Hector returned and was ready to start north to Jasper House.[1] Chief Factor Christie decided to accompany us as far as his own horse camp where we would stay overnight. He would inspect the Company horses that were being fed there during the winter.

They were a merry party that night. The two horse guards had a big slab of ribs, fresh doe meat roasting on a spit in front of their chimney fire, and boiled cold buffalo meat, and to be sure they would have enough, they added two jumbo whitefish to another spit to roast with the doe ribs. You can believe me there was little left of that bounteous feast to throw to the dogs.

The doctor, never one to cater to the official class distinction so carefully cherished by Company usage, included us all in the entertainment. Even Factor Christie lowered the bars to tell some interesting and amusing experiences, under the influence of the doctor's genial and companionable inclusion of all the men in a generous helping of rum, which he highly recommended as the best remedy for all our troubles.

I noticed the doctor took very little of his solicitous recommendations in the matter of the drinks but made certain the factor received his just share. My own refusal exploded an eloquent speech on the faults, illnesses and dire calamities of the whole human race due chiefly to men's refusal to accept known and tried remedies for the faults of obstinacy, stupidity and oddities of a teetotaller. It amused me greatly because the doctor knew for some time of my pledge to abstain at any social function, using liquor for medicine only.

Drunkenness in those days was a dangerous business and looked upon with a great deal more intolerance than it is today. Indulgence to excess was looked upon as a weakness and did more to lower respectable people's opinion than even theft or any petty larceny.

At daybreak, we were on our way west to cross the Pembina and thence north to the Athabasca River.[2] The doctor chose this route to cover new territory. He tramped on snowshoes with our guide ahead of Richards and me, who were with the dog teams. It was tedious work, over fallen timber and heavy brush. We sometimes had to cut our way through or go around. Our guide, Louison, showed poor judgement in his choice of a trail. He was a new man to my acquaintance but he was supposed to know this territory. I was to learn a great deal more about the man before the trip was over.

This was all new country to me but after a good deal of delay in the second day's travel, I suggested that we exchange places. The man seemed glad of the easier work and never suspected that I doubted his ability as a guide.

The doctor wanted to travel by compass. I suggested to him that it might be better if we kept the same general direction, taking advantage of the natural openings and lakes and not trying to keep a straight compass reading. He agreed and we reached the banks of the Athabasca early the following day.

We could have lightened our sleighs by caches for the return trip, as was the custom, but we would not be following the same course again; however from the river we would have to keep the same trail. The doctor had us make a cache there.

We travelled on ice with some pleasure after our difficult passage across from the Pembina. We made another seven miles before camping on the site of an abandoned post called Fort Assiniboine. There was nothing but the ruins to indicate where the post had been, but the name was carried downriver to a better location for trade.

Two days later we passed the mouth of the Mcleod River and here we met with the first bad luck of the trip. We had to climb the banks to avoid some bad ice on the river. In descending back down to the ice again, Louison lost control of the toboggan and the sleigh was smashed beyond repair on the rocks at the shore. The doctor did not say anything to Louison, even though it was his bad judgement that caused the accident.

The toboggan was abandoned and the load had to be shifted to the other one and the dogs strung out on the one toboggan.

Fortunately the load was considerably lighter after more than eight days travel. Where a steep descent had to be made, all the men were called to let each sleigh down. Richards was in the lead and the doctor and I were waiting to help him down but the other chap did not wait but tried to come down without help; the dogs, trained to outrun the sleigh, were too much for Louison's dragging weight and the load. Richards' command to the dogs to swing to the right was too late to save the toboggan but none of the dogs were hurt.

We had to make an early overnight stop as the delay over the accident had lost us mileage. The next morning Dr. Hector was provoked to find that two dogs had broken loose after chewing their tie straps. A short stick tied to the collars and to the tie line prevents a dog from reaching around to chew itself free. Louison had neglected this precaution always used on dogs known to have this bad habit. We had to leave them. The weight of our equipment and the load of pemmican and dog feed was too much for the remaining dogs, so we were again forced to make another cache to lighten the load.

I knew one dog loose would follow the others, but two dogs would take the trail to the first settlement at Lac Ste. Anne or St. Albert. Train dogs have been known to travel great distances to reach their homes. They develop a cunning far beyond any other breed of dogs, survive, and overcome obstacles where other canine breeds would starve or die of fatigue. I saw an Indian trained dog cross the Saskatchewan on drifting spring ice, jumping from one ice cake to another and finally reaching shore safely, unhurried and as unconcerned as if he were on solid land.

With three extra dogs on one sleigh, we made much faster time, stopping only for Dr. Hector to examine some feature of the terrain interesting or necessary to his work. An interesting mark on one of the trees at a noon stop was found by one of the men: "Mr. Jeffery, date 1852". We all went up the bank to look as the doctor told us about the man.[3]

We passed a camp of Assiniboine Indians, where the doctor traded some ammunition for a pair of snowshoes and some moose meat. They appeared to be in poor circumstances. I believe that these Indians were too far away to reach buffalo on the plain and had no horses, depending mainly on fish and the wild game natural to the northern woods. They did not develop the strength or energy of the tribes who had access to the buffalo meat.

From my own experience on that trip, the diet natural to the country, on which we were mainly dependent, did not supply the stamina that our staple food from the buffalo did on our prairie trips. We found that a day's drive left us tired, with little energy left for camp duties at night. No one seemed inclined to enjoy the evening talks that were always looked forward to each night after a good day's run. I questioned my companions and they agreed that they were similarly affected.

The doctor did not show any such condition but I think this was assumed for our benefit, because when we started to have four meals a day instead of three he made no objections but joined us in the meals. I had never felt the same fatigue on many much harder trails; in a matter of a few hours we grew ravenously hungry and unless we stopped for food, we became weak and shaky, unfit for the work.

We finally reached what was called Dead Man's Rapid. This was where Rolland had nearly lost his life. The snow from there on was not so deep, and we made twenty-five miles the next day. It was getting near the end of the month when we came in sight of the mountains. We were approaching the end of our journey and we all felt much better for that reason.

It was after we had left the rapids behind us that we found a camp of Iroquois Indians. They had been brought out by the fur traders as boatmen and had married native women and stayed in the country. They all appeared better dressed, healthier, and better equipped than the Assiniboines. Possibly they had acquired a knowledge and experience in their travels that fitted them better to their new environment. Perhaps Company largesse allowed them more privileges than the other less-energetic tribe. They were all good trappers and hunters, physically better-built men, and a great deal more active in their movements around camp than their indifferent slow neighbours, the Assiniboines.

Our last day before we reached Jasper House was memorable, because at Lac La Brule the ice was partially covered by a fine sand from the huge banks along the edge of the lake. We had to help the dogs pull the toboggan across the worst patches of sand where it drifted with the wind on the lake ice, like drifts of snow on the prairie.

We were less than four miles from Jasper House and it was getting dusk, but we had to cross a tributary of the Snake River, actually a creek that was open water. The doctor wanted to get there that night. Though the prospect was not inviting, there was nothing to do but wade across. Hector volunteered to go across first and start a fire, ordering us not to tackle it until he had the fire going.

I watched the man wading into that cold water with

something of amazement and a slight feeling of guilt. We had been hired to do his bidding, yet the man refused to listen to the protests of Richards and Louison. "Certainly the water will be cold but there is no need for us all to be freezing when one man can have a fire going, ready for the rest of you to change as soon as you have the load across. It will mean several trips for you fellows while I only have to cross once."

We carried the toboggan but had to unload some of the stuff. The doctor had a good fire started before he ordered us to start packing. "Leave the dogs to the last. I will have the sleigh packed and ready to go as soon as you fellows get all the load over."

The water was not too cold when one stayed in but as soon as the air struck your legs on the other side it froze stiff on the outer garments. The water was only a little above our knees, but open water in January was something I hardly expected to see in any of my travels.

"Peter, our people in England would be shocked at the discomforts of your western dressing rooms."

"You don't need to go that far to find a man that objects to cold water and outside bathing in January, but you know the water actually felt warm while we were in it."

We hurriedly changed to dry clothing. The doctor made us rub our legs thoroughly before we put on the clothes.

Everyone had retired at the post when we got there but Moberly the factor, and he roused a man to take care of our dogs when he learned of our plight. That was one night when I appreciated being under a good roof, with someone else to rustle the wood to dry our clothes.

The doctor and Moberly decided to make a hunting trip, as Hector wanted to investigate some features of the area further north. Moberly had horses and they outfitted for the trip, taking pack horses along. The three of us were left at Jasper House to occupy our time as best we could.

Louison was again to get us into trouble the week Hector was away. The post depended almost entirely on the products of the chase, and supplies were low. Fish was our main diet; only the remnants of moose and deer killed earlier in the fall offered us any change. Boiled for breakfast, dinner, and supper, it was served with very little salt. The meat had probably not been allowed to air properly and had an odd taste. The food became almost revolting. Our mouths fairly watered for a taste of pemmican but I knew this was impossible as it had to be saved for the return trip.

Although I had not been specifically authorized, I felt responsible as I was the oldest employee with the expedition;

the other men had been hired just for the trip. The doctor had told me not to expect him back for at least four days. I was checking over our supplies and equipment when I discovered our last sack of pemmican had been opened and considerably reduced.

We were in for a serious going-over from our leader. Louison admitted his guilt, but that it was his duplicity alone could hardly be believed from the amount gone, and trying to establish that Richards and I were innocent of the damage might just make matters worse, so we decided that all three take the blame.

Calling Richards into the conference, and with Louison wistfully standing by, he and I had a light meal; then I moved the sack to the custody of the Company clerk. We would await the storm with what tranquility we could jointly muster.

I had intended to remove the sack back to our own supplies as soon as we had warning of the doctor's return. Unfortunately they were several days longer away than expected. Growing tired of the idleness, Richards and I decided to go on a hunt of our own, hoping to get small game to change our monotonous food. During our absence that day the party returned, and Louison, poor stick, overcome with the enormity of his guilt, had exposed the whole thing.

We were in no position to defend ourselves, not knowing what explanations had already been made, so we took our medicine like the staunch conspirators we actually were. We were all banished back to Fort Edmonton. Richards and I both agreed the sentence was very severe, but as experienced travellers we had to acknowledge that the punishment was justified. Every precaution had to be taken to protect a party against any emergency that might arise in the course of travel.

Orders were orders, and in our pride we refused to offer any extenuating circumstance that might have improved our position with the doctor. However, we decided that Mr. Louison would run his legs ragged to keep up with our pace on the way home.

We carried our resentment to such an extent that we were forced out of pity to load him on the toboggan the last two days of the trail. He was completely played out and would have died of fatigue and cold if we had done otherwise. Louison at a later date was good enough to offer Hector a true explanation of the whole episode, which created a good laugh when the doctor told the story at a camp fire the following summer.

It was arranged the morning we left Jasper House that I would meet the doctor on the fifth of March. However, I carried a sealed letter to Captain Palliser that probably contained reports of his trip and the cause of our return without our leader. That was one date that I was determined to meet without fail. In fact I would be ahead of time to be certain of not disappointing him; that of course was my explanation to the captain.

The father was away on his trap lines when I arrived at Lac Ste. Anne, but my unexpected visit was made more enjoyable for its surprise. Nothing was lacking in my welcome and I was dined to the best of their hospitality. The doubts that had been bothering me vanished with her smiles. The prospect of a respectable land ownership grew in proportion to the influence of her affectionate attentions and vivacious personality.

The doctor arrived on schedule, late in the evening. He was tired after tramping twenty-five miles on snowshoes with a heavy pack containing his instruments and food.[4] He had hired an Indian and sent him back from where they had camped the night before.

"Peter, I will be ready to start back with you just as soon as we can get something to eat."

"We are invited to supper with some of my friends. They will consider it an honour if you will accept."

"Be glad to, Peter. A hot meal of home-cooked food is a most enticing thought after our scanty camp fare. Lead the way and I hope I do not shame you with my appetite."

The doctor certainly did justice to the food, which pleased the mother more than all the best compliments he could have offered. He was at his affable best, and I marvelled at the man's easy manner of speech, which drew the old lady and Florence into the conversation as if he had been an old friend instead of an utter stranger. Nor did he make the mistake of trying to pay for his supper, but thanked them both and shook hands as we took leave, expressing a sincere appreciation for their hospitality.

Stopping half way to the fort to rest the dogs and have a lunch, the doctor was out of the sleigh rustling wood for the fire. He was somewhat stiff from his run but in the best of humour. Our last meeting at Jasper House was not what one could call a happy circumstance. I was glad that he had apparently wiped the matter from his mind.

"Peter," he joked, "I have often wondered what the great attraction was that induced you to make these long trips for the factor when you could have claimed it to be outside your own employment. Now I know. Your lady friend is a very attractive woman and what is more important has plenty of good sense."

"This latter quality, Doctor, is what causes me most of my difficulty. She absolutely refuses to become the wife of a wanderer, or traveller, as they call it in Cree or French. I must become a farmer with a house ready and waiting before she will consent to any thought of marriage."

"Wonderful! Wonderful!" he repeated. "It's not often that you can find beauty and common sense blended with such perfection. The captain would be pleased to know that our views were supported by this winsome maid at the edge of the prairie and the big wilderness timber of the north."

The doctor wanted to drive the dogs while I took a turn riding but I refused.

"What would I have to boast about, Hector, if I allowed you to do that! After your high praise of my girl, I feel I could drive you to Fort Pitt with only a stop or two between here and there. You have already done your day's work. I've rested for two days and am quite fit, so you climb into the toboggan and let's get started."

"Very well, then. I'll not argue but I still feel a little run would do me good."

He wasn't in the sleigh more than a mile before I knew he was asleep again.

We had been at the fort for less than a week when the captain got word that one of the Company officials[5] was very sick and wanted Dr. Hector to go there. The request was urgent.

It was getting late for dogs in case the doctor had to stay for any length of time, and there was less than an average depth of snow, although no break could be expected till the following month. Finally he decided to take a five-dog team. The trail had drifted but dogs are very adept at finding an old toboggan trail, even with hardly a sign on the surface. They seem to be able to feel their way with uncanny instinct.

After the third day of travel, we had covered more than half the distance. The further east we travelled, the more snow there appeared to be. The fourth morning when we got up there was a regular blizzard blowing.

We had both been over the trail several times and decided we would recognize the land marks to keep on the right track. The wind was blowing almost at our backs and after we started visibility gradually grew less until the man breaking trail ahead of the dogs only appeared as a figure without form. Finally the doctor who had been doing his share of trail breaking, stopped and came back.

"Peter, I believe we're lost. It's impossible to recognize anything in this storm. We'll camp in the first sheltered place we can find and wait the storm out."

"Yes, I think that might be best. To continue might lose us

time, instead of gaining. I think we are south of the regular trail but I am not too certain."

"My compass can give us the direction but it's useless if we don't know where to start from. Keep close with the dogs. If we should get separated, we would never get together again."

We ran into a heavily wooded ravine a short distance from where we had stopped, and it was past the noon hour when we finally had the camp comfortable to wait out the storm. During the night the wind stopped blowing. The skies cleared but it was bitterly cold. I roused the doctor and informed him of the change.

"That's good, Peter. I'll be up in a minute and take observations in case the sky clouds over again before daylight."

"Breakfast is about ready. If you can get our location, we can be on our way before daybreak."

Our discussion at breakfast verified our conclusions that the wind direction had changed, and by keeping the wind at our backs we were off course nearly ten miles south of the proper trail.

We had only been travelling about an hour when we came to a lake which the doctor recognized as one he had camped on the previous year. With a fixed point to start from, the doctor brought us to Fort Pitt without further error. We took turns breaking trail, but the heavy snow slowed us down to less than twenty-five miles a day.

We stayed on at Fort Pitt after the doctor's patient had fully recovered. My own time was occupied with the hunters after fresh buffalo meat, besides short trips with the doctor in territory he had not fully covered. The doctor, busy with his ever-lasting figures and notations which never seemed to be finished, was mighty poor company. However, when we were on the trail, he appeared to shed his former concentration and obliviousness to his surroundings and became a brilliant conversationalist. His shrewd observations and witty remarks showed he had not been entirely engrossed in his work.

It was well on in April when the doctor finally said he was finished and we would return to Edmonton. We would ride horses and lead a pack horse.

Dr. Hector was a hard man on horses and men, but never asked anyone to do more than he was prepared to do himself. It took the best of my ability to control his speed to the amount of riding a horse could take without becoming exhausted. He had no intention of being cruel but always had a devilish energy or urgency that seemed to push him beyond reasonable limits. I often took pride in my own endurance on the trail but I have to

97

admit that the man was equal to anything I could take in hard trail punishment.

At Edmonton, we found the officials of the expedition gathered at the fort. Brisco and Mitchell were again with the party. I spoke to Palliser and advised him that I wished to attend to some private business of my own. "Certainly, Peter, you are free to take what time you need."

My sorrel was in prime condition and getting a fairly early start I was able to reach Ste. Anne before sundown. The family was at home when I arrived but shortly after I had received a lunch Florence and her mother excused themselves as they had promised a sick call to one of their friends and the father was left to entertain me. I realized later that this had been arranged. I had noticed an unusual coolness on the part of the women but the father was the same genial personality that he had always been.

I was going to ask him if he had found any location for my land when he brought the matter up himself. "There are two places along the Sturgeon River near the St. Albert settlers that I believe you would like, one on the north side of the lake and the other about three miles down river. There are of course dozens of other locations that might serve as well but in my own opinion it is as well to choose a place near good water. You must be familiar with the general appearance of the locality."

"Would you consider going with me tomorrow to look over the places you think are good? If I am satisfied, I would like to arrange with some men to start building this fall."

"Certainly I'll be glad to go with you or you can ask young Fred Bellcourt who was with me when I looked over the two places. But before you make any definite plans, I had better tell you that Florence refuses to consider marriage before you've definitely established a home for her. We both have tried to talk her out of this. Although her mother and I both assured her you'd be welcome to make your home with us until you had your own place prepared, she refused to consider any such arrangement. My girl has a mind of her own, and nothing that we can say will change her mind. I thought it better to tell you this before you say anything yourself."

There was nothing I could say in reply but I assured the old man that he need not worry about the matter. I was satisfied to allow Florence's decision to decide for us both.

No man likes the initiative taken away from him but under the circumstances the old gentleman's words had the effect of relieving my mind of a troublesome situation. I surmised from the tone of his voice and the manner in which he brought up the subject of marriage that the decision was already settled.

They had decided that my continued employment with Palliser showed a reluctance to carry out my intention of taking up land.

I could plainly understand that any further delay on my part would not help remove their doubts so I went and looked up Bellcourt and arranged with him for an early start in the morning. He took a pack horse and bedding; also a supply of food to last for three or four days.

We were away before any of the household were up. We shot some ducks and roasted them for our breakfast some ten miles on our way. We had looked over the first location, which did not satisfy me. It was too low and mostly slough grass. Bellcourt led the way to the second location, avoiding the settlement to the south of us.

The second location was an excellent choice, all high land and fronting on the river. Good building spruce timber was available within a short distance from a nice building site. The land sloped to the south near the river with probably forty acres of bottom land. The balance was level as a table. I could see no stones anywhere. We made our camp near the river and prepared to stay overnight.

The next morning we covered a wide radius of territory which was all semi-open land with an excellent growth of grass, pea vine, and vetch almost up to our horses' bellies. There were miles and miles of good range country. The location was ideal from every point of view. Yet somehow or other I could not feel any enthusiasm. I had a strange reluctance or uncertainty, not exactly a premonition but a depression that I could not shake off.

We were at our river camp only a matter of fifteen or twenty miles from the fort and I was tempted to pay my guide and return direct to the post.

My companion was good company and entertained me with all the gossip of the settlement, and slyly hinted that I had a rival for my girl's affections who was, in his own words, "A persistent dog but I hardly know whom he likes best, your girl or her mother. He visits there even when your girl is away some place."

This last information changed my mind immediately. We would go back to Ste. Anne as early as we could get started in the morning. I shot a couple of ducks on the wing and my partner cleaned them and boiled them ready for an early breakfast.

I stayed a week at Lac Ste. Anne and as before was treated with every kindness. Florence went everywhere with me visiting the settlement people. There was nothing in her conduct to indicate any change in her affections except in that one implacable determination not to marry me till we had a home of our own. My week over, I found my way back to the fort with admiration for the girl who made up her mind and stuck to her decision.

At the fort there was a great deal of activity as the fur packs from the northern posts had been brought in for shipment down the river with the annual fur brigade. The men of the post were busy sorting the furs and packing. Care in the proper packing was a very important matter and the men at Edmonton were experts at the business. My friend Bill Borwick worked early and late and had no time for any foolery about our private affairs as was customary in the evenings in our rooms.

The departure of the brigade was an annual event that brought a large number of people to the fort, as the wives and children who came with their men to bid them a gay farewell camped outside the stockade and pastured their horses on the flats below the fort.

Captain Palliser was impatiently awaiting the arrival of his man Beads, who was stationed at Fort Garry to pick up despatches with his instructions and appropriations for the summer expedition. He had orders to bring them to Edmonton with as much speed as possible. There was no word of Beads so the captain decided to proceed at once and wait for his instructions on the prairie. He wanted as large a crew as the previous year but the amount of work he could do and the number of men would depend on his allotment of funds.

The expedition started on the 24th of May, leaving the doctor and myself to await the arrival of Beads. We were camped at White Mud Lake at a distance from the fort where the feed was better for the horses and we could intercept Beads on the trail. The doctor was consumed with impatience and anxiously watched the trail, or had me do so while he worked out his anxiety on his never-ending calculations.

"Doctor," I told him, "you must remember that the man has over a thousand miles to travel and it would take him a month of riding, as the captain never allows any of his men to travel on Sunday. It's more likely that the great masters in England didn't hurry their despatches, judging their puny little island facilities as equal to our vast open prairies and waterways that could surround their land a dozen times."

Hector's glare as he turned towards me, from the now well-beaten path in front of our tent, set my body ready for action, then he burst out laughing. "Perhaps you're closer to the truth than you imagine. It is hard to get people to realize the vast extent of this country and the difficulties of mail or transportation."

Finally, after three or four days of waiting, I spotted a saddle horse in sight coming from the east. It was our man all right, and the doctor was happy again. I was glad that the session of waiting was over, as the doctor was getting quite hard to live with. His imagination had Beads sick or accidentally hurt or a half dozen other mishaps all quite as improbable.

Beads had made a remarkable ride; he had covered the distance in less than thirty-five days, yet had rested every Sunday according to the captain's instructions. The horse could have kept going the next day, but for once the doctor curbed his impatience and allowed the horse and his rider a full day's rest.

The captain had given us a general idea of their direction, leaving a bottle with further instructions under a campfire secretly marked at each main campground they had used. After the third day's ride we were given directions to find a cache of food and the location of their next permanent campground. The evening of the fourth day's ride we caught up with the expedition.

Shortly afterwards, the captain sent five of us on a scouting party for the purpose of alerting the camp to any hostile Indians in the area, and also to report on the general topography of the country.

The Indians acknowledged no line of demarcation except that set by their own tribal wars and peace treaties, although they were now beginning to understand the great difference in the Hudson's Bay Company's treatment of the Indians from that of the Long Knives to the south. Actually there was no authority on our side of the border, only the policy of the Company which was to hold a neutral position towards tribal wars; yet I know of very few instances of major crimes.

Horse stealing was looked upon as an honourable calling, practised between tribes but never to my knowledge by individuals outside of the tribes of Crees, Blackfoot, and Peigans. Theft or other petty crime was not a factor of much importance. In all my years of experience in later years, I never lost an article from my carts, although there was plenty of opportunity for things to be taken without my knowledge, as I often left them unguarded while I visited with friends among the teepees of camps on our way to or from Fort Garry with freight.

The American Indians, fighting an almost continuous war with the white men encroaching on their land, did not recognize the imaginary line we called our border, and consequently retaliated at any and every opportunity that presented itself for an easy victory over any inferior force they met with on our side. It was in such circumstances that I received my first and only actual wound from an enemy.

Our party was making a large circle around our camp, keeping within a radius of five to seven miles. The sun was getting low when we suddenly decided to return. Although we had found no sign of any other people in the area, I was not satisfied and I had an odd feeling of excitement. "Keep your eyes peeled, Sutherland," I said. "I can almost smell trouble."

We were passing through rolling brushy country. I was in the lead and I stopped my horse when I reached the highest point of the hill for a careful look. There I noticed a flock of chickens take flight from the brush about two hundred yards to our left; then I spotted movement between clumps. The others had pulled up their horses beside me.

"There is movement on both sides of that brush at the bottom of the hill. I think a band of foot warriors are trying to encircle us and may be already in place. We will ride straight at them on a dead run. See to your guns. Hold your fire till we are among them, then let them have it. We will take them by surprise."

We were at full speed when we struck the brushy slope. We caught them by surprise as they rose to their feet to head us off. We shot at the moving targets. I do not think that we hit any of them but those nearest dug for cover in a hurry.

The Indians had been all on foot. After a half mile or so of fast speed, I felt a stinging in my leg and glancing down I was surprised to see an arrow sticking in the calf of my leg. Three of the men dropped back to cover our retreat while Ballentine took a knife and cut the long end off and fastened a hasty bandage above the wound, as tightly drawn as he could make it.

"If you can travel a half mile with a whole arrow in your leg, you ought to make camp with only a part still in there."

I was in no position to argue, and the prospect of another in the back, if we delayed, was too likely to risk. The others slowed their speed out of consideration for me but wasted little time getting into the camp and alerting the others.

The doctor scolded Ballentine for not trying to stop the blood.

"It'll take more than an arrow in the leg to kill Erasmus," he responded. "Besides, he has two legs and I only have one back. Those devils can run faster than a lot of our horses. One chance like that is enough for me for one day."

"Doctor, those are exactly my own sentiments," I said. "He

did the best he could under the circumstances. I was as eager as the rest of them to put distance between the Indians and us. I thought it wise not to incur any further risk. We were outnumbered at least three to one."[6]

The captain never neglected any precaution for the safety of the camp. The wagons, or rather carts, were drawn up in a circle and guards were always posted at night.

We were still in the same camp a few days later when Paul Cadzeau[7] rode into camp at a hard gallop to inform the captain that a large band of about one hundred riders was approaching in our direction. Palliser ordered the men to prepare guns and take positions within the camp circle.

"Don't shoot until I give orders," said the captain. "Prepare your guns and see to your flints. If they attack, we'll sell our lives dearly. Be brave. This may mean life or death."

I heard the orders and hobbled out of the tent with my own gun. Palliser stood cool and as undisturbed as if nothing unusual was in prospect. He hadn't raised his voice as he placed his men in readiness for the riders. The Indians were all in war gear with painted faces and the horses marked with signs usual for a warrior. We thought they were Crow Indians, and our interpreter addressed them in that language.

"What do you want? We are the enemies of no man. We are out for pleasure, so come along and be peaceful."

Their interpreter replied in the Crow language.

"We are not Crow Indians. We belong to the Snake tribe. We are short of tobacco."

"Peter, bring two fathom of tobacco and give it to them!"

I brought the tobacco and gave it to their leader, who stood slightly in advance of his riders. One of the men got off his horse and distributed the tobacco among all the men. Every time any of us spoke English I noticed the head man took notice. One of our men made the remark: "They are as handsome a band of men as I have seen among the tribes." The leader smiled at that remark and I whispered to Palliser, "That man understands English."

Palliser said in English, out loud, "These men are a ferocious and bloodthirsty lot." As soon as the leader heard that he made a demand for ammunition, after he had spoken to the others in their own tongue.

"Now, Mr. Man, you are not an Indian," said Palliser.

"No, I'm not an Indian," the man replied in perfect English.

"You are a disgrace to your white blood and a bad example to the Indian."

"It's an easy life. I don't have to work and I am treated like a king. My leadership is established and my word respected. What more could you want?" As if to show us his authority over his companions, he gave a command at which they all swung their horses and rode away.[8]

The captain flushed with anger but said nothing more, very well satisfied that he had avoided trouble without endangering the lives of his men. He took every precaution that night and for several nights afterward. Double guards were placed and the horses tied up each evening.

We had again moved camp and were moving to a new location when one of the scouts rode back to inform the captain that he had spotted a small herd of buffalo a few miles west of our course.

The captain, Brisco, and Felix, the scout, started out after them. They killed four animals and we had orders to erect a temporary camp while the meat was fetched in and drying stages were erected to cure the meat.

A Sarcee hunting party met up with our men going after the meat and invited the captain to visit their camp. However, Palliser decided not to change his course but traded for some pemmican and dried meat to be certain we had plenty of supplies. These Sarcees seemed a friendly tribe though they were allies of the Blackfoot, who seldom made any overtures to any man except their allies and associates.

A day or so later, Brisco, Mitchell, Felix and Piscan [or William Munroe] killed five more buffaloes. Mitchell had killed a cow and had the best meat. The camp again shifted to where the kill was made. The camp was set up while the meat was cured and the horses rested. The captain's objective was the Hand Hills so as quickly as the meat was cured we moved again.

Palliser had a little difficulty with Felix Penlope.[9] It was the custom of the country where a stray horse was found that the man who saw him first could claim the animal. The captain had tried to explain the Queen's law with respect to property that belonged to other persons but Felix would have none of it and left the camp in a huff.

He was a valuable man, our interpreter, and a first class hunter. When the captain learned of his desertion, he sent a man after him. I never learned how they had patched up their differences but I suspect that Felix had time to review his position, cooled his temper and became more amenable to reason.

We had again moved camp and were in Blackfoot territory. None of the men liked the idea at all. Some expressed open hostility to the risk of entering the area with so small a crew, but the captain managed to quiet their anxiety by informing them that he was well stocked with presents that he felt sure would pacify any hostility they might show. Felix Penlope, our interpreter, was invaluable, as he assured the men that the Blackfoot would not interfere with their party since they were at peace with the Crees, and that the tribe knew about Palliser's expedition from the previous year and were only curious about the purpose of the party.

Shortly afterwards, we had a visit from about fifty Blackfoot horsemen, whom we were able to entertain without rousing their enmity. They challenged our men in some contests of sport. At the doctor's suggestion, we allowed them to win most of the games.[10] Some small bets were placed on these contests and the captain shrewdly made up the losses to the men of our party. So everybody was satisfied and the Blackfoot went away happy.

Our old friend Nimrod, who had been with us the year previous and now was with us once again, almost lost his life when he decided to leave the party. He was captured by a small party of Blackfoot riders who were taking him back to their camp when Mitchell and Sullivan happened to come along and managed to convince the Blackfoot that their prisoner was a member of Palliser's party and that Palliser would give them presents for his release. The Indians were invited back to the camp, and the riders went away satisfied to forego the pleasure of Nimrod's torture and death in exchange for the gifts.

We were near the Red Deer River when we had another visit from some Blackfoot chiefs and their followers. Their behavior was exemplary; no doubt the captain's diplomacy and well stocked store of presents of tobacco and trinkets were helpful. Felix's acquaintance with two of the chiefs helped a great deal in the early preliminary procedures that usually marked the successful establishment of good relations with these highly temperamental characters.

These two meetings with hostile tribes helped to quiet the discontent of the crew, and their fears were somewhat relaxed but not entirely removed. Travelling through Blackfoot country and meeting others of the Blackfoot and Peigan tribes, all of whom proved friendly, was certainly not to the liking of any of the men. The captain was worried that his stock of diplomatic tools of good fellowship might run short and any such catastrophe might become serious. The instability of Blackfoot tempers that the men feared from years of bitter experience was well grounded. Palliser did not dispute their convictions in this regard but decided to move on as quickly as possible out of that highly inflammable territory.

Hector, Beads, and I had caught up with the party on the 19th day of June. We arrived at the Gull Lake camp[11] after Oliver and Todd had left directions where to find the permanent camp at the Hand Hills. Previous to this they had had a great deal of trouble in keeping the camp provided with food supplies. There were times around the end of May when the matter of food was actually serious. However, after we joined up with them, food was easily obtained and in good supply.

During the balance of our trip that summer and after turning our direction to the west, we were always well supplied. The country traversed near the Red Deer River was very poor soil, cactus and sage brush, and in my opinion the poorest area in all the country we had passed through. At Berry Creek where I accompanied the doctor in his work, the grass was very poor and the soil wretched wherever we passed. I took particular notice because, except for the jackpine country of the north, I had always thought that all the southern prairie was good buffalo grass.

When we passed out of the arid area, our travel became more leisurely. The camps had visitors from the Blackfoot and Peigan confederacy, but they were all peaceful and the tribes offered no opposition to our progress.

I had cultivated a friendship with Felix Penlope for the purpose of learning more about these tribes and something of their language. This was my second year trying to get a working grasp of the language, and I could now follow the talk with a good understanding of its contents.

Felix advised me that considerable effort was being made by the American Indians to enlist the help of the three southern tribes on our side of the line for an all-out drive to push the whites out of the northern states, but up to now they had not received any encouragement as most of the Blackfoot and Peigan chiefs felt they were well entrenched in their own territory and had nothing to gain by joining the American tribes.

The captain now wasted little time in pursuing the westward direction, possibly fearing to run short of supplies and not wishing to test the discontent of his crew by too much intercourse with the Blackfoot that on each occasion grew more difficult to manage. The presents of tobacco and other articles were getting low. However, he considered the drain on his supplies a good investment which allowed passage of his party without trouble and investigation of the territory highly successful.

Considerable credit must be given to our interpreter Felix

Penlope in that he did not know the true purpose of our journey through Blackfoot territory but explained to his inquisitive kinsmen that Palliser and his men were out for sport and wanted to know the great Blackfoot people. In fact his boss had admitted, privately of course, that they, the Blackfoot people or Peigan if they were present, were the finest specimens of any race in his travels both in the United States and in our country. Also, Dr. Hector was a great medicine man who could see at night better than any man could in daylight. No doubt Felix Penlope's conclusion came from the fact that the doctor frequently made observations of the sky at night.

I did nothing to alter his opinion, but assisted in this regard by adding to his beliefs some imaginative creations of my own to enhance Hector's supernatural powers. Showing a preference for Felix's company and consulting the man in matters concerned with his mother's people who were Blackfoot, I learned a great deal about those people that was very useful in later years. Both the doctor and the captain assisted me in my schooling by assigning duties that included us both. Before the summer was half over, I was well able to check the trend of any Blackfoot or Peigan talks.

Although Felix had no education, he had a sharp mind and frequently adjusted his interpretations of the captain's words to flatter the ego and arrogance of his Blackfoot listeners. He never added to the basic facts but softened the militant harshness that was natural to Palliser's speech. The man's shrewd judgement of his people was most effective, and the results in my opinion justified his variations of the actual words to be interpreted. Felix and I exchanged talks when I questioned him about the liberties he took with the captain's speech.

He shrugged his shoulders and said, "Is it not my job to keep peace with our camp and the Blackfoot? They are not a people to be treated as children or hired servants. The Blackfoot are proud, independent, and very stubborn in their ways. They have no masters and will acknowledge no authority, only the force of numbers. How long do you think we would last if we aroused their anger?"

I had to admit the truth of his explanation and of course never brought the facts to Palliser's attention. I had no desire to risk my neck, or rather my scalp, in exposing the actual facts of Felix's interpretations which our leader might not appreciate. His military experience[12] and authority in our camp might not be accepted by the Blackfoot warriors in their demands on the captain's generosity.

We finally reached Chief's Mountain and turned north till

we reached Kootenay Pass, so called because the Kootenay Indians used it on their trips to the plains.

The captain's horse, a fine big bay with an O.T. brand, Oregon Territory, looked like a thoroughbred and probably was. No doubt there was a good story if his former ownership could have been traced. Palliser became very fond of the horse, fed him lumps of sugar, and made a great fuss over the animal. He looked after the animal himself for the balance of the summer.

We continued our way along the foot of the mountains and met with a camp of Stony Indians.[13] Though it was early on a Saturday afternoon, the captain decided to make camp near them over Sunday. There were ten teepees, and that evening we heard them singing hymns and praying. Palliser was surprised at this but I explained that a missionary by the name of Rundle had spent some years among the Indians, and these people were likely some of his converts. My inquiries with the assistance of Nimrod proved this was true. Although it had been years since any contact with a minister, they still carried on with his teaching.

The captain invited them over for service the next day. They all came. He read a portion of the scripture and asked them to sing their own hymns. They were good singers and they all joined in, their voices rising in a melody that was most impressive. Our men listened in amazement that these people far removed from any Christian influence should practise their Christian beliefs with a great deal more devotion than those of us directly under our own ministers and priests.

"Peter," said Brown a few days later, "those Stony Indians are a grand example of the Christian influence and a striking comparison with those black-hearted scoundrels they misnamed Blackfoot. I think I will be a little more respectful to our own priest and attend services more often."

The captain made a short address on the plan of salvation. The leader, an old man, spoke, and this I in turn interpreted to our men in English. They sang a few more hymns, and then the old man dismissed the congregation with prayer. The captain invited the old man and his councillors to stay and visit with him as our men retired to the tents and the others back to the teepees.

"We never hunt on Sunday," the old man said, "and we always respect a day of rest as our missionary taught us. We are following our teaching the best we know how."

"Yes," said Palliser, "You are doing right. God would not want us to do more than we know how. Your band is a fine example of Christian faith. I shall mention your people to the leaders of the church who sent your missionary among you. Perhaps they may send another to take his place."

The Stony Indians were very co-operative, giving the captain and Hector much information about the regions they called their hunting grounds. The doctor was a keen listener and made notes on the talks. It was through them that he learned of another pass through the mountains that he investigated the following spring.

It was around the middle of September[14] when the captain called a conference of the officials of the party and informed them that they had now completed work on the eastern part of the mountains, and that he had instructions for the western side. He considered it too late in the season to attempt any work on that side.

Dr. Hector wanted to carry out some projects of his own in the mountains. He asked me to go with him. I had never refused to go with him before, but after careful consideration I had to refuse.[15]

"Doctor, I hate to refuse to join your party but if you consider the condition of the stock, the lateness of the season, and the scarcity of pemmican and dried meat supplies to take along, you might understand my refusal. We would have to depend on game in the region. Nimrod considers it a risky business not to have plenty of prepared food to last the entire trip. It may well take three weeks to investigate the area. To take from the supplies on hand for your needs will make the other members of the expedition dependent on day-to-day hunting for food. I'm sorry but I just cannot do it."

The doctor was greatly provoked, in fact somewhat abusive. I had too much respect for the man to answer but turned away and went about my own business. It was not so much that he was angry at my refusal to go as that he resented my criticism of his judgment in not fully preparing supplies for the trip. He had other men as capable and perhaps far more reliable than I was to choose from. What he disliked more than anything was my outspoken explanation of my objection to going along.

Palliser took a neutral position when I was called in to his tent to explain my summary of the difficulties that would be entailed in such a trip and to justify my outright refusal to obey orders.

"Doctor," he said, "the success or failure of an expedition of this kind is largely dependent on the information and the honesty of the men we employ to carry out their duties. Their experience of conditions in their country is of vital interest to the safety of us all. Peter had a right to express his opinion. He is one of our oldest employees and has served us well in other times. Take any one of the others. I will employ Peter in other duties."

Turning to me, he said, "While I do not approve of rank disobedience in any of my men, and while your absence from the doctor's party will not in any way reduce its efficiency, I will uphold your decision. You will remain in camp until I have given the matter further consideration."

You can believe me, I was mad as the devil but managed to curb my temper. The flimsy canvas of the tent did not prevent some of the men from hearing the whole conversation, and it would be all over camp in a matter of minutes. However, I had won the battle, although I felt badly crushed over being restrained to camp duties. For three days Palliser kept me confined to rustling wood and water and other menial tasks around camp. The fourth day he ordered me to scout duties and hunting after game. I knew then that my punishment was finished.

I had done some thinking during my confinement to camp. Although the captain made no further reference to the incident and appeared to have completely removed it from his mind, I still felt a deep resentment for his high-handed manner of addressing me during my argument with the doctor. It was time that I prepared myself to ensure my independence from being just a hireling to any man's whim, whether right or wrong. Our experience in the mountains in the previous year of near starvation and the doctor's accident made me hesitate to plunge into a similar experience. Only Nimrod's sheer endurance and native sagacity had saved the situation. No man among the rest of us could have prevented disaster.

I spoke to Palliser, saying: "Sir, I resent the fact that under your contracts a man may be compelled to take risks against his better judgement and experience of years in this country. If I continue to work with your expedition it will be as a free agent not bound by slavish rules of superiors who know nothing about the conditions involved. I will take risks with any man, but your doctor is so fanatical with his work that realities do not exist in his mind."

Palliser surprised me by laughing out loud, a rare thing with him. When he had regained his composure he said, "Upon my word, Peter, you take my breath away. I admire your pride and independence. Your remarks have convinced me of your good judgement. As to those contracts, they do not mean a thing for there is no law in the country to enforce them. Of course I would not like to advertise the fact. They serve their purpose in impressing men who might otherwise quit when a difficult situation arose as it did this summer. The only clause

110

in the contract that is binding is that we can withhold a man's wage if he fails to complete a season's work. I could not allow your refusal to go with the doctor go unnoticed for the effect it might have had on the other men. Being confined to camp was the most noticeable way of impressing the men that I could think of."

The captain's explanation cleared my head of the brooding resentment over the whole incident. I felt inclined to go to the doctor and have a talk with him but my pride would not allow any overtures on my part. He had banished us from Jasper House without asking us if we had any explanation for the disappearance of the pemmican, and his hasty words over the mountain trip business were just a little bit too much, but after he pulled out without me I felt pretty bad as though it was my own fault; that is really what caused my anger and resentment but also the fact that he had appealed to the authority of the captain to enforce his will.

The captain called me in for a talk. "The doctor and I have discussed your situation fully and he has asked me to express his regret at losing his temper. He admits you showed much more self-control than he would have under the same provocation."

"Well, Sir, I am happy to hear the doctor holds no grudge, for I must admit that I have been very miserable over the whole thing. I think you realize that I have a great admiration for his physical abilities on the trail. I know of no man I would rather be with than your young doctor. My work with him has always been a pleasure except for that devilish urge, that always seems to be riding him, to be on his way regardless of what horse flesh, dog, or man can stand up to on the trail. The man must have a limit somewhere!"*

Captain Palliser and Dr. Hector planned to return to England from Victoria on the west coast. The captain would go through the Kootenay Pass and by way of Colvile[16] on the Columbia River. He took Vitalle[17] and two other men with him. Dr. Hector was going by Morley, then only known by its Indian name, which was on the south branch of the Saskatchewan River. He wanted to find a pass that the Stony Indians had spoken about the previous summer.

Dr. Hector and the captain had urged me to return to England with them to complete my education and take up a profession. Dr. Hector had first broached the subject during the summer while out on one of his trips, and later the captain had joined him in explaining their wishes on my behalf. Although at the time I felt flattered at their interest and had given the matter some serious thought, I had decided the whole idea was attractive only because it would satisfy my craving for travel.

I had quite a sum of money saved from my wages, but insufficient to carry me over the four more years required for such an undertaking. I would eventually be living on the charity of these two men, both having promised they would see that I would not fail for lack of money. It was a great temptation, but common-sense reasoning weighed against the inclination to accept.

I had no actual obligations except my mother, and she, I knew, was well cared for by my married sisters. Now, when I was actually faced with the urgency of making an immediate decision, I was shocked to realize that my girl had never entered my mind as a factor in any decision.

Having a great respect for the captain and feeling a strong friendship for the doctor were my greatest motives for accepting their offer. These men had always treated me as an equal, but I knew in England this might be different. As a dependent on their good will, I would be a curiosity to their associates and would probably be viewed in the same way as the specimens so carefully preserved by the party.

Most Englishmen of my acquaintance considered themselves made of superior cloth; even the most ignorant and pitiably helpless individuals faced with the ways of living of the West all looked down on the native inhabitants as inferior beings, even though they knew that their very lives were dependent on the good will and resourcefulness of our people. Except for the members of Palliser's expedition, most Englishmen of my acquaintance made no effort to conceal their intolerance for the native sons of the land with part European blood in their veins.

I informed the captain of my decision not to go back to England with them.

"Too bad," he said. "You are a man of good sense. With your disposition and ability, you would be an ornament to your people."

"Captain Palliser, let me say that I appreciate the offer that you have both so kindly extended but I am now twenty-six years of age. It might prove too difficult a task to adjust myself to conditions of your country; and a course of study, after six years of freedom on the plains away from books, might be more than I could stand. Perhaps I may yet find use for what abilities I have. However, I thank you both from the bottom of my heart for your consideration and thought for my welfare."

The very use of the captain's word "ornament" proved that my refusal was the correct decision. My pride and independence would be tied to their bounty. I would soon hate my position and in all likelihood would give physical expression to the condescending mannerism of the people and thereby bring disappointment and trouble to these good men.

Dr. Hector was disappointed but had a better understanding of my reasons for refusing to go along. "Peter, a man's decision must be his own. It would have been great fun to have you come along, but I think that the captain's use of the word "ornament" was bad." He smiled as we shook hands. I felt he understood my reasons as well as if I had fully explained all my reasoning.

I had mixed feelings of regret and more of relief in leaving the expedition. Perhaps I had missed an opportunity of bettering my condition. At any rate my pride soon established itself. Reading the captain's letter of recommendation I became convinced that I had made the proper decision. I would hold the respect and friendship of these two men, the better in their memories than would otherwise have been. I knew it would have been difficult to adjust myself to the attitude of a million Englishmen when, in my own environment, it took a lot of self-restraint to ignore the supercilious mannerisms of the few who found their way into my country.

The captain's letter read: "For his advantages, Peter Erasmus is every inch a gentleman and has rendered me a great service." I prized the letter and kept it for a number of years but never used it for any purpose. That letter and the doctor's statement about the accident were two things I kept for a long time.

The captain and the doctor had both given me their saddle horses. Both horses would make any man's heart beat faster. I was overwhelmed with their generosity when they handed me Bills of Sale to both animals. The horses had all been re-shod, including the two gift horses. Quickly I outfitted from the Hudson's Bay post where the captain's order gave me all my needs in food and ammunition.*

CHAPTER SEVEN

Gold

AWEEK LATER news was verified that a gold strike was on near Colvile. I was not greatly concerned as I knew nothing about mining. I was planning a trip to visit my home at the Red River settlement when two men, Peter Whitford and Butcheesh Annas[1] approached me to outfit them for a mining prospect.[2]

They offered me two-thirds while they divided one-third between them if we had any luck finding gold. They had no money of their own. It was suggested that I would furnish an outfit and money for the grub stake. They would provide the experience. In the mood for any adventure, I accepted without making much inquiry over the costs of doing so.

I turned the doctor's mare and the bay horse out with the Hudson's Bay horses and made arrangements for their care during the winter, picked up my sorrel, and made a pack horse out of the one I had ridden through the mountains; and the next morning we were on our way. They each had a saddle horse and pack horse of their own. I knew nothing of the two men but I liked their appearance. Whitford had a quiet way of talking and we were not on the trail for two days before I knew he had plenty of experience.

Butcheesh Annas, a French half-breed, was a wiry, happy-go-lucky, rather undersized chap, quick in his movements, who always seemed to be on the alert for danger. He had remarkable hearing and eyesight. Though I had passed through Blackfoot and Stony country without meeting any hostility, my companions used every precaution to avoid meeting any Indians. Whitford was a superb tracker. I thought that I had learned a great deal about reading tracks myself, but to him every mark had a meaning.

"You would be a dead man twice over, Peter, if you had our American Indians to contend with. One Indian track is just as bad as a dozen. Where you find one man there are certain to be others. The only safe way is to avoid the vicinity of any Indian camp regardless of what tribe they are. This country is big and gives us lots of room to manoeuvre. There is a big camp to the east of us. We have passed four unshod horse tracks. These are scouts for the camp. Notice the absence of buffalo of any kind. That means Indians have chased them out within the last two days."

I felt relieved of any responsibility and was glad to let him assume leadership, so replied, "O.K., you take the lead. I'll be content to follow your advice. Annas seems to have eyes and ears all over his body."

When we were at Colville, I learned that Custer,[3] the man in charge of the supply station, was well acquainted with both men and greeted them as old friends. I had time to think of what I was embarked on, and expressed my doubts to Custer.

"The man Whitford is very reliable. I have had occasion to employ his services and can personally guarantee his character. The man Annas is his devoted companion. Both are experienced miners. Whitford's long residence in the States was because of the mining. If there is any truth in reports of the mining prospect you can depend on them to get their share."

Whitford suggested that we have Custer draw up a mining agreement, after warning me that in case the venture proved unsuccessful, my loss would be considerable, as, under this kind of agreement, the risk was all with the man who put up the capital. They would supply all the work and experience. I would only be expected to take care of the stock, prepare a noon meal if I cared to do that, and assist in building the shack for winter. I could bring the stock out for the winter or stay in camp as I chose.

Although I was somewhat worried over the cost to be properly outfitted, I decided I had gone too far to withdraw now. So we signed an agreement and had it witnessed by two old men who lived in the vicinity.

"Peter," said Custer, "I advise you to buy an ox to help pack your outfit into camp, and later kill him for beef. If this strike turns out to be near as big as rumours claim, prices of food will skyrocket before the winter is over. Many fools will be there with no provisions to last the winter. Buy a better gun, and, if you are a hunter, you can double your money in sales to those who are less able to provide for themselves."

It took us five days to reach the mining location. Annas scouted ahead for the best way to travel. They chose a trail that they said would save us at least a week's time if we took it instead of going back to where the others had followed to get to the mining location.

Driving the ox ahead of us was tedious work, even though Whitford had nailed shoes on him to protect his feet.

"No use to hurry, Peter, if we expect to keep fat on his bones. There's no hurry, even if there are people ahead of us, there are probably only a few with any mining experience, and there will still be plenty of good locations for us to take."

Apparently he thought that I had caught the gold fever already, but he was wrong, for it was the unconscious adoption of the doctor's habit of hurry when he was on the trail that made me impatient with our slow movement.

We finally reached the site of the mining location. There were only about a dozen or so people there then, but it was hardly two weeks more before the camp took on the appearance of a small town. My partners immediately set out to locate our claims and left me to take care of the stock. It was late when we arrived the previous evening but at daylight they went out on their business. I got everything ready for a move as soon as they returned. They came back in the evening quite elated over their prospect. They had located three claims together. Mine would be in the centre. We moved to our claims and I started to cut logs for the shack while my partners started work on the claims. Almost at once they struck good pay dirt.

"By gar, Peter. You bring us luck. We work de two days and already we find de gold. Now me, I'm not sorry we leave all our tings behind."

This aroused my curiosity. Some time earlier, Whitford and Annas had undertaken to carry a packet for a man in Montana. While in the States,[4] their luggage had been searched during their absence, bringing them under suspicion of espionage, although they were quite innocent of the contents of the packet. Later they managed to get away through the assistance of the rooming-house manager, who had listened to the men searching the room and heard their conversation.

Already the forces that were to break out in the Civil War

were joining sides in a network of spying activities. Whitford and Annas had already made up their minds to leave the States when this incident made it imperative to move out of reach of the officers of the government. They left behind everything they owned except their horses and a pack animal which they had picketed in the brush out of town. They were well known in the district and could not take the chance of returning to their mining shack for their belongings.

I was kept busy looking after the stock and working on our winter shack. I was willing to build a fireplace but my partners were so enthusiastic over their mining that they grumbled at the delay in helping me with it. I was determined that our shack should be as comfortable and warm as it could be made. They helped me at last but good-naturedly complained about the extreme care required in placing the stones for the fireplace. Built of a clay-grass mixture on four poles, when the job was finished I was quite proud of my accomplishment. My first fire proved it a complete success, and when they came in for a meal they were as tickled as two kids with a new toy.

My partners certainly knew their business. They had located the diggings to take advantage of a small stream that entered into the main creek on which we had built the shack on the first bench above the water. They blocked this little stream with wood and stones and other debris to form a pool from which they drained the water through a flume made up of split dry fir; the centre they hollowed out with an adze, a tool that I had never seen used before. Whitford had paid twice the price of a good axe for it and had made the old man a promise to give it back when he left the mines.

I was amazed at the ingenious use they had made of the water and materials in constructing their flume and riffle where the gold was washed from the gravel. Each night they blocked off the flume to allow a head of water to build up for use the next day. It worked like a charm, and very soon I caught up their enthusiasm and found myself shovelling beside them.

It was back-breaking work and my hands became blistered and sore from the unusual work. They good-naturedly poked fun at my pains and aches and by every device invented easier tasks for me to do, but I stuck with it, determined to show that little Frenchman that I was as good a man as he was.

After a while they quit poking fun at my awkward efforts to help and as I grew hardened to the work, Butcheesh gradually took over the camp duties, first because he knew that I could barely move after a day's digging, and then because he realized that I hated the job of cooking the meals.

One day around seven o'clock Butcheesh threw down his

shovel and said, "By gar, Peter, you big ox! You tink your size will kill me with de work. Now you try to starve me smaller. No! I got enough for de day. I go to make one big supper."

I received a lot of satisfaction over his statement, which I knew was half in fun and half serious. Up to then they had treated me much as you would a small boy entertaining himself with the shovel and pick. Whitford sat down with a big laugh and started to smoke his pipe. "Do you know, Peter, it is the first time I ever heard Annas admit he had enough work, and he has been with me for nearly six years. I saved his neck once, the first time I ever saw him, when he was fighting two big men. Using his feet, he knocked both men down, and a third was drawing a gun to shoot him when I interfered. I shot the gun from the third man's hand, but do you know I had the devil's own time to get him to back out of that saloon. He has never left me since."

"Well! Well!" I said. "Who would have thought that little beggar had that much spunk. I hope he never gets angry with me. I know how those Frenchmen can use their feet. I once saw a bloody battle between a Frenchman and a big Swede. It wasn't pretty, even though they were both very drunk."

"He's been a great help to me. Saved my life twice by his quick eye and uncanny hearing. Dropped a savage across my legs once in the Dakotas, shot stone dead between the eyes. Told me to get him off my bedding before he messed things up, as cool as a cucumber when danger threatens."

We kept very much to ourselves, as the main diggings were up another branch of the creek further south to us. When we first arrived I was inclined to go out and get acquainted with some of the others, but both Whitford and Butcheesh warned against doing anything of the kind. After working with my partners a short time, I realized they knew more about the business than I did, so I stayed away from the other miners. They cautioned me not to disclose any information whatever if by any chance I met anyone.

There was no need to go among the miners, as Whitford's stock of supplies was quite sufficient for our needs. The summer was well into the fall when Whitford said it was time to kill our ox; our horses were giving us increased trouble as the feed got short. Our pemmican and dried meat had lasted well in spite of the big meals the work demanded.

It was up to Butcheesh or me to take the animals out to Colvile and neither of us wanted to go. Whitford took no part in our friendly arguments over who should leave.

At the first snow we still had not come to an agreement. "Look here," Whitford said, "I decided long ago that Annas must take the horses out, and you, Peter, will stay with me. I have just made a scout to see what's going on at the big camp. Half of those chaps will be starving before the winter actually sets in. Some of the shacks are flimsy lean-tos, unfit for the winter. We can't all leave or someone would jump our claims as soon as we left. Peter can hunt and sell the meat for a good profit."

"Good," said Butcheesh, "that what I want all de time but Peter he like to talk so I help him."

I suggested that Butcheesh take some of our store of gold.

"No," replied Whitford, "that's too dangerous a job for one man. When we leave, we go together, our guns clean and ready for use. Already there has been a bad knifing and a man dead. Wait till the work is over and they gather to drink and gamble, to while the time away — then you'll see trouble as bad as any in the States. The vultures already are preparing to take the miners. There's a big new log building for whisky and gambling. White savages, Peter, are the worst kind. The others don't know any better and it's a fight for their lives and living in the States."

"You know best," I replied. "This is a new game to me and I, for one, say you should be our leader. We will do exactly as you think best."

Butcheesh got up and said, "By gar, Peter, that is right. We shake the hands on dat deal now."

Butcheesh left with the horses, a small bundle of food tied behind his saddle, and only a couple of blankets underneath. He tied all the horses up late that evening and left before daylight in the morning. He claimed he would be in Colvile with only two nights' stop. Whitford instructed him to return as soon as he considered it possible for the horses to find feed.

We took a few days from the mining to build a strong log storehouse, with the only entrance from inside our other shack. We also killed the ox and stored the meat.

Whitford never left the mining site that winter when I was away hunting. When the water froze in the creek, all mining was suspended. Whitford shovelled a lot of worked-over gravel back in our prospect holes. I thought the action a stupid waste of work until a few nights later.

I woke him up and whispered that I heard noises up at the sluice box.

"That is exactly what I wanted. I expect there is someone up there to get a sample of our pile of supposed prospect dirt for a test. Give them ten minutes, then fire a shot over their heads. That'll scare them off and I don't think we will be bothered again."

Whitford's precautions in the matter of shovelling dirt back in the prospect holes, and in piles at the side was a wise move. Investigation showed where several samples had been taken during the night. My respect for the man's judgement increased and I made no decisions without his advice during the balance of our partnership.

Before the heavy snows came, I located the best area for game, and was pleased to find that moose and deer seemed plentiful. I saw several large flocks of mountain sheep, but these were not worth the extra stalking and trouble they cost in hunting. I was ready for the winter snows and tramped many miles in every direction to make myself familiar with the terrain.

After I started hunting for the big camp and made contact with a few of the miners further up the diggings, I learned that there was a rough element in the camp. There had been some bad fights and the disappearance of two miners who were among the first men to locate the strike. The miners organized and formed a committee. Four men who were suspected of complicity in the deaths and disappearance were advised to leave on penalty of death if they returned.

My partner was invited to join the committee. Apparently he was well known to members of the miners' organization. He sent word with me declining the honour, but said he would be glad to assist if any serious breach of miners' law threatened.

Prices of food skyrocketed as Custer had predicted, and I was well paid for the game that I was able to obtain in hunting. With so many people in camp, food became a serious matter.

There were bound to be some failures, men who came ill-equipped to stand the rigours of a long winter. The wisest ones pulled out as soon as the first snows came but others stayed on in hope of finding work among the biggest miners who could afford to pay wages to burn the ground and continue winter operations. The gold fever pushed men beyond the limits of good sense and judgement. Some of these latter I shot game for, and had them fetch it back themselves, after warning them against saying anything to their neighbours.

Some men who got gold in quantity appeared to be in a frenzy to rid themselves of it by drinking and gambling. They apparently placed no value on it as a means for easier living later, but seemed to judge the excitement of its attainment sufficient reward for the drudgery of digging it from the mother earth — much different than my partner who stayed in the solitude of the camp. When not occupied in improving the mining facilities for the coming spring, he piled up huge quantities of wood which he said he would use to melt the

120

ground as soon as the water started to run. He hardly seemed interested in the news I brought in to our shack from the big camp.

"Erasmus, come up and look at the improvements I have made in readiness for our spring work. Notice that the gravel riffle is larger. I have picked a large quantity of gum which I'll melt and plug up joints where we lost water last summer. Two weeks of hard work will about clean up the best of our prospect when Annas returns. Then we will sell as it stands. What do you think?"

"That is wonderful news," I answered. "I am already sick of these mountains and as you say, if we can clean up in that time, I may yet be able to catch the Saskatchewan boats going downriver. I was planning on a visit with my people at Fort Garry when you fellows talked me out of it, but this time I am going even if I have to ride horseback alone the whole thousand miles."[5]

Spring came early again that year. As soon as it started to melt in good style, Whitford started to burn the prospect ground with the wood. A week later Annas hit camp, a regular human dynamo.

"By gar, Peter, I work you two feet shorter and maybe fifty or one hundred pounds less wider," he said, making a motion of both hands to indicate my smaller size. In spite of my tramping through the woods all winter, he almost did, for I knew the harder we worked the quicker would be our release. I had lost interest in the gold and was burning to get a straddle of a horse on the way back home to the prairie.

Two weeks to a day, Whitford announced we had taken the best from our prospect. There were good day-wages still left, but he said he and his partner were not interested in that kind of money. He figured we had enough for our needs and that it was better to sell our claims now.

"By gar, Peter! You make me happy. I like de country but de neighbours dey make me mad, dey durty like peegs. Sacré, always dey ask de questions 'you make plenty money? You get plenty de gold?' You go find de buyer, I now make ready de packs."

To this emphatic speech I nodded my agreement, and Whitford without another word went after the men he had in mind as buyers. They returned in two hours to inspect our prospect holes. Our buyers were two big men, one named Carter, both dressed in work clothes; they were clean-shaven and had their hair trimmed. Apparently they knew mining and were greatly taken up with the way we had obtained our water for the sluice box.

"You have an excellent setup here. If you haven't cleaned up all the gold, it is ideal in every way. We will give you one thousand dollars provided you have paydirt here."

"Good," said Whitford. "Go to work. Everything is cleaned up and ready for new dirt. I know the dirt is there so we'll prepare to leave as soon as we get packed and our horses brought in. You take everything as it stands except this one tool. I promised this to a man at Colvile. Come down to dinner at twelve, but at two o'clock you must clean up and be ready to take over."

"That sounds real honest," said one of the men. "We will go one better and clean up at one o'clock before we stop for dinner; that will give you fellows a better chance to leave in good daylight."

"That will be fine," said Whitford, "but remember that I told you that while the prospect would pay good wages, it is no bonanza. Notice that the point of that rock shelf on which we are walking must at one time have been the original bed of the creek that cut its way down to the softer clay where it now runs. The lower portion still has room for another claim. I would advise you to file on that, which may give you far better than good wages."

"I'm a mining man of considerable experience and I believe that you may be right. The fact that you started work on this higher bench and got results is proof of your statement."

During all this time as I stood and listened to the conversation, I was afraid that their digging might prove barren and we would be compelled to delay our departure.

When we went back to the shack, I put my doubts in words. "How can you be so sure they will get paydirt, Whitford?"

"Because for the last week all dirt cleaned up showed a good wage, and is bound to continue the same way for at least another three weeks' work."

Butcheesh had no doubts about his partner's arrangements, and had the horses tied up waiting to get the packs adjusted as soon as we got word from the two men.

Our buyers had started to work at nine o'clock and at twelve they hollered down to us to get dinner ready, they would be coming in fifteen minutes. They were in excellent spirits when they borrowed our scales to weigh their gold, and estimated they had earned five dollars each for three hours' work.

"You fellows have a very good summer's work here. Why sell at this time of year?"

"Well," said Whitford, "to tell you the truth, Peter Erasmus, that fellow there, put up the money to grubstake us, and is burning to get back to the prairies. This is his first venture in mining, and according to him, his very last. My other partner Annas also has an itchy foot and no use for money. Says it only gets him into trouble, so in our partnership the majority rules - hence the sale to you fellows."

"Good," said the big man named Carter, "what is one man's loss is another's gain. You've made a sale. Here's your money in gold. Weigh it and make out a Bill of Sale for your property."

Whitford now called me to the table to make out the papers, while he weighed the gold.

We had a big dinner and Whitford brought out from under a loose-hewed slab in the floor a sealed bottle of good rum. I noticed Annas with a grin as wide as the door. I refused a drink. That created a lot of comment among the men. Apparently a man who didn't take whisky was a creature from some unknown origin. My action in refusing a drink somewhat cooled the ardour of the others. Whitford left the balance of that bottle to the new men for medicine, both of whom expressed the greatest appreciation for his thoughtfulness.

We had everything packed and ready for the road; the men were still around awaiting our departure when Whitford went to one corner of the shack, lifted another slab and took out two small leather bags of gold. I had very little idea of the value or weight of gold but the thought struck me that we had accumulated more than those two sacks. However I was too anxious to be out of the country to let the matter bother me.

Our only road lay through the main part of the mining field. I grew quite provoked, after all our efforts to keep our business secret, at my partners' delay in talking to all and everyone they met along the way. I could see no sense in Whitford's elaborate precautions to keep information to ourselves when they now advertised our departure so publicly. I finally lost patience and hollered back at them to get going unless they wanted to stay in town. I had the two pack animals on a lead rope, one tailed to the animal in front.

"Go ahead," said Whitford, "we will catch up in a few minutes."

They caught up after ten minutes or so and by this time a bend in the trail had left the camp out of sight. Now they seemed to be in a big hurry. Annas came up beside me and said to turn the pack horses loose to be driven.

Whitford said, "Peter, we have to make time from here on. We must make the big rock entrance to Crooked Valley before dark. We'll make our first camp there."

I flushed with provocation but said nothing, for I had learned that every move he made had a good reason behind it.

We reached his objective just at dusk, and as is customary, started to gather sticks for a campfire.

"No campfire tonight. We have everything ready for our supper and we can drink water. Tomorrow morning we will have our coffee. Turn the horses down the creek on the flat. Hobble them but use no bell."

The mystery was getting almost beyond my patience but I still restrained my irritation at all this foolishness that seemed without reason. We ate a cold supper in silence before we took the horses down to water and feed on the creek-bottom grass. It was about a half mile from the big rock entrance to this second valley.

When we got back, the packs had disappeared and our blankets. I noticed the reflection of a fire about a hundred yards back on our trail.

"Annas, what the devil does he mean 'no fire'? Look back there."

He just laughed and motioned me to follow him. "Look," said he. "Dat is a trap for our friends at the camp. Peter, he sure dey come tonight. We watch. You first, me next, and den Whitford take over. We never sleep tonight."

I looked at our little Frenchman beside me on our high perch among the rocks. He was fairly sparkling with anticipation of trouble, and hugging himself to keep from laughing out loud. Down by the fire I could see three figures of men stretched out with their feet towards the flames. In the reflection of the flames, I saw Whitford climbing to his station behind some brush on a ledge that would put the dummies in between us.

It took some time to get the whole picture in my mind, and when I did I got busy gathering rock to form a breastwork in case our expected visitors returned our greetings. Nights get desperately cold in the mountains and Whitford had only placed our horse blankets for our use. I soon begrudged those useless dummies the covering.

Whitford returned to give us last minute instructions after he had secured his own safe hiding place.

"Peter, you have the first watch. An owl hoot will be my signal that I have taken over from Butcheesh, but I doubt if any of us will get much sleep as I had to rob your bed rolls to make my dummies look like the real thing. If anything bothers those men beside the campfire, shoot over their heads, but if they return the fire shoot to hit low if you can. The main idea is to give them the surprise of their rotten lives."

"What makes you so sure that we will be attacked tonight?" I asked.

"Those two sports who bought our mine property were too agreeable. They could not wash out ten dollars worth of gold in the short time they were at it. Our own take for the three of us working twice as hard as I noticed they did was from eight to ten dollars worth of stuff. They handed over their thousand dollars too easy unless they meant to take it back the easy way. We would have been lucky to get half as much for the three claims."

"That's good reasoning and I think your last statement is the best guarantee of an early visit as any. Doggone them anyway. I thought they were real gentlemen. Perhaps I was wise after all in refusing to drink," I said.

"By gar, they return one shot and dey are dead men," said Annas — sentiments I heartily agreed with but kept to myself.

Although it was cold, I had trouble keeping awake. I still had a half-hour before it was time to wake Annas, who was sleeping as soundly as a babe. Then I heard a stone rattle on our back trail, but no other sound for a long time. I touched my companion who was awake in a second. He sat up listening, then reached for his gun. "By gar, they come," he whispered.

We watched a shadowy form approach closer to the dummies, then another from the other side. I saw the flash of the second man's gun. Then the bent figure of the first man raised his arm and drove it down into the nearest dummy. He gave a surprised yell to his partner. Then I saw Whitford's gun go into action. The two men ran twisting and zigzagging back down the bench to the trail. Butcheesh wasn't a second behind Whitford's shot. I finally had presence of mind enough to join my friends, shooting low as Whitford had instructed.

Butcheesh got down, saying he was going to make sure they had really pulled out. I watched on the trail but I could not see where he went. I was now not a bit sleepy. An hour after, my companion returned and I still hadn't spotted any sight of him till he spoke at the foot of our rock perch to warn me of his presence.

He came up chuckling to himself, saying he had beat them to their horses by cutting across along the creek bottom as the trail made a wide turn on better ground higher up. He had hid in the bush while they came to the horses. One man had been hit in the leg and was cursing and swearing at his companion for being such a damn fool as to waste their money on such a fool venture.

"Quit your whining," said the other, "we are lucky to be alive and we still have the claims."

"By gar! I could have shot them both stone dead, but Whitford he don like to keel a man. Sacre! Dos men dey are de

125

white savage. You kill or be killed. Dey never come back dos two maybe."

It was now well on towards morning. We heard Whitford's signal of an owl hoot. It was so natural that I wasn't sure it was not the real owl himself, but my friend had no doubts and told me to go to sleep and Whitford would finish out the watch. Again he fooled me for I presumed that the one set of crooks was enough for one night.

I lay awake for some time and the first thing I knew it was daylight and Whitford had come to wake us up. My bloodthirsty companion was still sleeping the sound sleep of the innocent; the minute he woke up he started to laugh as if he had heard the best joke of the season.

"Come on you chaps and see how they sprung our trap."

We both jumped up and followed him to the decoy campfire which he had left undisturbed for our inspection.

"This, Peter, is your souvenir," he said, as he drew a long scalping knife from the log that served as my likeness. It had been driven through the blankets and into the log. My assailant had been in too much of a hurry to try to draw it out.

"Butcheesh, you can dig a bullet out of that chunk of rotten wood that was supposed to be your head. You can boast about how a man shot through your cap into your head and never touched your skull."

He gathered the blankets of another log saying, "It looks like I got off scot free."

The dummies were dressed in our spare clothes, complete with caps, boots, and all. I shivered with thoughts of what might have been if my companions were not such thoroughly capable fellows. I kept the knife for a long time afterwards — it was a good lesson of acute and accurate observation that I never forgot and found very useful in later years.

We went for the horses as Whitford got the packs ready. When I returned he called me to help him move some rocks where he had lain on watch during the night. I wondered what next to expect but complied without complaint. "There, Peter, safe from early last winter, is our summer's work. Those two sacks I took from the floor contained just a good grade of ordinary sand. Our clean-up this spring is in the bottom of your duffle sack."

I had to laugh, for my duffle sack hung on my bunk in plain sight and contained — as I thought — only my dirty clothes and some cartridges for the new rifle that Cust had sent with Butcheesh when he returned with the horses.

"By gar," Annas added, "What you don't know, you can no tell. That miner business is one funny ting."

I guess you thought those two small sacks I took from the floor were all for a summer and winter's work. I placed the gold here for safe-keeping the night before that first big snow last fall in case we got into trouble when all that robbing was going on in the big camp. Those two men that bought our claims are owners of the gambling joint and are suspected of being behind or of leading the toughs in camp."

"So that is why you chose them for suckers in your sale. The head of the miners' committee must be a friend of yours to put you wise to all this," I remarked.

"Yes, he is an old friend from camps in Montana. He is the man that put us wise to our danger when we skipped out from the States."

"Well, well, Whitford. That explains a lot. I was beginning to think you had supernatural powers and that Frenchie here had the devil's hindleg. I am glad you are just human beings like myself, but don't think I do not appreciate what you saved me from last night. The quicker I get back to uncivilized savages the better I will feel about this business."

"Cheer up. We will be a long way from here by night or rather by midnight tonight, and I think our friends of last night have had a scare they will not forget for a long time. We take turns sleeping till we reach Colvile."

"You know Whitford, I agree with you. White savages are the worst kind. The Indian savage will take your scalp or your horse if you are his enemy but he will not steal among his own tribe. Few among the Indians will share a meal and then try to kill you first chance they get."

We had no further trouble on our way to Colvile. Annas trailed behind, hardly ever in sight except at meals and at night. Whitford never let us get careless at any time on the whole route. "That gang back at the camp may be better organized than we think, although our sudden decision to sell and move out may have caught them flat-footed, and the trail we are following is not a regularly travelled road. Annas, among his other many qualities, is a wizard at finding new trails in the mountains. His folks have been in the country for years, originally from Louisiana. In spite of the bad English he uses, he had a good French education. I suspect his impetuous ways have got him into trouble and he has formed the habit of bad English as a good disguise."

"Yes," I replied, "I have noticed that often he uses proper English mixed in with his other jargon. I have never known a man who enjoys trouble as much as he does. He expressed regret last night that you were against any unnecessary killing. Did he tell you he had beaten the men to their horses and hid him in the bush listening to their conversation?"

"No, but that is typical of him. He wanted to satisfy himself that the men were our buyers, that's why he was still laughing this morning. His sense of humour is quite beyond me sometimes. That is why I sent him to Colvile last winter to keep him out of trouble, for idleness is very trying to his restless soul."

I was more than satisfied to learn that my share, even after I deducted costs of the outfitting, came to more than my savings for the last five years and what they were for the next three years in addition. "Gentlemen, I think that I'm receiving more than my contribution justifies. All I subscribed to the venture was money, and but for you chaps I might have been dead now. The money I earned in hunting goes into the pot for you fellows."

"No," said Whitford. "If we had failed we would have been under no obligation to pay you a cent — which is customary in mining agreements of this kind. Your share will be exactly what the terms of our agreement call for. The one hundred and fifty dollars we got for the ox meat we sold goes directly to you. A one-third share of your profit in hunting we will accept but that is all."

Annas nodded his agreement as Custer weighed out the gold and gave us our shares. We all shook hands. I was too overwhelmed with the fairness and honesty of my partners to be able to say anything.

"By gar, Peter, you are one fine partner. Maybe you want to join us in de summer prospect, yes? We share everything in three parts."

"What about it, Peter? I second my partner's offer."

"Your offer is a fine compliment but I have had enough of the mountains. I am making tracks for the prairies first thing in the morning. I am going home to visit my old mother while I have the time and money to do so. Gold mining may be a fine occupation, as you men have proved to me this last year, but it is not as much fun as chasing buffalo. My back still aches and my muscles feel stiff as boards. Besides, I have no fancy for your white savages' long knives or short guns."

They all had a good laugh, Butcheesh loudest of all.

"No, by gar, Peter, you are mistaken. Dat Blackfoot, his eyes better dan de hawk. His knife zip, and your hair, she is gone. I keep my back to de rock, my hair she stay where she grow."

My partners offered to escort me back to Fort Edmonton, but Custer was going there himself[5] and his men would be along to care for the horses as he was going to Fort Garry on business. I refused their offer.

"No-one will recognize a gold digger in the buckskin

128

clothes that I have in Custer's storage." Pulling my coat off, I handed it to Butcheesh, adding "Now that's the last sign of my mining business."

Butcheesh, not to be outdone in a joke, put it on and strutted up and down the floor in a good imitation of my walk. Three sizes too big, it created such a big laugh that Mrs. Custer busy in the kitchen, came out to investigate and joined in the fun. Thus our partnership ended in friendly feelings of good fellowship.

CHAPTER EIGHT

To Smoking Lake

I WAS NOW FILLED with a burning haste to be on my way back to Edmonton and my associates in that area. I hardly expected to catch the boats when we left the Pandara[1] mining site. Downriver travel would be delayed by the lateness of the Saskatchewan breakup of the ice; a light snowfall in the mountains usually indicated slow movement of the ice flow.

There were a number of Pigeon Lake Indians at Fort Edmonton when I arrived there. They told me that Mr. Woolsey had gone to Whitefish Lake to confer with Mr. Steinhauer about starting another mission on the north side of the Saskatchewan River. I learned later that the authorities in the East had ordered him to move from Pigeon Lake as they considered the territory too dangerous under present conditions. There had been considerable war activity among the Blackfoot, Peigans, and Bloods against the Crees' increased arrogance, and some provocation against the peaceful Pigeon Lake Crees. No doubt Woolsey's report to the home missions had impressed on them the danger of allowing their missionary to continue his work there.

Mr. Woolsey was backward in leaving his mission and the people at Pigeon Lake, but Sinclair,[2] who carried on the work after Rundle had left, was forced to leave. Two of his men had been killed by Blackfoot, but Sinclair had been warned by a friendly Cree in time to escape with his family. He moved to Lac La Biche and started a mission there.

After listening to the young men gathered around me to renew our acquaintance, I suggested that it might be better for them to move their hunting grounds with their missionary.

"No," they said together. "We have occupied our territory for fifty years. Our chief has always adopted a peaceful attitude to all the tribes. We have never stolen their horses or committed a warlike action in our memory, but if we are forced to fight we are ready and quite able to hold our own against any who attack us, as you well know, for you have lived among us and you, Peter, have been with us when we scouted a Blackfoot camp. Did we do any wrong to others when you were with us?"

"No," I replied. "You have not and I know of an occasion when you found a wounded Peigan rider with a broken leg and almost starved. You took him into your camp, nursed him, and escorted him back to his own people. Another time you saved a Blackfoot who would have died only for your help."

The contemptuous attitude the other tribes held for the Pigeon Lake Indians on account of their declared policy for peace was growing irksome to these trained young warriors, and I feared they would break out in open defiance later, especially since they had lost the influence of their minister. The old chief and his council were bound by the ethics of their Christian faith, but failed to influence a like faith in their young men.

The pride of these young men, the persistent training and watchfulness in guarding their camp, was at variance with the declared policy of peace at any price held by the elders. I was saddened by the thought that there were dark times ahead for these friends and companions, my good teachers of wood craft with whom I had lived as one of themselves. I sympathized with their independent spirit and their determination to protect their own hunting grounds, even though they knew they were facing a stronger foe.

My experience during my travels with Rev. Mr. Woolsey gave me a knowledge of their ability in hunting and tracking and scouting. Their athletic development made it certain that they would not for long endure the contemptuous and provoking acts of other young men of the Blackfoot and Blood tribes. A single overt act might provoke reprisals that would have serious consequence to the whole Pigeon Lake tribe.

I was never again to see many of these young men, as three years later, under a war chief from Fort Pitt, they were drawn into battle with the Blackfoot. Although they won the battle, many of the Pigeon Lake men were killed, and the tribe so decimated that living at Pigeon Lake so near to Blackfoot territory made that area unsafe for many years.

The first man I met after reaching the fort was my friend Borwick. We exchanged greetings but I detected a seriousness in his manner that was in contrast to his usual cheerful humorous teasing. It was quite late in the evening when we arrived after disposing of our horses. I was glad of Bill's invitation to share his room. We had made a long hard ride to make the fort that night.

"You have made a fast trip, Peter. Though I made considerable effort to dispute the rumour that you were going to England with the captain, I actually didn't expect you to return. I'm afraid the story has had disastrous results for your immediate plans."

"What on earth are you talking about?" I exclaimed. "Out with it! I never knew you to be serious about anything before. Why all the secrecy of closed doors and even your low voice, as if I was about to be charged with murder?"

"Well, maybe it's not as serious as I thought. But after a man has spent all and every spare minute of time for three years chasing to Lac Ste. Anne and the girl finally gets tired of waiting and gets married to another man, who wouldn't think it was serious?"

To say the information was a shock was putting it mildly. However, I managed to convince Bill that it was not too important.

"Yes, Bill, I've got to admit I was sorely tempted to accept their offer. In fact if I had the news you now tell me, I probably would have gone with the captain. I cannot say whether I am more disappointed or relieved. Forget it, Bill, as I intend to work more interesting prospects."

"Peter, you sure got me puzzled. I could have taken an oath that you loved that girl but she fooled me just as bad. She wept on my shoulder and refused to be consoled and promised me she would wait to give you time to get back, but a week after that she was married. If that's what they call love, the good Lord deliver me from the affliction."

"Cheer up, my friend! Life does play funny tricks sometimes but take it from me, your turn will come. Then I can return your sympathy."

Bill, like the rest of the fort inmates, escorted his friends to the boats. They were now ready, and at a signal from the leader, swung out into the stream, one behind the other in a long single file, the men waving their hats and paddles to those on shore. The swift spring freshet of water in the Saskatchewan soon carried us around the first bend of the river. Someone started a French boat song and the others joined in — a rollicking melody that expressed my own feeling of the joy and freedom of the prairies. I was thrilled to be a part of this happy good fellowship of the crews.

I heard the song break down in a chorus of yells from the lead boats and soon I saw what occasioned the interruption. Fifteen or more riders appeared on the flats that approached to the first cut banks of the river. I noticed they were mostly girls and young women. They made a picturesque sight as they reared their horses, circled and manoeuvered their horses in a wild show of horsemanship. I was delighted with the scene for I knew that most of the young Metis women could handle horses and use a gun with facility — it was not mere showmanship. The men all cheered, lifted their paddles high in the air in a salute, then dipped them deep in the water to drive the boats ahead with speed that soon carried us out of sight around the next sharp bend.

These men knew the river, every rapid, bend, and channel. Had they not traversed its banks in the tedious and back-breaking job of towing cumbersome loads upstream? As we shot over the rapids I had an uncomfortable feeling under my belt as the water whirled and gurgled, the boats within a few feet of a huge protruding rock. My enjoyment of the superb handling of the boats soon settled any worry from my mind: laughter and song down the river, sweat and strain and swearing up river, all a part of their work.

They all pulled into shore for their noon hour meals but supper was delayed until well past dusk when they camped for the night; breakfast at daylight and again on our way. Many places along the shoreline were piled high with huge ice cakes where the ice had jammed and the water backed up, lifting tremendous chunks of heavy ice far back into the timber of the shores, shearing large trees off at their roots, scoring hundreds of others, twisted and bent in the relentless force of the annual spring break-up of solid river ice.

During the first few days of my stay with the crew, I came in for a lot of teasing, as most of the men were from Lac Ste. Anne and St. Albert, and I knew them all by their first names. My happy-go-lucky friends soon forgot the matter when I did not react to their thinly veiled references to the unhappy outcome of my steady pursuit of one of their most popular young women. I volunteered no information but learned that my lucky opponent was not too well liked. The marriage had been as big a surprise to them as it had been to me. Their opinions, expressed in some colourful French expletives, helped salve my wounded feeling, although I knew the result was entirely my own fault. Their resentment helped bolster my pride.

At Fort Pitt and again at Carlton, the brigade was joined by other boats. All were heavily loaded with furs, buffalo robes, tanned moose hides, and deer skins. The fur catch that winter was described by the factors as excellent, the best in several years.

I enjoyed the short stopover at Fort Pitt and got an invitation to a dinner of beaver tails, buffalo tongue, or a choice of fresh lake trout and smoked sturgeon. The menu reserved for high-ranking officials of the Company aroused my curiosity as to my changed status in Company rating. The contrast was so striking it stirred my egoistic impulses. Apparently as a man of substance, my native antecedents were entirely removed.[3] My share of the gold venture had been deposited with Company officials at Edmonton. I was sorely tempted to ask if my sudden prestige had been Company notification of my credit standing, but managed to curb the thought; besides, the experience was extremely gratifying.

At Carlton there were fifty teepees pitched just east of the fort. A large band of horses were being driven down to water when we came in sight of the place. The usual pack of innumerable dogs that were always a part of a Cree encampment barked notification to all that the boats were arriving, and aroused the inmates at the fort and in the teepees to form a host of welcoming people that lined the banks in front of us for a considerable distance both ways.

The sudden appearance of so many people made me thankful that they were peaceful Indians. The bloodless conquest of Indian good graces by the Company policy of fair treatment and straight-forward dealings was a tremendous contrast to conditions just across our invisible border. Here then was concrete example and evidence that the general policy of the Hudson's Bay Company had merit above my own private prejudice against certain personal practices of some of the officers.

Having had no experience of American policy towards the Indians of the States, I had listened with amazement tinged with unbelief to the stories told by Whitford and Butcheesh of things done in the southern border country. I happened to mention my contempt for the small gun and its uselessness for this country. Whitford didn't say anything but gave me a demonstration of speed and accuracy that left me gasping and completely convinced.

"Americans have an unwritten code of conduct that makes this size of a gun a necessary part of their wearing apparel. In my opinion this is nothing more or less than licensed murder. The fastest gun becomes judge and jury and final right. Your opponent must be wearing a gun and be shamed or excited into its use, or at least a try. The fast gunman shoots a man down and walks away, his reputation increased to the extent of another murder. The sheriff or marshal of a town makes the most perfunctory examination of the shooting — no more than in establishing that the victim was in possession of a weapon. That ends the matter as far as the law is concerned.

"Few of them consider the Indian as a human being with any rights of living in the country at all. The Indians across the line are doomed to extermination unless the government at a place called Washington on the eastern border of that country can establish an authority greater than the fast gun or the Sharps rifle that can pick an Indian off his horse at a distance of a half mile.

"When I left the country there was much talk of a war to free the coloured people on the southern plantations from slavery. It's a funny situation, Peter, the very men who are willing to give up their lives to give a Negro freedom in the States, think nothing of killing an Indian for target practice. Hunting and killing Indians is practised with all the relentless power of superior arms and manpower that can be assembled, yet they fight at the drop of the hat; the minute a southerner meets a chap from the north they get arguing over the merits of either side."

My mother was almost speechless with happiness when I finally arrived at the old home. I knocked on the door and waited to see if she would recognize me. She stood for a moment as if she couldn't believe her eyes, then with a glad cry said, "It's Peter, my boy Peter!"

I heard a scramble in the house and my two married sisters rushed to the door to greet me. It was a glad homecoming and I received such a deluge of questions from them all at the same time that I couldn't answer any. "Hold on there. Wait a while. Let me get my breath! I am going to be here for a long time and will answer all and every question in turn but I cannot answer all at the same time."

My sisters laughed and grabbed both my arms and pulled me into the house while my mother sat down and had a good cry as I suppose is the way with all mothers when their cup of happiness overflows. Then it was my turn to ask questions as I inquired about all the relations and my friends. The youngest children were still attending school and my married sisters lived in the settlement as did my oldest brother, Henry. The sisters took their leave and planned for a big get together the following evening. I was glad to know our mother was not left alone but was well taken care of by her sons-in-law who held the old lady in high esteem.

I sat back in my chair and watched with enjoyment as mother busied herself preparing a meal. My pack contained some special edibles that I thought might take her fancy, and I was well repaid in the delight that lit up her face as I dug in my heavy pack and placed them on the table. Also among the presents was a fine Hudson's Bay shawl that I took out and placed over her shoulders and which claimed her attention more than anything else. The dress goods she declared were too good for her use but would make some fine dresses for the younger sister.

"No, that won't do. I bought these for you and the little sister has her own at the bottom of this bag."

Just then the door burst open and the young lady herself appeared. She was in the middle of the floor before she noticed a stranger in the house. She slid to an abrupt stop that almost gave her a tumble, somewhat flustered at her impetuous entrance, embarrassed that a stranger should catch her in such unlady-like manner.

"You must kiss your brother Peter, who has come to get you to wash his dishes," her mother told her.

The young lady never took her eyes off me as she came forward, very hesitant, trying hard to overcome her embarrassment. I let her off with a hand shake but when she turned away with a delighted giggle, I strode after her and demanded my rightful kiss, making certain that my beard brushed her cheeks in doing so.

"Ouch!" she yelled. "Those bristles, Ma, are just awful."[4] She rubbed her cheeks in a grimace of mock pain but with a glimmer of mischief in her eyes that belied the hurt. Her expression quickly changed when mother showed her the presents and said I might have something in the bag for her. I made a pretence of having difficulty of finding her parcel and when I finally handed it to her, she hugged it to her bosom, making no attempt to see what was in it.

"Open it up. You'll never know what it contains unless you open it up."

At last her curiosity got the best of her as she slowly untied the cotton that held the presents together. A ready-made dress, pieces of print for other dresses, several different colours of ribbon, a string of neck beads, and combs and a brooch to match the dress. After gazing at her treasures, speechless, she carefully gathered them together and placed them on the table. She rushed back and threw both arms around my neck, and kissed me whiskers and all. "Oh, brother, that is the nicest present I ever received in my whole life. You must be awful rich to buy such terribly expensive gifts."

I had made inquiries through the factor's wife at Fort Garry, who had a daughter just the age of little sister. The dress was one she had just finished for her own girl for a birthday gift. She let me have it when I told her what I wanted it for, going into the store to help me pick gifts her own daughter would like. Mary Anne and I became great friends after she tried the dress on and found it an exact fit.

"You must be the wisest man in the world, for how else could you know my exact size." I didn't tell her how I had arrived at the right size of the things she would most prize.

My stay would only be for a few weeks but Mary Anne's incessant teasing and questions were unending. Her interest in all my travels never abated but usually ended up in an enquiry as to why I never found a wife, like everybody else in the settlement.

"Brother, in all your travels you still haven't found a wife, surely they cannot be too ugly for you. If I didn't have to go to school, I would go and keep house for you. I would mend your socks and cook meals but I wouldn't wash dishes. Huh! I hate washing dishes."

I had to laugh at her curiosity. She asked me questions and seldom waited for an answer. It was impossible to make her understand that I had no home or that a house of my own was unnecessary. I had presents for all the family, and gave them out the next evening. The thought that I could afford to give was the nicest thing of my whole experience, and I only then appreciated the value of our lucky mining venture.

The family gathered the next night after my arrival and it was a wonderful evening. Mary Anne played hostess to the guests with all her new finery proudly displayed. She was a picture of sober propriety. Being twice her age, I was amused at the serious attentive service all our guests received at her hands. She soundly cuffed the ears of one of the younger nephews who attempted to belittle her new position. For the first time in my life I felt a kinship with my homeloving relatives and an appreciation of home life that I had never experienced before.

My interview with the bishop was on an entirely different plane. His attitude to the church of my former employer had softened. His searching questions in regard to the Christian Indians of the West revealed a much broader opinion than he had expressed at the time of my last visit with him.

I arranged with the bishop for a sum of money to be paid to my mother each month, a larger sum if there were any special need, thinking this was best, for I was afraid that a lump sum might induce others to take advantage of our mother's generosity. The transfer of a sizeable sum would be arranged by the factor at Edmonton to the chief factor at Fort Garry, from which the bishop could present my order for the trust fund.

Renewing my acquaintance with my old friend Murdoch Spence, I found him a little less energetic but still healthy and rugged for a man of his age. The red-headed wife had been to the house the evening before and made me promise that their house would be next on my list of visits. Mrs. Spence excused herself and told me that she promised help at some settlement community work and would be gone for the afternoon but would return in time to prepare supper.

I gave him a full report of my travels, especially the gold-hunting venture. The latter experience opened up memories of his own adventures when he was employed by the North West Company. His face flushed with excitement as he recalled and lived over the most memorable of those encounters with their opposition, the Hudson's Bay Company, many of which were amusing subterfuges to best their opponents for the Indian trade. It was not all one-sided, and his laughs at instances of his company being outfoxed in the game were quite as hearty as when he had been on the winning side.

It was the most interesting and exciting entertainment of my stay, the more so since I had been over some of the places he mentioned and heard or knew of some of the men referred to in his stories.

The old man grew quite serious as he brought me up to date on all the angles of the growing political pains of a young country preparing for the advent of civilized government.

"Peter, the people of these parts have been through some bad times. Twice they have been driven from their homes by the policy of greedy fur companies who considered that settlers would be bad for their fur trade and made every effort to discourage and destroy their beginning. The sad part of that business is that some of the employees in the North West Company were in sympathy with the settlers, and had friends and even relations among those driven out. I was among those in the last raid that completely wiped out years of work by those struggling settlers. I saw the misery and hopelessness of men losing their homes through the avarice and stupidity of men in control that were far removed from these parts.

"I settled here after my retirement from the service and hoped to live out my span of years without the turmoil and sorrow of such bad times. Now I fear that trouble will again fall to the lot of this country by the same ill-considered action of people intent on their own selfish interests."

"Surely, Mr. Spence, you would not try to block progress and the further expansion of the settlement of lands that are as yet untouched by human habitation other than the wandering bands of Indians? My two years of experience with an expedition sent out by the British Government surveying and mapping the country, indicates some action along these lines before too long."

"No, Peter, that is not what I meant. Lord Selkirk was ahead of his time in bringing settlers into a raw wilderness, unprepared and ignorant of conditions that prevailed in the country at that time. The rivalry of the fur companies with no clear authority as to who actually owned the best right to these territories; the assumption by the Hudson's Bay Company that they were the real authority despite their laxity in expanding forts to assert that authority in areas claimed under their charter; and then their sudden change in their policy to drive everyone else out when they found that others were employing and benefitting from more aggressive methods — all these changes have had their bad effect.

"However, the people came, lived through all the sacrifices, discomfort, semi-starvation, and trouble, and again and again came back. The first settlers grew up in knowledge of hardship and self reliance. Now the descendants of these people are a race of independent hard-willed men. They are not likely to submit with the same meekness that was forced on their forefathers. There is a great deal of talk against the Hudson's Bay monopoly of all authority and trade. Others take the reverse position. There are factors and factions taking shape in this very settlement that are bound to cause friction."

"I was born in this settlement," I responded, "and though I have been away a great deal of my time since I left here as a boy, all my experiences are memorable for the good times and happy associations of the people of this settlement. I am afraid you are taking a dim view of portending trouble for the settlements. What do you mean?"

"There are men in the Red River settlement and its precincts who are still bound to old loyalties. Others who worked with the North West Company, like myself, who, because of the company policy had to carry out instructions, even though now the companies are one, are still looked upon with suspicion. The French half-breeds, who are the most numerous, are led by a young firebrand who had become somewhat of a leader among that class. . Many of the Protestant people associate his activities with the Catholic Church. This in itself is ground for division and strife. My opinion is that unless the government in Canada uses men of judgement and discretion when they take over this land from the Hudson's Bay Company, and shapes policies to fit the various interests, we are bound to have trouble."

"Surely, Mr. Spence," I replied, "there are prominent men in this area that can be depended on to make representations and to advise the government of these conditions, so they will adopt policies that will be to the best interests of our people."

"That, Peter, is easier said than done. All leaders in the various factions will no doubt make their claims separately, and thus confuse the proper solution that much more. There are people who refuse to believe that the easy living of the prairie buffalo-hunting days is about over."

"Anyway," I cut in, "the transfer of the territories to other authority may be a long way in the future. Let us not worry about it at the present time."

"No, you are wrong, Peter. The pressure of people hungry for land is growing. I think that those people back east are becoming aware of the growth and sweep to the west of the American settlers to the south of us, and will make haste to establish their own authority by settlement as quickly as possible. To do otherwise would leave our area open to American penetration and eventual ownership. Our fertile prairies will not lie dormant very long — possibly five years but certainly not more than ten years from now."

I changed the subject as I saw it was useless to argue against a man who I believed made politics a hobby and had many sources of information that were impossible for me. His library of books occupied two walls of the room. A hasty glance over the titles showed names on subjects that I did not even know the meaning of, never having any time to read. I was nevertheless deeply impressed and at the same time curious to know what was the background of the man. He must have had a private income. The freight on them alone would have cost a small fortune. Actively living the life of the West yet he retreated into a world of his own as contained in the largest assembly of books I ever saw. In fact his shelves contained more reading than could be brought together in the whole of my western travels and I dare say in the whole of the settlement itself. Even the collegiate library would fill a small space in the man's study.

My visit had extended to almost a month when I received a letter from Rev. Mr. Woolsey offering me employment as an interpreter at a new mission he was starting at a place called Smoking Lake. I was beginning to get restless at my prolonged idleness, and as the cart brigade would be returning as soon as their stock were rested, I decided to return with them when they were ready to leave.

I bought a saddle horse and rigging from a man in the settlement and made arrangements with a man from Ste. Anne to carry my luggage which included a new gun of the latest manufacture. I tried my new horse out in making the rounds of the settlement to visit my friends and relations to inform them of my departure.

Our family was all gathered at the old home place the morning of my departure. The younger brother and sister had been excused from classes to see me get started. The boy was a big strapping lad who would probably outgrow my size and height. Mr. Spence was quite enthusiastic over the way he had taken over the management of the stock on the farm. He proudly gathered them together for my inspection and I found that they had increased in number and quality. My mother had told me of the old man's interest and help to the youth during all the years of my absence.

The young man and Mary Anne were great chums as I noticed when she broke down and started to cry; it was to my younger brother she reached for support. She begged me not to go again. This scene almost broke my own composure.

"Never mind, little sister. Don't cry. I'll be back as soon as I get a chance but you must be sure and send for me when you get married."

Like the sun shining through a shower, her tears were banished and she flung at me, "You find a wife for yourself first before you try to marry me off to some traveller with scratchy old whiskers."

Her remark made everybody laugh and thus a serious tone was changed in a twinkling to a happy, laughing goodbye as I turned my horse and rode away.

I arrived back in Edmonton almost four months after my start in the spring. Woolsey was waiting at the fort quite impatient to be on his way. However, he allowed me two days to rest and conclude my business at the post.

"I have assembled all the things I think we will need but I'd like you to check them over to see that I've not missed anything we may need later."

I found everything in order but added some things of my own choosing that would contribute to our comfort and pleasure, among which was a stock of tobacco and some additional articles that could be used in trading for food with the Indians. These latter things were of course kept from the knowledge of my employer. Because of his strict adherence to Company rules against trading, he might offer serious objections. The gentleman was too inclined to accept his daily prayer for food in much the same way as the Israelites did with the manna from heaven, whereas I knew from bitter experience that material provision for your future needs was an important law of survival regardless of the missionary concept of these things.

Turning the Fort Garry horse out with the Hudson's Bay herd, I took the other horses. The captain's bay was in fine fettle and the roan mare was fat and sleek with their long rest. The sorrel would be one horse too many to manage so I sold him to Borwick who had overcome his dislike for riding and now was quite a horseman.

Bill had apparently caught the bug from me and was now seriously engaged in a pursuit for double harness, a situation which he had persistently warned me against. He was married two years later and true to his former ideas took up land near the fort, although it was not quite within the shadow of the brass guns; years afterward he profited by the growth of the town over his choice of land.

The roman-nosed roan horse that had given me so much trouble when I first joined Woolsey at Fort Pitt had been stolen the previous winter. I hoped the Blackfoot that raided the Cree horses where Woolsey was visiting when he lost him would be cursed with his ownership as much as I had been. The Blackfoot had left his mare as not worth taking, but actually she proved the most valuable of the two horses.

It was a beautiful Indian summer day when I went to fetch the horses for an early start. Woolsey's pack horse and my own would be too loaded, so I suggested that we pack his mare as well and he could ride my roan mare. This pleased him a great deal as he stroked her nose and petted and made a fuss over the animal.

"She's a beauty, Peter, and such a sweet disposition. This mare is as easy to ride as a rocking chair."

"Yes," I said. "My mother has one of those things. I never rode in it since I almost broke my neck as a youngster when it tipped backwards with me playing horse with my brother Henry. I don't like your reference one bit."

Woolsey had chosen the site for his mission the previous summer. We were to locate the place on the northwest side of the lake. We followed the north side of the Saskatchewan River until we reached a place that was later to be called the Lobstick settlement. I had never been in that area before, but we got our directions from some Indians who were camped in what is called Sucker Creek. It seemed to be all heavily wooded country with an occasional prairie hardly big enough to deserve the name.

We passed through some fine stands of spruce trees almost three feet in diameter interspersed with heavy poplar and elms. There were a lot of sloughs where ducks of many species swam in utter indifference to our approach. Later in the evening we saw partridges high up on willow clumps picking diligently for last-minute suppers before the approach of darkness. I could have knocked their heads off with a good dogwhip, for they appeared to be without fear.

The last day of travel before we reached the building site we started a herd of deer, seven or more in the bunch. They ran a short way then turned and watched us pass as if they had never seen a human being before. This was in my opinion a hunter's paradise. The country was slightly rolling with a few really rough parts.

We built a log shack twelve by sixteen with a fireplace at the back end of the house. A good stand of straight young pine was close at hand. We skidded the logs in with an improvised harness of shaganapee lines and made a breast strap of birch bark covered over with a part of a blanket.

None of our horses had worked in a cart. Woolsey's mare being the quietest, we tried her first but her cougar-like contortions in harness, bucking and rearing and clawing the air with her front feet tested even the missionary's patience. He got so exasperated that he grappled a pole and whacked her over the rump so hard the stick broke in his grasp.

"Dash it all, Peter. I think the devil incarnate had possessed this beast." But whatever it was that inspired her performance, no coaxing or abuse could make her tighten a tug. We had to abandon our efforts and get another horse.

My pack horse proved more amenable to reason, though he too offered some objections. We finally were able to get him to work. I was amused at Mr. Woolsey who was more provoked at losing his temper than at his mare refusing to work, and would not let me turn her loose but tied her to a tree all the time we were working the other horse.

"Perhaps she will learn by example," he said. "She is not going to enjoy the grass while this other fellow does her work."

We moved into our new house on the twenty-sixth of September, 1861.[6] I remember the date, as Woolsey inscribed it on a log with his pen knife. "Someday, Peter, historians of church history will be arguing over the date of our mission work in this area. Here will be irrefutable evidence to remind

143

ourselves and others long after we have moved to other fields of endeavour, that we took possession of this humble abode on that date. Too bad we have no way to cut your name on the stones used on that excellent chimney. That way we could preserve our record for a hundred years after we are gone."

I advised Mr. Woolsey that it would be necessary to move our stock back to Edmonton for the winter, as slough grass in the bush country was poor feed to keep a horse in condition if the snow was deep and the weather severe. It would be better to have a good dog team.

"Yes, I agree with you and I have arranged with an Indian to have a supply of fish on hand when we need them. Little Whitefish Lake is quite near here and is a good whitefish lake as well as good for other species of rough fish. My own animals will have to take their chances here as I intend to buy two cart horses and carts when I go to Fort Garry for supplies next summer. Once the mare gets used to the range, her wonderful leader instincts will come in useful in holding the others from straying."

"I suppose that mare is contrary enough to live against all odds," I said, "but I must take my horses away as I have already arranged for their care this winter. I'll try to trade for a dog team for our use this winter after the first heavy snow comes."

"Certainly a good dog team would widen the scope of our work, as the Indians of this area are more or less camped in permanent places and will do no travelling except on their trap lines," he said. "I don't think the authorities back east would allow such a large expenditure of funds without first giving their consent. However, if you think you can manage, I can assure you that they will pay rent for their use. My own horses will have to make out the best they can."

"Well," I replied, "they will probably make wolf bait before spring, but if a Blackfoot wouldn't touch that mare I doubt if a self-respecting wolf would bother with her anyway."

"Perhaps you're right. For it is plain to see that the animal is too proud to be a common cart horse but I know she is a born leader. Everywhere I have been the contrary beggar gathers around her horses like a hen with a brood of chicks. I was provoked enough to kill her when she refused to help skid logs but I'm rather proud of her independence. Her gift of leadership will be valuable in this heavy bush country. I believe she would tackle a wolf as I have seen her chase some big Indian train dogs and send them howling back to camp."

"Very well then, Mr. Woolsey, as soon as the first snowfall comes, I will take my horses back to Edmonton and try to pick up a dog team."

An Athabasca Cree was at the fort with a fine team of matched husky dogs when I arrived. He had brought a traveller to Edmonton and was enjoying his new wealth with abandon, perhaps not realizing that he was a long distance from his home base until his earnings had been spent on Company rum and fancy nick-nacks that were useless when he got hungry on the road.

He was backward in parting with his team. He tried to borrow enough grub for his trip back but Company policy did not allow the extension of credit to Indians not within their own particular regular-customer area. Bill told me about the man's predicament so I offered him a good price for his outfit — my Fort Garry horse with saddle rigging complete, food for the trip, and also goods, traps, or anything he wanted that would be payable by the Hudson's Bay factor in his own area.

After seeing the horse and outfit he finally consented to the trade, but Mr. Sinclair, the factor, had some difficulty in convincing him that the medicine bag that wrapped a sealed letter in a little buckskin sack would, on presentation to the factor in his home area, carry out the promises we made to him here. I felt satisfied that I had given him a fair price for his dogs and had provided him with a means of reaching his destination. He started next morning but not before he came and thanked me for helping him out of his difficulty.

So I returned to Smoking Lake with my fine dog team. The dogs were all a light silver grey colour. The leader was a big brute, but the others were young dogs and would be as big as the leader before another winter. I had traded in the harness and equipment that came with the dogs for a brand new outfit, including the toboggan and harness, decorated with tassels and bells for each dog. Train dogs like the bells and react to the decorations with quite the same human frailties as do their masters.

It had given me much satisfaction to know that I could afford to buy the best of everything that made up my outfit. The two silky buffalo robes would make my employer's travels a luxury and not an endurance test in cold or stormy weather.

Woolsey spent the rest of the afternoon making friends with the dogs, five in the team. I warned him these huskies were not the same docile creatures that followed their masters to the plains, but he appeared to disregard my warning. I was astonished to see him petting the leader, the one that I considered the most vicious of the lot.

The howling, yelping brutes that were always loose around an Indian camp paid very little attention to him but concentrated their fury on me. I was greatly provoked one day

145

when one of the skulking brutes tore a chunk out of my leggings and scratched my flesh in the attack. I landed a swift kick under his jaw at the next attempt, sending the dog rolling and howling in pain.

"Peter, you must learn to control that temper of yours," Woolsey told me. "That poor brute only wanted to greet you. You ought to be flattered at their attention. Notice they never seem to look at me." And in an amused contrite tone, he sighed and added, "Apparently they consider my poor dry bones not worth tasting." I had to laugh but I made up my mind to carry my loaded dog whip for the next taste they craved.

I enjoyed making my purchases in Edmonton, knowing that I could well afford the things I wanted: a pair of new snowshoes for us both, some badly needed warm clothing for the Reverend (in fact, a complete outfit from head to foot), and a new capote for myself from the best Hudson's Bay blanket material. I placed Woolsey's outfit on his bed while he was still outside.

The minister was embarrassed by the pile of stuff when I told him it was all for his use. He gave me a severe scolding for what he described as foolish and extravagant spending.

"Peter, you have spent more than a half-year's earnings that you haven't as yet earned. The price of the dogs and toboggan alone must have cost you a small fortune and now these clothes that I doubt the bishop could afford — it is entirely too much."

"Hold on, Mr. Woolsey, let me explain before you commit yourself further. The clothes are my contribution to God's work with you as His instrument, and when you feel inclined to strip yourself of clothes for the benefit of some undeserving beggar who plays on your mistaken sympathies, remember that the clothes belong to the Church and you just have them on loan till they wear out."

He gave me a startled look as if shocked at my temerity in replying to his tirade, but his face broke out in a kind of rueful smile.

"I guess, young man, you have the best of me at that, but I still do not understand how you can spend more than a half year's salary that you haven't earned yet."

Then I told him of my lucky break with my partners at the Pandara mining venture, revealing only what I thought was best for his rather strict opinions. He listened with avid interest to the whole story, then made this comment: "Well! Well! Gold apparently has its compensation for those who know how to use it well. I thank you with all my heart and am glad that God has blessed your fortunes. I was honestly beginning to believe that your sudden generosity and affluence had its source from some less-respectable support."

I had to smile at his half-serious, part-joking relief over my explanation of why I could afford to spend, as he said, "so lavishly." The next day, as if to show me his pleasure, and, I presume as an unspoken apology for the severe scolding he had given me, he asked me to hitch the dogs as he wanted to try them out on the lake. He was busy inside while I got the team ready; then he came out dressed in all his new finery. "Peter, I have to get used to the feeling of these new Pandara garments before I make a public appearance."

He came back in about two hours as pleased as if he had converted a half-dozen medicine men. "That team is the best I ever rode behind. They fairly take your breath away with their speed. The leader leaps to commands as if he were bridled and reined from the toboggan. I can't understand their former master parting with such splendid animals."

I did not offer any explanation of how I had bargained for the outfit — it might have spoiled his pleasure. I'm certain he would have condemned me for taking advantage of the Indian's predicament, though I had paid their full price.

From that day on he took over the care of the dogs, feeding and chaining them up again with as much unconcern for their vicious snapping teeth as if he were tying a well-broken saddle pony. I watched from a distance of a few yards with the loaded whip in hand to interfere the moment the dogs made a false move. Strangely enough it was never necessary. In a few days they would whine their happiness at his presence, yelping and jumping with pleasure. The leader would always place his front paws on Woolsey's shoulder to be patted and fondled before he received his food. I was amazed and perhaps a bit jealous at his demonstration since they gave me only their barest tolerance. They respected my whip, nothing else.

We visited a number of Indian camps, two or three teepees at each place where Woolsey held services, then were directed to the next camp after a stay of one day or so. The camps were spread within a radius of forty miles of our home site. Moose, deer, and game birds were plentiful that winter and the Indians were enjoying a full living. Fur was getting scarce which meant further distances to travel to attend the trap lines.

CHAPTER NINE

Mission Work

A<small>FTER CHRISTMAS</small>, Woolsey sent me to Edmonton to get two men to prepare timber for a better mission building. I brought a carpenter named Nelson and a man called Monkman as a helper. The Rev. Mr. Woolsey left with Monkman for Whitefish Lake where the Rev. Mr. Steinhauer had carts. It was Woolsey's turn to go for supplies as Steinhauer had made the trip the previous summer. They had agreed to make alternate trips to Fort Garry for supplies needed for both missions. Woolsey was to send back a helper from Whitefish Lake to help me whipsaw lumber for the new building.

Peter Whitford turned up four days later, bringing a wife along. He had been married since I saw him last. Pete was an enthusiastic duck hunter and kept the camp well provided with game birds that added variety to our food. I kept the pemmican that I brought from the fort as an emergency ration.

The Indians brought dried moose meat and deer meat in exchange for tobacco that my scrupulous employer would have objected to had he known. His faith that the Lord would provide for our daily needs took no recognition of the fact that the Indians of this area had no belief in the powers of prayer. Instead they believed that a one-sided gift was a highly dishonourable act; therefore, regardless of the difference in value, an exchange was the proper etiquette. It took considerable subterfuge to arrange these exchanges, but the natural secretiveness of the native readily lent itself to this harmless deception. However it often amused me to hear Woolsey praise the generosity and thoughtfulness of the Indians in sometimes travelling long distances from their camps to bring us the offerings of their hunt. I never took any furs but insisted on food alone as the only acceptable means of trade, and thus kept in line with Company rules.

There was little variety in food, yet sickness was seldom a serious consideration. Perhaps it was the outdoor life we led that kept us healthy. Our main diet was of course meat cooked in a variety of ways. Fish and game birds always provided a welcome change.

Any sickness among the tribes was treated with herbs and roots taken from the ground. Conjuring as reported by many writers was actually a ritual that had no real connection with the medicines actually administered to the patient. That show was more to impress the relations of the potential power of their treatment. Your psychiatrist of today may scorn the statement that his early predecessor was the so-called conjuror. The rituals these men practised did not depend entirely on that portion of the treatment that may have been based on the hypnotic effects, but were always supported by medicine, with, in some cases, remarkable effect. Quacks there were among some of the medicine men, as there are among the whites of today, and the mistakes of diagnosis are similar in both cases. The dead patient can make no protest.

Toothaches and the common ailments were hardly heard of before the advent of white men's food. I never had a toothache in my life, have been wet to the skin hundreds of times, yet never had a cold until I settled down to what is now known as civilized living. Indians had purgatives, mild or severe as the occasion demanded. Bladder troubles, another white man's inheritance, were unknown among the Indians. Of course this all had reference to the time before the advent of the settlement of white men in the country.

Whitford and I whipsawed all the lumber required by Nelson, the carpenter. The main part of the building and roof were complete except for the installation of windows and doors. The carpenter worked from daylight till dark as he wanted to have it ready when Woolsey returned. Windows in those days were unbreakable. They were on special order from our Indian friends. They were bullet-clear parchments of deer or elk, whichever was most easily obtained, scraped to a thinness of glass. It was surprising how well they let the sunlight in and kept the cold out.

Whipsawing lumber was almost as hard as shovelling gravel in our mining operations. A frame was built on a hillside on which the big logs were rolled. One side was hewed to a flat side first, placed face down. A slab was then sawed off and again rolled until there were three square faces from which the lumber was sawed. A man stood on top and a man under. The man on top followed the mark and the man under, usually the tallest, followed his lead. Some of this lumber had a face of eighteen inches. The wider the board the less lumber required for flooring and roofing. The carpenters of course reduced their width to their own needs.

One day Monkman walked into the camp to call us to help him cut the road the last four miles into camp for the carts. Peter and I had already opened about three miles near where the carts were but Monkman had missed our trail by going too much to the east. We all went back with him, Pete's wife as well. She was as good with the axe as her man and we were able to bring the carts in that same evening.

Mr. Woolsey was delighted with the progress of the work, and expressed his approval with some elaboration. He went from one place to another examining Nelson's work. He was particularly delighted with the desk for his books and writing material. Had he known this work was all Sunday spare time work, he might not have been so pleased.

In two weeks everything was ready in the new building. Whitford was released and Monkman went away to visit his family but promised to be back later in the winter. Nelson stayed on to complete seats that we both tried to tell Woolsey would not be used. His disappointment was almost comical when on the first Sunday that he held a service in the new building, his guests pushed the seats back against the wall and took their usual posture of sitting on the floor with their legs crossed. "How will they ever learn to get on their knees to pray to the Almighty God from that position?" he ruefully exclaimed.

We visited a wide range of camps that winter of 1861-62. The hunting area extended thirty miles east of Smoking Lake and almost that many miles to the west and northwest. The Crees by agreement always respected the rights of others in their trapping areas. The gathering of different camps at the site Woolsey chose for his mission was largely for the purpose of conferring with each other in regard to any dispute that might arise or assigning new areas if such were requested. The name

Smoking Lake derived its name from these yearly gatherings, usually in the spring of the year when trapping was finished. The name of the lake and town has now been shortened to Smoky Lake.

Fur animals for some reason unknown to the Indians had been for several years getting scarce, though the game animals were plentiful. A number of families had moved out of the region to more profitable trapping. Those remaining in the area that winter numbered twenty teepees, perhaps one hundred souls in all, not near the number served by Woolsey at Pigeon Lake.

Woolsey was a man past middle age, and though he was not a robust person, he had a toughness not outwardly visible. The rigours of continuous travel that he insisted on that winter, regardless of weather or storms, had sapped his strength more than he would admit. He had an unquenchable zeal to carry out his mission that pushed him beyond reasonable limits.

An elderly Cree medicine man who was reputed to be a dispenser of bad medicines, used for spite or revenge, protested to Woolsey that he was killing himself to be on the trail on such a day.

Woolsey replied, "My life is as nothing if one soul can be saved on such a day."

The medicine man, with whom Woolsey had frequently expostulated about his evil ways, had been so impressed that he asked to be instructed in the plan of salvation that Woolsey so devoutly followed. Later he was baptised and became an outstanding exponent of its principles and precepts among his followers.

Woolsey was greatly excited over his success with this hardened old sinner, and was inspired to greater effort, if that were possible. I had to force him to restrict his labours by refusing to take him out when his health began to fail. Oddly, he complained but did not force the matter to an issue.

The Indians were good to their children. They often expressed astonishment in their talks with me that their children, always shy with strangers, quickly grew friendly with the minister. This gave him great influence with the Indians. To my notion the children were a nuisance, but not to this man. For him they were a blessing and joy, and he never seemed bothered with their persistent attention. No doubt this very fact was his best means of obtaining the respect and hearing of their elders.

I was often faced with questions by individual Indians that were beyond my ability to answer, such as this:

"How does your master expect us to do what he and

Steinhauer say is right for the Indians when white men who have known about their God all their lives refuse to believe or live according to the teaching of these men? We know they are good men but we all have beliefs from our fathers and the fathers before them, and we were content with the laws handed down to us from the oldest memory of anyone in our tribe. These men now teach that our beliefs are wrong, yet his people refuse to adopt the ways he says are right. I ask you why is that?"

Perhaps I may have been of some help to Woolsey as I gave him a report of these difficult questions. I recognized the trend in the sermons I interpreted for him later.

I make no attempt to paint these people with exceptional virtues, but I am forced to admit that they lived up to the traditional rules of association in the band or in their family life with far greater adherence to their beliefs than any comparable number of whites under a similar situation.

True there were breaches by individuals as in all societies, but the punishment was prompt: banishment from the band and being stripped of their possessions to pay the offended party. Few of the boldest ever risked such a calamity and no Indian of my knowledge ever questioned the justice of the proceedings.

Mr. Woolsey never seemed to get any grasp of the Cree language. I was called upon to sit out long afternoons and evenings interpreting the words between the teacher and his interested listeners. He did not actually use a program of church services but carried on conversations much the same as they do today in the Sunday schools. He read passages from the Bible and explained the meaning. At first it was hard to get them to ask questions, but after a few visits with the same people they appeared to enjoy the informal talks with the minister, and questioned him on lessons of a previous meeting. There were very few among the various camps who did not give him respect and an attentive hearing.

There were some who gave him some difficult questions to answer but he never failed to give a satisfactory explanation. He had a gift of adaptation to Indian understanding and an intimate knowledge of Bible passages on which he depended for inspired answers. This often astonished me in that he appeared to anticipate the questions and was ready with the appropriate answer before I properly interpreted the question, though I am positive he never learned the language.

The winter was not too severe, although we had some bad storms and a few weeks of very cold weather, but the long hours Woolsey spent in the camps were a heavy drain on his health. He was fairly comfortable in the toboggan, wrapped in good buffalo robes, but I noticed that he seemed to sleep a lot during the rides between camps. It was unusual for him to do so and at our campfire stops between visits we always engaged in some discussion of the previous day's work. I realized he was a sick man, though he never complained.

We had reached the furthest end of our usual camps to the east of us, a place called Island Lake. There, four teepees were situated, and the Indians told us about a new camp of two more teepees about ten miles further northeast. Woolsey planned on visiting these people in spite of the fact that he had developed a throat ailment and could hardly swallow food.

He had spent a sleepless night and immediately dropped off to sleep when I started out in the morning. We would have to follow the same trail for several miles before turning north to the new camp, but instead of turning north I swung back on our home trail. I knew he had a poor sense of direction and if he did wake up, might not notice we were heading in the wrong direction.

It was about time for the noon stop when he finally woke up. Unfortunately he recognized the location at once. I knew he was provoked but the condition of this throat prevented the scolding that I fully expected to receive. I was thankful when we reached our own camp that I had gone against his orders, for his face was flushed and he showed every indication of having a fever. I carried him into the house, robes and all, while I started the fire to warm up the room.

I stayed up and watched my patient all night as he tossed and rolled in his blankets, alternately shaking with chills and at other times stripping his blankets because he was too hot. I could not induce him to taste the broth that I had prepared. I was getting more worried by the hour, especially when he grew delirious.

I was desperate to know what to do. I had stopped at the old medicine man's teepee and explained my employer's condition, and the old chap prepared a powder that he said could be given him with meat soup. Woolsey had a deep prejudice against all Indian medicines, a feeling that was shared with most white men. Perhaps his refusal to take any nourishment was connected with my delay at the camp.

When I noticed that he was being wracked with a jerking of his body muscles that fairly shook the bed, I heated the broth and shook the medicine into the container, first tasting it carefully before presenting it to the sick man. There was no taste other than that of the meat.

I took the contents to his bed, lifted him to a sitting position, and ordered him to drink it. Again he refused.

"You are no baby, Mr. Woolsey. You will either drink of your own free will or I will pour it down your throat by force. Take your choice and do as I say."

He looked at me in astonishment, and I sunk my fingers into his slender shoulders to emphasize my determination and threat of force. He steadied the bowl with his hand and drank to the bottom without another word, though it took him some time to do so. He never said a word but I guessed his throat was so swollen that he probably couldn't talk anyway. I laid him back gently with a sigh of relief, hoping all the time that the old devil of a medicine man knew his herbs and was really converted. I had grave doubts about both. I was plenty worried that the effect of the medicine might have the reverse action than that of a cure. Having forced him to drink, my guilt would have been heavy on my conscience.

After an hour or so he drifted into a natural sleep. It was now nearly morning, yet I was not the least bit sleepy. I didn't even feel tired as I walked out of the hot room to get some fresh air. I went to the storehouse and chopped a large chunk of pemmican. I had completely forgotten my own supper in my worry and care of my employer. A full stomach usually banishes needless or exaggerated concern. Whatever the result, I had done my best; as Woolsey frequently stated, "If you have done all you can then the matter rests with God."

Going again to my employer's room, I found him still sleeping. He lay quietly and there was no more twitching in his body. I placed my hand on his forehead and found it cooler to the touch. I felt like a condemned prisoner must feel when he is reprieved from a death sentence. My combined breakfast and supper was one of the most enjoyable of my experience.

Early the next day, Woolsey's old friend the medicine man drove up to the door. His son had brought him with a dog team. I was glad to see the old beggar but wondered how he would handle the patient.

"Oh, ho! my friend. At last you have burned the fires of your body too long. I have come to make you well again."

"No, no," Woolsey exclaimed, "I am all right now. A little weak but that is all."

"My friend," the old man replied, "you gave me medicine for my soul with God's word but now I must give you medicine for your sick body so more of my people who are living in darkness can be brought to see the light. Lie back, my friend, I shall not leave you till you are on your feet again; that is the least I can do to repay you for the joy that you have brought to my heart by your teaching. You are my friend and it pains me to see you sick."

The medicine man questioned me as to the effect of the powder I had added to the soup. He appeared satisfied and got busy making a kind of paste that he applied to Woolsey's throat. The patient seemed resigned to his fate and offered no further objections to the proffered treatment. His recovery was rapid, and in three days he insisted on having his clothes for a walk to get a breath of fresh air.

Finally the medicine man declared his patient was completely well, and asked me to drive him back to his camp. I made certain to slip a generous supply of tobacco and some other articles I thought would please him in the toboggan beside him. This was done of course without the knowledge of my employer. He likely would have objected, as this might be construed as a breach of Company rules against trading with the Indians.

I was grateful for the old chap's help, for now I felt certain that without it the poor man's sickness would have proved fatal the first night of his illness. A strong man might not have stood for any length of time the terrible twitching and fever that seemed to be burning him up. I had grown fond of his pleasant companionship. His witty remarks enlivened many weary miles. He seldom complained, and our only differences were over my treatment of the dogs: they remained vicious to my handling, and had I relented in my continuous watch over their behaviour I would have been rewarded with a slashed hand or some other mark of their uncertain dispositions.

Woolsey was always grateful and appreciative for every little act for his comfort. I admired the man for the sincerity and zeal with which he carried on his work with the Indians. He always tried to do his share of camp duties when we were on the trail. His patience and perseverance in spite of difficulties in overcoming the prejudice and ill will of a few of his contacts always won their friendship even if he failed to make converts out of them.

When Monkman returned in the early spring of 1862, around the last of March, I decided to go to Whitefish Lake. I had wintered my horses at the lake with Woolsey's three animals. Nelson had gone back to Edmonton shortly after Christmas but promised to return later in the summer to complete the rest of his finishing work on the building.

After a talk with Monkman, in which he said that he was willing to take over my work with Woolsey, I informed Mr. Woolsey of my intentions and received his permission. I told him I would leave the dogs and outfit for him for the rest of the winter and take the horses.

"You have been longest in my employment and are entitled to a choice, Peter. If you wish to go I think Monkman can handle your dogs. I will travel only when the weather warrants safe passage. I do not wish to cause the old medicine man friend of mine the excuse for more experiments with my body."

"Surely, Mr. Woolsey, you do not doubt the potency of his cures. Or is it that you question the sincerity of his confession of faith?"

Smiling broadly he replied, "Well let us say that I do not care to go through another spell of sickness as severe as the last."

I felt tempted to tell him of my own doubts in the matter but managed to keep quiet, only expressing my disapproval of his apparent ingratitude over his friend's treatment. If the man only knew the torture that I had gone through both before and after I had used the medicine, he would have had a good chuckle over the whole episode.

I caught up the horses and packed my equipment ready for an early start in the morning. I planned on going across country direct to Whitefish Lake, confident that I would find my way without any trouble from the lie of the land described to me by the Indians.

Leading a pack horse and riding the bay, I thought the mare would follow as she always did, but I reckoned without the persistence of the minister's mare - she ran after the horses, circled and tried to stop them by kicking them from the front. She whinnied and succeeded in driving the roan mare back to the others. Finally I caught up with the roan and tied Woolsey's favourite up to a tree but she still tried to climb the tree and break loose.

Monkman said he would ride part way with me and would hunt game on his way back. The heavy timber scraped the side of the pack, making it impossible to lead two horses abreast. After Monkman turned back I tied the roan to the tail of the pack horse, but the roan still continued to whinny and show her reluctance to leave that miserable little cayuse Indian pony that Woolsey described as a born leader. After that last exasperating experience, I would never doubt his word.

It was provoking, at the same time funny. She was nothing but an undersized Indian pony yet these two wellbred horses were completely under her domination. She kicked and fought the biggest horses and was the uncrowned queen of any herd she happened to be with.

I was lucky in finding my way without too much trouble, and was invited to dinner at one of the camps. They directed me to a pack trail that was recently travelled and made easy work for the horses, so that I reached Whitefish Lake just at dusk.

Steinhauer was home and invited me to stay with him. After I had given him a report of Rev. Woolsey's work and informing him that I had left the man's service, he offered to hire me.

"I have some work that you can do for me till spring really arrives. Then I want you to make a trip to Fort Garry for the mission supplies for the two missions. It is my turn this year but I don't like to take the time away from my work with the Indians not only here but out on the plains. Travelling with the buffalo hunters, I'm able to meet many of the tribes that have never had a missionary among them. I will have nothing to worry me if you are in charge of the carts."

"That will suit me fine as it will give me a chance to visit my people in the Red River settlement. I was worried about leaving Mr. Woolsey, for he has been very sick this winter, but I believe if he takes proper care of himself he will gain back his strength. Monkman is a good interpreter and a capable guide."

"All right then, if you are satisfied to make the trip for me, I will have to start preparing to go out on the plains. A third cart with Woolsey's two carts will be enough for all our requirements from Fort Garry, if you can buy another one down there. I will bring pemmican and dried meat sufficient for Woolsey's needs from our hunt."

I was getting ready and anxious to be on my way to Fort Garry when Monkman arrived with the carts. Rev. Steinhauer engaged two Indians to handle Woolsey's carts and gave me an order to purchase another cart at Fort Garry. We took an extra cart horse for the return trip. I took both saddle horses, as I didn't want to take a chance of them straying while I was away.

The snow was almost all gone when I left for Fort Garry but I was informed that the ice on the Saskatchewan was still holding in the river so I followed the north side to Fort Pitt. There was a well marked cart trail now, unlike my first trip when the tracks were hardly visible.

By the time I reached Fort Pitt, the ice was gone from the river so I forded the river and crossed over to the south side which was a much better route, not cut up with creeeks and ravines as much as our trail on the north side of the Saskatchewan.

When I reached Fort Garry I disposed of my orders for the goods and supplies required for the two missions, when I was informed that a Rev. George McDougall was anxiously enquiring about the arrival of the mission carts.[1] I was barely out of the building when I met a man whom I recognized immediately as a minister. He introduced himself and his son John, and when I told him my name, he said he was well acquainted with my work from Mr. Woolsey.

"We have been waiting here for quite some time and are anxious to get started on our way to the two missions at Whitefish and Smoking Lake."

"I am sorry, Mr. McDougall, but I must disappoint you. It will be impossible to start back up the trail until the stock have been rested and our carts repaired. I have my instructions from Mr. Steinhauer and cannot complete his business in less than four days at least."

"Let me remind you, Mr. Erasmus, that I am superintendent of missions, and my authority supersedes that of ministers under my control. We must get started at once."

"Your authority may cover the ministers but in no way obligates me to go against common sense and the conclusion of our business that I have been sent nearly a thousand miles to perform. If your business is so urgent, there are other ways of travel that are available. However, if you will come with me and examine the stock and equipment, I think you will agree that the delay is absolutely imperative."

The reverend was extremely provoked, for his face grew very red, but nevertheless he followed me back to where we were camped. When there, he grudgingly admitted the stock showed a need of rest. A broken filly on one of the carts and loose spokes on the others convinced him that it was useless to think of starting back the next day as he had proposed.

The Rev. George McDougall was destined to travel many a prairie mile in a Red River cart and to learn that these vehicles, though useful conveyances, required patience, perseverance, and some skill to keep repaired and suitable for use. When fording rivers and creeks, the wood swelled in the water and the hot sun dried the wood rapidly so that spokes came loose and damaged the outer rim. A plentiful supply of shaganapee line was soaked in water and bound around the wood to prevent further breakage until a birchwood replacement could be made. The Red River cart had no iron on any part.

I was with McDougall on the prairie in later years when he ruefully admitted his former ignorance in his first trip with me from Fort Garry. This was after a particularly exasperating break with a loaded cart in which he had forgotten to load some repair material that was always carried in case of trouble. It had been necessary to travel back almost ten miles to fetch the wood left behind before we could proceed on our trip.

I was able to make a short visit with my folks while our carts were being repaired. My mother was in good health and Mary

Anne was the same bright vivacious young lady but more of a tease than ever. She had decided that I was a hopeless matrimonial prospect, although she expressed her utter inability to understand why I was so unattractive to women. She finally decided it was my whiskers that were the real reason for remaining a bachelor. She refused to accompany me back to the West just as she had refused the first time.

"I will not go out to such a barren region where men have so little appreciation for women. I'll stay right here where there are a dozen fine young men to choose from, not one who allows a scratchy beard to grow past the second button of a dirty shirt. So there, brother Peter, you have my opinion."

"Hold on there, young lady! That's going too far. This is a brand new Hudson's Bay shirt of the best quality. None of your young men could afford such a nice shirt nor could they support such a fine beard, washed and combed to a texture of fine silk."

I called on my old friend Murdoch Spence, who brought me up to date on the Civil War in the States. Whitford of the Pandara mining venture had been right in his predictions of a war between the North and South over Negro slaves. He had left the States just in time to avoid being drawn into taking sides. Mr. Spence was still worried over the growing dissatisfaction and outright boldness of some of the agitators in the Red River settlement. Representations were being made by the different factions to the Government of Canada but no action as yet was in sight.

I rode back to our camp and found that Jackson had our carts ready and two already loaded, so that we could make a start in the morning. I was able to buy a good used cart for Steinhauer in the settlement, and the man brought it in that same afternoon. I went to McDougall's and told them if they brought their luggage next morning we would be on our way. They had a lot of stuff but we managed to find room.

We stopped at Fort Carlton to pick up some goods that happened to be in short supply at Fort Garry. There we received an invitation to dinner with the factor.

We sat down to dinner and started to eat when John said, "Will you pass the bread, please."

The factor smiled and replied, "I'm afraid you will have to do penance for bread in this country, young man." This caused a good laugh. Though John was somewhat embarrassed by the incident, he took it in good humour, and when it was explained laughed as hard as the rest of us.[2] John McDougall was to learn in the months and years ahead of him that bread had no part in the meals he would be eating for quite some time in the future.

McDougall drove one of the carts, Jackson and Sparkling Eyes one each, and I had the last one. John rode one of my horses. Travelling with the loaded carts was a slow, tedious task. Between twenty and twenty-five miles was a good day's travel where the prairie road was dry and there were no sloughs or hills to pass over. Where travel was good I had one of the men trail my cart horse and I went out after game birds to vary our food. John did some hunting but on that trip he didn't seem to have much luck.

The Rev. Mr. McDougall soon adjusted his haste to the slow movement of our carts. In fact he became the most talkative of us all, once he had dropped the stiff-backed officiousness of our first meeting. Each day as we travelled he seemed to take a fresh joy out of our camp life and the vast open spaces that lay before his view on every side without a single sign of habitation in our way. He was almost boyish in his exuberance, and I began to form a new opinion of the man. Our first meeting had rankled me sorely.

John was a young man. He could speak Swampy Cree and was an eager listener as his father questioned me as to my knowledge of the tribes with whom I had been in contact. I decided this young man would have no difficulty in grasping the essentials that were required for western living. He had none of the eastern prejudices and had an open mind. He was physically fit to cope with any hardship of trail endurance. There was no question in my mind that he would adjust himself to our people and conditions with far greater success than his father would or could.

I had a feeling he was not imbued with the same denominational prejudice that was in my opinion the greatest obstacle to the Christianization of the Indian. The Catholics taught their way as the only way to salvation. The others were equally free with their criticism of the Catholic. Yet both claimed the same God, much to the confusion of the untutored Indians who were quick to grasp the incongruity of such a situation. With the exception of Father Lacombe and Mr. Woolsey, the others were openly hostile to each other, though all claimed to be brothers working for God's will.

I often thought that a sensible division of the fields of service and their operation would have clarified the situation and greatly speeded up the work of all churches. There were thousands of Indians without any religious direction and hundreds of miles of space to carry on the work.

In due course, we arrived at Whitefish Lake. Mr. Steinhauer was greatly elated over the arrival of the chairman of missions and arranged a special service in his little church to honour

McDougall's arrival in the West. Mr. Steinhauer's influence greatly impressed the chairman by the large number of people who attended that service on such short notice. Mr. Steinhauer despatched riders to summon the people to assemble to hear the great man preach his first sermon in what was later to be called Alberta.

Mr. McDougall wanted to hire me to guide him to Smoking Lake with Woolsey's carts, although Steinhauer told him he was sending Jackson and Sparkling Eyes with him.

"Well," said McDougall, "I was not thinking of the carts alone. I want Peter to work for me as an interpreter and guide, as I want to establish a mission of my own at some strategic place to contact as many Indians as I can."

"Peter can please himself in that regard, Mr. McDougall. I hired him to make the trip to bring in our supplies and some other business at Fort Garry, all of which he has completed very satisfactorily, and I am of the opinion that if you need a man you can do no better than hire him to go with you. However, if he wishes to stay, I will provide him with work."

After discussing the matter with Mr. Steinhauer, he advised me that he did not have any work that actually could not be done by any other man among the tribe, but I could be of far greater benefit to the church work by attending as interpreter and guide to Rev. McDougall, and he would not like to deprive McDougall of my services.

I had not forgotten our first meeting at Fort Garry, but under Mr. Steinhauer's persuasion I finally consented to go with the man. I liked John and I think that is what overcame my reluctance, but I was afraid that a second instance of his arbitrary instructions might again cause me to resent openly such treatment.

We found Woolsey a sick man when we arrived at the Smoking Lake mission with his supplies. I was sorry to see my old friend in such bad health, in fact I was shocked at his appearance. Monkman had allowed him his own way and taken him on trips before he had regained his strength. His old friend the medicine man had warned him that he must not travel until he was completely well, but he had persisted, with the result that he was now perhaps permanently incapacitated.

I had a talk with Monkman and scolded him for not taking better care of Woolsey in spite of my warning to keep him from overdoing himself. I had also told him to get the medicine man's help if he took another attack like that I described to him in detail.

"Woolsey refused to allow me to call the man for help to doctor him, in fact he ordered me not to go. I thought he was a goner several times but somehow he pulled through, but the sickness left him as you see today."

"I know he's difficult to handle, but I told you the man was not strong and was subject to those attacks. You saw how it shakes his body beyond human endurance. The old man's medicine took immediate effect and his recovery took only a few days afterward. The man does not know his limitations. He is fanatical in his work. You did wrong in not asking for help in spite of his objections. The medicine man handled Woolsey before and he would have been only too glad to have helped again."

"Peter, it's all very well for you to talk but when I take a man's pay for work I do his bidding if I can. If not, I quit. The minister is not a child. He should know what he is doing."

He had me there so I said no more. Actually I was feeling guilty of neglecting Woolsey when I knew that I should have stayed and helped him through the balance of the winter, instead of leaving him in other hands. I knew that Woolsey preferred that I stay with him rather than have Monkman take over.

The mission chairman did not approve of the site at Smoking Lake. Woolsey's Indians were not of numbers satisfactory to the cost of supporting a mission so far from the travelled trails. By questioning those camped around the mission at the time he ascertained that fur-bearing animals in the region had been getting fewer for several years. Many of the former inhabitants had moved to more profitable areas. The regular occupants of the region served by the mission totalled fewer than twenty teepees or one hundred souls. The gathering that spring had been only ten teepees.

"We will go to the Saskatchewan River where the Indians tell me there's a good ford. It may be possible that we can find a better location nearer regular trails. Also we would be in a better position to take advantage of the boat service for obtaining our supplies.

"I consider," added McDougall, "that the time spent during the summer going to Fort Garry for supplies is time wasted that might better be used travelling with the Indians, the majority of whom, I am told, spend their summers on the prairie. At least we ought to be able to obtain our supplies of pemmican and dried meat from that source; that is why I wanted you, Peter, to accompany me as interpreter, guide, and buffalo hunter. What is your opinion, Erasmus?"

"The money you have spent here will much of it be wasted, but a great deal of the new building can be saved and used at the other place. However, in all other respects the advantages of a

162

better location will in due time pay for the loss and give you a much larger field for missionary work. The cost of processing the meat on the prairie will have to be paid to the Indian women who do all the work. If you pay the Indians for the work they do, it can only be in trade goods, for money is not known to them. If you do that then you will become entangled with the Company rules preventing any missionary from trading with the Indians."

"Peter, you have summed up the matter in a masterly style, but I did not take over this task without considering there would be obstacles and I certainly do not intend to let Company policy cripple my work. I will face the problem when it becomes a reality."

While his statement was exactly my own opinion, I could not help but feel the difference in moral principle of the two missionaries. Woolsey would not in one single thing deviate from the rules governing missionary conduct in the West, whereas this other man proposed to explore means to defeat this great handicap to independent action that was faced by all individuals outside Company jurisdiction. Even in the simple effort of providing one's living from the vast herds of buffalo on the plains, the Company, by its policy, had control.

The rest of the day was spent in preparing for the trip, sharpening tools, and sorting anything else that would be required if a suitable location was found.

We were up at daylight the next morning for there would be four of us making the trip. Nelson had returned a few days previously to complete his unfinished work and was hired to go along. The minister expressed some doubt as to his ability to ride that far but I gave him the roan mare to ride, and after we started he was delighted at her easy gait and gentle handling. John rode one of Woolsey's cart horses, a good plug but not a saddle horse. I had brought my own pack horse and by dividing the load among the saddle animals we managed to carry all our needs.

When McDougall confessed to having developed some pains at the noon hour, I told him about my own suffering on my first ride form Fort Pitt to Saddle Lake and Woolsey's advice that helped. He laughed and said, "These pains are the first of the obstacles I mentioned to you yesterday."

Crossing from the north-east end of Smoking Lake to the Whitemud River[3] and thence directly south, we passed through where the little town of Smoky Lake is located today. It was an easy ride of about eighteen miles but the minister was glad to reach our destination before dark that evening.

We had no difficulty in locating the ford as the water was

163

low and quite clear all the way across. I rode half way across to test the depth of the water and could pick the shallows a long way ahead of the horse. The deepest parts only came to my stirrups without lifting my feet.[4]

Mr. McDougall was well satisfied and expressed his delight over the location. He kept repeating, "It is a beautiful spot and the very place we need. It will give happiness to our people just to live here."

The next morning we went up in search of suitable timber for our first building. I knew of a stand of spruce about six or seven miles upriver. When I came down with the boats we had a meal there and two of the boatmen and myself walked through the stand. My companions were quite enthusiastic over the straight, even-sized growth and said that the trees were just the size for building logs.

We made a camp on the north side of the river and started building a raft to carry our tools over. John and I proposed a small raft but Nelson refused to agree with us. "We have to cross several times, and if the weather gets colder, swimming twice a day across the broad expanse of that water would be foolish as well as dangerous. We'll build a raft big enough to hold three people. I'll burn up that surplus energy of yours as soon as we get into the timber."

Later on he commented, "We have cut sufficient timber the first day. Peter, you like swimming so much, you rig up a harness for one of the horses tomorrow morning and bring him across to do the skidding. John and I will cross over and roll the logs nearest to where we will build our raft and start the foundation frame to hold the logs together."

The third day we had all our timber assembled in a raft. John and I both wondered how such a cumbersome craft could be controlled. We had to cross over to the north side of the river where McDougall proposed building. All we had were short shaganapee lines. If we did get across the river, how would we manage to get it snubbed?

Nelson did not volunteer any information, but after he was satisfied that the raft was solidly fastened together he rigged up two sweeps, one for each end, bored pine in the cross timbers to form rowlocks, doubly secured by pieces of the rawhide straps to reinforce the pine. Then he gave us a briefing on how to use the sweeps. Our raft was ready to be floated.

I then swam the horse back over the river while John and Nelson brought the small raft over to carry me back. Nelson said it would take all three of us to handle the big raft. McDougall was to gather the camp equipment together and meet us at the ford.

We had difficulty in getting the big raft afloat, but John and I stripped off our clothes and waded in the water with pries to edge it away from the shore. We finally pried it loose and scrambled up as the raft started down stream. We were away and riding down current. John and I both yelled our triumph and made the shores ring with our enjoyment of the free ride.

Captain Nelson shut off our joy by yelling in an exasperated tone to seize the sweeps or we would be aground again. He gave us no time to put on our clothes and cursed us soundly for our clumsy handling of the sweeps. We just managed to miss the next bar when he roared out again for us fool savages to get our clothes on again. The language he used was hardly suitable to address a preacher's son, but it was effective in curbing our exuberance.

Nelson was more than a little disturbed when he slipped and almost landed backwards in the water. We laughed harder than ever at his comical appearance as he waved his arms and fought to keep his balance. I learned later that he had never learned to swim, hence his terror and aversion to the water. I had no sympathy for anyone who neglected to learn to swim which was a necessity in those days of our travels over unbridged streams.

Our captain had previously picked out his landing place where we would skid the logs to where they would be needed, and he indulged in some fancy language to inspire our efforts at the sweeps and land his craft at the exact point required. I felt the raft grind to a stop. We had grounded on a point close to the north shore. The man was now all smiles, whereas a few minutes earlier he had been a raving maniac.

McDougall, who had not yet arrived with the horses, might not have approved of Nelson's abuse of the Queen's language. I wondered what the preacher's son thought about such abusive terms, but apparently the success of our landing justified Nelson's excitement and he did not appear at all ruffled over the man's heated orders. To have missed landing where we did would have meant the complete loss of all our work, for we had no way of snubbing the raft any further down. To skid the logs any further would have been impossible, as the banks were cut straight down so that a horse could not climb up dragging logs.

In a short time we had the logs up and the roof and chimney built. Nelson and I whip-sawed boards for the window and door casements. Mudding and the chimney were the slowest and most tedious aspects of the work. John worked like a trooper; it was all new work to him and he blistered his hands using the axe, but he persisted and did not complain. He was a likeable chap, always in good humour, who seemed to enjoy working.

165

This was the first house to be built in a Protestant settlement west of Red River.[5] Two years after McDougall started his mission there, the first of the people who were to form the Victoria and Lobstick settlements arrived and continued to come in and occupy land that spread twelve miles upriver.

Woolsey wintered at Smoking Lake but his health remained very poorly and he was unable to carry on the work as he had done in the two previous winters. In the following spring of 1864 he was relieved of his work and took passage east with the boats. Monkman had stayed with him as helper and took care of the stock Woolsey had gathered for his work.

We were kept busy that winter of 1863-64 preparing timber for a larger building to be erected the next summer. We used single sleighs made for one horse. The logs were tied on the top of the sleigh and the ends dragged on the ground. This was slow and tedious work but we had a choice of the best timber in the country and a stand of good spruce on the south side river banks, not far from the mission.

There were jumping deer that ranged in a heavy jack pine bush about four miles east of the home place. They were in bunches of as high as fifteen to a herd. Not being hunted, they were tame and a dependable source of excellent meat when necessity required. However, no meat could replace our main diet of buffalo meat which was the standard food and occupied a place similar to the grain flour of today. The other game meats did not have the quality or taste to satisfy your hunger as did the buffalo meat.

Woolsey had arranged with an Indian to keep my dogs during the summer at Little Whitefish Lake, and as he was in no condition to do any travelling that winter, I brought them to the mission at Victoria where I used them in hauling provisions on the prairie and whitefish from Saddle Lake. They had been well taken care of during the summer and were in excellent condition when I got back.

John McDougall had adapted himself to conditions of travel with excellent aptitude, and was good company on the trail. With more experience I felt that he would be a good westerner, though he sometimes irked my feeling by his tendency to boast of his prowess. However I did not attempt to discourage this tendency for I believed that a man who sets himself a high objective is quite likely to obtain some success in the matter.

The Rev. George McDougall named the location Victoria, I presume in honour of the Queen, and so it was called for many years afterward until the name came in conflict with Victoria in

British Columbia and the advent of civilization and the royal mail, when the name was changed to Pakan.

The Rev. McDougall returned overland with his family towards fall.[6] His wife was a Quaker who used the words "thee" and "thou" in all her conversations. She was a very kindly woman. She hardly ever raised her voice to correct the children. They were a happy family and soon made the place ring with laughter and happy voices. An older daughter was at school in the east. The son David was living with his uncle back in Canada.

The family lived in the small house while Nelson was finishing the big new house. They were badly crowded but I never heard a word of complaint from Mrs. McDougall. However she was a happy woman when she was able to move to the new place.

The slopes along the banks of the Saskatchewan were loaded with high bush cranberries, raspberries and saskatoons, and chokecherries and red cherries later in the season; they made a pleasant variety to our food. Mrs. McDougall was a very adaptable person and quickly learned to use many of the native ways of preserving the fruit for later consumption. Her cooking was a most welcome change from our own hasty preparation and saved us a lot of time for other work. Mrs. McDougall's arrival was decidedly a wonderful event in that it left us free to carry out other duties.

Rev. McDougall had done no travelling among the Indians, meeting none except those who in the course of their travels called at the mission or camped near there. He was now making preparations for a buffalo hunt to the prairies, hoping to meet up with bands out on their fall hunting. During this trip, which lasted well on into December, the minister was successful in meeting several bands of Crees. He was well received and highly pleased with the reception his ministry appeared to arouse among the people. Few of them had ever had the Gospel preached to them.

I had some difficulty in adjusting my interpretation to McDougall's manner of speech. Mr. Woolsey's sermons were always carried into the Indian's own realm of understanding in simple language that made interpretation easy. However, after a few sermons by McDougall, I was able to render a good interpretation of his text. When he became better acquainted with his audience, their customs and beliefs, and their way of thinking, I noticed a great deal more interest and understanding among the people.

An Indian was always a good listener but seldom exposed any emotional effect from the most impassioned eloquence of

167

the speaker. It often came to my mind that it was hopeless to get behind the thinking of these stoic masks of indifference that appeared before us, though they sat with every indication of thoughtful attention.

We arrived at the mission before Christmas, and McDougall was pleased to find everything in good order. The family was in good health but somewhat worried over provisions that were getting short. We had no sooner unloaded our packs than they were raided by the children, whose bedlam of delight gave me personally a great deal of satisfaciton. The Reverend George paid no heed to the excitement but gave his good woman a long account of the trip.

When I went to the house on an errand only a few days before Christmas I found Mrs. McDougall weeping. It was too late to withdraw without her knowing I had entered the house. I was in a quandary to know what to do. She was always so happy and cheerful that to find her in that state was a great surprise.

"I beg your pardon, Mrs. McDougall, but what is it that makes you grieve? Is there anything that I can do to help?"

"No, Peter," she replied after some difficulty in getting control of herself,, "it's the children. This will be the first Christmas they'll have without presents and all the things that make Christmas memorable for them. I never thought about Christmas when we left Norway House to come here and now we can get none of the things here."

"Look here, Mrs. McDougall, I have never had a Christmas tree or presents since I was a boy of fourteen years in the Red River settlement. I think it is about time to do something about it. I'll speak to John. He'll have some ideas and I think the children will have the best Christmas of all their lives."

"I think that would be wonderful, Peter. I do not mind for myself but I hate to think of the children not having their Christmas tree. Mr. McDougall is so busy that I hate to bother him with my small worries."

John and I were quite close friends, and when I confided the state of things with his mother he was all ears, and immediately started making plans.

"We will need some money, so I suggest we each donate ten shillings towards the presents that will include father and Mr. Nelson as well. Mr. and Mrs. Flett[7] should be good for another ten shillings each, that ought to give us enough to make this the biggest event of the year."

"That's fine with me," I replied, "just as long as you take over the collection of the money. We will have a tree from across the river where I saw some good ones up the creek aways. We can get some white hair from that white mare of Woolsey's if we can persuade her to keep her feet out of the skies while we cut her tail. Your Santa Claus wig and whiskers can be made by your mother and Mrs. Flett, so we are all set for the big day."

"Hold on there, Peter! I get all the worst jobs and you just help make up the audience. Is that your idea of a fair distribution of the work?"

"No, it was my idea and you took it away from me, so abide by your own choice. There will be lots of work for us both before the idea becomes the real thing." .

John's approach to Nelson and to his dad met with their high approval and brought promises to help, with each adding some new suggestions of their own to the general plan. Mr. McDougall wanted to include some of the other camps in his Christmas list of presents and was taxed ten shillings each for him and his wife and an additional twenty shillings for charitable donations by the church. He complained about the severity of John's sentence but kicked through with the full amount. In fact he went further and ordered all the work stopped for Nelson and me until after the celebration on Christmas day. We were to devote the balance of our time entirely to the preparations.

Mr. Flett and McDougall were elected to the committee to make a list of the Indians in the five camps around the fort and to purchase presents from the Hudson's Bay store that might be suitable for the occasion.

The time was set for the early evening of Christmas Day. Invitations were sent to the camps that contained about twenty-five people, most of whom were Christians from Woolsey's mission at Smoking Lake, except one old man who was visiting one of the camps.

The presents, assembled under the tree, contained small parcels of tea, tobacco, cotton shirts for the men and dress goods for the mothers, trinkets for the children, and other articles which I have now forgotten. Mr. McDougall explained about the old man who always visited the people at this time of year. The white people believed he came purposely to see the children. His story was much the same as today except that he adapted the wording to the understanding of his Indian audience.

At the ringing of a bell, Santa Claus was ushered in from behind a curtain that sheltered the fireplace. The whole performance was realistic as the attention of our audience was centred around the ringing of the hidden bell, which the minister manipulated with his foot by a string. The McDougall children clapped their hands and couldn't contain their

169

enjoyment. The younger children among the Crees were somewhat frightened; but the older ones, following the lead of the white children, soon laughed and clapped their hands at the funny old man with his long flowing beard.

When Santa gave them an address of welcome in the Swampy Cree language, the elders gazed in astonishment. I had to speak to them in Cree and explain that the man could speak in all languages for he visited all countries over the Big Water. The presents were handed out and Santa took his departure, which, I explained to them, ended the entertainment.

It was in every respect a fine Christmas day. Mrs. McDougall came to me when the others were busy with the guests departing, and with tears in her eyes said, "Peter, this is the most wonderful Christmas that I ever had. I will never be discouraged again. I will remember this day and will always be thankful for what we have."

CHAPTER TEN

Married Life

W OOLSEY CAME TO VICTORIA in the spring of 1864 to wait for the arrival of the boats. He was feeling much better and was quite cheerful, though I could see that he was not happy over having to go back East. I think his chief worry was over his saddle pony. He asked me if I would see that she wasn't abused. I promised him that I would take care of her and make certain that she would do nothing except carry out her chosen occupation of leadership with the band. The other horses were mission property, as well as their equipment, so he had nothing to worry over on that score.

I was sorry to see my old friend leave but I was glad that henceforth he would have things much easier. I felt guilty for his illness in that I could possibly have protected him against his overzealous efforts among the Indians. I was convinced that he could have been saved his present misery if he had not been so prejudiced against Indian medicines. A fine character, kindly and unselfish, but strong-willed and determined far beyond the powers of his physical strength to support. His influence with the Indians was tremendous. History will never record the extent of his labours.

Having travelled hundreds of miles in all kinds of ways and

weather conditions, I always found him cheerful and happy, although there were times when I thought that we might have curtailed the length of his grace at meals or his prayers in the morning and when camping at night. Extreme cold, blizzards, or buckets of rain never affected his customary supplications on these occasions, much to my own impatience which by his example I learned to accept without complaint. I admired the man for his sincerity and I knew it was beyond him to boast of his work or the privations he had suffered travelling to reach his migratory flock. He would never dwell on the sacrifice of comfort or of his endurance on the trail to impress his eastern superiors. I hope that these few words may remove some of the obscurity that hides his work among the Indians.

I was thirty-one years old in 1864 and still unmarried. My companions and friends frequently commented on what they considered this oddity, especially in a person who they thought was well able to support a family. Early marriages were the custom of the times. Most young men were married before they were twenty-one years old. Girls were considered at a marriageable age at sixteen years.

The Rev. George McDougall's eldest daughter was married to Richard Hardisty at the age of sixteen years. Though she had been raised and educated in the East, she soon adapted herself to western conditions. Her honeymoon trip by cart trail to Edmonton and saddle horse to Rocky Mountain House from Victoria was an event of historical fortitude that any present day bride might well envy.

During my stay with the Rev. Mr. Steinhauer, I had been greatly attracted to a young lady among his congregation. The thought of that girl had been a weighty consideration in my first refusal to work with McDougall. However, the girl was so much younger than I was that I hesitated to make any advances that would seriously show my intentions.

Charlotte Jackson was a very pretty girl. Her mother was a widow and supported her family with a trap line. The girl was half white, a fact that gave me considerable thought, in that it was the basis for much of my prejudice against Hudson's Bay factors in general, many of whom felt no moral obligation towards their offspring that were not uncommon among Indian women with whom they had contact.

The incongruity of their attitude that held up their own prestige as Hudson's Bay factors or chief clerks to a high position of honour among all white visitors to their forts, while at the same time they deemed Metis associates and servants beneath the levels of ordinary respectability, was always quite beyond my understanding.

Perhaps my church training and my subsequent association with ministers of the gospel had emphasized the immorality of men who had children born out of wedlock with native women and took no responsibility for the children, yet held themselves in higher esteem than us ordinary mortals though they found no shame in co-habitating with squaws in an indulgence of their physical desires. True, there were Indian maidens who took pride in the fact that their child's father was a white man and in no way felt obligated to hide the fact. However, the background of tribal custom that held women as mere pawns was some justification for this attitude. A woman's position in the life of the tribe up to the entry of Christian missionaries and church marriages was at best insecure. Continuous raids by any successful war party usually netted some young women. A choice of adoption into the tribe or an axe in the head became an accepted custom of tribal warfare.

Charlotte's father had been a Hudson's Bay factor. This was no secret among the tribe and possibly I was the only person who held any resentment over the truth of the matter. I held these views long before I knew there was such a person in existence. I had a deep intolerance for men who took advantage of their situation to indulge in such a despicable practice. Few people of today realize the tremendous power officials of the Hudson's Bay Company held over the people in those early days. These men were the only law or authority on the western plains and therefore felt themselves immune from any moral or material responsibility for their actions. Many of the reports concerning the native people were obtained from Hudson's Bay Company officials. Naturally their information would be tinged with prejudiced views reflecting on the moral instability and loss of virtue among the natives and the Metis women. The facts of my experience give no support for such a view.

My personal experiences among the tribes with whom I have been in constant contact through my work with the missionaries does not bear out this generally accepted viewpoint. Had I made any advances to intermingle with the young women of the tribes without stating my intentions towards marriage, I would without doubt have endangered my life. Certainly I would have received immediate notice to depart for other places. The code of conduct among the tribes was strict in this regard. Any departure from the unwritten code was promptly penalized: banishment from the camp and confiscation of the offender's chattels.

I informed Mr. McDougall that I wished to get married and wanted time off from my duties to ascertain my fortunes in that regard. The missionary was very co-operative; he highly commended me on my decision, offered all the facilities at his disposal to speed me on my way, and told me that when I was married, I could have the use of the first house we built as my home.

Getting an early start the next morning, I arrived at Steinhauer's home at dusk. I had saved many miles by cutting across country. The bay horse from Captain Palliser was a good fast walker, big and strong. The light snowfall that winter hardly delayed his stride. Mr. Steinhauer was at home with his wife when I arrived. I was welcomed into the house and as was customary the women immediately started to prepare a meal while I was questioned about the progress of the Victoria mission. I had hardly finished my meal when Mr. Steinhauer and his wife excused themselves, saying they had promised to make a sick call. Little did they realize how opportune was their visit, or my own purpose in being here at this time.

Charlotte Jackson was busy clearing the dishes after my meal; she was working for the Steinhauers. You can believe me that I lost no time in getting acquainted with the charming young lady, and let this be sufficient explanation and excuse for my expression of regret for my hosts' departure that my suit was accepted and plans for an early marriage were already underway when the Steinhauers returned about two hours later.

Mr. Steinhauer was delighted, although somewhat surprised, but Mrs. Steinhauer teased us both about taking advantage of their absence as Charlotte and I, holding hands, informed them of our intentions. I could see they thought a lot of the girl, but were prevented from further intimate conversation by the entrance of the younger members of the Steinhauer family from a toboggan slide that was the chief interest of youngsters at that time. They were all immediately banished to their rooms and bed, a little surprised at their mother's sudden orders for their departure but they all obeyed without a murmur. They were scarcely out of the room when Mrs. Steinhauer launched into a thorough instruction and advice on the duties and proper conduct of a husband to his wife.

Mr. Steinhauer with an amused gleam in his eye stopped his wife with the remark, "My dear woman! You'll frighten the man out of the notion if you keep on. Do you realize that Peter is at least ten years in arrears of his duties as a married man?"

The next day I went to the mother to get her consent and to see Charlotte's uncle, who was her tribal guardian. Sam Jackson, my instructor in that first buffalo hunt at Hairy Hill, was glad when I met him and told him of my intended marriage to his niece and saddled a horse and came back with me to make arrangements and set a date for the marriage. Somehow I had lost all my former reluctance and hesitation, and was now happily anxious to proceed at once to Edmonton to draw on my account with the Hudson's Bay people for all the things I was told were necessary to have for the wedding. The list of articles from Mrs. Steinhauer was long but when I informed Mrs. McDougall of my success and showed her Mrs. Steinhauer's list, she added others of her own and I began to realize that marriage was a costly procedure. Mrs. McDougall expressed disappointment when her husband advised her that half the stuff on her list could not be obtained short of Fort Garry. That was about the only time that I heard her complain in front of her husband about conditions under which we lived in the territories.

My trip to Edmonton with a single horse sleigh and another horse trailed behind for changes to hasten my trip was made with dispatch. My visit with Bill Borwick was brief. He was married and lived in quarters of his own. His wife turned out to be an old acquaintance from Lac Ste. Anne. They both were enthusiastic over my own coming marriage, and convinced me they were happy and wished the best for me.

I had my five dog team when I left Victoria for my wedding at Whitefish Lake. Woolsey had returned the two silky buffalo robes when he went back East. Ribbons and decorations were packed in the toboggan ready for the return with my bride. Both Mrs. McDougall and Mrs. Flett had assumed complete charge of my affairs and planned every detail of my trip with the gravest concern which left me helpless to add any suggestions of my own even if I had cared to do so.

"Remember, Peter! You have one day to reach Whitefish, one day to rest and arrange for your wedding on the morning of the third day. You must return here at dusk of the third day without fail. The wedding supper will be waiting and the guests assembled for that time. Nothing must interfere with this schedule."

When I arrived at Steinhauer's home in the evening, Mrs. Steinhauer immediately took charge of the parcels of finery and other articles which the good mothers at Victoria deemed absolutely necessary before a proper marriage could be performed. From the exclamations of delight by the women, I presumed the selections were quite in order.

The mystery and excitement of all the fuss being made over the event was beginning to affect my confidence. The calm matter-of-fact attitude that Mr. Steinhauer took to the whole excitable business was a great help in calming my own disturbed nerves. The matter of visiting my affianced before the ceremony was considered impossible and not to be allowed under any circumstances. I had to be content to assume a very minor part in the arrangements and leave everything to the capable hands of Mrs. Steinhauer and the others.

The marriage was performed in Steinhauer's little church on the high slopes of the Whitefish Lake hills early in the morning, where I was ushered by my attendants but had to listen to a hurried briefing by Mrs. Steinhauer before we left the house. By the time I arrived at the door of the church, I was in a daze. I do remember that Charlotte was attended by her uncle, Samuel Jackson, and a crowd of relations who filled the aisles and made way for my attendants as they pushed me into my place before the minister's altar. I was nervous in spite of my efforts to appear nonchalant and self assured. I stumbled over my answers and the Rev. Steinhauer had to help me over the rough spots. Not so for my bride, who amazed me with her calm acceptance and clear answers. Her conduct that day was typical of her attitude to all the problems of our married life.

The Reverend Mr. Steinhauer's strict code of serious Christian conduct of a solemn marriage ceremony did not allow of any show of exuberance frequently displayed at weddings in this day. We were escorted to our toboggan which had been previously decorated and prepared by my attendants and brought to the door for our convenience. Shaking hands with all those present and of course kissing the women of all of my relations while my attendants held the restive dogs in place, took quite some time. Meanwhile my bride had been subject to a lot of kisses while she was tucked in comfortably by her numerous helpers. I was finally free to go. The dog whip and the trail line were handed to me. The dogs were then freed and we were on our way.

The downhill course from the church to the lake gave me a few anxious moments. To have tipped the toboggan as the excited dogs raced to keep ahead of the sleigh would have been considered an act of ill omen and a bad example of my fame as an experienced dog driver.

Our noon-hour stop was brief but my wife insisted on making tea for me, and laid out a delicious meal of choice viands that her people had provided for our noon lunch. There was more than enough to have fed a boat crew. The weather was mild for that time of year and I could see that she was enjoying every minute of the trail as we passed over lakes and through heavy spruce timber and poplar.

I was a little worried about how my bride would act at the reception that was prepared for us when we arrived at the mission, as she then could not understand a word of English. Mrs. Flett and Mrs. McDougall, warned by the noise of the guns as we passed the Hudson's Bay post, were outside to greet us when we got there. The warmth of their greetings and the hugs and kisses they showered on my wife were most gratifying. Charlotte accepted and returned the welcome with the calm self-assurance that was always to amaze me in a girl of so little experience.

Later in the evening Mrs. McDougall came to me and said, "Peter! You are more flustered than a youngster. Stop worrying about your wife. Look at her. She's as contented and self-reliant as the best of us. I wish I could meet utter strangers with half her self-confidence."

I quit worrying and started to enjoy my evening. Nearly fifty miles of road gives a man a relish for food that makes eating a pleasure. The women had certainly gone all out to prepare a good meal. The highlight of the evening was a plum pudding, and of course other edibles prepared by skillful kindly hands.

George Flett and Mr. McDougall vied with each other under the influence of good food to make the evening a happy and memorable event. Although the wife could take no part in the conversation, she enjoyed watching the smiling faces and attentive activities of their wives for her pleasure. They had won my wife's heart, for as soon as we returned to our rooms she said, "Peter, you must teach me to talk English as soon as possible so I can thank these wonderful women for the presents they have both given me."

My wife insisted that I talk English to her all the time. Sometimes to my exasperation when I spoke to her in Cree she pretended not to hear or would not answer. I was surprised at the speed with which she picked up English. I teased her by saying big words to hear her attempt at pronunciation, but I soon quit that as she demanded to know their exact meaning or their Cree equivalents, which was sometimes just a bit hard.

We took up residence in the first log shack. Everything had been tidied up and a new coat of whitewash was on the walls. My bachelor shack had received a transformation for which I was thankful, having completely overlooked the matter myself. I only then appreciated the great importance women placed on detail in matters concerned with marriage.

I was luckier than I deserved. My wife's surprising adaptation to any circumstances was a never-ending pleasure and wonder in the years to come. Self-reliant and understanding, her patience and appreciation of the smallest kindnesses that she received from her new friends was a revealing characteristic that made me feel ashamed of my hesitation in entering into this marriage, which had its basis in the condescending attitude that I recognized now as completely misplaced. I am afraid that my approach had been distorted by the mismatches entered into by careless and thoughtless people for whom marriage with Indian or Metis women was a mere convenience and not a responsible duty. As Steinhauer had said, "Marriage was a sacred and holy responsibility, not to be lightly entered into or carelessly carried through life."

During the balance of that winter of 1864-65, John and I were kept busy building stables for the cattle and horses belonging to the mission. My own stock were left out on the range. Just as soon as we had completed one piece of work, Mr. McDougall had something else planned for us. We had occasional breaks from the routine work when we went after fish at Whitefish or Saddle Lake, or out on the prairie for fresh buffalo meat. We were a large household, and with the many visitors to the mission, it took a lot of food to keep us from need.

McDougall renewed his trips out on the prairie during the summer to visit the wandering Indian camps, and to provide cured meat for our own use. The matter of exchange for Indian women's help in preserving our hunt did not in any way become an obstacle to the minister's work, a matter I did not refer to in any conversation after that first time at Smoking Lake when I had pointed out the Company rule about missionaries not trading with the Indians. His solution of this problem was very simple — he just ignored the problem until such time as the Company brought the matter to his attention. I was curious to know why Company officials did not act in this breach of their laws but found out later that there had been and was at that time considerable representation being made to London against a renewal of their monopoly over the fur trade. The Company probably did not want any incident to influence a decision not in their favour.

We had just returned from a trip on the prairie to the Victoria mission when a few days later McDougall called me into his study for a talk.

"Peter! You have been with me nearly three years. The expense of starting here has been heavy and I have instructions to reduce my costs in every possible way. I think you should consent to accept a lower salary."

I was then receiving $250.00 a year (at that time money was counted in pounds and shillings).[1] I did not make an immediate reply but allowed him to continue his argument in support of his proposed reduction of salary, the tone of which tended to emphasize the great benefit I had received in his

178

service and the favours he had rendered me personally and also the heavenly rewards stored up for all the people who engaged in the work of Christianizing the Indians.

"Mr. McDougall, I would like to ask you one question before you proceed any further. Just how much do you propose to reduce your own salary?"

His reply to this question was a clear evasion. He came back with a tirade about ingratitude and a lot of other remarks that reflected on the value of my work while in his service.

I replied with some heat, "Mr. McDougall, if you think I have not given good value for the money I was paid, I can quit right now. Being a married man, supporting my wife and myself by my own resources, I cannot consider your proposition for a moment. I'll prepare to leave your premises as soon as I round up my horses and pack our few articles and clothing."

The reverend gentleman was very wroth indeed, unprepared for such a definite answer, and he spoke some high words hardly in keeping with his office. I did not interrupt until he was finished.

"Sir, I am surprised at your use of such irreverent words. You forget that I am a free agent and not a bonded slave. A cut in my salary that does not reduce your own is not appealing to my sense of justice. I see no reason why the high objectives and heavenly rewards you expound so forcibly do not apply to us both. I have earned every cent you have paid me and the kind of gratitude you demand from me is not in my being. I will be subservient to no man's will. Goodbye, I will leave this place as soon as it is humanly possible!"

John and I were good friends, and he tried to patch up the quarrel between his father and me, but I refused to reconsider my decision. The old man had gone too far in wounding my pride. I have always given my best to my employers, regardless of the hardship or toil entailed. I never counted the hours in a day's work when on the trail, and kept on the trail regardless of weather conditions in summer or winter, with the least delay possible, frequently travelling half the night to reach a destination to be at work the next morning at the usual time.

When I informed Charlotte of my change of plan and asked her to prepare our packs for the road, as we would be leaving at once, she never asked a single question but started immediately to pack our stuff. We had three horses of our own and Woolsey's white mare that he had offered as a gift in a letter written back from the East. My dog team had been sent to the care of an Indian at Little Whitefish Lake about twenty miles north of Victoria.

Flett remarked, "I'm sorry to see you leave, Peter, but under the circumstances you would be foolish to stay. To accept lower wages after three years' work is hardly an enviable position."

After we were on the road for some time and I had time for reflection, I realized I was in a bad position, as I had no home to take my wife to. I decided to go to the Rev. Mr. Steinhauer's place at Whitefish Lake. We didn't even own a tent. It was time that I built a house of my own. I had no worry about money as I still had a considerable sum to my credit with the Hudson's Bay Company from the Pandara mining venture. My salary from the mission work had added to the account and I could get by for some time until something came my way to make my living.

The Steinhauers were glad to see us when we arrived and offered us their home as long as we cared to stay, after I had explained the situation at Victoria.

"We will accept your offer for a few days but I want to get permission from the chief to build a house of our own along the lake shore some place. We have been asked to join a buffalo hunt, and as soon as we get back I want to start building."

Just then Chief Seenum put in an appearance and Steinhauer spoke of my wishes for a place to build.

"Yes," the chief replied, "I will go with you in the morning to help you pick a site for your house. We'll be glad to have you join us and I feel sure my council will assign you a trapping area, as I know your wife is quite a trapper in her own right. She and her mother have supported themselves for several years with a trap line."

I was very thankful that one of my problems would be solved so easily, and thanked the chief for his interest and kindness in offering his help.

We were up quite early the next morning, and shortly after breakfast the chief called and asked us if we were ready to take a walk with him. I had our horses ready to ride, but he said as it was only a short distance we need not bother with horses. We walked less than half a mile from the mission when the chief led us off the trail to a high-level bench above the lake shore. It was a well-drained, high piece of land in the centre of a small prairie of probably three acres. It gave us a nice view of the lake, and a long point of land a few hundred yards to the south gave us a nice sheltered bay. This was an ideal spot in every way.[2]

"This is yours," said the chief. "There at the edge of this little prairie is a fine stand of straight spruce trees that contains all the building logs you need. There is enough land here for gardening purposes, there are fish in the lake for the taking, and game in the woods handy for your gun. With a house and a beautiful wife to cook your hunt, what else could a man ask for?

This place is yours for as long as you or your family want to live with my people."

I thanked the man with all the sincerity that I was capable of expressing; by his generosity and kindliness we had chosen our home that was destined to be, for many years in the future, the source of much happiness and the centre of my future activities.

There were now quite a large number of Indians permanently located around Whitefish, Goodfish, and Reed lakes, where there were some large hay meadows. Probably two hundred and fifty souls had been encouraged to live there in an area served by the Rev. Henry Steinhauer's mission. When he first located at Whitefish in 1856, there were only three families, two of which were Steinhauer's and Ben Sinclair's own families.

A starting date for the hunt had been arranged. As we went south we were joined by the various families, until at our first stop there were twenty teepees. Charlotte and I had no cart of our own, only pack horses and a six-skin buffalo teepee that was too cumbersome to pack on a horse. William Bull offered to pack it for us. We agreed provided he and his wife would share it with us on our trip. There were only two of them as their family were all grown up and married. It was a nice arrangement as they were a fine old couple. The man was a great storyteller and had a remarkable memory. They were both devout Christian people and now with my last worry removed, I began to enjoy the trip in a true holiday spirit.

I felt strangely footloose after all my years of steady employment. I could hardly get used to the idea that I was my own boss and that time was my own to do with as I wished. At last I had realized my early ambition. I was no longer a wage slave and not at anyone's beck and call. It took me some time to adjust to the new idea.

We crossed the river at the Saddle Lake ford where I had made my first attempt at swimming a horse across a river. Samuel Jackson was along on this trip and entertained our family group by a recital of my experience of that trip. The tale had lost nothing in spite of the lapse of ten years of time. They all had a good laugh at my expense but I decided there and then that Mr. Jackson would have to extend himself this trip to beat me at killing buffalo.

In recalling my first travelling in these parts, it seemed strange that now I was married to one of their most attractive maidens and that I was out on a buffalo hunt for a living and not a sport. I recalled "Nigger Dan" Williams's hunger for his beloved mountains, when he was on the prairies with the

Palliser expedition,[3] and his eloquence in extolling the beauty of the wooded mountains in comparison with the prairies which he hated, whereas I never liked mountain travelling a little bit. The narrow ledges we often had to pass over tested my courage to the limit. I never conquered my fear of precipitous heights and felt buried in the dark spaces among the big trees that shut out a view of the open skies above.

The coloured man's singing when the trail and weather were good and his swearing when things were bad had been a constant source of amusement. He did not indulge in the ordinary vulgar expressions, but his eloquent and spontaneous substitutions were impressive if not edifying. He was a wonderful singer, with a repertoire of songs that was amazing. Hector never seemed to mind or pay attention to Dan's outbursts of swearing, which probably amused him as much as it did the rest of us. I noticed he enjoyed the man's singing as much as we did.

Dan was a mountain man, and, though he knew nothing of the mountain region we passed through, his mild suggestions of the better course always proved to be right.

"Look at dat, Peter. Ain't dat sure grand, and she changes every minute. Not like your old prairie, always, always de same ting, only worser." I always had a feeling of being bound to a small space and crowded in with overhanging cliffs that surrounded you on every side, shutting the sun's rays away when yet the afternoons were only half spent. The coloured man's ecstasy over those things was something I could not share or understand. This was my country and it was with sadness that I remembered Captain Palliser's predictions of the great changes that were bound to come to these as-yet-untouched wide-open spaces.

Ten years ago, on my first hunt, there had been a herd of more than three hundred animals less than ten miles from the Saskatchewan River. Now we had to travel more than thirty miles further south before we spotted buffalo and this was a herd of only fifteen animals, whereas there had been small herds of from fifteen to fifty head all along our route from Saddle Lake crossing to near the Fort Saskatchewan ford.

Already a settlement was gathering along the river near the Victoria mission. Samuel Whitford, Turners and Howses, half-breeds from the Red River settlement, had investigated for land and planned on bringing other families out the following year. Revard Rose Norn, a Scotchman and employee of the post at Victoria, had picked a piece of land on which to build three miles up river from the mission.

There were many of the Protestant people who were

dissatisfied with the growing discontent and trouble being stirred up in the region of the Fort Garry and Red River settlements under a man called Louis Riel, a French half-breed and Catholic, which to their minds was a strong argument against anything he might represent, regardless of other causes.

The founding of the Protestant mission and the Hudson's Bay post at Victoria was to prove an attraction to settlement, as the land in the vicinity was very good and timber easily available for building purposes, making the location ideal in all respects for people leaving the Red River and Fort Garry regions. There would be others without a doubt once they learned of the new area. I realized the transition had already started. My own plans would have to be implemented without delay.

I still had the captain's horse and had trained him to run buffalo. Though he was not a young horse now, the light work that he had done in the last five years had left him sound in limb and wind. I was determined to show my early instructor that I could beat him at his own game. The other horses were not in as good a condition as mine, as they had been used for all purposes under the saddle, while mine had done very little work all summer.

During the hunt, I killed four animals the first run, two cows and two young bulls. One of the cows was a dry fat animal. Samuel happened to kill the only old bull of the lot, but knocked down two younger bulls. The other two men managed to kill one animal each, both yearlings. The other members of the hunt joined me in making the best use of my luck, for they had all heard Samuel tell the story of my tough luck in that river crossing.

"Well, anyway," Sam ruefully remarked, "I taught the man to kill his first buffalo and I am glad he hasn't forgotten my teaching."

All the rivalry was in good-natured fun as it was the custom of the tribe that the meat of all animals killed would be divided equally among all the carts. You were allowed your first choice of an animal, provided you killed more than one beast. It was share and share alike. I was pleased to see that the women all joined in helping my wife prepare the pemmican and dried meat and also helped in sewing the new sacks to contain the finished product.

In less than two weeks we were successful in obtaining all the meat we could pack home. It had been a profitable and most enjoyable hunt.

It was well on into October when we got back to Whitefish Lake. William Bull delivered us to the site of our new home and helped us erect the teepee which, I forgot to mention before, was a gift to us from Charlotte's mother. The next morning bright and early I was out cutting logs for the new house.

William Bull came along shortly after I got started, packing an axe and saying he was there to help me. We had been called to dinner when a horse and cart pulled up and I was informed that there were four others coming behind with their tools in the cart ready to help.

I was glad of the offered help but worried as to how I would be able to pay them for the work. When I mentioned the matter of pay, they said they were only returning the help I had given them in killing buffalo. Of course I protested that killing buffalo was not work and I was glad that I could share with them any luck that I had in hunting.

William Bull spoke up and said, "Say no more about pay, Peter; we decided to build your house when we were still on the plains. You are only the hired man here and have nothing to say. When your house is finished you can then talk all you want."

The next day the walls and roof were complete. They even brought lumber for the door and material for the two windows. I could see they had done some previous planning before coming to my place. On the second day, other men showed up. William, acting as foreman, assigned each man a task as he arrived. I was ordered to assist in directing and helping build the chimney. They even had a hammer for breaking and fitting stones in the chimney place.

All who arrived brought food with them, and two of the younger men brought their wives along to assist Charlotte in preparing the meals. They were a merry, willing crowd of workers. My first house must have held the record for fast construction, but, under William's supervision, everything had to be done in first-class workmanship.

The plastering and walls were whitewashed inside and out. There is a deposit of marl along the mouth of Whitefish Lake from which the Indians took the white mud. On the third day a fire was lit in the chimney and our foreman declared the job an excellent piece of work. We were warned not to move in until we had kept fires going a few days to let the whitewash dry. We were proud of our house but as the weather remained mild, we stayed in the buffalo teepee until the plaster was thoroughly dry. We built a fire in the chimney each day. Finally we moved into the building as my wife was anxious to get settled.

The next morning when we got up it was snowing and blowing a blizzard outdoors. That day, I believe, in spite of the storm, was one of the happiest of my life. We owned a home of our own. At least for me it was a great event. My thoughts went back to the Red River settlement and my younger sister who could never seem to understand why I did not own a home of my own.

The windows were covered with parchment and the door had only rough lumber, but, it was well made and fitted snugly in the door jams. It was nothing elaborate and cooking utensils were pitiably few, but, as my wife remarked, why should we care? We had food and shelter, horses, guns, and ammunition — a lot more than many people had all their lives. We could get all the things we required by our own efforts. Our trap line would provide all our needs. In this regard I was not too enthusiastic as I knew my limitations along that line.

The years I lived at Whitefish Lake with Charlotte were the happiest and most contented of my life. She had a surprising faculty of adjusting herself to the inconvenience of bare necessities in household utensils, never demanding more than she knew we could afford or obtain. Her happy and joyful acceptance of what we had or could improvise, cooking by the open chimney fireplace in winter and the open campfire in the summer, were part of her duties as a good wife.

The country in those early years was overflowing with animals and the lakes teeming with a variety of fish to satisfy any man's appetite. There were marten and mink to be trapped in the winter. Muskrats were plentiful but held a very low price. There were lynx and foxes but no beaver, although their old dams crisscrossed the area in every direction where there was any water flow. Beavers had been over-trapped as the demand for their pelts by the Hudson's Bay Company was high and hunters had made no provision to allow for their natural increase.

Seenum's council had met and we were assigned a trap line directly east of our home, towards the area that was to become many years later the districts of McRae and Sugden. It was heavily timbered rolling country, mostly with huge spruce and tamarack with some groves of heavy poplar and balsam. I rode through the area on saddle horse to investigate its possibilities and came back delighted at the prospects for fur-bearing animals.

I had cached my traps at the Smoking Lake mission. I had bought quite a number of traps in Edmonton with the intention of doing some trapping, but had such poor luck that I had given the idea up after a trial of a few weeks. I decided to go after them and bring my dogs back at the same time.

Sam Jackson laughed at me when I told him that I was going after traps that I had cached away four years ago. "Man, you are crazy to think they will still be there, and even if they are there they will be rusted so bad that they will be useless. Sure, I'll go with you but I still think it's a long way to travel for nothing."

"Well," I answered, "I still have to go after my dogs at Little Whitefish Lake and pay the man for taking care of them anyway, and another ten miles further on is not going to kill our dogs. So let's get started tomorrow at daylight."

"All right, but don't sleep too long as I'll be there before breakfast, but you had better get ready tonight or you'll have to run to catch up with me at Lone Pine where we'll stop for noon. I know a toboggan trail by Goose Lake and Island Lake. I intend to kill a couple of deer or maybe moose. This will not be a wild goose chase for me anyway."

We were a long way up the trail following a well beaten track when it became thoroughly daylight. Sam must have attempted to catch me in bed as he had threatened the night before, but I had his breakfast waiting when he arrived at my door. Our good toboggan trail petered out at an Indian trapper's shack near Goose Lake. We had travelled nearly thirty miles on a fairly good trail and decided to stay at the shack.

Cardinal, the owner, and his partner came in shortly after we finished our supper. Jackson knew both men but they were strangers to me. They appeared glad to have company, shaking hands with me and telling us that we were welcome to anything they had; of course Sam had to tell them about the wild goose chase after my traps.

I was beginning to be a bit peeved about Sam's references to a useless trip. "It may be that I'm wrong about finding my traps where I left them but I'll tell you this much. I will not be satisfied until I know for certain that the traps have been taken. I've travelled with your people for several years and assure you that I have known more Indians than any of you chaps up north here are likely to meet in a lifetime. Yet I have never met a man among them yet who could steal an article not belonging to him. Steal horses, of course, but that is a war act and requires bravery and skill and is, as far as their beliefs go, an honourable calling."

I possibly spoke with some heat, as the three men looked at each other in surprise. Cardinal said, "My friend, you shame us with your faith in our people. I hope with all my heart that your trust is justified. I have never been to the prairies but make a good living in these parts and have no need for your buffalo. Perhaps what you say may be true of the prairie Indians but in these parts there are a few men that I know cannot be trusted."

I had had enough of their conversation, and being tired

went to bed while they stayed up with Sam and talked practically half the night.

I was beginning to have my own doubts when I reached the Cryer's shack where my dogs were kept. They were in very good condition as he had given them some work to fit them for winter use. I had trouble making him take payment for their care, as he claimed they had earned their keep twice over since the first snowfall. However, I gave him an order on the Hudson's Bay store at Victoria and added a generous bonus of extra sugar, tea, and ammunition for Christmas treats for the family.

Jackson left his dogs at the Little Whitefish camp, and I wanted him to stay and rest there. "Oh, no!" he said, "I want to see how you keep traps safe four winters and three summers without rust or theft."

The traps were as I had left them, well greased, inside a huge fallen pine log that had a hollow centre. I had cut a green tamarack log to plug the hole.

He that laughs last, laughs best. I couldn't help but enjoy Sam's amazement when I exposed my find. I scraped several years accumulation of dirt from the logs, part of which I had shovelled over the butt to hide my marks. I could have placed a hundred traps in the large cavity instead of the fifty that I had hidden there.

"Peter, you beat any Cree at hiding your tracks. Only a huge forest fire could have spoiled your cache and I think the muskeg surrounding that island bush would stop a fire before it reached your tree."

We stayed over at the trapper's shack while Jackson went out with Cardinal's partner after a moose. Cardinal and I went out after deer and were successful in getting a nice young buck and a doe. They would only take one quarter from the young buck and refused to take any of the moose meat as they claimed they had all they could use. We were now well satisfied with our trip but it took us an extra day to get back to Whitefish with the heavy loads.

There were quite a number of lakes in our trapping area and several small creeks. My wife insisted on going along with me to set the traps. Of course I made no objection as I did not have any experience in setting traps, except the first winter I was with Mr. Woolsey at Pigeon Lake. I had been with the Indians while they made sets, but had been not greatly interested and consequently learned very little from them.

We found plenty of signs of marten and mink, and I was more than a little bit excited over the prospect of a good catch. My wife warned me against disappointment later if I grew too

187

enthusiastic before we even had the traps set. We had barely covered half the distance we planned on when we found sets for all the traps we had brought. Under Charlotte's instructions I built two deadfalls for lynx, using fish as bait.

I was surprised that the area showed such good signs of game and was so well populated with fur-bearing animals. I hadn't thought we would be given an area so rich in fur prospects. However, it is possible that the whole area was similar in the matter of game and fur animals.

The next day we went back and set out the balance of our traps. When we had these distributed, I could not restrain my impatience to see if we had made any catches with the traps we had set the previous day. My wife advised against disturbing the sets till the following day but none of her arguments could change my mind. We found three marten and two mink in the traps. One deadfall for lynx had been set off but had missed its quarry.

"Charlotte, my good woman," I exclaimed, "I have told you several times that you have brought me luck. Now look what we have already."

"Oh, Peter," my wife exclaimed, "don't be too sure of yourself. We have a long winter ahead of us and we cannot be so fortunate all the time."

Beginner's luck or not, we continued to have success, until by spring we had accumulated sixty marten and forty mink, two fisher, and two lynx, besides a number of weasels. The fisher was a fur-bearer that was already very scarce in the country. There were only four others caught by all the Indians in an area probably fifty miles square.

We had earned a year's salary in a matter of a few months. However, my wife must take full credit for our wealth of furs, for without her knowledge and skill, my own efforts might have been a different story.

CHAPTER ELEVEN

Free Trading

O UR FIRST CHILD was born in April of 1867. We had planned to visit my folks that summer, but my wife decided that she would not risk a trip of such distance with our little girl. Steinhauer asked me to take care of his carts in bringing his supplies from Fort Garry. I traded for two horses to haul a cart as I wanted to buy two carts of our own and not be dependent on others when we went after meat on the prairies. Steinhauer hired two Indians to drive his carts so I took my two saddle horses.

I was glad of Sam Jackson's help in packing the furs, as I wanted to ride on ahead when we got to Carlton. I learned from Sam that the experienced packing of furs to be carried a long distance was as important as preparing the pelts after catching the animal in your traps.

We were making an earlier start than was usual, for it was customary to wait till the grass was well started before taking the horses out on the trail. Mr. Steinhauer considered the horses had come through the winter in good condition and with some grain twice a day would do well until the grass was better.

He had been successful in persuading the Indians to cultivate some few plots of grain, barley, and vegetables. Their farming tools were very crude, mostly homemade of wood.

Factor Christie had presented Steinhauer with a plough made with steel shares and wooden beam which was in great demand after the people learned that a little grain fed to their ponies on winter trips increased the stamina and strength of their animals.

The rich, fertile soils of the Whitefish and Goodfish Lake districts,[1] even with the crude tools used, gave big returns. Once the Indians learned the value of the grain and the increased relish that vegetables added to the fish and meat diet, there were few who did not try to cultivate some land. They pooled their power in ponies to pull Steinhauer's plough, but it must have been heart-breaking work to train these animals to pull a load. My observation of some of the harnesses used showed considerable ingenuity in the use of materials at hand.

Our trail to Fort Pitt was again on the north side of the Saskatchewan, as the ice was still solid in the river at the end of April. I travelled with the carts till we crossed over the river at Pitt, and then packed the cart horses and went on ahead.

At Carlton I caught up with Cuthbert and McGinnis,[2] two independent traders. They told me of an independent trader who had a store at Fort Garry, a man by the name of Inkster. I wondered if he was my old collegiate friend who had sided with me in our escapades at college. Almost the first man I ran into at Fort Garry was this very man, whom I recognized at once.[3]

"Hello, there! If it isn't my old friend Peter Erasmus, then it must be his brother. How are you, Peter, and what brings you here?"

"Oh," I said. "I have two pack horses with furs for sale."

We talked for a while of old times, when perhaps I intimated that I was a pretty good trapper. From then on he was all business, and named a price for each species of fur contained in my packs.

"I'm sorry but I promised the factor at Lac La Biche to give their man here a chance to bid on the furs. I'll have to see him first."

"Very well, Peter! I know it's useless to talk to you until you've kept your promise, but do not sell before I have a chance to examine your pelts. If they are prime skins and well stretched, I can do better than my first offer. Whether you sell or not be sure and come and see me before you leave."

The Company price, after a careful grading, was much lower than Inkster's blind offer, so I bundled them up and went back to Inkster.

Sam Jackson had graded the furs at home and I had made a careful calculation of the approximate value I would receive. Inkster's valuation was a lot more than what we had estimated the total value would be, so I sold to him without further argument. Three dollars a pelt for marten, two dollars for mink, and four dollars each for fisher, with a good price for the other furs. As I had traded my guns and some riding equipment to the Indians as well as a spare horse for extra furs, my total sales came to over four hundred dollars, with an offer of a substantial reduction on any goods purchased if I didn't demand payment in cash.

I bought two carts in good repair for ten dollars each, and two sets of used harness for eight dollars. They were practically new and had been well taken care of. You'd better believe me, I was quite proud of my bargains. I also bought a ninety-pound keg of sugar, a half chest of tea, a few sacks of flour, some prints, dress goods, and clothes for myself, and numerous other articles. I replaced the guns I had sold, and last but not least bought some cooking utensils for the wife and some extras along that line for trade.

Inkster saw my carts were light and offered to give me a hundred dollars worth of trade goods on credit to be paid back the following year. I agreed, and he chose stuff he thought most required by hunters and trappers: a lot of ammunition, fish twine, some prints, blankets, beads and other trinkets for the women. To these last I objected, as I considered those things useless and a waste of room in the carts. "Look here, Peter. If you're going into this business, you will have to sell what people want and not what you think they should have. There is a good profit in this stuff and you will find that you could sell twice the amount I have given you. Besides, I want my money back and I think I am entitled to use my judgement and experience in giving you what will sell. You can bring back anything you can't sell."

In the face of these arguments I had nothing more to say, and let him have a free hand until he had loaded our carts. Steinhauer's carts would not arrive for several days so I took the opportunity of visiting my folks.

I found everyone in good health, including my friend Murdoch Spence and his red-headed wife. The old gentleman was more than ever disgusted with the state of affairs in the settlement. Government surveyors from Canada had been sent out to survey the land and were dividing it up in quarter sections regardless of ownership or interference with the river-lot system of extended lines back from the river front.[4] He predicted dire calamities in the future of the settlement unless sane heads could control the hotheads that were threatening to act on their own.

I was becoming a little tired of his gloomy predictions and

soon excused myself on the grounds that my men would be waiting for me unless I got back to the fort.

The next day, the three men arrived; their stock was in splendid shape. They had taken the precaution to cache some of the grain for the way home and were quite enthused over the wonderful effect of feeding horses grain on a trip as long as ours. These men would be great exponents for Steinhauer in his efforts to induce the tribe to do some farming. They had averaged thirty miles a day from Fort Pitt whereas the usual distance was about twenty to twenty-five miles in dry weather and on good prairie roads.

We made excellent time on the return trail, even though we were heavily loaded. The weather favoured us and we travelled early and late, though we gave our horses plenty of time to feed. Samuel Jackson, William Bull, and another young fellow they had brought to drive one of my carts were just as anxious to get home as I was. They never complained even when I gave orders to hook up in a wet drizzle or rain. Usually when it rained travellers stayed in camp and let the horses feed.

Charlotte was almost speechless with pleasure when I started packing all our new purchases into the storehouse. When she opened the packs that I brought into the house for her particular inspection, she was in tears, especially when she opened her new cooking utensils.

Having made an extra-early start on the trip to Fort Garry and making good time on the return with no delays for bad weather or breakage, we were in time to join the regular fall buffalo hunt. All of us married men had our wives along as was customary in those times. With our two carts I had room for some of Inkster's trade goods.

My visit with Inkster had convinced me that there were good prospects of profit in trading with the Indians for their furs and skins, whilst doing some trapping during the winter for myself. Quite by accident, I had stumbled into an occupation that would give me independence and a home life with my family. Inkster assured me that the monopoly long held by the Hudson's Bay Company would no longer be kept in the matter of trade with the Indians. The whole country would be open to any man with some capital and experience, but he advised me, "You must begin in a small way, learn the demands of the trade, and above all, you must teach yourself how to judge fur. Paying high prices for poorly handled pelts and inferior furs can ruin you in a hurry."

Having finally come to a decision over my place for the future, I felt greatly relieved of my past worries, and found myself enjoying the company of my fellows on the buffalo hunt with exuberance, almost with youthful energy.

There were twenty teepees in our camp when we crossed the Saskatchewan River. Chief Seenum was in charge of the camp and immediately sent out scouts to locate buffalo or any enemies who might be lurking in the locality. All the unmarried young men were used as scouts.

We were about two days' travel from the river when one of the scouts came in to report a herd of ten animals only a few miles from our next camp that night. Chief James Seenum and Hunter came to my cart to ask if I thought it advisable to change our course to try for these few head.

"By all means," I said, "We have a better chance to pick the best from a small herd than from a large one. There are some of your people who only have dried fish and nothing else."

Five of us saddled horses for the chase the next morning. The chief came to where we were making ready and said, "You're right, Peter, some of our people have very little food. We could use all ten head if you could get them. You're in charge of this hunt, and I expect a good report when you return."

We found the animals in an excellent position to approach quite close before we would start them. They were feeding in a long flat between ridges high enough to hide our horses until we were ready to run them. The buffalo were all feeding upwind, fairly well bunched together. Sam and I crawled to the top of the ridge to size up the best way to get at them.

"Look here men, the chief said the camp could use all ten animals if we could get them. I propose that we do just that. We'll split up. Three of us will start the herd, after two men have got in place at the far end of this draw and flashed back a signal that they are ready. We will spread out and try to drive them towards the others, killing as many as possible before we reach there. That means we must get two animals each. Are you all agreed?"

"Yes," they replied almost as a chorus. They were getting the spirit of the game I had proposed.

Then Samuel spoke up. "Peter, we all know you have the longest-winded horse of any of us, so I'd say you kill as many as you can of the cows and leave the calves to your partners. The bulls will hold together, if you do not crowd them too fast at the start. My mare is almost as long winded as your horse so I will try for two, leaving the others to my partner "

"That sounds all to the good, Samuel. Now you go ahead and get in place. Don't forget to flash a signal when you are ready."

After about an hour we got Samuel's signal. A pocket mirror flashed in the sun can be seen at a great distance. The Crees were very good, using a kind of code in talking to each other across long distances. Taking advantage of every cover, we got quite close to the buffalo before they noticed our approach. We were riding about forty yards apart when they started to stampede, and then we raced after them. The bay of mine was not a fast starter. Most horses could outrun him for a quarter of a mile, but after that distance he steadily gained speed. One cow left her calf and followed the bulls but the rest were holding together.

I began to think I would lose the race without a shot; then I saw the cow drop back. I rode beside her and knocked her down from a distance of three yards. I kept after the others. Then I saw one of the bulls being outdistanced by the others and urged my horse for more speed. Old bulls are bad actors when they get winded, so I took no chance and took a shot at him from ten yards away. He fell head over heels but I kept my horse headed after the others. They were now too far ahead for me to hope for another shot but I kept running them to keep them going in the right direction.

Suddenly I saw one of the animals drop to his knees, then fall head over heels; he jumped up and started running again but he had slowed enough that I caught up with him and got in a fatal shot. The other two animals were still running strongly but were too far away for a winded horse to catch, and anyway they were running close to where the two men were waiting behind the ridge. One minute afterwards I saw Samuel and his partner taking up the chase.

I looked back over the flat but could see no live buffalo running. It looked like we had accomplished our objective. Shortly after, the carts appeared over the ridge where they had been waiting for us to finish the run. I found out afterwards that they had watched the whole thing from behind the ridge. There was plenty of help to dress the carcasses so I rode slowly ahead to find out how the others had made out. From the ridge I saw them both dressing out their kill, so I went back to my last kill to prepare the animal for the carts. I found the bull had a broken leg; he had stepped in a badger hole, and that's what had delayed him long enough for me to catch up.

When the carts came up, they told me that we had made a clean sweep of the herd. The other two men had killed a cow each and had easily finished off the calves. If we did a little boasting that night, we hardly could be blamed.

Charlotte, as I presume is the way of all wives, did not think it such a wonderful stunt. "It was a shame to kill the last animal in a herd and especially those poor little calves."

I remarked that possibly she was the only person in camp who thought about it that way, but, unlike her people, I had learned that one must provide today what you are likely to need next week. I was possibly a little sharp with my answer.

"Oh, Peter!" she exclaimed, "don't be offended. I hate to hear you boasting. Let the others do that. I know you are the best buffalo hunter in the country but you do not have to talk about what they already know."

I was somewhat mollified by this remark but still doubtful of her actual meaning. I looked at her rather sternly; finally I had to laugh it off. Nevertheless, it had the desired effect for when I felt inclined to join my companions in extolling our luck and boasting as they were always inclined to do, I curbed my own inclinations and remained silent.

My wife was full of surprises. I never could tell whether she was making fun of me or really thought I was that good, and I never did find out.

Seenum decided to move the camp nearer to where the animals were killed. The flat where we had run the buffalo drained into the Vermilion River; I have been told that a railway passes along the route of that buffalo hunt. That night two of the scouts came into camp and reported only small scattered bunches of buffalo for many miles from where we were camped. It was lucky that we had killed what we could, for otherwise we would not have had enough to feed the camp and certainly not to fill our carts.

The other scouts also arrived in camp, and their story was the same: only a few scattered herds of from five to ten animals. They had covered the prairie in a radius of forty miles in all three directions, east, south, and west. The Indians called a meeting and decided to move to the west and thus be on their way home as soon as the meat was prepared.

I had expected to meet up with other Plains Cree, but apparently they had gone a long distance south in search of buffalo. Chief Seenum came to our teepee and said I would be in charge of the buffalo runners, and intimated that if our men could repeat the performance of that first hunt he would be satisfied that it might be good management, instead of just luck. Apparently my wife had been talking to the man, although he made his remarks in a kind of joking way. I made up my mind that if planning could do the trick, he would have to swallow his jokes.

I called the men into a secret conference, and repeated the

gist of the chief's remarks. They entered into the spirit of the test with enthusiasm and agreed with me that in the right locality and with a small herd it might work again.

The matter of having the scouts count the next herd they spotted was for my wife's benefit. If it was humanly possible, we were determined to repeat our performance. I suspected the wife had enlisted the chief in her efforts to curb my boastfulness.

We had been travelling west for two days but found no buffalo. Finally we made camp about forty miles south of the Saddle Lake ford. There the scouts came in to report a small herd of about ten animals northeast of our camp.

My fellow conspirators met again to discuss further details with as much careful deliberation as if they were planning a campaign against their ancient foes the Blackfoot. My orders were to kill no calves, only mature animals.

Our plans worked to perfection and we were successful in killing eight mature animals, leaving four calves. The camp knew about the results of the hunt before I entered my teepee. If I was expecting praise for our record, I was doomed to disappointment. "Peter," Charlotte said, "You ought to be ashamed of yourself, leaving those poor calves to starve on the prairie by themselves. It would have been better to have killed them all."

Perhaps that was once when silence was the best policy, but I could not help but tell her that leaving the calves was her idea not mine. I was only trying to please her when I ordered no calves killed. It would have been a waste of time to have explained that the buffalo cows weaned their calves at the first snowfall unless they were not in calf.

Eighteen head of domestic beef would have been a lot of meat, but when you realize that there were over a hundred people to feed and that the meat was all processed into dried meat and pemmican, and the bones roasted and broken for the marrow and poured into pemmican sacks, it was not surprising that we required a lot of buffalo to fill our needs. There was nothing wasted. The green hides were placed on frames, and the hair removed and made into parchments partially dried for tanning when we reached home.

Each family had brought dried saskatoons to mix with the pemmican and marrow fat for at least one sack, which was considered a delicacy. The berries were reboiled before being added to the pemmican.

We were almost all loaded when the chief decided to turn homeward, taking a roundabout course, in hope of running into a few more head to fill our carts to capacity. Our scouts located a herd of about twenty but this time our leader gave strict orders that we were to kill only four of the best animals. We got two cows and two young bulls. While I was restricted from making any boast, I made sure that my wife would have the benefit of the full story. Thus ended my first real disagreement with the good woman.

It was the custom of James Seenum's band to share their hunt with those unable to join the hunt for lack of means of travel, sickness or old age. The prepared provisions were brought home in the fall and were kept over for winter, if possible.

A successful hunt was a great blessing, as was suitably expressed by the minister's sermon the following Sunday. The church was crowded and I do not think that I ever witnessed a more devout congregation in all my experience. Mr. Steinhauer's sermon gave all the credit to Divine Providence and very little to the poor instruments who were used to bring this about. Whether by accident or intent, my wife's elbow sharp in my ribs expressed her complete agreement with this portion of the minister's otherwise wonderful sermon.

I think it had been during the winter of 1867 that a delegation of five men had come to have me word a petition to the Wesleyan Mission Board in Canada seeking assistance for support of a regular teacher for the children of the Goodfish and Whitefish Indians. The men were Benjamin Sinclair, Sam Jackson, Frederick Hawk, Jacob Stanley, and, if I remember right, John Long. They were successful in obtaining a regular teacher, or at any rate funds were provided for a teacher.

A man by the name of Snyder was their first regular teacher. He had little of the spice of human kindness or patience in his make-up. One day young Arthur Steinhauer ventured to remonstrate with the man over an unmerciful whipping that he had given one of the younger children. This was after school had been dismissed and the teacher was on his way back to his shack. Snyder lost control of his temper and attacked Arthur, who, being a capable athlete, was more than willing to respond in kind. He thoroughly thrashed the teacher. Snyder threatened to report the matter to Rev. Steinhauer. Arthur, realizing the seriousness of the situation, as his father the Rev. Steinhauer would certainly take action in the matter, came to me for advice. I told him to say nothing about it until I interviewed Mr. Snyder.

Mr. Snyder, who by this time was feeling the enormity of his bad behaviour, was painfully administering sedatives to his physical ailments when I strode in at his door without knocking. I explained my business and suggested that as there had been no witnesses to the encounter he withdraw his threat to report to the minister, as he had placed himself in a bad position in forcing a fight out of school with one of his pupils. He had by this time cooled off and was more amenable to reason. He agreed to keep the incident a secret and promised me that he would use more discretion in giving way to his temper.

Mr. Snyder was a newcomer to the West, and, after giving him a light lecture in the matter of his treatment of Indian children, I pointed out to him the grave danger to his life if he should arouse the enmity of the parents. There had been but a short lapse of time since the Indians had come under the influence of Christian teaching. I expressed some doubt as to the effectiveness of Steinhauer's influence should their recent savagery be aroused. The man listened with growing consternation on his face and promised to be more patient with the children. The man's conduct was a great deal more satisfactory but I always related the most gruesome incidents of Indian warfare and horse-stealing activities to keep him reminded of his danger.

I had a much more difficult time to persuade young Arthur to continue his studies under Snyder, but when I suggested that by not attending school the next morning he would release Snyder from his promise of secrecy, he finally agreed to give school another try. A few days later I found the two of them out in a boat fishing together. The teacher was smart enough to ask the boy's advice on fishing and hunting ducks and rabbits, and to allow Arthur the use of his very good eastern equipment. I was pleased to see them become friends. One good trouncing had done wonders for the man Snyder.

Whitefish in the lake spawn late in the fall and there was almost an entire migration of people around the lake for this last harvest of their bountiful year. They pitched their teepees in little towns of from five to ten teepees with all their families. If the weather remained mild and the fish wouldn't keep, they were cleaned, dried, and smoked; otherwise, in cold weather, they were strung on poles that pierced the tails.

The nets used were pitiably inadequate for a big catch. However, the fish were so plentiful that even the poorest nets got results. Among my purchases at Fort Garry were two factory-made whitefish nets. Having no nets of my own the preceding fall, I had had to depend on the generosity of my friends, which of course was not lacking. With these good nets, I could repay their help with abundance and share with those less able to provide for themselves.

My wife praised me for my generosity, little realizing how little effort it took with good nets to double and sometimes triple the catch of those with shorter, hand-made nets that were much inferior to mine. However, basking in the sunshine of her approval, I did not inform her as to those insignificant details.

During the winters of 1867 to 1870 I trapped furs and made a further trip to Fort Garry during the summer to sell my furs and obtain more goods for trade and supplies for my own household. Inkster doubled my credit that year and refused to share in the profits of the sale of his goods, charging interest only on the price of the goods taken. You can believe me, I was more than grateful for his treatment. In fact, I was just a little ashamed that I did not protest more and was so easily convinced, especially when he offered to let the Hudson's Bay man bid first on my consignment of pelts. This latter suggestion I refused, except that I told him that I had a standing account with the Hudson's Bay Company for one hundred and fifty dollars that I thought it only fair to have from their store.

"Certainly, Peter, that is perfectly all right with me. Totalling the share of the goods sold and your fur sales, you will have slightly over four hundred dollars of your own to buy as you see fit. I will give you two hundred dollars' worth of trade goods in addition, which I will choose as best suited to your needs in that region. With purchases from the Hudson's Bay Company, you will need another cart and horse. I have an outfit you can have very reasonably."

"Well, that will be fine," I replied, "but I must see your outfit first. I am rather particular about the kind of horse I use."

He laughed and said, "Of course, knowing you as I do, I hardly expected you would buy a pig in a poke."

All things taken into account, we had made a very profitable year's work. The goods I purchased from the Bay stores contained guns, traps, nets, and other articles used by trappers and hunters. These guns were greatly in demand as they were of later manufacture and not the previous muzzleloading long-barrelled atrocities that were formerly traded to the Indians.

Weather conditions were bad on the return trip. Roads consequently were in the worst condition possible. We were heavily loaded and could only make twenty miles a day, often times less than that. It was late in October when we finally arrived at Goodfish Lake, still eight miles from home with one horse played out. Sam Jackson was a welcome sight when he came along riding saddle with a horse on a lead line. "Peter, you take my saddle horse and hit the road for home. You became a father of a big son while you were fooling around on the trail. I will camp with your outfit tonight and take them through in the morning."

"Thanks, Sam, for your good news and help. But how on earth did you know I was here?"

"You were spotted on the trail at noon today by some duck hunters and they called to let me know."

This was typical of the many ways that the Indians of those days treated each other and those they thought to be friends; they never hesitated to put themselves out to perform some friendly act of neighbourly kindness.

Charlotte was all smiles and happiness when she presented our son for my inspection. "Peter! You must pick a name for him now. What will you call him?"

"James Bancroft Erasmus, because he is a tall baby and will have to grow to fit his name."

The balance of the winter of '69 and '70 followed the usual procedure: fishing in the fall, trapping and trading with the Indians, and planning for the annual trip to Fort Garry after trade goods and supplies. I had been too late to catch the fall buffalo hunt, but I had flour, tea, and sugar to trade for pemmican and fresh buffalo meat during the winter.

It was around the first of April 1870, when a man from the Victoria settlement came to Goodfish and told the people that Louis Riel had organized the French half-breeds and formed a government at the Red River settlement. He had appropriated the Hudson's Bay stores and had formed an army of his own to resist the constituted authorities of Canada. He had arrested a number of settlers from up the river and had condemned several to death for trying to resist his authority.[5]

The rumours grew with various other confused reports, so I saddled up a horse and went to see the man myself. This man had come to his brother Thomas Sinclair to warn him against going among the Indians as smallpox had broken out among some Plains Indians. He had obtained his information about Riel from two people whom I knew would not spread rumours unless they had some basis in truth. They had returned from Fort Garry a few days before his visit to Goodfish Lake.

There was no question in my mind that a trip to Fort Garry at this time would be risky, so I made up my mind to go with those who were preparing for a buffalo hunt. Our few carts from Whitefish Lake gradually increased, and by the time we had left Saddle Lake and crossed the river our teepees numbered thirty-five. By arrangement the hunters from Lac Ste. Anne and St. Albert were to join us at a point about thirty miles southeast of Beaver Lake.[6] They were already camped and waiting for us when we arrived.

As was customary when two or more groups joined

together, a meeting was called to elect a leader for the whole group, which now counted over fifty teepees and tents. The leader would have authority to enforce rules and regulations for the general good. The safety of a camp depended largely on the experience and good judgement of the man elected. The leader was chosen by the total vote of all the heads of families and any of the young men who were old enough to take responsible positions of trust in the duties of guards in camp or scouting for the camp.

The yearly decrease of buffalo made it necessary for us to travel much further south into the territory of the southern tribes to obtain supplies, but the larger party made it highly improbable that we would be attacked. Horses had to be guarded and scouts were sent out to find buffalo or keep watch for any enemy tribes who might be in the vicinity.

There were only three candidates mentioned for leadership in this election. Our party with James Seenum were in favour of a man from Lac Ste. Anne, a Scotch half-breed whose nickname was Ma-cheesk and whose given name was John Whitford. I had never met the man and did not know the other two men from Saddle Lake. Big Louis was one and the other I've long forgotten.

Apparently John Whitford enjoyed a reputation for leadership and was trusted for his judgement far above the other two. I was anxious to meet him and made inquiries as to where he could be found. No-one seemed to know where he had gone. I finally located his teepee but his wife informed me he had left before daylight with three other men but had promised to be back in time for the meeting that evening.

The other candidates I noticed were busy among the teepees, much the same as white men in present-day elections soliciting support. John Whitford's supporters were growing anxious as the time approached for the meeting and he did not put in an appearance. Our crowd from Whitefish would vote for him if he turned up, but failing that they would give their support to Big Louis.

The whole camp had assembled and were patiently waiting for the hour. There was a lot of talk going on among the Saddle Lakers but I noticed our crowd and those of Lac Ste. Anne and St. Albert anxiously scanning the prairie for their man. I watched all this with considerable interest. I asked Chief Seenum what would happen if the man failed to show up.

"No man can be chosen unless he is here to consent to his name," he replied, "but don't worry, he is sure to be here exactly on the hour."

Time was set by the position of the sun at the horizon. I thought to myself if Mr. John Whitford intends to be here he is cutting time very close.

I was talking to the chief when I heard a shout by a number of voices behind me. We both stood up to see what all the excitement was about.

"Yes," said the chief, "there is our man now and it wouldn't surprise me if he had found a herd of buffalo for the hunters tomorrow."

The chief was right on both counts. Whitford grounded, hitched his horse, and walked among the Lac Ste. Anne outfit while the other men joined where their friends were standing. One of the Goodfish Lake men came to Chief Seenum and told him they had found a small herd of fifty buffalo a half-day's ride east of our camp.

Chief Seenum strode to the centre of the circle, announced that it was time for the voting, and asked if they were satisfied to let Peter Erasmus count the votes. They all agreed. They were asked if they wanted to vote by a show of hands or by the use of sticks. It would be up to the three candidates to decide.

Big Louis said he preferred the sticks. Whitford agreed. The third man withdrew and left it between the other two. Each man was provided with two sticks, a short and a long. From the appearance of the sticks they must have been previously prepared, for they were distributed from a bulky deerskin sack. The chief explained that the short stick dropped in one bag would be for Whitford. Long sticks voted for Big Louis. Neither of the candidates were given any sticks. I presume that their votes offset each other.

I was handed two open sacks, one tied to my left belt for the no votes and the other to contain all votes cast for the two men. The two candidates sat together and took no part in the voting. However each man was represented by volunteers, one each to explain and supervise proper procedure. This was my first vote in any election up to that date, and I made certain the votes should be cast exactly as their rules called for.

My two helpers and I moved out on the grass away from the crowd while I counted our wooden ballots. Whitford was the winner by a majority of ten votes. Then I announced the winner without declaring the number of ballots in majority. Big Louis rose to his feet, shook hands with the winner and announced to his supporters that they should all give the leader now elected all the help and co-operation they were able to give. It was a unique experience for me; the election had been handled in a manner that would have shamed many of my latter-day experiences in what were called civilized elections.[7]

Whitford, as was the custom, announced that Big Louis would be second in command and named one man each from the other areas represented in the camp. Chief Seenum was his selection from Whitefish, Samuel Jackson from Goodfish Lake, another from Saddle Lake, and one from St. Albert. As he announced the selections, the crowd cheered their approval. I was delighted with the reception of Whitford's selection and his choice of members of his council.

Whitford was a man of great energy. The organization of the camp was accomplished in short order, each of us being informed by our representative on the council of our duties. I do not know when the man slept as he was always last to bed and the first man out in the morning. Arthur Steinhauer claimed you never knew when he would come around at night to check on the alertness of those doing guard duty.

The leader elected by the whole camp had complete authority in decisions for the camp's safety. Those selected on his council had advisory powers only. In the absence of the leader from camp in performance of duties connected with scouting or for any other reason, then the man he appointed as second in command would assume his duties and authority. Custom had established that the advice given in the advisory capacity of the council would be heard by the leader, but his final decision was law which must be followed.

A few days later I had the opportunity to witness a rather exciting example of the leader overriding a recommendation of council. We were a week at our first kill and were again moving south in the region of the Battle River when Whitford came in sight at a fast gallop. I was riding saddle alongside the long string of carts, so I rode up the lead cart to hear what caused his fast riding.

"There is a camp of Blackfoot directly in our course. Turn your carts and head due west."

The Crees and Blackfoot were supposed to be at peace that year and some of our Saddle Lake Crees protested this change of plan. The driver of the lead cart, a Saddle Laker, picked up his lines and loudly declared his refusal to abide by Whitford's order, at the same time lashing his horse straight ahead.

John Whitford wheeled his horse and levelled his gun at the man's chest and in a voice like a crack of a whip said, "You will follow my orders or die! It is better for one of us to die than risk the lives of everyone in this party. Turn your cart around now."

The man swung his horse around and headed for the west, lashing his horse unmercifully to show his anger.

We never stopped until we were ten miles away. Whitford rode in the lead and I thought foolishly exposed his back to the angry man in the lead cart. That evening the camp was assembled for a meeting which I presumed had been organized by the malcontents who resented Whitford's peremptory orders.

People had been gathering for a considerable time before the hour set for the meeting. All the men from Saddle Lake as well as a full quota of men from Lac Ste. Anne and St. Albert were present. There was an air of expectancy and excitement, and contrary to custom, many had guns at their side.

The loud talking and the murmur of many voices died to a complete silence when Whitford appeared among them, exactly on the time set for the meeting. Each side moved back to open a lane for him to the centre of the inner circle. He carried no weapons, not even the hunting knife common to the wardrobe of every man present.

Big Louis from Saddle Lake waved Whitford to the speaker's position and rather impatiently ordered silence among his own crowd, who had again started their angry arguments when our leader stepped into position for speaking.

His complete indifference and calmness in the face of the marked hostility and the many guns held by men in an ordinary camp meeting was amazing. When Big Louis had established order, Whitford stood silent, looking among the crowd as if in search of something. We all expected him to make a speech in defence of his threat to the cart driver. Finally he named a man among the Saddle Lakers and ordered him to come to the front and explain what he had seen and heard while riding with Whitford that forenoon.

The man very reluctantly came forward and explained that he had been on scout duty that morning riding with Whitford, to whom he had reported when he saw signs of a strange camp in the vicinity. They were following the signs when a Blackfoot Indian appeared, who, from a hundred yards away, warned them not to approach any closer. He told them their whole camp was infected with smallpox; many had died, even the hunters trying to keep the camp supplied had died out on the prairie. The man was barely finished with his story when Whitford spoke in a loud voice so all the men could hear. He ordered absolutely no contact with any person outside their own camp: "No-one from this camp will touch or handle anything belonging to others outside this camp." The Blackfoot custom of leaving a tent set up with a dead person's belongings which often was his gun and horse equipment made this order necessary.

Whitford went on with his warning: "Every dog in this camp must be tied up. Any dog found loose will be shot on sight. No-one will leave camp except under my orders or those of Big Louis, and every person returning from scout duty must report to Big Louis first before entering his own teepee. Big Louis will be on duty all daylight hours and I will be on hand during all the night hours. We will set up a special teepee to which every person leaving camp or returning will first report."

We were now actually prisoners in our own camp. Whitford then asked if there were any questions. Big Louis spoke up and said he would answer for his band and would see that the orders were obeyed. Chief Seenum said his band would follow orders without complaining. Whitford then stepped forward, and as before a lane opened for him to pass through.

I stayed on to see what reaction there would be among those chiefly concerned with calling the meeting. They were a chastened bunch. Now they turned their anger on the man who had failed to explain before the meeting Whitford's order to reverse the direction of travel. The poor fellow got a bad browbeating from his own crowd. It was useless for him to try to explain that he had returned from his scout duties just prior to the calling of the meeting.

I was not required to perform any scout or guard duties during the first few days of travel as Jim Jackson and I were assigned duties as buffalo runners for our party. We each had two of the best buffalo-running horses in our camp and consequently were picked by Chief Seenum for that task. Whitford had picked the men for various duties: camp guards, scouts, horse herders, and, of course, buffalo runners.

A big camp such as ours only allowed from four to eight men to take part in a buffalo run. The camp was divided in teams according to the size of the herd sighted. I noticed with some satisfaction that no-one grumbled or complained about the work assigned him. All accepted the various duties with alacrity. The night-camp guards were usually elderly men with experience, the scouts younger men who could stand lots of riding and at times camp out on the prairie. A buffalo runner could be any man with a good horse and gun and experience as a killer of buffalo. These latter men took turns in making kills in order to divide the work and give the horses a rest between runs.

Our scouts came in one day with word that they had located a good herd about a half-day's travel to the northwest, so the whole camp advanced in that direction the next morning. If we were successful in this hunt we would have sufficient meat to fill the carts and could then return home.

Whitford called all the buffalo hunters in together to advise us that he would double the usual number taking part in the hunt and that this would be our last chance to fill the carts. The council had decided that they must return as soon as they could as everyone was getting anxious about their people at home. There was a herd of over a hundred animals in a good position to use all the men for this final hunt of the year.

I had a black horse with a white face and three white stockings that had been raised by the Kootenay Indians. He had been picked from a hundred head owned by the chief. When I learned where the horse had come from, I doubled the price the man had paid for him and bought the animal. I knew of the former owner and the kind of horses he raised.

Bellerose from Lac Ste. Anne owned a beautiful roan mare. For conformation and build she was easily the best animal in camp. I had been urged to match my horse against his animal in a race for speed but I had consistently refused, for I knew that our Indians would bet their last blanket on a race of that kind. However, Bellerose was not in sympathy with my reasons for refusing to race, and had become increasingly boastful about the better quality and speed of his animal. The pressure was becoming somewhat irksome as I kept refusing to race my horse against his mare.

This would be the first time I would be teamed up with Bellerose in the hunt, and that day would put both animals to the test without hurting my friends. I had killed buffalo off his back and knew he was long winded and had a nice easy long stride but it had never been necessary to demand his full speed.

As I was riding out the next morning for the hunt, I told Jackson that it was my intention to try out the roan mare on the run after the buffalo. He was delighted over the prospect as I believe he resented the boastfulness of the Lac Ste. Anne crowd more than I did.

The buffalo were feeding over a ridge of hills about two miles from the camp. It was customary for all those taking part to wait in line for all men to get the same start, but the Lac Ste. Anne men were about fifty yards ahead when we came in sight of the buffalo. They started at once without waiting.

My friend Hunter riding behind me yelled, "Are you going to let those braggarts beat you?" At the same time I lashed my horse over the rump.

The decision was fairly taken out of my hands. The horse, already excited, plunged after the others in one breathtaking leap, then settled down to a race. We had approached to less than half a mile when the buffalo started to stampede. At a quarter of a mile, the roan was still ahead. I had now gained control of my black and he was still running strong and free. At the moment I was less concerned about killing buffalo than I was about beating the roan mare.

I thought to myself, the man has foolishly wasted her speed on the first quarter mile. I figured she was too light to hold a long-distance speed. We were catching up to the buffalo. I had to beat the mare before we merged with the herd. Hunter, who had kept close behind me all this time, now yelled, "You have got to beat him, Peter. My horse has no more speed."

For the first time now I touched him with the whip. The result was great. The black really responded, stretched his rather long neck, and within a few strides caught up the roan and passed her. I couldn't help but wave to him as I passed, hoping he would painfully squirm at his outright defeat with ten other riders to witness my victory.

We were among the herd before I could gather my wits about me. For some reason the herd had scattered and seemed to be running in two directions. I sighted on a cow that was crossing my path and the shot took such immediate effect that I had to swing my horse to avoid a collision. I heard a warning yell from behind me.

"Peter, look out for that bull!"

The warning came seconds too late to avoid his blind running. The huge fellow was charging straight at my horse. I just had time to free my feet from the stirrups and try to pivot the horse to avoid him, but I was too late. He struck the horse a glancing blow in front and knocked us both to the ground. I managed to clear my legs from being pinned under. The horse jumped to his feet but stood trembling and breathing very heavily. I tried to see through the cloud of dust what was going on around me. I picked up my gun that I had flung to the side while trying to clear myself away from the horse.

I walked around the horse, then I saw the blood squirting from a horrible gash on his shoulder. His shoulder muscles were ripped as if cut with a knife. I hastily made a pad with my horse blanket to stop the bleeding, but I could see it was useless as the bull's horn had pierced between the ribs. Hunter and Bellerose came back as they both saw the bull charging my horse. Bellerose raced his mare back to the camp for medicine to stop the blood, riding a fresh horse back on a dead run, but it was all for nothing; the horse was bleeding inside and died that night in spite of everything we did to help.

I believe Bellerose felt as bad about the accident as I did, for he stayed with me and helped all he could till the horse was dead a few hours afterward. We both knew that we were to blame. Racing our horses to beat each other, we had not watched ourselves; we were more interested in running our horses than attending to our work of killing buffalo. Fortunately the other riders had killed sufficient for our needs and we would be on our way home as soon as the meat could be cured.

It appeared another small herd had been feeding and resting just over the ridge where we stampeded the big herd. They had jumped to their feet when the other buffalo crossed their path. A frightened bull when suddenly aroused or excited will charge anything in his path and apparently I was in the line of his maddened flight.

I was feeling pretty bad when I returned to my teepee, not so much at the loss of the horse but at my own stupidity and foolish pride in trying to win a race when I had other business at hand.

My wife said, "Forget it, Peter. You ought to be thankful that your life is spared. You might have been trampled to death or badly hurt. As long as our children are healthy and we are both well, we ought to be thankful to our Master for all the good things we have and for sparing your life."

Curing the meat took another five days. Then the camp broke up and we started for home. We travelled together to a point a few miles from where we had held the election for leader, and then the Lac Ste. Anne and St. Albert people turned north to their home while we turned northeast to the Saddle Lake Crossing. I took particular notice of the cordial manner in which Whitford's early opponents parted with him. We had made a successful hunt and had met with no enemies. We all had full carts and everybody was satisfied and in good spirits.

CHAPTER TWELVE

Smallpox

T HIS WAS NOT TO LAST FOR LONG. A rider caught up with us to bring bad news. Whitford had sent the man to give us the warning: smallpox had broken out at Lac Ste. Anne. The messenger told us to take every precaution against any contact with other people and to continue the same vigilance throughout the balance of our trip home. Even after we got home we would have to make every effort to keep our people free from the disease. Touching the clothes of a sick person, or living in the same teepee was dangerous. Complete isolation was the only preventive, as there was no known cure.

It was depressing news as very few Indians of Seenum's band had ever had any experience with the disease. At our first camp the chief called a meeting which everybody, men, women and older children, were ordered to attend. The chief asked me to speak on what I knew about the disease. There was little I could tell except to emphasize the need to avoid contact with other people, even their own relations who would be waiting at home. I told them that their only hope was to separate and take their families into the bush if they would save themselves. They would have to shoot their dogs or keep them continuously tied up.

There were two men present who had contracted the disease

and had recovered. They were asked to explain anything they knew about the symptoms or a possible cure. One man's graphic description of the horrors and futility of attempting anything except complete isolation from other Indians made a deep impression on the people, but I knew that the close ties of relationship among my Indian friends would be too strong to let them cut themselves off from the children and old folks left in their homes.

It was a hopeless situation and the more depressing because I knew there was a preventive serum which was impossible to obtain in time to save many of these people. The Indians were doomed by the very qualities that were admirable: their loyalty to relatives; the sharing of their things with the band; their devotion and sympathy for any sick person; their continuous visiting of any ailing person, and kissing of children and women who met together even after a parting of a few day's duration. I knew that habits of a lifetime could not be thrust aside, except by the bitterest of experience. The people of James Seenum's band practised far greater consideration of Christian sharing in their joys and pains than many white people of my later experience.

Smallpox had already reached Saddle Lake, and Big Louis sent riders with us to escort us past any possible contact with Indians of his locality. He kept his own people in camp, isolated from the others, until he could find out the true situation among the people there.

We found that the smallpox had also started at Whitefish and Goodfish Lakes. Cart drivers who had been hired to take carts to Fort Garry for the Hudson's Bay Company had contracted the disease on their way and had been turned back from Fort Pitt.

Peter Makokis, one of the men who had come back sick, had banished all his family to the bush in order to keep them free from sickness, and warned others to do the same. He had pitched a tent on Cardinal's Point to avoid passing the disease on to other people.

I dreaded the thought of exposing my own family, but as Steinhauer had gone to Canada in the early spring, he had left me the responsibility of his household and some of his duties; I felt that I could not leave, as many others were doing.

We heard of Peter Makokis's helplessness as soon as we arrived near our home. I spoke to the wife about the man staying by himself away from any help in his sickness, and the responsibility left me by Mr. Steinhauer, but she begged me not to put myself in danger as it was the responsibility of his relations to take care of him. When I told her what the man had done to save his own people, she withdrew her objections.

"Peter," she said, "if you feel it is your duty to see after the man, then you must go. We can only pray to God for our protection and yours. You will have to stay by yourself. Should anyone come here, I will tell them you are away looking after sick people. I'm sure no-one will come near after that. We will be all right here till this is over."

There was a terrible fear among the Indians. Few had ever been exposed to the disease. Makokis being the first man to fall sick, his warning had been taken seriously. Many had followed his advice but others refused to heed the warnings and suffered losses in consequence.

I found Makokis in a bad way, his body completely covered with pox from head to foot. It was a revolting sight, though he was still capable of moving around. He scolded me for risking my life in coming to his aid. However, later, his gratitude was pitiable in such a strong-willed man who had voluntarily sacrificed all ties with his family, knowing he might never see them again. My arrival that afternoon seemed to improve his condition and he slept well through the night. The following morning he took some nourishment and was visibly cheerful, and I grew hopeful of his recovery. He asked me to read portions of the scripture and later on he again took food.

The evening was advancing towards night when he called me back from the outside campfire and gave me explicit instructions for the disposal of his property; judging by those days' standards he was quite well off, with horses, cattle, and carts. I pointed out to him that he had showed a great improvement since I came and tried to persuade him that he would get well.

"No, my friend! There is no need for us to hide the truth from each other. I knew my death was certain when I parted with my family. It will be enough if they survive as I have prayed day and night that they would be saved." Strangely enough his prayers were answered, for none of his immediate family suffered from the pox.

That night he grew delirious and by morning was dead without regaining consciousness. There were other deaths at the two places but none with the extreme suffering of Peter's case. Some of the more stubborn refused to heed the necessity for destroying all clothing of the sick persons, even though they were in some cases lightly affected, and others caught the disease with much more severity.

A Stony Indian named Pan-eza Sa-win came to my assistance shortly before the death of Makokis. He was an elderly man and told me he was not afraid of the sickness as he

211

had got over it several years earlier. When he heard I was with Makokis he came and offered his help and said he knew a medicine that would make us safe from catching the disease. He had us both stripped naked and we washed our bodies with some solution of his own. He warned me not to come in contact with any part of the corpse. I had no faith in his medicine, but whatever the reason, I did not catch the disease. We rolled the bodies onto a parchment and carried them to previously dug graves. Sa-win, though an unbeliever, insisted that I say a few words at each burial.

We burned everything used by the sick people after they had recovered or were dead. Sa-win made all those who survived wash themselves with his solution before they were given other clothes. I am confident that the old chap helped save many, whether his medicine was effective or not, because the fact of his confidence in its potency and the cheerful way that he inspired faith in his cures sparked a hope that certainly was effective.

At last the epidemic was over. The terror and fear that had gripped the people was gone and no new cases developed. The people who had fled to the bush returned with the colder weather. Life went on as before except for the scattered graves and the missing places of those who were gone. I was grateful, happy, and truly thankful for the escape of my family and myself. I do not think there was any time in my life that I was more aware of God's divine reality than at the moment of being united with them again. We went to our knees and most fervently thanked God for his mercy and protection and prayed for comfort for the bereaved, who had lost their protectors and loved ones from their homes.

There were fifty of Seenum's band who died as the result of smallpox that year, not all of whom were at Whitefish during that time. Many had been in other areas when caught with the disease. It was not till the following year that a full accounting of the people could be made with any accuracy. Those who had escaped the pox gave clothing and bedding to those whose clothes were burned. Our own household was stripped to the essentials to help the survivors.

Due to the sickness there were few people able to do any trapping. Our own catch was very poor and we deemed it inadvisable to make the long trip to Fort Garry.[1] We would have to depend on food supplies natural to the bush country, but there was no danger of starvation. Whitefish and five other species of rough fish were numerous in the lake. Prairie chicken, partridge, and rabbits were plentiful that winter, and I knew that the lakes during the summer would be dotted with ducks in their thousands.

I still had a good supply of powder and shot and a fair amount of lead bullets used for bigger game. I thought I had enough ammunition to keep all the band from need with a little care in rationing each man's share. The hardest part would be getting along without flour, sugar, and tea, once considered a luxury and once thought unnecessary to our living. As a youth of fifteen, I had given my tea away because I disliked the taste, but kept the sugar as it was a novelty to my existence up to then.

My brother Henry came to visit me and I had him stay for the winter to join me in the trapping. In the spring he offered to go into partnership; he would do the travelling and share in the purchase of goods for trade. I accepted, as I was tired of the months lost by being on the road. I also wanted to do some building. I could then stay home and take care of the family.

Henry started for Fort Garry on a saddle horse with pack horses to carry his duffle and the furs. He would buy two carts to bring back the supplies and trade goods. He carried what was left of the two winters' catch which would amount to about four hundred dollars in value as my share. It was arranged that I would meet him at Fort Carlton in August.

In July I joined a small party of six carts and was successful in finding a small herd of buffalo northeast of where the town of Vegreville was later built. We loaded our carts and were home in less than two weeks.

Each year I noted the buffalo were getting harder to find. On this trip our scouts covered a radius of twenty-five miles each side as we went south to where we found that small herd. The vast herds that crowded the banks of the Saskatchewan River and crossed over even into the timber country fifteen to twenty miles north of the river were no longer to be found. The words of Captain Palliser and Dr. Hector often occurred to me. I had not believed that the vast herds could possibly be killed in so short a period of time. Only eleven years had gone by and there was now less than one animal for the hundreds that could once be found within a few days' ride of the North Saskatchewan River. The Crees with whom I had talked carried the same tale of the rapid deterioration of buffalo numbers that reached to the borders of the United States. They also told stories, carried from one to the other among the tribes, that great herds of skinny cattle, with horns longer than both arms of a man could reach, were being driven into the prairies of the south border country. Captain Palliser had said, "Vast herds of long-horned cattle from Texas will take the place of the buffalo." I had no doubt now that all the things he and Hector had predicted for this country were about to take place.

213

I started with two carts to meet my brother at Fort Carlton. William Bull had asked to go along. He said, "If you will take some tanned buffalo robes and my few furs along, I will handle one of your carts."

Bull was a grand story teller, and the whimsical, humorous way he told his tales of the former glories and exploits of his tribesmen in their wars and horse stealing raids made his company an interesting and entertaining way to spend rainy days and long evenings while we rested our horses. William Bull's knowledge of the Bible, which he had acquired from the Rev. H. B. Steinhauer, and our many discussions brought out facts that suggested that his people were one of the lost tribes of Israel. He had a story of the flood, an Indian version that was most convincing. He demanded that I account for their story of the Ark. Why did his people have a knowledge of something that he had only learned to be true because it was written in the Bible? Steinhauer had also told him that certain of his tribe's rules concerning women had a similarity to practices of the Jews. He had other arguments that all the church education I had received could not refute, yet he was a man who could neither read nor write.

We reached Carlton hoping to meet my brother, but there was no word of his presence on the trail. There were several carts just returned from Fort Garry. Then Richard Hardisty arrived. I inquired if he had heard any word about Henry.

"I'm afraid I have bad news for you. I had a long talk with Inkster and he told me that your brother arrived with the furs and sold them, paying off your debt, but had drawn the balance due and took the money with him. Later he was seen drinking with two strangers but when he woke up next morning, he was stripped. He didn't have a cent. The men were arrested but the case was dismissed for lack of evidence."

I was shocked but managed to say, "Oh, well! He is my brother and it will do no good to go there now. I will have to return empty handed."

Hardisty expressed sympathy, and offered to load my carts for delivery to Lac La Biche, paying two dollars and a half per hundred pounds. This was a big help, so I bought what supplies I could afford and started on my way home.

I hated to think of Charlotte's disappointment when I told her the bad news. I was keenly disappointed over my brother's carelessness. I knew of his addiction to liquor but thought that he had outgrown the weakness. The thing that made me so angry was the fact that he had fallen for one of the oldest confidence games of the West. Whisky was used by every unscrupulous crook in the country to take advantage of any unsuspecting victim for his money or furs. Many carried out their various schemes under the guise of being free traders.

The southern portion of the country in Blackfoot and Peigan territory was polluted with so-called traders whose unbridled use of rotgut whisky was creating havoc amongst the once-proud Blackfoot nation and their allies.[2] The Americans from across the border of Montana had established so-called trading posts within our border and had accomplished what the thousands of Crees had failed to do in their best days, namely the subjugation of the southern tribes. The American long-range rifles and their speed with the short gun while they plied the natives with whisky and cheated them out of their belongings was a disgrace to a civilized nation.

It was with horror and impotent rage that I had listened to a recital of the growing power that these degenerate adventurers who acknowledged no authority but their unmerciful use of guns and whisky to victimize the natives. A man named Felix Monroe, who had been a Blackfoot interpreter with the Palliser expedition in '58, spent half the night telling us of the many misdeeds going on in that part of the territories.

I was in those days indifferent to the need of government, but now was fully awake to the fact that nothing could save my Indian friends but some authoritative action to oust these American vagabonds and leeches who were sucking the very life blood of the southern tribes.

My old friend Spence had kept me informed of the controversy raging in the settlement of the Red River and Fort Garry that ended with the Rebellion of 1869-70, the final outcome of which I had learned on this trip. During the transition of authority from the Hudson's Bay Company to the Government of Canada I had taken a neutral stand, not joining with any side in the disputed matters concerned with this change. I deemed the whole question was not of my concern, living in the western Territories. It would be some time before we were affected.[3]

The matter of annexation to the States was a different matter. Its accomplishment even to a minor degree by the usurping of authority by these unprincipled traders in our territory fairly made my blood boil as nothing had in all the years of agitation, petitions, and what-not that had predated the Riel Rebellion. I welcomed the news that a high official of the Government of Canada was being sent out to the West to investigate actual conditions and report recommendations.[4]

It was variously rumoured in Hudson's Bay circles that as a result of this investigation a police force would be made available to the Territories and that some form of authoritative government would be established. I found myself adopting a completely different attitude. It had now become a personal matter by the loss of two winters' labour in trapping and trading.

The continued decrease of buffalo on the prairies was creating considerable resentment among the Indians whose livelihood depended completely on the buffalo. Though poison bait was unheard of among the northern tribes, a supply was being used and made available by these southern traders. Indian dogs had been killed by the baits set out for wolves and coyotes, and it was a common belief that horses had been poisoned by eating grass where an unrecovered carcass had decomposed. If horses could die, they argued, then buffalo would also be killed.

Isolated among the northern tribes, I had not given these matters much thought. My personal loss by one of these rogues filled me with a resentment almost beyond my control. At the moment I did not credit my brother's weakness for drink a factor of any importance. I had fervently expressed my hearty approval at Carlton and Fort Pitt and definitely stated that it would be easy to recruit help to route those whisky traders and crooks who were engaged in that nefarious business.

When we got back home, Charlotte received my bad news with her usual fortitude. "Well, Peter! Using your own words, it is tough luck. We are both healthy and we can still hunt and fish. We will leave our two boys with my mother and make that trip to Beaver Lake that you claim is swarming with mink."

"Look here, woman! It will be impossible for you to go along. We will have to go on saddle horse and bring our stuff on pack horses. How can you take the girl along? Three children will be too much for your mother and I will not allow it."

"Forget your objections," she replied, "I have made up my mind. If there are as many mink on that creek as you claim, you will have no time to trap, skin and prepare the pelts as well as cook your meals, and besides we both have to work to recover our losses this winter."

The weather was very mild for that time of year in the latter part of October 1870, after a sharp period that froze the small lakes. I made a last effort to change my wife's idea of braving the trip but it was useless. "We can be at that creek in four days. We have a good tent and the weather is mild. Look at this fur-lined bag that I have made for our girl. Hundreds of Indian children have been carried for centuries in this kind of thing. My mother helped me make it. Besides, she is only too eager to have our boys in her care while we are away."

I gave up the argument but I slammed the door good and

hard to show her that I was not fully convinced, but I came back with an extra saddle horse for her. I knew it might be a tough trip, for it was over one hundred and forty miles to where I expected to set our traps.

The weather remained mild all the way till we reached our destination, which was a creek that entered into Beaver Lake on the north side. I was glad to find signs of mink as I was a little afraid the place had been trapped as I had been there almost three years ago. The ice was marked in many places where the mink had been on to the shore ice to eat fish. We picked a good campsite among young spruce. I cut pine brush for a mattress, then ate a hurried lunch that my wife had prepared while I was making the tent ready. I was anxious to make some sets before dark.

The place without any exaggeration was swarming with mink signs. I made a dozen good sets within a short distance. My wife had a big supper ready when I returned at dark, quite elated over the prospect of a good catch. She was all smiles over my enthusiasm. It must have been a welcome change for her after my conduct of the last five days. I guess she must have been happy that I had finally dropped my miserable brooding and dismal thoughts.

The next morning our twelve traps netted eight mink, all large pelts. I was delighted, as my investigations up and down the creek showed every indication of continued good luck. We would soon recoup our losses at the rate we were catching mink.

We were soon on our knees for our morning devotions, thanking God for our health and continued success; I prayed forgiveness for those whose evil had brought us misfortune. As we went about our preparations for the day's hunt, I noticed tears of joy in my wife's eyes, for at last she knew I had overcome my resentment and anger. Strangely enough my mind seemed cleared of its dark thoughts. I felt happy and eager to start the day's work.

We moved our camp only after trapping out sections of the creek. By the middle of December we had sixty mink pelts of excellent grade and now had nearly exhausted all the best mink runs. We were getting short of provisions. It would be a day's ride to Edmonton but I did not care to leave Charlotte and the little girl overnight without protection. It would take two days for the trip.

There were moose in the Beaver Hills and red deer but I did not have too much confidence in my ability as a bush hunter. My best chance would be to locate an odd buffalo that might be sheltering at the edge of the hills along Beaver Lake.

I was making ready for a hunt when Thomas Makokis rode in on a saddle horse. He was the first human being we had encountered since our arrival on the first of November. You can imagine how glad we were to see him. I abandoned the hunt for the day and turned my horse loose again.

"I'll go with you tomorrow, Peter, if you'll let me have a horse as my own is tired from the long ride."

"That suits me fine," I replied. "If we don't find a buffalo tomorrow, we can try for a moose as I know you're a good bush hunter."

I was not too hopeful of finding buffalo within a day's ride from our camp but I knew of a place from previous hunting trips where I had always depended on finding a few animals. So I had to prove myself wrong. Makokis was riding about a mile to the east of me, walking his horse back and forth on a ridge as a sign he had found something. I rode over to where he was waiting.

"Peter, I've found fairly fresh tracks of two buffalo. We may be in luck yet after all your gloomy talk when your favourite area proved empty."

After back tracking for a short way we came to the conclusion that the buffalo had been ranging in the locality for quite some time. The tracks were only a couple of days old. We went back to where we had first tracked the animals, made lunch and left our packs there. Within a mile we saw two buffalo feeding close to a clump of willow and poplar trees. We made a wide detour to get the bush in between us and the animals in order to get as close as possible before they stampeded. We were almost a quarter of a mile away when they came around the bush in plain sight.

We gained another one hundred yards at a walk before they saw us. Immediately they whirled and both raced away. My horse, Whitey, was a replacement for the black I had killed in the race. This would be the first time I had ridden him in a chase after buffalo, although the former owner claimed the horse was one of the best he ever rode. He seemed to be very slow, as in the first quarter mile I hadn't gained any distance on the two animals, but after about a half mile he gained rapidly. I realized Whitey knew his work, for as he drew alongside one of the buffalo I could have almost touched it with my gun barrel. I aimed for a vital spot and let him have it. The bull ran a few yards then dropped in his tracks, and Whitey tore up snow and almost unseated me as he whirled to take after the other animal that had turned in another direction. I had trouble getting my horse under control as he reared, grabbed at the bit, and pranced sideways in his eagerness to get on with the run. I was

218

well satisfied that his former owner had not exaggerated his value.

Thomas was in the meantime taking a leisurely gait to come up to where I had killed the bull. I asked him why he didn't try after the other animal.

He said, "I was keeping my ammunition in reserve in case the Blackfoot owner of that appaloosa horse should show up."

I had bought the horse from a Saddle Laker who claimed to have stolen him from the centre of a Blackfoot camp while tied to the owner's peg lines.

I figured that we would skin the buffalo, take a chunk of meat back to camp, and come for the meat with pack horses.

"No need of that," said Thomas. "While you're roasting a nice piece of meat, I'll make a pair of toboggans to take the meat back with us. You go for some grey willow poles, four of them slightly longer than a fathom; bring them back and then get busy on that roast. I'm starving for a taste of fresh meat."

I rode to the nearest bush to get the sticks he wanted and when I returned he already had the hide off and was cutting the meat up in quarters and laying the pieces aside in two piles. By the time I had the roast nicely browned, he was cutting the hide in half lengthways and with the sticks was shaping what looked like a boat, with slits cut at the edge of the hide and the sticks inserted in place and laced with shaganapee strips and the meat placed inside as he drew the sides together. I could see it would serve the purpose though I still had my doubts about how hard it might pull behind a horse.

I called him to start on the roast; in spite of his declaration of hunger he reluctantly left the job and came to eat. After we had eaten a good meal and drank several cups of tea, Makokis said that by the time I brought the horses, he would have things ready to go.

"Better get on your horse while I fasten him to the load. Whitey may have objections to becoming a cart horse after being a big Blackfoot chief's riding horse. Watch yourself. He may decide to go back to the Blackfoot if he gets a look at what's behind him. Only a gun shot will stop him if he ever gets started."

I was not too sure that the shaganapee-improvised harness would stand much of a load. I had even used my leather gun cover for a breast pad. Whitey showed no liking for the new rigging but when I climbed on his back he quieted down and let Thomas fasten the straps to the load. The horse didn't like the new work at all. He plunged ahead a few steps, then stopped and lashed out with both hind feet. He finally settled down to going ahead with only an occasional kick. I was surprised how easily the load pulled through the snow. Thomas waved to me to keep going. His horse was a good cart horse and I knew he would have no trouble.

After a time I stopped and rested the horse without too much trouble. Thomas caught up shortly before we reached our small packs and advised me against getting off the horse.

"Stay on your horse. I wouldn't trust a Blackfoot or his horse in the best of times. If that beggar gets a look at what's behind him, he'll throw you sky high and kill himself running away from the load."

It was long after dark when we finally reached the camp. Thomas still insisted that I stay on saddle until he had unfastened the tugs. We scraped the snow away and gave the horses a good feed of barley, but Whitey continued to snort and show his disapproval all the time he was eating the grain.

The wife was still up and had supper waiting, delighted at the news of our kill. She and Thomas had a good talk, all about the things at home and about the children, as he had gone to Whitefish from Saddle Lake, and then came directly to our camp from there.

The next day there was a regular blizzard blowing and it grew steadily colder. Our discarded tin container that did duty as a stove could hardly keep the tent warm though we banked up the sides with pine brush and snow. The wife was worried about the little girl. She was listless and wouldn't eat anything all day, just lying quietly without making any fuss. She had been always full of play and talk.

We finally decided we would try to go home as soon as the storm let up. We had Thomas take care of the girl while we went out and brought our traps in. The wife had caught ten more mink since Thomas arrived, and we took two more out of the traps that morning. We now had seventy-two mink pelts — and they would be quite a bulky pack.

Five mink for each of the two days she had attended our sets, a great deal better than I had been doing, as I could get only one or two a day. There was no doubt who was the better trapper; even after six winters I could not equal her results.

The snow was now quite deep, and as we couldn't take much of the meat along we made a cache, covering the pile of meat with snow and brush and packing it solid; then we froze water over the whole thing. By morning it would be impossible for wolves or coyotes to dig into it. We would direct someone to where we had left the cache so that it need not be wasted.

We made a late start when the weather cleared but we made twenty miles that first day. Thomas was leading on a pack trail that cut off many miles. He knew of a trapper's shack that had been used the previous winter. It had a tiny fireplace and we were quite comfortable that night. The girl did not cry but seemed to sleep a great deal more than was natural.

During the night there was another heavy snow, the weather had turned much warmer and it was still snowing when we started out the next morning. Travel was slow, though we followed each other in single file and frequently changed places to break trail. We had set our next stop for a place that was later to be called Andrew but all the horses were getting leg weary plowing through the deep snow. It was growing dusk and we were still several miles from our destination. Thomas was some distance in the lead and I saw him stop, turn his head in a listening attitude. I was curious to know what he heard.

"I hear dogs barking north of us. Perhaps we had better go there and get your girl into a warm tent. Our horses are too tired to make much further."

"Go ahead," I said. "Anything is better than risking a night camp without a fire in the tent for the girl. I'm afraid she is very sick and Charlotte must be terribly tired but she refuses to let any of us carry her."

We came in sight of two buffalo teepees in less than a mile of travel. The barking dogs roused the inmates and four people came out of the teepees to greet us. They invited us to camp. An elderly woman walked up to my wife and took the girl from her arms. The young man recognized Thomas and asked him to share their teepee, offering to take care of the horses. They had hay and a barn, though they kept no horses.

The elderly people apologized for not being able to provide us with much food but said they would share what they had. Their hunter had been unable to kill any moose or deer. They had rabbits and nothing else to eat. They wouldn't hear of us using our own tent.

"Our teepee is big enough for all of you. Besides I want the little girl where I can watch her and take care of her during the night. That child is real sick."

I was too weary and worried to reply. When we had stripped the saddles and packs from the horses, I took a good chunk of buffalo meat to each tent. Imagine the joy and thankfulness with which this was received. It is a pitiable thing to see children's hungry eyes shining in anticipation of food after semi-starvation.

The cold weather and the thick crust had made it impossible to get within range of a moose with the gun they had in camp, a muzzleloader of ancient vintage that from its worn appearance would not be accurate at fifty or sixty yards.

221

When I re-entered the teepee where my wife and girl were, I heard the woman say, "Do not worry, daughter. I will have your little girl laughing and playing before the sun sets twice more."

Charlotte broke down and cried as if her heart would break. I didn't realize what a strain she had been under, blaming herself for taking the little girl out when I had been so much against it. I said nothing but I made up my mind that these kindly people would be well repaid before I left their teepees. Somehow I felt confident that the woman would make good her promise to the wife.

I do not know if the women folk slept that night, but I talked with the man past midnight and then lay down fully dressed except for removing my footwear. Charlotte woke me when breakfast was ready, placing her finger on her lip for silence. She beckoned me to the child's bedside. The child was sleeping soundly and breathing naturally again. Her mother had a look of utter contentment and happiness that I shall never forget as she turned back to assist with breakfast.

"Your girl," said the woman, "has been very sick. She will get well now but it would be unwise to travel with her for at least five days. Then you will have to have a sleigh and keep her warm all the time."

We were in a serious predicament. The amount of food we had with us would not feed seven adults and five half-grown children. It was up to me to plan up something to relieve the situation.

After I had a talk with Thomas, we decided that I would make a trip to Victoria, which was only ten miles northeast of us, to trade for some supplies. Thomas would take my gun and lend his own to the young man in the other teepee. The new snow and the milder weather would give them a better chance to stalk moose.

We all started from camp together but after a few miles they turned west and I continued north to Victoria. I was riding Whitey and leading a pack horse in case I could get a sleigh. I wondered what changes there would be since my last stay when working for McDougall. I had heard scraps of information about settlers in the area but as our hunting was in a different direction we did not often meet.

I went to the Hudson's Bay post first. A man by the name of Adams was in charge but his offer for my furs was not good enough so I went to an independent trader by the name of McGillvery.[5] His offer was much better so I sold to him. The two buffalo robes that I had to sell he advised me to take to the Rev. Mr. Campbell who had inquired about robes.

The Rev. Campbell was busy in his study when I called. He was a very pleasant mannered man, quite cordial but altogether too voluble for my business of selling the robes. I did not mention my name as I knew this might touch off another volume of questions and answers. I was getting impatient and finally had to say, "Do you want these robes or not, Mr. Campbell? I have business to attend to that requires my immediate attention." I planned on starting back as soon as possible.

"Oh, the robes. Yes, certainly I want them. Did I not say so? I will give you a year-old steer for the robes and that chunk of buffalo meat you said you had. You return me a good roast from your calf, if you care to. Now will that be satisfactory?"

"Your offer is more than satisfactory, sir, and I appreciate your generous terms. The beef will solve our immediate needs."

"Oh, well," he replied, "you cannot let people starve if you can help it, can you? By the way, sir, you speak remarkable English for this part of the country. What is your name?"

Now that I had accomplished my purpose I was willing to tell him who I was. It cost me another two hours of time although I did not begrudge the loss, in that he gave me a lot of information regarding the settlement and the work of the McDougalls. My only source of information was by word of mouth; there was no mail service. Victoria was only fifty miles from Goodfish or Whitefish, yet the two areas were as isolated as if they had been hundreds of miles away. My two hours with the minister was not enough to cover all the information we had to exchange.

I learned that there were now quite a number of people in the area who had settled along the river at Victoria and up to what was later to be called the Lobstick settlement, about twelve miles along the Saskatchewan: Norns, Whitfords, Turners, the McGillvery family, Howse, Andersons, Favolls, a man by the name of Thompson, and a Norwegian bachelor who was starting a ranch with horses and cattle. Samuel Whitford was a man I knew from the Red River who had several married sons. Plans were being made to build a school which would serve a dual purpose as church as well, three miles up the river. The minister was enthusiastic over the attendance at his church services at Victoria.

John McDougall had taken charge of a mission at Morley the year previous, in 1872. I was told that the Wesleyans had decided to open a mission for the Stonies on the Bow River. Rev. George was permanently resident at Edmonton. Thus I was brought up to date on the church work and exchanged news of Steinhauer's work at Whitefish Lake. Only the urgency of getting ready for an early start the next morning forced me to leave.

I butchered the calf that night and sold the hide to McGillvery. He loaned me a sleigh and harness to take my load back, saying I could return it at my convenience as he had another and wouldn't need it that winter. Picking a generous choice roast the next morning, I sent it over to the mission by messenger as I was afraid if I went myself I might be tempted to continue our talks.

The road was heavy and it took me nearly all day to reach the camp. Thomas and the other man had killed a moose the day before and had wounded another and had gone again to fetch some of the meat and track up the wounded animal. They returned shortly after I reached camp in high spirits. I could hear them laughing and talking long before they reached camp.

"You must have been in luck today by all the noise you are making," I said.

"Yes, we're happy," replied Thomas. "We got a dry cow we wounded yesterday and there is the proof," as he slung a sack at my feet. Sure enough I found the bag filled with inside fat that could only come from a dry cow at that time of year. A person's body craves for fat when they are on a diet of lean meat and very little else.

I was anxious to be on my way but wanted to be certain that the little girl was completely well before leaving. However, these kindly people urged us to stay.

"I can see you are getting restless, Peter, but I'll tell you just as soon as I think it is safe to travel with your child."

Thomas took three of the horses and the old man drove the dog team to go for the balance of the meat. They wouldn't let me go with them.

"Your Whitey is useless to pack. Besides, I couldn't be bothered to look after you and the Blackfoot horse. You had better stay home and get ready for when we start home again. All we have to do is load the meat and return to camp."

Not feeling too happy being teased about riding a stolen horse, and also irked by Thomas's disregard for the rather exorbitant price I had paid for the animal to the former owner, I turned and walked back to the teepee. The young Hawk, who occupied the neighbouring teepee, set out the next morning to fetch the meat we had left at Grassy Creek. It was a two day trip across country the way he would have to go.

We had been in camp six days. I was growing more impatient at the delay and idleness each day. I could see nothing wrong with our girl and wondered if we were being delayed for a purpose. That night the Hawk got in with his load of buffalo meat and we were told that the girl would be ready to travel the next day. It appeared they were holding us back until the young man arrived with the meat.

I refused to take any of the buffalo meat except a few choice pieces for the road. Finally the old gentleman said, "We will keep the meat if you will accept two tanned moose skins as a gift." To have refused would have insulted their hospitality. I left them all the remaining powder and balls that we had.

"Thomas, give your gun to the young man," I said. "I have another newer gun at home of the same calibre. You can have it in its place. They will not refuse the gun and I would like to express my appreciation to them for helping our girl." They were a grateful and happy family that bid us goodbye and they were true friends for years afterwards.

CHAPTER THIRTEEN

The Last Big Buffalo Hunt

T HE BALANCE OF THE WINTER of '73 I spent trapping on our assigned trapping grounds. I built a new log house in the summer of '74, and went out as usual on buffalo-hunting parties after provisions. The buffalo were getting so scarce that it was doubtful if we could come back with full carts or half loads. There was not the choice that we once had. We had to be satisfied with anything that we could get.

In 1874, news spread among the Indians that the Queen Mother had sent out Red Coats, Police, to drive the whisky traders out of the country. There was much speculation among the people. For myself, I was delighted when I heard the news. However, opinions were divided among the James Seenum band in regard to the restrictions that might be placed on their travels and hunting. The Rev. Mr. Steinhauer did much to calm the fears of those who were worried by the show of authority on the prairies.

I was frequently at a loss for answers to questions about government that I faced from my Indian friends. It was difficult to explain to those people the necessity for control of the unscrupulous traders who were ruining the Indians with bad whisky and unbridled murder. My own information was very meagre in regard to the policies that might be in effect once the Police were established.

Referring to the Queen as the one person who was head of the government I knew would not be acceptable to these people. No woman could have any part on the council. To say that we were ruled by a woman would be scorned as impossible and her representatives in this country would be deemed unfit to be taken as wise men or respected in council. That is why the Queen was always referred to as the Great Queen Mother by the men who negotiated treaties at a later date with the Indians. Women were respected among the tribes after they became grandmothers to a degree hardly in keeping with their early years of service with the tribe or as mothers raising families. Although Seenum's band under the influence of the Rev. Mr. Steinhauer's Christian teaching gave more consideration to the women than was practised in other tribes, there were a few men yet who gave their women less consideration than they would their beasts of burden, dogs, or horses. Of course these were the odd few still holding to their old traditions.

The Riel Rebellion and the appearance of soldiers to establish government authority did more to convince or rather to impress the natives with the fact of the authority of one big chief over all the people than any other factor in my knowledge.

In one conversation in which I was asked to express an opinion, I emphasized the weakness of intertribal wars that had decimated their people over the years, the devastating effect of the smallpox, their helplessness in fighting against such unknown diseases, and the debasing effects of the American whisky traders who had victimized the once-strong people of the southern tribes. The gradual extinction of the buffalo was caused by their slaughter in the thousands just for their hides in our neighbouring country. To these people this was an unbelievable thing to do. Destruction of food was in their minds worse than the murder of a man's own family.

I seldom made any attempt to widen the scope of their understanding except when directly questioned. Government in their understanding meant rules set up by the big chief and his council. This was the nearest comparison to anything they would accept. To have entered into discussions or to have tried to express my personal views would have placed me in opposition to their own views and convictions of proper government. I adopted a neutral attitude. I had faith in the good judgement of Steinhauer and his influence among the Indian leaders.

There was a growing resentment among various native

people that men from the Hudson's Bay Company, such as Christie, should be called into consultation with the big chief while the Indians and half-breeds, those chiefly concerned, would be ignored completely. It was worse than useless to try to justify these facts or explain them to native thinking.

The Whitefish chief was a man of keen understanding who sought out every way to increase his knowledge of factors that might affect his Indians. It was rumoured that the Indians would be asked to give up their rights to the land. None of them could understand why they should give up what had been their right to enjoy since the earliest memory of the oldest story of their tribe.

In 1875 I made another trip to Fort Garry, as we had accumulated quite a valuable assortment of furs, only selling what was necessary for my customers and my household in tea and sugar which had now become essential to the tribe.

Inkster was still doing a splendid trade and was glad to see me return and continue our business after such a long absence. My helpers were young men who had asked to go along to see the country. They wanted no wages as they had fur to sell of their own. However the price of furs had increased so that I could well afford to give them a liberal allowance for their time. These young men found so many things to buy that money from their own furs soon ran out.

Visiting my old home, I found them all in good health. My younger brother had handled the stock and farm work so well that he was now of quite independent means. My young sister was now a grown woman, wearing an engagement ring, proudly displayed for my inspection. Teasing her I said it was a very good glass.

"Brother, I don't care if it was wood taken from some blockhead. The man that gave it to me could tie you up in a knot. So there, you know what I think!"

No visit would be complete without Murdoch Spence's comments on current events. I found the old man a little more aged and somewhat less inclined to walk back and forth on the floor fervently expressing his fiery opinions when he was excited. It appears that one Alexander Fisher, a selfish grasping fellow, had, while the buffalo hunt was being organized, slipped out ahead of the others during the night and scattered the buffalo, making it necessary for the big party to travel a great deal further to obtain meat to fill their carts.

Gabriel Dumont, the elected leader of the party, had suspected that Fisher's activities were to blame for the scattered herds, from where they had been previously located, and had hunted the man down and confiscated some of his property. It was the unwritten law amongst buffalo hunters that no man could separate himself from a party for his own advantage in obtaining buffalo.[1]

Lawrence Clarke, then a member of the government, put in a strong report to Ottawa on Fisher's complaint, declaring the action of Dumont a minor revolt. A man of Clarke's experience in western living conditions should have known that authoritative reprisal at the instigation of Fisher would arouse the half-breeds' discontent to serious proportions.

Gabriel Dumont was arrested and the man never forgave the Police for having caused his detention. The whole incident was sufficient to convince every Metis and Indian in the party that there was no justice in the law and that the action of the Police was clearly prejudiced in favour of a man whose selfishness and greed were openly held in contempt by the majority of the people of the settlement and surrounding areas.

I knew from my own experience of many years with the tribesmen and Metis people that these rules of the hunt were necessary and important for the well-being of the majority. The communal sharing regardless of the number of animals killed by any one man was the accepted practice. No-one in my experience ever disputed the rules and regulations that were enforced by the leader chosen by the vote of those taking part in the hunt. The above story is an example of ill-considered action by officials that aroused the hot-blooded supporters of Riel to open rebellion again ten years later.

Spence continued: "I am not in accord with the choice from the Hudson's Bay Company officials as our representatives. Clarke's report was stupid, prejudiced, and inexcusable. It would be different if he were unfamiliar with the customs of western living. His bitter condemnation of Riel as a foolish Catholic agitator was difficult to understand in view of his own adherence to that Church. Riel's sympathetic support for Dumont was based on my own concept of what was best for the majority of the communal sharing of organized buffalo hunts and the rules adopted to enforce this concept."

This visit with Murdoch Spence was the last time I was to see the man, as he died the following year, in his nineties. A remarkable character and the main source of my political information, always intensely loyal to the British Crown, he was strongly intolerant to the attitude of officials sent out to the West by the Government of Canada.

Early in March of 1876 I received a letter by courier from Mista-wa-sis (Big Child) and Ah-tuk-a-kup[2] (Star Blanket) asking if I would consent to act as their interpreter for a treaty that was proposed for the coming summer. Their men explained that I had been recommended by a man named Clarke as the best interpreter in the whole Saskatchewan valley. I was not personally acquainted with either of them but I knew them by reputation as the two main chiefs of the Prairie Crees.

I gave them a letter of acceptance and explained to their agents that I would be glad to act for them, provided that they let me know when to be at Carlton where the treaty was to be negotiated. They promised to send a man to notify me of the date of the meeting.

We again had quite a successful winter hunting and trapping of '75 and '76. Trading with the Indians had left my stock of trade goods almost depleted, but as I had promised to go when the chiefs called me, it was difficult to know what to do. My wife suggested that we send our furs with Mr. Steinhauer, who always went along with his carts when I was unable to make the trip. He gladly undertook to handle my business and see that my carts were taken care of. I hired Sam Jackson and gave him an order on Inkster for his wages. He had two of my carts and his nephew drove one of the horses.

Our family now consisted of two boys and two girls. Jimmy, the oldest boy, though only seven years old, was big for his age, quite tall, would likely make the six footer that I had humorously predicted at the boy's naming. He was a big help to his mother and at the same time caused her considerable worry, for he had no fear of a horse and could ride like a trooper — and did at every opportunity he could get his hand on an animal. His mother frequently demanded that I assert my authority to discourage his love for horses.

The sheltered bay which our house fronted on usually froze, forming a nice sheet of ice. I made Jimmy a pair of wooden skates, which he quickly learned to use. He was enthusiastic over his new sport, and when he loaned his skates to his friends, the parents were deluged with requests for the same kind. The fathers and uncles were kept busy making models of Jimmy's pair.

A piece of wood was shaped for the feet right and left, somewhat in the shape of a canoe. Holes were bored through the main part in two places through which strings were passed to lace on to their moccasins. An incision was made down the centre into which a piece of barrel hoop was driven, slightly curved up at the ends. The blades sharpened made very good skates. I was amused at the innovations these youngsters made to improve the skates. One young inventor captured his grandfather's worn moccasins, cut them down and fastened them to support his ankle in much the same way that skiers do today.

Jimmy's popularity grew and our house became the meeting place for all kinds of adventure, much to his mother's disgust. However, I noticed the boys were always served a hearty lunch after a session of skating.

When the summer was well on the way, Jimmy watched me swim out after a duck that I dropped in flight. He demanded to be taught to swim. He was on his third lesson and could already swim some distance by himself when his mother dropped in on us.

"Peter, come out of that water! Don't you think that I have enough to do keeping track of my boy without you teaching him a new way to kill himself?"

Her disapproval was very plain. Jimmy's disgust at my meek obedience to his mother's orders was almost laughable. It would never have done to teach him disobedience to his mother's wishes.

Not being able to swim seemed characteristic among this northern tribe, and I was determined that none of my boys would be thus handicapped. It was very hard to convince Charlotte that learning to swim at an early age was as important as learning to walk or run. A little mild flattery in regard to the superior physical development of her son over other children of the same age won the battle.

Later Charlotte's enjoyment in watching Jimmy and his friends, who soon followed his example, swimming, ducking, and diving with effortless ease was quite equal to my own. She was, without too much outward demonstration, quite proud of another accomplishment for her eldest son, though she insisted that I fix stakes in the water beyond which none of the boys would be allowed to go.

It was an ideal life of abundance and good health these northern Indians enjoyed. They were not as the other tribes solely dependent on the buffalo for a living. Their hunting excursions to the prairies gave them additional security and provided a good reason to get together in the social band life that they all loved. They shared the proceeds of these trips with the less-fortunate people at home. Contributions to the minister, teacher, and all the old people were a regular practice, and these were distributed with an equality that was just and fair for those who actually went on the hunt.

The women without a doubt were the hardest workers, but did not consider themselves abused. They were happy and contented with their allotted tasks. They vied with each other in friendly rivalry for an abundance and variety of food on their tables. Any woman who did not supply her husband with the best in gloves, moccasins, or other wearing apparel and did not

231

keep those in the best of condition, was soon teased or shamed into a renewed effort to mend her ways. When any woman was sick or in confinement and was unable to carry out her duties, she was ably assisted by friendly neighbours till she was on her feet again.

The Indians were friendly and peaceful among themselves, although as among other people there were a few who tried to evade the social restrictions and habits that had become law for their tribe, but these few instances that came to my notice were of a minor nature and were soon severely dealt with by the chief and his councillors. I make these statements as dealing with times leading to and prior to the settlement of white people in the country.

There were plenty of wild fruits: strawberries, raspberries, blueberries, black and red currents, gooseberries, and three different kinds of cranberries. The Indians had no way of preserving except by drying in the sun, and adding water and heating over a slow fire during the winter to add a relish to winter foods.

Buffalo meat from the prairies was used as a supplement to deer, moose, and bird game in those days, the latter including geese, swans, waveys, cranes, and a dozen different species of ducks. Partridges were numerous but there were not many chickens, as the prairie chickens moved north in the winter to feed on the cranberries of the muskegs. Fish were numerous in the lakes. In the spring, I have seen rough fish, such as jacks, actually push each other out on the shores by the masses that drove up the creeks. I believe that the variety of food was a leading factor in the health and energy enjoyed by the people of James Seenum's band.

Flour as we know it today was a luxury, and never considered a necessity. Even when flour became more plentiful, bread was actually passed up for other food. Even the children showed no preference for bread. Flour only came into general use after wild game got scarce and the buffalo were gone.

It was getting well on in August and I still had not heard from Big Child or Star Blanket. I decided they must have made other arrangements, so joined with a large party being made up from Seenum's band and those at Saddle Lake for a buffalo hunt.

We had three carts and my two saddle horses. Peter Shirt drove one of the carts and a young man called Red Head (for what reason I do not know as his hair was black as a crow), drove the other cart.

Peter Shirt was a boy I had picked up in a Peigan camp in 1863 while on a trip to Fort Garry before I was married. I do not know what prompted me to take pity on the lad as he stood crying his heart out at the grave of his last relation. I had witnessed many harrowing scenes previously that never affected me with any feeling of responsibility before, but that time I was filled with the overwhelming desire to help the poor boy.

I went to the chief and asked if I might take the boy with me.

"Yes," said the chief. "Come with me and ask the boy if he will go with you."

"Will you come with me as my son?" I asked.

"Yes," he said. "If the chief will say that I can go."

The chief took him by the hand and brought him to where I was standing. He took my hand trying to control his crying and walked with me to where my carts and men were camping.

The chief said, "I am glad you can give the boy a home, as my own teepee is full and he has no relatives in this camp."

I could readily believe the chief had no room, as he was reputed to be supporting three wives already. Another addition to his teepee would certainly complicate matters in the management of such a household.

That was the last time I ever saw the boy cry. In all the years since that occasion, he never gave me any reason to be sorry for my impulsive act. The boy adapted himself to his new situation with amazing rapidity. In the matter of a few days he became very useful in our camping places. He was eager to learn and anxious to please me in every little way he could. When I took him into the store at Inkster's and fitted him with clothes from head to foot, his eyes fairly danced with joy, although the assumed dignity and facial soberness of the Indian was a contrast that was almost laughable.

"Father," he said, the first time he had used that word, "I wish those big boys could only see me now. They would laugh in a different way."

That was the first and only reference that he made to his former life. It was as if those things had never existed. The remark was very revealing and I was glad that I had brought him with me.

I was in somewhat of a quandary as I then had no home of my own and wondered what on earth I could do with him. Then I thought of the Rev. Steinhauer. I would ask him to take Peter and send him to school while I paid for his board and clothing. Steinhauer gladly accepted his care. Later, when I was married, Peter came to live with us.

Now he was a grown young man. His affection and loyalty to his foster parents was above question. I hardly had realized how much I depended on him for the care of the family when I was away from home. He had turned out to be a devout Christian and a fine example of the great work Steinhauer was doing amongst the Indians of James Seenum's band.

We were camped at a lake about fifty miles east and a little south of where Vegreville now is situated. It was deemed advisable to remain where we were, rather than disturb the buffalo that were using the lake for water and appeared to have established a range around there. I did not know then that this trip would be the last organized buffalo hunt that I would take part in, but, this being so, I can probably remember details with greater clarity than many of the others.

My wife was about to be confined and I was quite worried. Strange as it might appear, though we had four children, this would be the first time when I would be near my own abode when a birth was imminent. Charlotte was not worried in the slightest manner. When I failed to hide my concern, she scolded me for not going out with the men in my work of helping kill buffalo.

"Mrs. Hunter will take care of me, Peter. You know this will not be my first baby nor am I the first woman to give birth to a child. Go on with your work. There are people depending on you to kill buffalo for them."

During the night a few days after our talk, I was roused from my slumber to a realization of my responsibilities as head of my household by my wife's voice. "Wake up, Peter! Wake up! You must go and call Mrs. Hunter at once!"

Now thoroughly aroused to the gravity of the situation, I jumped up and made a bolt for the door in all haste. I was stopped in my tracks by my wife's laugh.

"Peter," she said, "you have lots of time to dress properly. I can hear people up already and if you appear as you are, you will be the joke of the whole camp."

The wisdom of this advice was only too apparent but not greatly appreciated under the circumstances. However, I dressed with more than customary speed that morning but lost some time in fumbling with the outlet in the tent flap. Forgetting our tent faced another where Peter Shirt and the children were sleeping, I almost tore the tent down when I stumbled over the peg lines.

Mrs. Hunter was already up and on my appearance grabbed a bundle already prepared and left the teepee. It puzzled me how the lady read my errand without me having to say a word.

John rose from his couch fully dressed. "Sit down, man. Sit down! This is one occasion when men are not needed. There is nothing to worry about. Your wife is in capable hands. The wife has successfully brought more babies into the world than

234

you have fingers and toes, so sit down and rest yourself while I get some breakfast ready."

"Do not bother," I said. "I'm not hungry."

"Huh," he grunted, "Stop worrying. Healthy good women in our tribe never have trouble with babies. When you married one of our girls, you did not marry trouble. Your wife has had four children without your presence, so why trouble yourself now?"

This remark of the old gentleman had its desired effect in cooling my nervousness. Under his cheerful conversation which avoided the matter uppermost in my mind, we began eating. I forgot my lack of hunger and my usual good appetite asserted itself, much to the amusement of my optimistic friend. The gleam in his eye reminded me of my former protests against eating any breakfast.

It was now broad daylight and everybody was up and about their duties. I watched the old gentleman's clumsy efforts at washing the dishes. Then he turned to me in a grumbling voice and said, "You have my wife working for you and I have to do her work, so you had better go after my horses as I need them this morning."

I had a long walk after his horses. It took quite a search to find them but I brought them in for him at the Hunter teepee. Mrs. Hunter waved to me to come to my own tent.

Charlotte gave me a weary smile and said, "Peter, I am glad for you. It is another boy and I want him named David."

I was so relieved and glad that she was all right that I would have consented to the name Ebenezer had she asked.

Hunter I noticed just tied his horses up till noon, then turned them out again. He had merely sent me after the horses to keep me occupied. I was grateful for his clever management that had kept me busy and free from needless worry.

Two days later a couple of strangers arrived and made inquiries as to my whereabouts. They were guided to Hunter's teepee by one of the camp guards. Hunter immediately offered them the hospitality of his teepee, placing robes for them to rest in a reclining position. A good meal was prepared at once as was the custom when strangers were guests. The guard had shown them to Hunter's tepee knowing how matters were in my tent, this with far more consideration and tact than I experienced among white settlers in later years.

John sent his wife to call me from my tent without saying just what was wanted.

"These men," said Hunter, "are sons of Mista-wa-sis and Ah-tuk-a-kup; they have been up to Whitefish Lake and have followed you here."

I shook hands with both men saying, "My friends, you have come at a bad time. I'll have to talk with my wife before I can promise to go with you."

Discussing the matter of the arrival of these men, my wife's answer was typical of the way she faced all our problems.

"You have given your word to their fathers, Peter. There is nothing for you to do but go with them at once. I will be all right with Mrs. Hunter to look after me. Peter Shirt and Red Head can look after the carts and we will return with the others. Thanks to our friends, our carts are loaded and the others are almost ready."

I went back to the men and told them that I would be ready as soon as they wanted to go. "We are ready now," said one man as he rose to his feet from where he was resting. "My father has already started for Carlton and we may be late if we delay."

Packing a few things in a bag for extras, I went with the clothes I was dressed in, hurriedly packed food and cooking utensils on a pack horse and riding Whitey, my buffalo runner, I was ready to start. Peter had fetched the horses while I was packing my duffle for the trip. I bid the family goodbye and gave some last minute instructions to Peter in regard to the care of the family and equipment. These latter orders were hardly necessary as I had long since been dependent on the young man for the care of everything while I was away. Of course a man likes to assert his authority, especially with strangers present.

Hunter decided to come along with us as he wanted to listen to the treaty negotiations. I was just a bit worried that the fast trip would be too much for him but he was well mounted as we all were and if he grew too tired I could leave the pack outfit and he could follow up at an easier gait. I need not have given the matter any thought for he stood up to the trip as well as any of us and his saddler turned out to be the best riding horse of the lot.

We arrived at Carlton the evening of the fifth day of hard riding and long hours, but our horses were all in excellent condition to start with and stood up well to the trip. A large encampment appeared, and separated by a lane were the various tents and canvas shelters that housed the traders. Apparently they had anticipated an agreement on treaty terms and had come prepared to do business with the Indians.[3] Later I learned that my youngest sister was there also. She had married a trader, a big strapping Swede by the name of Pederson. Though I was kept pretty busy, we managed to get together for a visit.

A comfortable teepee had been set up for our use with buffalo robes, new blankets, cooking utensils, and even prepared food. Mr. Hunter was particularly impressed with the care lavished on us for our stay. Certainly it was the best hospitality that could be provided. The camp crier rode among the teepees and announced our arrival. He was riding on a gaily decorated pinto pony. He was telling the people that their interpreter had arrived and that the chiefs and councillors should get ready for the meeting the next day.

I decided to take a walk around camp and saw Governor Morris walking in front of the Hudson's Bay post. There were over 250 teepees on the Indian section of the grounds. It was an impressive sight. I had never seen so many teepees in one locality before. There were hundreds of horses feeding on the flats, some picketed close by their owner's teepee with the usual assortment of dogs which appeared to have barked themselves to exhaustion as they lay before each teepee.

Peter Ballenden and his brother Sam came to the chiefs and informed them that the Governor desired them to meet him at the fort that evening. I had just returned from my walk when Mista-wa-sis came to my tent and asked me to accompany them.

"I have been told," said the chief, "that the Governor has hired two other interpreters. However, we have decided to pay you ourselves, even if the Governor does not."

The chiefs were dressed in all their finery, feathers, plumes, and ermine-decorated coats. I felt a little out of place among the tribal costumes; and when we came before the assembled officials, they also had quite as great an array of finery as our Indian chiefs. My work clothes, though neat and clean, when compared against all the other finery were indeed inadequate. I wished that I had come better prepared for this situation.

When I saw Peter Ballenden and the Rev. John McKay seated among the official group, I presumed they were the interpreters the chief had mentioned. I was not too greatly concerned, as I knew both men; their ability as interpreters to a large gathering such as we would be faced with on the morrow would be tested to the limit.

Governor Morris, Hon. James McKay, Clarke, William Christie, now retired from the Hudson's Bay service, and a Dr. Jackes were all seated at the table when we entered.[4] Clarke jumped up and came forward to introduce our party.

I was standing beside Mista-wa-sis, but Clarke paid no attention to my presence while he was conducting the introductions. Although Clarke, Ballenden, Christie, and the Rev. McKay all knew me by name, they did not offer any sign of recognition.

The Governor advanced and shook hands with the chiefs, saying, "I have come to meet you Cree chiefs to make a treaty with you for the surrender of your rights of the land to the government, and further I have two of the most efficient interpreters that could be obtained. There stand Peter Ballenden and the Rev. John McKay."

His words were interpreted by Peter Ballenden.

Big Child answered, "We have our own interpreter, Peter Erasmus, and there he is. Mr. Clarke (he pointed directly at Clarke) advised me that Peter Erasmus was a good man to interpret the Cree language. Further than that, he recommended the man as the best interpreter in the whole Saskatchewan valley and plains. Why he did so, only he knows. On Clarke's advice, though I have no acquaintance with the man, I went to a great deal of trouble to fetch him here and though I know nothing of his efficiency, I am prepared to use his services. All our chiefs have agreed."

"Is that correct?" asked Governor Morris of Clarke.

"Peter Erasmus lives several hundred miles from here and I did not know that the chiefs had sent for him; therefore I hired these two other interpreters."

"It was quite unnecessary to send for the man," said the Governor. "We have two interpreters hired by the government and it is up to the government to provide the means of communication."

I had quietly interpreted these side conversations to the chief and he was prepared for an answer.

"Very good," said Mista-wa-sis, "you keep your interpreters and we will keep ours. We will pay our own man and I already see that it will be well for us to do so."

This latter statement by the chief, I interpreted to Morris directly, not waiting for Ballenden to misinterpret the chief's meaning.

"There is no need for you to assume this extra expense for an interpreter when the government is willing to pay for the interpretations," reiterated the Commissioner.

The chief replied rather heatedly, "Our man will interpret as well as yours. I can speak Blackfoot and I know what it takes to interpret. If you do not want the arrangement, there will be no talks. We did not send for you, you sent for us."

I was quick to translate the conversations before waiting for Ballenden's hesitant and slow interpretations. The Governor's party were huddled at the table in low conversation, none of which I could hear. In the meantime the chiefs gathered together and were about to leave the room when the Governor looked up and saw they were going to leave.

"All right," he said. "You can have your interpreter. My tent will be pitched on the prairie where we will meet. There will be a band playing to notify you of our presence."

CHAPTER FOURTEEN

Treaty No. Six

T HE GOVERNOR'S TENT was pitched on a slight rise some distance from the fort. Most of the other officials were already waiting for him in the tent. Then the Governor's carriage appeared, accompanied by the Mounted Police and led by the promised band. The Police, dressed in their smart scarlet uniforms and riding well trained horses, made a big impression with the Indians. In fact the great prestige of the Governor was somewhat overshadowed by the smart appearance of his escort.

Many Indians of that camp were seeing the Mounted Police for the first time. Though small in number, the Police were to be an important factor in establishing in the minds of the tribes the fairness and justice of government for all the people regardless of colour or creed — something they had no concept of in its broader sense.

The Indian's own rules were handed down from the dim past, their oldest traditions accepted without question. The chiefs and councillors were chosen for outstanding qualities of character. Bravery and ability were the sole measures by which their leaders were qualified to take positions of trust. A son of a chief assumed office following the death of the chief only if he had proved himself qualified under these standards of office.

The Indians recognized and respected the personal qualities

of the individuals comprising the Force as being the qualities they demanded in their own leaders. The administration of impartial justice without regard to colour or creed, and the tenacity of its members in carrying out their duties, soon became a topic of Indian campfire conversation. The small number of this Police Force would have been utterly incapable of handling the thousands of Indians if they had attempted to employ force to compel obedience.

The chief and his councillors administered the laws for their band and the tribe recognized the necessity for rules governing individuals who at times broke the rules set by their leaders for the benefit of the majority. That, in my opinion, is what made possible the successful role that this small Force played in the progress of settlement of one country.

Our approach to the Governor's tent was delayed by certain ceremonial proceedings that have been far better described than I feel capable of doing. However, let me say that these ceremonial practices had a deep significance to the tribes and can only be explained as a solemn approach to a vital and serious issue for discussion.

Few people realize that those so-called savages were far more deeply affected and influenced by their religious beliefs and convictions than any comparable group of white people, whose lip service to their religion goes no deeper than that. The forms of ceremonial behaviour with which the Indians approached the Governor's tent were based on practices whose actual meaning has long since been lost. The ceremony in the crowning of the kings and queens of England would have little meaning were it not for the benefit of a written language.

We were finally seated on the grass in a large semicircle in front of the Governor's tent crossed-legged, a position that seems to be the most restful and relaxed manner of listening to a speech. I have seen quite old men rise to their feet to speak from this position without the use of their hands or arms to assist them, all with apparently effortless ease. My own attempts in this regard were never graceful or even easy. I always had to use my hands and arms to assist me. It was a physical feat that I never successfully conquered.

We were patiently awaiting the Commissioner's convenience when the Hon. James McKay came to the front and called Peter Erasmus to come forward to interpret the Governor's speech. I rose to my feet and said, "I object, Sir. It is my impression that I am not employed by the government but am acting only on behalf of the chiefs assembled here. Therefore, I refuse to interpret the Governor's speech; that I consider is the duty of its paid servants." I then faced the Indians and repeated my words in Cree.

McKay again insisted but I just as promptly refused.

Mista-wa-sis turned to me and in an undertone asked me if I thought that I was capable of interpreting.

"Certainly I can, or else I would not be here. Let their own men talk first and then you will understand why I refuse to do their bidding."

Big Child and Star Blanket on each side of me nodded their agreement. The former rose to his feet. There was considerable stir among the Indians at the delay. Voices were noticeable from those seated furthest away from the stand. As soon as Big Child stood up there was immediate silence. He was a commanding figure of a man, not tall, but he stood straight and his wide shoulders spoke of strength. He didn't say a word until there was complete silence. Showing his closed fist with index finger protruding, he spoke, "This is number one," indicating "one" with the raising of his hand for all to see. "Already you have broken your word on what you have agreed."

I stood beside him and interpreted word for word as he spoke.

All the Indians rose to their feet and crowded forward behind their chiefs. The Police were kept busy keeping them away from the table. They were like a forest as a gathering storm of words rolled forward. I was thoroughly angered at the manner in which the Governor had been inveigled into this situation.

I had expected neither the strong reaction from the Indians nor McKay's determination to have his own way. I knew that Peter Ballenden had not the education or practice to interpret, and his voice had no carrying quality to make himself heard before all this large assembly. The Rev. McKay had learned his Cree among the Swampy and Saulteaux. While there was a similarity in some words, and I had learned both languages, the Prairie Crees would not understand his Cree. Further, the Prairie Crees looked down on the Swampy and Saulteaux as an inferior race. They would be intolerant at being addressed in Swampy or Saulteaux words. I knew that McKay was not sufficiently versed in the Prairie Cree to confine his interpretations to their own language.

The Rev. Mr. McDougall was busy trying to calm Bear Skin, the most irate and the loudest of any of the crowd.[1] Both leading chiefs stood without saying a word while all the fuss went on. Finally Big Child was satisfied that the Government party had been sufficiently chastised. He waved to those immediately surrounding him to be seated, and as before, with a few words, restored order.

The Governor was quick to take advantage of the lull after Mista-wa-sis had waved his people to silence. You could almost feel the strong tension that still remained. Governor Morris started his address with the Rev. McKay interpreting.

"You nations of the Crees," he began, "I am here on a most important mission as representing Her Majesty the Queen Mother to form a treaty with you in her name, that you surrender your rights in these northern territories to the government."

He went on to explain that treaties already had been signed by other tribes, naming those that had been treated with. He mentioned the Touchwood Hills Crees and some of the others, saying that he had been chosen because he was familiar with Indian conditions.

McKay's interpretations were mixed with Swampy and Saulteaux words. I mentioned this in English to the table, and the Honourable James angrily shouted, "Stop that, or you will rattle him!"

Mista-wa-sis, after listening for a time, jumped to his feet and said, "We are not Swampy Crees or Saulteaux Indians. We are Plains Crees and demand to be spoken to in our own language."

McKay understood, was confused, and sat down. The Governor turned to me and asked what the chief had said. I explained the chief's words. The Rev. McKay again tried to continue, got mixed up with Saulteaux words and took his seat.

Ballenden was now called up. I was delighted, for I knew the man quite well. He was a good man to interpret personal talks but I knew he would be completely out of his element as an interpreter for such a large meeting, where a man's voice had to carry to reach the men furthest from the stand.

His attitude of the previous evening in not showing me any recognition; and Clarke's conspicuous neglect of a formal introduction, even though he was personally acquainted with me, had fairly made my blood boil. I had no pity for the men who had contributed their share to having me discredited with the Commissioner. Ballenden did exactly as I thought. He made an excellent interpretation of the Governor's words but in a voice so low that it could not be heard beyond the first ten rows of men seated on the ground. The men in the back rows got to their feet and demanded that he speak in a louder voice; again there was some confusion and the two chiefs beside me got to their feet and ordered the men to be quiet. Ballenden tried to raise his voice, choked, and then sat down. My revenge at that moment was sweet but I could read consternation on the faces of my impolite friends at the table.

The Governor, who I could see was growing exasperated at these frequent interruptions to his talk, said, "All right, Erasmus. Let this be your chance to justify your chiefs' confidence in your work."

I immediately rose to my feet, stepped beside the Governor's table, faced the Crees, and spoke in Cree, reviewing the text of the Governor's speech to them. Then I motioned to the Commissioner to continue his address. I knew my voice had suffered nothing from my heated veins or the exultation that I felt at the complete disposal of the slight so desperately manoeuvered by these men sitting around the table. The Governor spoke for an hour or so explaining the purpose of the treaty and its objectives, and describing in some detail the terms. He especially emphasized the money each person would get. There were no further interruptions.

Once during a pause in the Governor's speech, the Honourable James differed with me over an interpretation of one word. However, his brother supported my interpretation in the matter and no further objections were expressed during the whole of the remaining treaty negotiations. Though that first day I felt high strung and angry over the treatment I had received, I was determined that nothing would prevent me from doing my work with credit to my employers and justice to the Governor's talks.

The Indians had retired to their teepees or were sitting in groups discussing the treaty terms. Hunter was around somewhere with the other Indians. I was reclining in our tent trying to calm my ruffled feelings and assess the value of my contribution to the talks when the Governor's cook stuck his head in the tent flaps and said that the Governor wanted to see me. I was about to give the men a curt refusal, thinking that sending the lowest man on their staff to summon me to the great man's presence was another effort to emphasize my status. Then I heard the Hon. James McKay, Christie, and Dr. Jackes questioning the cook, asking if he had found my tent. He answered in the affirmative; then they all came to the tent and said they were there to escort me back to the Governor's quarters. Entering, I stood without making any comment, awaiting the gentleman's pleasure. "Well, Mr. Erasmus. I suppose you are slightly exhausted over your labours this forenoon?" I thought I detected a slight hint of sarcasm in his tone and immediately answered, "No, Mr. Morris. Not by the work but by the preliminaries that led up to the work."

He smiled and I heard laughs in the background. Then he

came forward to where I was standing and handed me a glass of brandy, which I accepted, for to have refused would have indicated that I was still nursing a grievance in the face of his apparent effort at appeasement.

"Mr. Erasmus, I called you here to congratulate you on your work. You are the first man I ever heard who interpreted to such a large audience without making a mistake. I see you have friends around here, although our first impressions may have discouraged this view."

It was pretty much of an after-dinner speech. Some of the Governor's guests applauded but I noticed that Clarke and Ballenden were not among them. Mr. Morris advised me that, beginning that day, I would be in his pay for the balance of the talks.

"Thank you, Sir. I hope that I may have better co-operation in the next few days. I promise to give you the best I have, and assure you that today's unpleasantness will not be repeated from our side."

I begged to be excused and took my departure without further words.

The next day the Police band preceded the Governor as before, but there was not so much pomp and display from the Government party. Even the Governor walked unescorted from his carriage the short distance to the stand. The Indians were already in place in their usual postures of comfortable listening as on the previous day.

The Commissioner formally opened the meeting by stating that today he wanted to hear what they had to say, adding, "I cannot go any further in regard to the terms I explained yesterday."

Poundmaker, who was not a chief at that time but just a brave, spoke up and said, "The governor mentions how much land is to be given to us. He says 640 acres, one mile square for each family, he will give us." And in a loud voice he shouted, "This is our land! It isn't a piece of pemmican to be cut off and given in little pieces back to us. It is ours and we will take what we want."

A strong wave of approval came back from the seated Indians at his statement. Some braves in the last row rose to their feet, waved their hands and arms, shouting, "Yes! Yes!" in Cree. Apparently these were Poundmaker's followers. It was some time before the main chiefs could restore order.

The Commissioner was visibly shaken by this demonstration that erupted at the beginning. His assumption had been that the Indians had completely adopted his treaty terms, which by his own words he was not authorized to change in any

244

form. I thought to myself, "A boxer sent into the ring with his hands tied."

The Governor went on to explain that unless certain lands were set aside for the sole use of the Indians, the country would be flooded with white settlers who would not give the Indians any consideration whatever. He made references to other areas where settlement was growing very fast. Morris's speech and explanation were couched in simple terms for the understanding of the Indian people. His manner held a sincerity that was most effective in impressing his audience. Knowing the Indians as I did, I could see that they were receiving the message with a growing understanding of its purpose.

Standing at the Governor's table I was able to observe the reactions of some of the listeners. I felt that Big Child and Star Blanket were both convinced of the fairness and justice of the terms explained to them by the speaker. I had an increased confidence in my interpretations, my sympathies transferred to the Governor's side, and my early animosity to the party was completely gone. The translations came to my tongue without effort and I seemed inspired to a tension that made my voice heard in the back rows where I had placed Hunter to give me a sign if my voice was not being heard distinctly.

Mista-wa-sis rose to his feet at the conclusion of Morris's detailed explanations of the treaty terms and answers to questions that arose during the proceedings, saying, "We heard all you have told us and I want to tell the Governor how it is with us as well. When a thing is thought out quietly, that is the best way. I ask this of him today, that we go and think over his words."

Governor Morris agreed with the chief and the meeting was adjourned till Monday. It was now Saturday.

The Indians did not hold a council on Sunday. The main chiefs said it was better to let the people have time to talk things over among themselves before calling a meeting. So word was sent to the Governor that they wanted to postpone the meeting till Tuesday. Permission was granted and a council called for Monday.

I was asked to attend the council with them and was personally escorted to the meeting by Mista-wa-sis and his ally Star Blanket. They said that I might be called upon to explain the talks, in case of any misunderstanding of my interpretations of the treaty terms. "There are many among us who are trying to confuse and mislead the people; that is why I thought it best to give them lots of time for their bad work. Today they will have to come out in the open and will be forced to show their intentions," said Big Child.

245

The chiefs were in agreement that it was better to bring about an understanding among their own. people before meeting with the Commissioner.

Whether the treaty was actually misunderstood or deliberately misconstrued I know not, but the meeting was hardly underway when Big Child motioned me to disprove any wrong statement by those opposed to the agreement.

There were immediate objections to my taking part in the council but Star Blanket got up and spoke most emphatically. "Mista-wa-sis and I fetched this man here at a great deal of trouble to ourselves because we were told that Peter Erasmus was learned in the language the Governor speaks. You all heard and saw the other men fail to interpret what he tried to say. He, Peter Erasmus, is the people's hired man. He is here to open our eyes and ears to the words that you and I cannot understand. Mista-wa-sis and I have asked him here to keep us right on what was offered in the treaty terms."

Ah-tuk-a-kup's words had the immediate effect of silencing any further attempts to confuse treaty terms. There was then no further need to dispute any statement intended to be misleading by those opposed or trying for better promises under the agreements.

The talks went on all day, only adjourned for a short noon-hour meal. Indian eloquence had full play that day. Many of the council men spoke in addition to the chiefs. There was a Chipewyan Indian present[2] who argued considerable time away and was supported by Poundmaker and The Badger until a council man rose and objected to his interference.

"This man is not a chief and has no authority to speak for his band. Why should he be allowed to interrupt the council and waste so much of our time?"

There was loud assent from many voices and that silenced the voluble Chipewyan, whom I judged to be the main troublemaker.

Poundmaker and The Badger led the faction who were strong in their objections and refused to grant the possibility of existing by agricultural pursuits. These men had most of their support from those with less than thirty lodges to their count. Late that afternoon, I thought there was little hope of reaching an agreement. I was getting tired and about to ask permission to retire when I saw Ah-tuk-a-kup nod to Big Child.

Mista-wa-sis rose to his feet. All afternoon he had sat without taking part in the speeches. All those who were taking part in the previous arguments sat down. There was silence as the man stood and waited for every person to be seated.

"I have heard my brothers speak, complaining of the

hardships endured by our people. Some have bewailed the poverty and suffering that has come to Indians because of the destruction of the buffalo as the chief source of our living, the loss of the ancient glory of our forefathers; and with all that I agree, in the silence of my teepee and on the broad prairies where once our fathers could not pass for the great number of those animals that blocked their way; and even in our day, we have had to choose carefully our campground for fear of being trampled in our teepees. With all these things, I think and feel intensely the sorrow my brothers express.

"I speak directly to Poundmaker and The Badger and those others who object to signing this treaty. Have you anything better to offer our people? I ask, again, can you suggest anything that will bring these things back for tomorrow and all the tomorrows that face our people?

"I for one think that the Great White Queen Mother has offered us a way of life when the buffalo are no more. Gone they will be before many snows have come to cover our heads or graves if such should be."

There were loud groans and exclamations of despair at the latter statement from many places among the group. Mista-wa-sis continued after waiting for the murmur to die down.

"I speak the tongue of the Blackfoot. I have been in their lodges. I have seen with my eyes and listened with my ears to the sorrows of that once-proud nation; people whom we have known as our enemies, the Peigan and the Bloods who are their brothers. Pay attention, listen hard to what I am about to say. The Big Knives of the south came into Blackfoot territory as traders; though few in number they have conquered these nations, and that, all the Crees in the days of our fathers and their fathers before them failed to do. How did they do it? Listen closely, my brothers, and you will understand. What was done to them can be done to us if we throw away the hand that is extended to us by this treaty.

"These traders, who were not of our land, with smooth talk and cheap goods persuaded the southern tribes it would be a good thing to have a place to trade products of the hunt, the hides and tanned goods. The traders came and built strong forts, and with their long rifles that can kill at twice the distance of our own and the short guns that can spout death six times quicker than you can tell about it, they had the people at their mercy. The Blackfoot soon found out the traders had nothing but whisky to exchange for their skins. Oh, yes! They were generous at first with their rotten whisky, but not for long. The traders demanded pay and got Blackfoot horses, buffalo robes, and all other things they had to offer.

247

"Those traders laughed at them for fools, and so they were, to sell their heritage for ruin and debauchery. Some of the bravest of the Blackfoot tried to get revenge for the losses but they were shot down like dogs and dragged to the open plains on horses to rot or be eaten by wolves.

"The Great Queen Mother, hearing of the sorrows of her children, sent out the Red Coats. Though these were only of a number you could count on your fingers and toes, yet the cutthroats and criminals who recognized no authority but their guns, who killed each other on the slightest pretence and murdered Indians without fear of reprisal, immediately abandoned their forts, strong as they were, and fled back to their own side of the line. I ask you why those few men could put to flight those bad men who for years have defied the whole of the southern Indian nations?

"Surely these Red Coats are men of flesh and blood as ourselves and a bullet is just as effective on them as on any Blackfoot. Why of course, they are of flesh and blood. They could be killed as easily as any Blackfoot, but ask yourselves why the traders fled in fear from so few men. The southern tribes outnumbered this small Police Force one hundred to one, but they were helpless in spite of their numbers.

"Let me tell you why these things were so. It was the power that stands behind those few Red Coats that those men feared and wasted no time in getting out when they could; the power that is represented in all the Queen's people, and we the children are counted as important as even the Governor who is her personal speaker.

"The Police are the Queen Mother's agents and have the same laws for whites as they have for the Indians. I have seen these things done and now the Blackfoot welcome these servants of the Queen Mother and invite her Governor for a treaty with them next year.

"I, for one, look to the Queen's law and her Red Coat servants to protect our people against the evils of white man's firewater and to stop the senseless wars among our people, against the Blackfoot, Peigans, and Bloods. We have been in darkness; the Blackfoot and the others are people as we are. They will starve as we will starve when the buffalo are gone. We will be brothers in misery when we could have been brothers in plenty in times when there was no need for any man, woman, or child to be hungry.

"We speak of glory and our memories are all that is left to feed the widows and orphans of those who have died in its attainment. We are few in numbers compared to former times, by wars and the terrible ravages of smallpox. Our people have

248

vanished too. Even if it were possible to gather all the tribes together, to throw away the hand that is offered to help us, we would be too weak to make our demands heard.

"Look to the great Indian nations in the Long Knives' country who have been fighting since the memory of their oldest men. They are being vanquished and swept into the most useless parts of their country. Their days are numbered like those of the buffalo. There is no law or justice for the Indians in Long Knives' country. The Police followed two murderers to Montana and caught them but when they were brought to the Montana court they were turned free because it was not murder to kill an Indian.

"The prairies have not been darkened by the blood of our white brothers in our time. Let this always be so. I for one will take the hand that is offered. For my band I have spoken."

There was a deep silence after Mista-wa-sis had taken his seat. No one appeared to have anything to say. Then, finally, Star Blanket rose to his feet and for a long minute stood with his head bowed as if in deep thought or as if he had been profoundly impressed with the former speaker's words.

"Yes," he said finally, "I have carried the dripping scalps of the Blackfoot on my belt and thought it was a great deed of bravery. I thought it was part of the glory of war but I now agree with Mista-wa-sis." Then he raised his voice so that it rang with the power of great conviction, "It is no longer a good thing. If we had been friends we might now be a host of people of all nations and together have power to demand the things some of you foolishly think you can get and insist on now demanding.

"No, that is not the road we took, but killed each other in continuous wars and in horse stealing, all for the glory we all speak of so freely. The great sickness took half our lodges and the dreaded disease fell as heavily on our enemies. We are weak and my brother Mista-wa-sis I think is right that the buffalo will be gone forever before many snows. What then will be left us with which to bargain? With the buffalo gone we will have only the vacant prairie which none of us have learned to use.

"Can we stop the power of the white man from spreading over the land like the grasshoppers that cloud the sky and then fall to consume every blade of grass and every leaf on the trees in their path? I think not. Before this happens let us ponder carefully our choice of roads.

"There are men among you who are trying to blind our eyes, and refuse to see the things that have brought us to this pass. Let us not think of ourselves but of our children's children. We hold our place among the tribes as chiefs and councillors because our people think we have wisdom above others amongst us. Then let us show our wisdom. Let us show our wisdom by choosing the right path now while we yet have a choice.

"We have always lived and received our needs in clothing, shelter, and food from the countless multitudes of buffalo that have been with us since the earliest memory of our people. No-one with open eyes and open minds can doubt that the buffalo will soon be a thing of the past. Will our people live as before when this comes to pass? No! They will die and become just a memory unless we find another way.

"For my part, I think that the Queen Mother has offered us a new way and I have faith in the things my brother Mista-wa-sis has told you. The mother earth has always given us plenty with the grass that fed the buffalo. Surely we Indians can learn the ways of living that made the white man strong and able to vanquish all the great tribes of the southern nations. The white men never had the buffalo but I am told they have cattle in the thousands that are covering the prairie for miles and will replace the buffalo in the Long Knives' country and may even spread over our lands. The white men number their lodges by the thousands, not like us who can only count our teepees by tens. I will accept the Queen's hand for my people. I have spoken."

With the last of his words, the councillors of both main speakers rose to their feet, together held up their hands as a gesture of acceptance, and again took their places. Other chiefs among the assembly spoke a few words in agreement. The greater majority with a few exceptions had accepted the views of the two main chiefs.

Mista-wa-sis adjourned the meeting by saying, "It is good that my brothers go back to their teepees and study these matters with care. We will not be hasty. You will have a chance to ask questions on things you want cleared up. We will have our interpreter mark down the things we think we should have."

To this the Indians agreed. Dismissed, many of the chiefs came up and shook hands with Mista-wa-sis and Ah-tuk-a-kup, thus expressing their unanimous approval of the speeches of the two men that had swung the meeting in favour of treaty terms. I noticed that Poundmaker and The Badger were not among those who came forward to shake hands.

After I had retired to our tent, I lay awake thinking of the things spoken by the two chiefs, and marvelled at the confidence they both felt in the fairness of the justice carried out by this slender arm of the Queen Mother. The statement that

250

the Police had the same laws for white men and the Indians was true of our country, whereas only the previous year some Americans had committed murder on our side of the line. They had been followed to Montana and arrested but when they were brought before the Montana court, in spite of all the clear evidence of their guilt, the case was dismissed. The men had only killed Indians and that was not considered a crime on that side of the line.[3]

On Tuesday the Indians were slow in gathering at the Governor's tent. Poundmaker and The Badger were trying to gather support for their demands in the matter of treaty terms. Majority opinion had forced them to a grudging consent at the meeting. The Chipewyan was again active wherever he could find an audience, and backed by the other two men had regained his former boldness. But I noticed he was having difficulty in getting anyone to listen.

The Governor did not waste any time on preliminary talk but said he was ready to listen to the people and was prepared to clear up any question about which there was any doubt. Poundmaker immediately spoke, asking help when the Indians started to settle on the reserves. The Badger took up the theme with more elaboration.

"We think of our children. We do not want to be greedy but when we commence to settle on the reserves we select, it is then we want aid and when we can't help ourselves in case of trouble."[4]

Sakamoos[5] and others spoke, referring to portions of the treaty in regard to settlement on reserves, the need for medical help, and guidance in regard to the new project of agriculture. A summary of their remarks meant that they wanted assistance to get established in their new occupation of agriculture, not only financially but also in instruction and management.

Then the Hon. James McKay, in a somewhat arrogant tone, admonished them in Cree for their demands. "In my experience you always want more than you were promised in the first place and you are never satisfied with what is given you." He made other biting remarks detrimental to the character of the Indian.[6]

In view of my knowledge of what had transpired at their council I thought his speech most unfortunate and very harmful. His very attitude insulted the intelligence of his listeners. There was distinct murmur of disapproval all over the crowd. McKay had hardly taken his seat when The Badger leapt to his feet.

"I did not say that I wanted to be fed every day. You, I know, understand our language and yet you twist my words to suit

251

your own meaning. What I did say was that when we settle on the ground to work the land, that is when we will need help and that is the only way a poor Indian can get along."[7]

The speech that McKay had made was not interpreted into English but Morris could see that it had made a bad impression on the people by the angry stir that prevailed. I interpreted all Indian replies and said, "Let McKay, the Honourable James, explain his own speech." However, I noticed the Governor did not take the trouble to inquire into the contents of McKay's speech that had so roused the Indians.[8]

"You will remember the promise that I have already made," he said instead. "You will get the seed and you need not concern yourselves about what your children will eat. They will be taught and be able to look after themselves."

Big Child spoke, "It is well known that if we have plenty in our gardens and crops we would not insist on getting more provisions, but it is only in the case of extremity and from the ignorance of Indians in commencing to work the land that we speak. We are in the dark. This is no trivial matter with us."[9]

"The things we have talked over in our Council, we think are for our good," said Star Blanket. "I believe that the good councillors of the Queen Mother and her commissioners know what is best for them. I was told that the Governor was a good man and now that I have seen him and listened to him talk, I know I heard right. He has removed some of the obstacles to our understanding and I hope he will remove them all."[10]

Star Blanket paused in his discourse as Big Child rose to his feet and demanded silence from the back where the Chipewyan was again causing a disturbance.

Star Blanket continued, "We want food in the spring, when we begin to farm; according as the Indian settles on the land and as he advances, his needs will increase. I would now ask the Governor to give us time to consider all the things that he has told us today."

This was granted, with a warning from the Commissioner that he could not spend too much time with them as he had other tribes to treat with that would be waiting for him. He further stated that he had heard that the buffalo were near and they would want to be on their way to get their winter provisions. "Food, my friends, is getting scarce in camp."

The Governor now turned to the Chipewyan who had been making a disturbance in the crowd. "You are only one of those people you claim to represent. You are no wiser than your tribe who have already accepted treaty terms with the Government. If you have anything to say, I will speak to your people after I have finished with the Crees."

Teequaysay on the following day got up at the outset of the meeting to say, "Listen, my friends, all of you sitting around here, be patient and listen to what our interpreter has been instructed to tell you. What he will tell you are the things our main chiefs and councillors have decided to ask for and have agreed are for our best interests. There will be no more talk or questions asked of the Governor."[11]

I first explained to the Commissioner that the document I was about to read had been prepared by the main chiefs and their councillors and actually contained little more than what already had been promised, but I had been asked to read the petition to all the people for their agreement. Thus I interpreted the contents to the Indians before handing it to the Governor.

The Governor then spoke at some length as he dealt with each section of the petition and gave reasons for the few of the things that could not be granted. However, he consented to a grant of one thousand dollars to assist those actually engaged in farming land on the reserves, but this would operate for three years only. This would apply to each band. They would receive a plough and harrow for three families under the same conditions. They would be at liberty to hunt and trap on government lands the same as before. The things they would be getting would be a present on top of what they had before nor would they be compelled to go to war except on their own free will. A medicine chest would be placed in the house of every agent for the free use of the band.[12] Each band would get four oxen, one bull and six cows, one boar and two pigs. After a band had settled on its reserve and started to raise grain, they would get one hand mill. Each chief would get one horse, harness and wagon.

Most of the chiefs expressed agreement, but Poundmaker was still not satisfied. Joseph Toma asked for guns and said he was speaking for Red Pheasant.

Morris replied, "When the list of things the interpreter read was handed to me, Red Pheasant sat in silence and I presumed he was satisfied as the others were. Then the principal chiefs expressed approval. I cannot grant your request."

Red Pheasant got up and repudiated the statement of Joseph Toma's as his own and not by his permission. That terminated the discussion in the formation of the treaty terms.

The Governor thanked the Indians for their attention and co-operation in all the proceedings and stated that the additional requests would be written in the treaty in all things he had agreed to. These special provisions were added into the draft of the treaty before the signing began. There were fifty signatures to that historic document and other adhesions followed the same wording as that signed at Carlton. The reading of the treaty took a great deal of time and required the services of all the interpreters but this time there were no fireworks in the matter of words used, nor the objection to Ballenden's voice. Half the Indians were not concerned.

Mista-wa-sis had called me aside and told me to keep a close watch on the wording to see that it included everything that had been promised. However, the other chiefs appeared satisfied that the Governor would carry out his promises to the letter. I was able to assure Mista-wa-sis that everything promised had been included in the writing. He was satisfied and his name was the first in the signing.

The following day the Governor was at his tent at ten o'clock while the chiefs' uniforms were issued, complete with medals and a flag. The councilmen were to receive theirs at the Hudson's Bay store. The Governor gave them a short discourse on the meaning of the uniforms, which in substance meant that they were now representatives of the Queen Mother and to see that their people should receive justice, and on their part to fulfill the obligations contained in their positions. There would be an issue of uniforms to the men that they chose from time to time to represent them as chiefs and councillors.

There was a great deal of hand-shaking and some fine compliments exchanged on both sides before the Governor took his departure. Mista-wa-sis and Star Blanket, I knew, meant every word they said, as did the Governor. Poundmaker was equally well versed in complimentary words but I felt certain that he didn't mean a word he said; in this I was right, for eight years later he served in jail for his activities in the Riel Rebellion.[13]

Treaty payments were started immediately after the signing. Christie was in charge and retained me for the balance of that day to assist in the interpretations. "Peter, the Governor wishes to see you at the fort this evening for a private talk and I believe Clarke has something to say as well," he advised me.

Later in the evening I made the call.

"I'm proud of you, Erasmus," said Clarke, "the way you handled the first day of the talks. I was in a bad spot after hiring those two men. I could not go back on my word."

"Well, as it turned out there was no harm done, but I hope you realize that your actions almost created a riot and could have wrecked the whole business. Trying to pretend you did not know me that first evening I considered a rank insult, and that, my high-minded friend, I do not take without repayment.

Further, you should know that you cannot treat men like Mista-wa-sis and Ah-tuk-a-kup as children, and the manner in which the Honourable James spoke during the meeting was equally as stupid."

"Well, Peter, I hope you hold no grudge. You can understand the position I was in at the time. I hope you will forget the whole miserable business."

"Certainly, Clarke. The victor is never the man to bear a grudge; it is always the loser, and I hope you bear that in mind."

Later in the day I had an interview with the Governor which was more than satisfactory, as he shook hands with me and told me to take a seat. Christie was present and appeared to be busy with treaty business.

"Your salary will be five dollars a day, as you have interpreted for the Indians as well as the government."

"He has done two men's work," said Christie, "so he is entitled to that money as well. And the man has travelled several hundred miles to be here — he should be given something for that."

"You are right, Mr. Christie," replied the Governor. "Put him down for fifteen dollars for four days' pay. He will be paid at five dollars a day during treaty negotiations and a travel allowance until I am through at Fort Pitt."

This was indeed good news and the unexpected support from Mr. Christie was, you can believe me, more than ample compensation for my real or imagined slight of the first evening of the talks.

"You may go with me to Fort Pitt by way of Battleford or you can go direct to Fort Pitt and meet me there. You will be paid at the rate of five dollars per day for travelling and the same for interpreting when I arrive."

"I would prefer to go direct to Fort Pitt as I have a friend with me who will take care of some supplies that I intend to take back to my people."

So it was arranged to meet at Fort Pitt.

Hunter, during all our stay at Carlton, had taken care of our horses, and also made himself useful in keeping me informed of all the latest developments in camp in relation to the activities and opinions in regard to treaty talks. I was thus free to devote all my time to a study of the treaty terms in the conduct of my duties. He had cultivated a friendship with Mista-wa-sis and Ah-tuk-a-kup, and I suspect kept them fully informed on all angles of their opposition.

On the morning of the twenty-fifth, we were making

preparations to go to Fort Pitt when the two main chiefs called at our teepee to inform us that they had not collected all the money from their Indians for our pay.

"We were waiting for the Indians to receive all their treaty money before we started collecting your money."

I replied: "We will have to start today or this evening as it will just give us time to meet our appointment with the Governor."

"All right," said Star Blanket. '.We will start at once and see what we can do. You must wait until we see you later in the day."

They handed me two hundred and thirty dollars that afternoon, and with the sixty I had received from the paymaster Mr. Christie, I felt well paid for my trip. I thanked them for the money and told them I was well satisfied with the amount they gave me.

An Indian stopped me while I was making the rounds of the traders' stores and offered to buy Whitey, my buffalo runner horse. "I want a hundred dollars for him without the saddle or bridle," I said.

He accepted at once and handed me a roll of bills for me to count out the money. I called Hunter to witness the counting, as he had been instructed in the use of money. The animal was good value for the price but I mention this incident to show how easily at that time the Indians could have been cheated out of their money.

I bought a good stout cart horse harnessed to a cart for fifty dollars to carry our duffle and the goods we bought. The traders were getting ready to move to the next trading spot at Fort Pitt and were offering some good deals to lighten their loads. I bought a shotgun practically new for about half the asking price from my new brother-in-law, then loaded our carts with staple articles of food and a stove. This would be the first cooking stove we would have since our marriage.

At our evening stop I took the gun and presented it to John Hunter; his pleasure was something to see, as he alternately polished the blued steel of the barrel and took aim as if to get used to the feel of the gun. Then I showed him a handsome piece of good print for dresses for his wife and some household utensils as well, but when I showed him all those things his former pleasure evaporated and he looked very grim.

"Peter," he said, "I cannot accept this gun with all the other things that you have bought for us. I never could match such a gift with a return. It is too much. My wife shall have all the things you bought for her but I am sorry you must take the gun back."

"That gun, my friend, is not a gift. It is in payment for all the work looking after the horses and your trouble mixing with the Indians to bring back a report of what was going on in camp. You have earned the price of that gun five times over. Without your help, I could not have prepared my interpretations or made myself familiar with all the things the Governor had to tell the people in that paper the chiefs and councillors signed."

"Yes," said Hunter, "but I was doing those things for my own pleasure and didn't know that it was any help to you. I would have looked after the horses in any case."

"You must not think," I said, "that I would be so ungrateful and selfish as to take all that pay and not give you something for all your wife has done for us and all the kind friendly acts you have done for me personally." Assuming an angry tone, I said, "Throw the gun away if you wish. It is yours to do what you like with it. I do not need another gun as I have one at home just as good."

He was profuse in his apologies. Luckily I had hit on the only theme that could dissolve his ethical beliefs that a gift must always have compensation.

"You must give those things to my wife as a gift. Do not give her those things as payment for care of your wife, or she will be hurt and refuse them even as a gift." I had not thought of it his way. Such delicate management hadn't occurred to me. To pay his wife for what they considered a friendly service would be putting a price on friendship that would take away the pleasure of doing things for your real friends.

We were both happy on the first leg of our journey towards home. We were well satisfied with our trip. John Hunter was a chief in his own tribe. His name interpreted in English was Little Hunter. He was not a small man as his name would indicate but I found that the name may have been received as a child. He was not a big man but he certainly wasn't little either in physical stature or in character.

"Poundmaker," he said while discussing the meeting, "is not satisfied, nor will he ever be satisfied. He does not think but just talks and keeps on talking. He and some of the others will make trouble. Times will be hard for the prairie Indians once the buffalo are gone. They will have nothing and will not settle on the land until they are nearing starvation. Steinhauer has often told us that we must learn to farm and raise animals to support ourselves for the day when the buffalo will be no more. Now I have to believe him. We are lucky that we already know something about raising grain and vegetables, and besides we still have bush game and fish.

We arrived at Fort Pitt ahead of the government party. A detachment of Police was already camped on the north side of the river and I counted a hundred Indian teepees camped on the flat near the fort.

We crossed the river with a boat that some traders were using to carry their goods across. Although the river was unusually low that fall, crossing goods over safely always gave some concern. By assisting the traders, we got the use of their boat that made the crossing a simple matter.

On the morning of September the fifth, the Governor and his party arrived with a Police escort that had gone out to meet him. All the tribes that were to meet there had not yet arrived but they had sent riders ahead to tell the others of their coming. Finally on the sixth, the last of the tribes pitched their teepees with the others.

I was resting under my cart when William Bull of the James Seenum band came to where I was resting. "The chiefs have called a meeting and have sent me to bring you to speak to them."

I thought it necessary for one of us to stay with our cart as there was a host of prowling dogs around. Train dogs are cunning beasts and I always said that I thought they would sooner steal than be fed in a proper way.

"Go ahead," said Hunter. "I can keep your shady couch warm till you return. Then we will move in with the chief Seenum and William who have invited us to share their teepee. We can get a canvas and bind our load for safety."

I was questioned at some length about the attitude of the tribes who signed the treaty at Carlton, about details in reference to treaty concessions, and the terms agreed upon, which by that time I had memorized by heart. I gave them a review of the discussions of the council meeting of the chiefs at Carlton, reporting the objections raised by those who opposed the signing, and spoke of the petition that had been drawn up for the Commissioner, with the points agreed to and those refused. I mentioned Poundmaker's and The Badger's efforts at trying to block or misinterpret the terms of the treaty, at which there were some expressions of disgust about their attitude.[14] Then I wound up my talk by a report of the two speeches made by Mista-wa-sis and Ah-tuk-a-kup that had swung the whole opinion of the assembly in favour of the signing.

I could see that the content of these two speeches had a tremendous effect on my audience, as I had reserved the latter for the last before sitting down.

Sweet Grass, who was the most important chief among

those gathered in council, rose to his feet to speak to their people.

"Mista-wa-sis and Ah-tuk-a-kup, I consider, are far wiser than I am; therefore if they have accepted this treaty for their people after many days of talk and careful thought, then I am prepared to accept for my people."

Chief Seenum then took his place and spoke. "You have all questioned Peter Erasmus on the things that have taken place at Carlton. He is a stranger to many of you but I am well acquainted with him. I have respect for his words and have confidence in his truthfulness. Mista-wa-sis and Ah-tuk-a-kup both sent their sons all the way from Carlton to where he lives, and he is married to one of our favourite daughters. He was not at home but they followed him to the prairie where he was hunting buffalo with our people. Little Hunter is a chief and brings back a good report of his work during treaty talks. He would not tell us something that was not for our good. Therefore, as those other chiefs who are in greater number than we are have found this treaty good, I and my head man will sign for our people. I have spoken."

Each of the other chiefs with their councillors expressed agreement, each man expressing in his own words ideas that conformed to the general acceptance of treaty terms. They were all willing to sign the treaty and there was not a single dissenting voice.

There was some delay on the morning of the seventh, which was the day set for the meeting with the Governor, as it was found that there were insufficient young men for the manoeuvres that always preceded a gathering of this kind as at the meeting at Carlton. Finally two young men volunteered their help. They were in training but as yet were not considered fully qualified.

The riders were performing in front of the people who were advancing to the Commissioner's tent when suddenly the two young men got confused in their movements and crashed their horses into each other. Both men were thrown to the ground, receiving injuries, and the horses were hurt. Fortunately there was a Police doctor on hand who took charge of the injured men. One had a dislocated hip while the other had only minor injuries; as they were taken care of the proceedings went ahead.

To an inexperienced person, viewing it for the first time, the show would appear to be a disorganized, undisciplined, crazy display of horsemanship, but this was not true. I had watched them training from a slow walking speed; all movements had an exact timing that was finally speeded up to manoeuvres that were carried out with a speed and intricacy of movement that was most confusing to those watching for the first time.

When the people were finally seated in their usual posture, sitting cross-legged, the Governor opened his address. There were no interruptions, but quiet attentive listening. At the conclusion of his talks, he asked the people for their opinions, but no one responded. There was a considerable pause as he waited for their reaction to his words. Morris looked puzzled, or rather "disappointed" might be the better description of his attitude. At other places he had received many objections and a lot of questions.

Finally Chief Eagle got to his feet, faced the people, and told them not to be afraid to speak their minds. If there was anything they did not understand or wished to know, this was the place and the time to express their thoughts. However, there was no response; apparently they had made up their minds the day previously.

Sweet Grass made a speech of some length, expressing his willingness on behalf of his people to accept the treaty terms and summed up his address by saying, "I am no wiser than my brothers at Fort Carlton who have accepted the Queen Mother's hand. I will sign for my people."

James Seenum spoke with some feeling, referring to the plough he had received as a gift from Mr. Christie some years previously. He stated that they had pulled the plough by manpower when their ponies had refused to work, had used the roots of trees for hoes, and had now learned the value of growing grain and vegetables. He was greatly pleased to know that now they would be furnished with better tools and the means to work the land.

Chief Seenum asked for a large tract of land. "For my part, I wish to say that I want a large area to settle all the Cree — the Woods Crees and Plain Crees — who may not now be taken in by the treaties at this time."[15]

Apparently he wanted a general reserve that would accommodate all Indians who might not at this time be willing to choose land and which would be set apart for this purpose. The chief went on to say, "I want an area from the Whitemud River to Dog Rump Creek, extending back as far as the Beaver River and its southern border to be the Saskatchewan River."

The Governor replied that he could not promise such a large tract of land without consultation with his superiors. The area selected was beyond his instructions. "It is not in my power to add clauses to this treaty, no more than you have already been promised, but I will bring your request before the House at Ottawa. However, I know it will not be accepted. As you said so, being a chief, I will bring the matter to the attention of my superiors."

Eight years afterward, in June of 1884, James Seenum engaged me to accompany him and interpret in regard to his request for a large area as requested in this treaty at Fort Pitt. We went to Regina where he was successful in getting the Saddle Lake Reserve lines extended to take in a block of land to the east. He had amended his claims considerably but won his demands for better farm land, because the Whitefish and Goodfish Reserves were not large enough to accommodate the young people according to the average per-person allowance by treaty terms.

On September 9th, the treaty terms were read and explained to the people. The chiefs agreed to sign, and so the treaty was quickly completed with none of the dissension that had occurred at Carlton. The paying of treaty money and issuing of uniforms took the greater part of two more days.

Governor Morris advised me that I would now be in the government service and that he would recommend me at a salary of fifty dollars per month. I would act for the government in the distribution of rations and goods in fulfillment of the government's part of the treaty terms. I would also be called upon from time to time to interpret the treaties to those chiefs who had not yet signed. I was to remain at my present abode at Whitefish Lake for the purpose of handling matters concerned with Indians of that area and its precincts.

This information was most agreeable and an entirely different prospect than that I was faced with on my first appearance at Carlton. Governor Morris further advised me that I would be on call for any assignment for which my services might be required. To all this I agreed, suitably expressing my appreciation of his confidence and assuring him of my fidelity in the accomplishment of my duties.

The departure of Governor Morris and his entourage was attended by all the chiefs and their head men, with considerable show of appreciation and good wishes from the Indians at Fort Pitt. For myself, I felt that all the chiefs there would carry out their obligations with sincerity and would make every effort to assist their people to become established on the reserves that they would choose the following summer. This was verified in later years when I had an opportunity of visiting some of their reserves.

The camp now broke up. William Bull came to me and said he wanted to travel home with me. I was glad and arranged with him to drive one of the carts. I bought another cart and horse from a trader at a very low price as he had sold out his goods and did not need the outfit on his return to Fort Garry.

I also bought five sacks of flour from the government stores from stock they had on hand to meet requirements of the Indians in the treaty negotiations, a half keg of tea, and a half keg of sugar from a ten gallon barrel. I took all the tobacco I could get, as there had been a heavy run on this luxury item. Taking advantage of the lower prices of the traders anxious to clear their stocks for the return journey, I was able to practically name my own price for the things I wanted.

The cart that I had purchased from Alexander Kennedy was iron bound, the first to make an appearance in the trade, so I was not afraid to load heavy. I was very well pleased with myself as I made the rounds of the traders preparing to leave, picking up bargains wherever I could. Money, my friend, had a great deal more value in those days and I still had money in my pocket when my carts were loaded.

William Bull was usually the best of companions but for the first few days I thought he was very quiet and somewhat despondent. Actually he seemed to be occupied in some deep thought, so I finally asked him what was troubling him.

"The chief has asked for a great stretch of land about which he now speaks as if it had already been promised to him. I listened carefully to your interpretations of the Governor's answer to his request. The Governor stated that he had no authority to grant any such request and merely stated that as James Seenum was a chief and had asked, he would pass the request on to his superiors. Is that right, Peter?"

"Yes, it certainly is. To have an unrestricted amount of land for one chief would have broken the terms of the treaty to all those others who had already signed. Surely Chief Seenum does not think that he has been promised the land from the Dog Rump Creek as far west as the Whitemud River, with the Beaver River at the north and the Saskatchewan River as its southern boundary?"

"Yes! That is exactly what he told me only the last night before the camp broke up. I tried to explain to him that this was not true but he would have none of my explanation, and we had some words between us. That is why I asked to go along with you. It would be a good thing if you would speak to him about the real truth as spoken by the Governor."

"Well of course I will talk to him, but if he does not listen to the words of his own councillor, how will he listen to me? If he is not satisfied with the terms of the treaty why did he sign? It seemed to me that he understood everything that I spoke about the night of the first council of the chiefs." I explained to them that each man, woman and child then living would be apportioned eighty acres each,[16] according to the number of Indians then belonging to his tribe.

"I and the others all understood exactly as you now explain. Further than that, the Governor also mentioned the amount of land each Indian would be entitled to when they picked their reserves next year. For myself, I can only occupy a small portion of the land my family would be entitled to, but I understand that all the land, regardless of the amount each family uses, will belong to the band and can be used by our children's children."

"You are quite right, William. I know the chief is a stubborn man but surely he is a man of his word. He has promised to abide by the agreement that all the other chiefs signed. He signed for his band and so did you."

"This thing will someday make trouble for us, mark my word," said William Bull, "for the man is not easily turned from his way, once he makes up his mind. I am afraid he will persist in claiming that the land was promised by the Governor, and many of our people will follow his lead. You and I both know differently but will the people believe us? Suppose they did, can we go against our chief?"

"Well, William, we will cross the bridge when we come to it. In the meantime, I do not think we should bother our heads about it. All the Governor promised, as I said before, was that he would bring his request to his superiors, and he also said that he was certain that they would refuse."

We were heavily loaded but by travelling early and late, we made good time. The weather remained clear and our stock stood up to the work. Our equipment did not give us any trouble or cause of delay. My iron bound cart proved an excellent improvement over the other all-wood carts.

My family was not yet home by the time we arrived at Whitefish, so we unloaded our carts and arranged to have my new horses taken care of. I caught up a fresh saddle horse and started out to meet the buffalo hunters.

I shot a black bear near where the village of Spedden is now situated. He was standing on his hind legs eating saskatoons on a side hill. He was bending the branches with his paws much as man would do. I shot him just behind the front legs in the body. He dropped and rolled almost to my horse's feet from about twenty-five steps away. The thick growth of grass had deadened the sound of my approach. It was a tempting shot but a foolish one. If our party were not on this side of the Saskatchewan, the meat would spoil before it could be used. I felt guilty of a crime against all the laws of prairie life — unwritten laws, but nevertheless lived up to by all the tribes of my acquaintance. Wasting animal life without cause was looked upon as the act of a stupid and unthinking person.

Fortunately for my conscience, our people were close at hand and I met them within an hour's ride. My family was well. My newest son showed his objections to being stopped on the trail by a lusty show of lung power that wouldn't stop till the cart moved on. There was one son who would follow his father's footstep — he loved travelling before he could even crawl. The party camped early that evening and some men went out to bring the bear back to camp for distribution among the people.

CHAPTER FIFTEEN

Rebellion

I WAS EMPLOYED by the Indian Department from 1876 to 1879 at Whitefish Lake, working from my own home; then I was transferred to Edmonton to assist a new agent at that place. There were several reserves under his agency. I left my family at Whitefish as there was no accommodation for a family man available that fall.

During February of 1880, a messenger arrived to inform me that my wife was very sick. He had a letter from Mr. Steinhauer which plainly indicated that her illness was serious and my return urgent. I rode out alone that very hour after informing the agent of the necessity of my departure. He offered no objections. Had he done so, it would have made no difference. Steinhauer's letter had an added postscript, "Make haste, if you hope to see your wife alive."

The animal I rode was grain fed and lasted as far as the Lobstick settlement, where I hired another horse, arranging with the owner to bring my horse to Victoria and take his horse home. I knew Louis Thompson had some good horses and I hoped to get one from him.

There were no lights in any of the houses I passed but I knew it was long past midnight. I rode up to the door and got stiffly off my horse. A big smooth-haired dog tried his best to drive me away. Louis must have been a light sleeper for I had scarcely finished a loud knock when he opened the door to let me in. I told him my business and explained the urgency of my trip.

"Wait till I get a lantern. Take your horse to any empty stall you find. I will start a fire and get you something to eat. There are several good horses in the barn. I am not much of a rider but you can have your choice."

After I had taken care of the horse, I saw a light in the other house. I entered and saw a roaring fire in an open chimney place. There were two Lac La Biche men who were on their way to Edmonton freighting for the Hudson's Bay store at that place. I asked them if they had heard any word about my wife. Yes, but only that she was very sick.

Thompson came in and called me back to his home; my breakfast was ready. "I've been thinking, Erasmus, that in your condition after riding from Edmonton you would make better time with a team and light sleigh. The road should be fair, as this is the second outfit to pass over the Lac La Biche trail this week."

"Yes, it would be much better and a lot easier for me. I have done very little riding in the last two years. My bones ache most unmercifully and my leg muscles cramp almost beyond endurance."

"All right then, you will go to sleep until we have the outfit ready. We will call you at daylight."

The hot meal, the first since leaving Edmonton, made me very sleepy after being out in the cold all day and part of the night. It seemed only a few moments when the hired man came to wake me and say the outfit would be ready as soon as I ate some breakfast. I was very grateful for the use of the sleigh. The team was well fed and eager to go but I held them down to a reasonable pace before allowing them a free rein.

Six hours later I drove up to our home. My wife was still conscious. She gave me a glad smile of welcome, and with a satisfied sigh dropped into a coma from which she never awoke.[1] It was a hard blow coming as it did without any previous sickness, for she had always been healthy, happy, and full of enthusiasm for the things that made up our life together. Charlotte was always proud of her family. She had a deep Christian faith and followed a strict observance of its principles. She brought her family up and shaped them into men and women, so that in later years they were known as honest straight-forward individuals whose word could always be accepted.

The Rev. Steinhauer took complete charge of the arrangements, even in the matter of the care of the children, and installed a housekeeper whom the children had learned to like. He thus made it possible for me to complete my contract with the government. I had been engaged in a contract for two years when I agreed to go to Edmonton. It would be almost a year before my term would expire. You did not quit your employment whenever the whim possessed you as is done in these days. Your responsibility to your employers was moral as well as financial.

It was late in the afternoon when I arrived at Thompson's and took care of the team. My own horse was in the stable and I was saddling up to continue my trip when Thompson came to the stable.

"What are you doing, man? Saddling the horse at this time of day. No man leaves my place at this hour. Strip that saddle off and come to my house for supper and bed. You can leave at any hour tomorrow morning, but not tonight."

The man spoke with a harshness and a tone of voice that would brook no refusal but I felt that those emphatic words covered a sympathy and hospitality that I had heard of long before I became acquainted with the man. Actually, this was the first time that I had any dealing with him. I knew it was not because I was leaving without offering payment, for I had offered to pay him before I left with his team. He had curtly refused to accept a cent and had said, "No, I don't want your money. You can do as much for me or any man that needs help in trouble like yours."

Thompson had two big log houses, one for his family home and another for use of travellers. A big fireplace occupied one end of the stopping place with kindling and wood ready for any traveller to start a fire. There were bunks on the lower floor and wooden beds upstairs to be used when the place was crowded. Travellers using the place were supposed to leave it cleaned up when they went away. There was never any charge for this service. Of course, by the custom of the times, travellers usually bought a hamper of whitefish from La Biche, a leg of some game animal or similar treat not available to a man who was not a hunter. They were likely to find a chunk of pork or a large slice of pickled sturgeon tucked under their canvas covers on their way home.

It was during my conversation with Thompson that night that I was persuaded to take up a river lot two and half miles upriver from his place. This was the first land that I was to own although I did not live on it until several years afterward. My oldest son Jimmy completed homestead duties when it became necessary to register land, and still lives on the land as you take these notes of my travels in this year of 1924.

During the winter of 1881, while I was still attached to the Edmonton Agency, I had orders from the Hon. E. Dewdney[2] to go to Fort Pitt. There I was instructed to leave for the Cypress Hills to endeavour to persuade the Indians who were camped there to go back to their reserves.[3] Big Bear did go to Frog Lake, where he had chosen a reserve, and a few of the eastern Indians left, but we failed to get the others to move.[4]

Many of these people were in very poor circumstances, with no means of transportation. The officials responsible seemed to be very reluctant to provide any means of travel. I decided it was a hopeless task. As my time was about to expire, I sent in my resignation to take effect immediately at the end of my agreement. I wanted to go back to my family at Whitefish Lake, but before arriving home, I met up with Hardisty, who offered me a position buying furs at Whitefish Lake. He would put in a stock of goods for trade and I would work under the Hudson's Bay post at Lac La Biche and receive a commission on my purchases for fur and the sale of their goods.

The offer sounded all right and I said I would try it for one year. If both parties were satisfied at the end of the year's trial, then we would continue for an indefinite time. He agreed and thus I went into business where I would be at home where I was needed now that my family were growing up. The arrangement lasted till the Rebellion of 1885.

I returned home early in the spring of 1882.[5] I was forty-eight years old and tired of travel. Many of the happiest days of my life were centred around the quiet precincts of the wooded country at Whitefish Lake. I was eager to meet my old friends among the Indians of that locality. My children would be strangers after an absence of almost two years, but I now found myself as eagerly looking forward to meeting them as I had been reluctant to face the vacancy in our home a year after my wife's death.

I had been delayed at Fort Pitt, awaiting confirmation of my resignation, but was able to send a message to Peter Shirt, my foster son, that I would be returning as soon as I received my release. I found him camped on the trail a day's journey from home. He had come to meet me. He offered no explanation of how he knew when I would arrive. He had camped there the afternoon before and was hunting ducks while he waited.

I thought it odd that he had guessed so exactly my approach to home, for I could see that he had made no preparation for a prolonged stay. He just laughed and said, "Oh, this is a nice place to get ducks and it made no difference which direction I went; I chose this way in case I should meet you."

However, I knew that in those days you didn't have to ride twenty-five miles just to get a brace of ducks. They were numerous three miles from home. I had to be satisfied with his answer for I knew I would get no other. I was glad to see him and happy to hear all about the children and the people around there.

In a few weeks a consignment of freight arrived from the Hudson's Bay at Edmonton, with instructions in regard to sales and the credit-rating of our customers; other detailed instructions would be forwarded from Edmonton in due course. It surprised me how much detailed information their reports contained about the personal integrity and earning capacity of each of my potential customers that would be included in my area.

My first year working with the Company proved to be quite satisfactory to them, as it did for me, so I continued expanding our business to include most of the Saddle Lake Indians who used the region north and west of Whitefish as far west as Island Lake. This included Indians who used an area south of the Beaver River, about in the location where Glendon and Mallaig are now situated.

The years from 1882 to the Rebellion of '85 were quiet ones at Whitefish Lake, in which I did not travel to any extent except in the spring, when I went out on local trips. Usually some well known trapper sent word that he had a large pack of furs for sale, so with a saddle horse and pack animal to carry some trade goods I would make an overnight stop and then return.

In the year 1884, Chief James Seenum insisted that I accompany him on a trip to Regina to interview the governor with respect to the land that he still insisted had been promised to him, although he had somewhat amended his previous claims. The survey of the reserves at Whitefish Lake and Goodfish Lake did not contain sufficient land for the listed population of Indians under James Seenum's band. I pointed out to him that he could establish a claim under that heading and that he was entitled to more land. An extension of his present boundaries at Whitefish would not greatly benefit his people as it was practically all bush land. They had the free use of it for their hunting and would likely have it for many years in the future. The reserve boundaries at Saddle Lake had also been surveyed, but there was a large strip of land on its eastern boundary still unoccupied, which contained much good hay land and quite considerable good open farm land. The chief then decided that he would pursue his claim along those lines.

We were very cordially received by the officials, all of whom I believe were quite anxious to satisfy the chief's complaint without complicating the original treaty terms. After pointing out the deficiency of the land granted at Whitefish Lake for the number of *bona fide* members of the chief's band, the vacant land available near the Saddle Lake reserve boundaries, and Chief Seenum's wish to take the land there for his Whitefish Indians, an amicable settlement was arranged. Of course the whole matter would have to get final ratification from Ottawa, but we were assured there would be no trouble on that score.

Meanwhile, immediate steps would be taken to reserve the land against settlement while arrangements were completed in Ottawa. I had some difficulty in convincing the chief that another formal signing of a paper was unnecessary. I thought that we had been very successful in getting what we had. The chief's band at that time took in practically all of those people dealing with my store at Whitefish Lake. In fact my list of names in that trading account was referred to in compiling figures for the land shortage by population that the chief "demanded" or, rather, interpreted by me, "requested".

Later, on our way home, the chief grumbled that promises by government people were like the clouds, always changing. However, I was able to convince him that he had received a great deal more than could be rightfully established, if they took the trouble to tabulate listed names on their treaty accounts. Knowing the slow processes of government business, I carefully planted in his mind the fact that he would get no results in less than a year's time. Setting the land aside and closing it to settlement was the first and most important step that would in time ensure success. It was almost two years before the request was finally officially settled.

My foster son, Peter Shirt married, had one son, and now lived in his own home about three miles from my place. A good hunter and trapper, he had his own hunting area around Lone Pine west of Whitefish Lake, then called Little Whitefish; this lake and that of Lone Pine were about twelve miles from my store. Though he lived in his own place, he continued to look after our stock and the things around the place just as if he still stayed there. He never returned from a hunting trip without calling to leave a share of game, moose, or deer that were plentiful in that area.

Peter had been home for some time when he came to visit me. It was around the beginning of March, 1884. He seemed troubled and, as I could see, somewhat hesitant in speaking of

270

what was on his mind. I thought he was in need and backward in asking me for help.

"What is troubling you? You should know that if you are in need of anything at home you have but to mention it and it is yours."

"No," said Peter, "it's not that. We have plenty right now. I have had an odd dream that bothers me a lot. I have had other dreams and have forgotten them almost as soon as I woke up, but this dream has stayed in my mind and memory as clear in every way as if the things that I saw were actually happening when I was awake. I cannot forget any part of it."

"You are a sensible Christian man; you live a Christian life," I said. "Surely you have not gone back to the beliefs of the tribe from whom I brought you away?" They practised many strange things in those days and still do even in this day.

"No, father! That's not true. I have done nothing to provoke or entice such thoughts in my mind. It was just a dream that I cannot forget."

"All right, then, let me hear what you dreamed. Perhaps then you will forget it afterward."

"I dreamed that a very old man came to me and, taking me by the hand, led me to the top of a high hill. 'Look to the east,' he said, 'and tell me what you see.'

"'I see many black clouds churning and rolling in many queer shapes and forms. Yet they seem to cover the same area and are not drifting with any wind. What does it mean?'

"'It means that there will be war and bloodshed and troubled times for many people. Now look to the west and tell me what you see.'

"'I see a big valley along the Saskatchewan River. There are many tents, wagons, and Police. They are very busy and there are a lot of horses picketed to one rope. I think I know the place. Yes! There are buildings and a church there. It must be Victoria.'

"'If you take your people to that place, all your people will be safe from the trouble and death that is coming from the East.'

"Then I asked the old man when this would take place. How would I know? 'Your family will own a white horse. The horse will die. When that happens, then you will know that the trouble has already happened. Take heed that you follow this warning!'"

I said, "Well, Peter, that is a strange dream, but it is unlikely that the dream will repeat itself in your mind. Don't worry. There have been some strange happenings in my experience that I have failed to account for or begin to understand.

271

Christian prayer is the only relief that I can recommend to you. I depend on it to drive away my own worries. Try it, Peter, it always works for me."

During the summer of 1884, Peter and some others were out hunting moose and deer about twenty miles west of my place when some Indians passed and stopped to purchase a few articles. They were going further north and wanted to trade a horse. He had sore feet and was very lame. They would take anything that could carry a pack and was not lame.

I went to look at their horse and was immediately taken with his splendid formation and attractive, intelligent appearance. Though thin and run down, he was young and had every indication of being an excellent saddle horse. I gave them a bigger roan for their horse and they went away perfectly satisfied that they had made a good deal. I was pretty well delighted at my horse also, and it wasn't until they had been gone a half-day's journey that I recalled Peter Shirt's dream. The horse was a pure white, with pink nostrils and the same around the eyes. I felt a little uneasy but shrugged it off as a stupid superstition. Yet I had some difficulty in not dwelling on the peculiar coincidence of the whole business.

The next day Peter Shirt returned from the hunt alone and as usual stopped at my place to leave us some meat. While he carried the meat to my ice house, I wrapped up some articles, tea, and sugar in return for his thoughtfulness.

"Father," he said, "you have traded for a white horse?"

"Yes," I replied. "I have and a fine animal he is. I got him in trade for that lazy mare you always complain is more trouble to drive than she is worth. But who told you about it?"

"No-one knows about it but yourself, for you must have him tied in the stable."

I was angered at the positive and vehement way he had spoken, as if I had done something shameful behind his back. "Of course he is in the stable but what on earth has that got to do with you?"

He turned and started to walk out of the store but at the door he stopped, speaking over his shoulder with anger in his voice: "I knew you had the horse for I had that dream again last night. This is the last time I will confide my thoughts in you for I believe you think that I have been lying to you."

He had gone away without the parcel which he knew I always had ready every time he brought any meat. It would be useless to approach him in his present state of mind. This was the first time in our lives that he had ever been guilty of disrespect or that I had uttered an angry word to him. I felt bad over our disagreement. I knew that he was badly hurt that I didn't believe in his dream.

My horse grew fat and sleek on the lush grass of the range, never strayed from our other horses, and could be caught out in the open any place, though he was a strong high-lifed beast, easy to ride and gentle under the saddle. I grew quite fond of the horse and I'm afraid somewhat boastful of his qualities.

Peter Shirt came back to visit me not too long afterwards, but neither by word or sign ever mentioned the cause of our slight difference or ever again referred to his dream, except once the next year when I directly questioned him about it.

"It bothers me, Father, that I remember every part of the dream but cannot recall one thing about the man's face except that he was a very old man and was not dressed as our people are. That part I remember quite clearly."

I looked at him with some surprise as he said these last words for I was reminded that the people from his tribe scorned the use of white men's goods and dressed in native costumes of their own tanned leathers and furs. The men dressed with little more during the summer than a breechcloth that merely covered their loins, with a light robe at hand while resting to cover their shoulders.

It was curiosity to see the way they were dressed that had originally induced me to go into their camp. William Bull, who was with me at the time, had told me about their attitude towards white men's dress. That was when I had taken the boy from the camp.

"Those people are Peigan Indians," he said with something of contempt in his voice. "They conjure and believe in dreams. Their medicine men are very powerful and the men all have two or three wives. Their chief has four wives, the youngest barely a third of his age and the oldest could be his grandmother. "Yes," added Bull with some pride, "we Christian Indians have learned to adapt ourselves to the best things and have thrown away many of our worst customs. Those people camped there cling to the bad and refuse to accept the better things for their people."

I had never told Peter about the people of his tribe and he had never evinced any interest about the matter. Inquiry established that their main chief had died a number of years earlier, and that with the extinction of the buffalo they had been forced to adopt white men's clothes and an adaptation of living conditions similar to the other prairie Indians.

The year of 1884 was eventful in that we buried the Rev. H. B. Steinhauer and his good friend and companion Benjamin

Sinclair. They died within a day of each other and by the common wish of both families were buried in the same large grave.

Rev. Mr. Steinhauer had joined Sinclair at Lac La Biche in 1855 but Steinhauer, in passing through Whitefish Lake on his way from the Saddle Lake crossing, had been greatly impressed with the location as an ideal place in which to carry out a plan of a permanent settlement for the migratory Indians he had come to serve. The same fall they had returned to Whitefish to prepare logs for the mission and then moved down the following summer where they had lived almost continuously till the day we buried them.

During March 1885, Peter Shirt came to invite me to a dinner at his home. I closed the store, caught up a horse from the corrals, and rode along with him. There had been very little business for several weeks and the spring furs were not yet due.

I owned around six head of horses that were running on the range. I kept only one horse at home for an occasional trip, inspecting the horses or visiting Indians in the course of my business. I decided that we had time to look up the horses that ranged along the creek and hills between Peter's place and mine. We found the horses almost at once but the white horse was not with them. Shirt suggested that he could not be far as he had seen him just a few days ago. Perhaps he had strayed with some other animals. I asked Peter to help me locate the horse. We searched the surrounding area quite thoroughly, saw other horses, but no sign of the white one.

"It's getting late. My guests will be waiting for me. We'd better cut across to my place from here and I'll get some of the young men to come and look for your horse."

"All right," I replied. "The horse has probably got in with some other animals. All the others are in good condition and the white horse looked the fattest of any two weeks ago. Lead the way."

"No," he said. "You go ahead. I have a mink trap to look at near the creek."

We were following a long chain of sloughs considerably south of where our horses usually ranged. It was open country and avoided the bush. This chain of sloughs came out near Peter's house and was the easiest way direct to his home. Peter had not yet caught up with me when I found the horse. He was lying on his back, stone dead. He had been rolling and got caught in the snow. The marks showed that he had put up a good fight trying to turn over on his feet, but the more he struggled the deeper he became embedded in the snow, and more hopeless his chances of escaping.

Neither of us had a word to say but I could see that Shirt was deeply affected by my loss or, more likely, convinced of the significance of the accident in relation to his dream. I had become fond of the animal but it was nothing to get gloomy about, yet Peter was like a man bowed down with gloom.

There were several people standing in groups in front of Peter's house when we got there. I was surprised at the number of people he had invited, especially when we went inside. The house was packed and excited voices came from all parts of the room. Peter had told me that there would be only a few people, just a few close friends and his wife's parents. When our entrance was noticed the talk died down.

Big Louis came forward to greet us. I knew for certain he was not among the invited guests. We shook hands with him.

"My friends, I bring you bad news. The half-breeds under Louis Riel have taken up arms against the government and there has been fighting. Big Bear has joined and is sending out riders to stir up all the tribes he can reach. There has been a massacre at Frog Lake. They killed two priests and several other white men. Some Saddle Lakers have gone to join in the fight. Others are planning to make a raid on the Hudson's Bay store at Victoria. The rebels want possession of all the Hudson's Bay posts. The rebels claim a victory against the Police. I came to warn you in case they send men here."

Shirt had been silent during Big Louis's report. Now he turned and looked at me with an unspoken question in his expression. Only then did the significance of his dream register on my mind. It was all the more astounding in view of the dead white horse that he had mentioned almost twelve months before to a day. If I had given the matter any thought at all, it was with irritation and annoyance that his education and all his Christian faith could still leave him open to such utter nonsense. Now I was faced with facts beyond my ability to understand or in any way account for as accidental or mere coincidence.

At that moment Samuel Jackson came into the room, walked up to Shirt, and told him that Acam-escen-is had taken two horses and told people he was going off to join the war. Now others came forward and told him that the man had taken Peter's gun from the store house and had gone away with it in his hand.

Sam Jackson had his gun with him. Shirt borrowed a rifle and saddled a fresh horse, and they both started after the thief. The man was reputed to be a famous warrior and horse thief in the days of Indian raids and possibly thought that no-one would be brave enough to try to stop him. The man had taken

275

his time preparing for the trip. They caught up with him shortly after he left the reserve. Over-confident of his safety, he had shot a chicken for his supper and neglected to reload. He had been an easy capture for the two angry and vengeful attackers.

They laughed when they came back leading the two horses and I asked them what had happened. They told us that for a famous warrior and horse thief, the man must have been badly out of practice. They had watched for him as he came along a narrow part of the road. They jumped him from two sides, disarmed him, and set him afoot with a warning that if he ever appeared in these parts he would be killed.

Big Louis was an influential man among his tribe at Saddle Lake, and though not a chief at that time, was active in working for the betterment of his people. He listened quite attentively to my arguments against any chance of the rebels winning a fight. Having worked with the Indian Department, I thought that the various chiefs were generally satisfied with their treatment in adjusting themselves to a new way of life. The government had not adopted a penurious attitude or a hide-bound policy strictly in adherence with treaty terms, but had instituted a more liberal action according to the needs of the people actually concerned. He listened with a quiet appreciation that made me feel my information was in accord with his own convictions.

There was a quiet determination about my foster son now, that I could not help but notice. Always he had come to me for direction and advice. Now he was giving his wife instructions for the conduct of his affairs that indicated a long absence from home.

"Peter," he said, "your store will be the first place these raiders will attack. Jackson has agreed to notify me as soon as Big Bear's men arrive on this reserve. We will ride and see the chief at once. I am not sure just how he will take our news."

Jackson immediately rose and went out and shortly after came back to tell us that our horses were ready. It was quite apparent that Peter Shirt had lost confidence in his foster father and now assumed leadership as if it had been a natural attribute of our former relations. Strangely enough, I felt no resentment at this new attitude — rather I felt relieved of the responsibility of the tense situation we were facing or likely to face in the near future. Calling me by my first name in addressing me emphasized his changed status, as he seldom if ever used anything else but "father".

The three-mile ride to the chief's house was a fast, silent

one. Shirt gave the chief a complete report of all that had happened and the news Big Louis had brought, but I noticed two things he omitted: he said nothing about the white horse, and he did not mention anything about the victory against the soldiers that had been claimed by the Metis.

The chief was not disturbed by the news; rather he took it as if it were a verification of something expected or of which he had previous knowledge. I was puzzled over the mild indifference he displayed over the drastic handling of Acamiscen-is. Many of the chiefs of my acquaintance were quite zealous of their authority and any encroachment was resented.

The chief asked us what he had better do. At this question, Peter turned to me and asked, "How much ammunition have you got?"

"A half keg of powder, about twelve pounds, very few balls, and only a small quantity of shot."

"You will go to Lac La Biche and try for some ammunition there while I take care of the store. That, of course, will be the first place the raiders will strike. They will do this in order to promise plunder to those of our Indians who will join them and to intimidate all of us who talk peace. I am prepared to protect your store until this is all over."

There was nothing more to say. The chief merely nodded his head and we took our departure without further conversation. I started for La Biche before daylight in the morning, and arrived early in the afternoon.

The trader Young[6] received my news with consternation, and at my request for ammunition said, "Man, I have none, but it explains why there has been a heavy run on powder and balls these last few weeks." He saddled a horse and rode to the mission to notify them of the news I brought, and also to try to get some ammunition from them.

The mission had already received a messenger informing them of the Frog Lake Massacre and they were busy preparing to evacuate their people. In fact they had sent several boat loads to an island. The balance of the women and children would leave that evening.

It was late when Young got back, accompanied by Peachie Pruden who would take care of the store and immediately move Young's family.

"We will have to go to Edmonton," said Young. "I don't think the rebels will get here before we return, but at any rate there's little we can do to protect Company goods without ammunition. There are not enough boats or men to remove the goods to safe hiding and even if we did, it would serve as an excuse for them to attack our people. It will not take much to stir up trouble among those rascals at Beaver Lake. There is nothing else we can do."

"Can you get sufficient loyal Metis people to protect your store till we get back?" I asked.

"Certainly I could but without sufficient ammunition it would be risking their lives and those of their families, and would probably inflame the whole country. No! I cannot do that. If they damage Company property it is replaceable; human lives are not. Bishop Faraud[7] concurs with me that it is better to move our people to safe hiding on the islands and take every boat with them. There they can be more easily protected."

"Sir, I consider that as good common sense but hardly in keeping with Company policy," I replied.

"Who cares for Company policy at a time like this when human lives are at stake? My family and those of our people are more important than all these goods. Besides, the government will pay damage for goods destroyed in an insurrection."

Thus Young expressed his opinions and with a lot of emphasis.

There were no new developments when we returned to Whitefish Lake, but Young took time out to give Chief Seenum a talk about keeping his Indians from joining the rebels. We changed for fresh horses and picked up two pack animals that Peter had already rounded up and had stabled awaiting our arrival. Apparently there was nothing that the man hadn't figured out.

The factor had a good rifle of the latest manufacture, but my gun was only a rim-fire rifle with but a half-dozen shells. When we reached Fort Saskatchewan, Griesbach was in charge.[8] He gave us a couple of revolvers and ammunition for our rifles and short guns. At Edmonton we found General Strange had arrived with troops.[9] We were able to get thirty-five pounds of powder, sufficient balls, flints, etc., and two new guns and shells.

On our way back we went by Victoria, as we thought we might get some news of the people there, but every house was vacant and there were no people around. We stopped at Mill Creek, so called because the Hudson's Bay had a flour mill there. The big water wheel was silent and there was no-one around. From the appearance of things at the mill, the miller and his family had made a hasty departure.

We were about to ride on when the Rev. Mr. McLaughlin put in a cautious appearance. He was the only man we had sighted since leaving Edmonton. We welcomed him to our camp and stirred up the fire to give him something to eat. We learned that all the settlements from Lobstick to Victoria were camped across the river. They had set up guards and had scouts patrolling the hills for any sight of the rebels. One of those had spotted us, recognized me, and informed the minister.

McLaughlin said he wanted to go with us to find Yeoman,[10] the teacher who was the only white man in that area. He feared the man might be killed. We told him that there was little danger for Yeoman with Peter Shirt taking measures to protect the people. At the first suspicion of trouble, Shirt would send him into hiding with some friendly Indian.

He told us that the Saddle Lakers had come to Victoria, with the intention of raiding the fort, but the guards had warned them off. Actually there was only one man there at the time. He had bluffed them by yelling at them to keep off and firing a few shots over their heads to show them he meant business. They left in a hurry. They had gone a half mile downriver, where they killed a big steer, repaired a York boat with the tallow, and took the meat back to Saddle Lake. That was the extent of any damage at Victoria.

It was nearly dark when we reached the White Mud River where we camped that night. We planned to cut across country after leaving our camp. This would save considerable mileage but would be considerably rougher travelling. At noon the following day it started to drizzle with a light snow. We soon became soaked from the lashing willows that we could not avoid, and by four o'clock, though we were only a few miles from the first of the Indian settlements, we were all in a miserable condition. The minister was worse than any of us, as he had not come prepared for adverse weather conditions, and had joined us for this long trip without a scrap of food in his saddle bags, even though the camp he left had had plenty of food supplies. He had been ten years in the country and his negligence in the matter of providing his food was inexcusably stupid. The Rev. Mr. McLaughlin was an excellent marksman, considered by many of his admirers to be quite a man in the hunt. I was provoked that he had run us short of food by this thoughtlessness. We had deliberately restricted our pack loads in weight to contain only the necessary things required in our intentions of protecting our property. We were rationed on food to last until we reached my place at Whitefish. I thought with some satisfaction that the pangs of hunger affected him as much as they did me, and was just a little amused that he always said a word of supplication at each of our meals for the Lord to supply us with daily food and inspiration to our souls. Yet a little common sense before he left camp would have placed some food in his saddle bags and not run us short.

Whitefish was deserted. My own home was vacant; the door lay open and the front window was not closed. I jumped off my horse to investigate.

"Take it easy," said Young. "I will go with you. There may be some of the rebels around."

I was too cold and hungry to pay any attention to his warning, although I went towards the side with no light. I listened carefully but couldn't hear a sound. I stepped into the door and stumbled over a pack of rat hides. We found the place littered with furs. They had dislodged them from the upper rafters where I had them carefully sorted and stored waiting shipment.

There wasn't a scrap of food in the store, nor on the premises. I suggested that the people might be camped at Cardinal's Point but there were no people around when we got there. I kindled a fire at the edge of the timber, out of sight from the settlement shores, but the minister would not come near the fire.

Young urged him to dry out his clothes, saying, "I would rather be killed by a bullet than freeze to death. Our fire cannot be seen from anywhere except from the west and there are no roads or approaches from that side." The minister finally came to the fire. I was almost tempted to pull the trigger of my short gun behind him when he cautiously approached the blaze.

There was not much prospect for sleep that night as it continued to drizzle with a mixture of snow for good measure. The minister stirred a bit of admiration from Young and a little forgiveness from myself as he laboured all night to keep the fire burning, while we drowsed half asleep and half awake waiting for daylight.

As soon as it was light I caught a horse and told the others I would go among the houses to see if I could get some food. I went first to the mission house, and passing the graveyard, I noticed a freshly made grave. I knew then why all the people had fled the area. There had been a killing and Peter had somehow persuaded the chief to move his people out of danger.

I knew the direction they would go if Peter had anything to do with their flight. I cut across country and in a mile or so had verified my conclusions. Riding back among the houses, I tried to find some food but all I could get were some potatoes from Sinclair's cellar.

I started back to the point when I heard shooting, several shots closely spaced. My companions were in trouble so I raced my horse to another crossing that would bring me to the point from another direction. The horse was foaming when I leapt off his back about two hundred yards from where I left them; I crept noiselessly through the brush till I approached within sight of the camp. Imagine my anger when I saw both gentlemen standing by the shore calmly discussing why they could not hit a diver. I gave them a piece of my mind. Both looked like two small boys caught in the act of raiding the cookie jar. I finally had to laugh, partly in relief, but mostly because they both looked so guilty as they realized the seriousness of their careless action.

"Get your horses while I make the packs ready. We had better get out of here as soon as possible."

I led them back to where I had tied my horse, dug into my saddle bag and handed each man two raw potatoes. "This is your reward for so valiantly routing the enemy. Your bravery in action deserves a suitable acknowledgement."

Without replying to my sarcasm, they each took knives, peeled the tubers and ate them raw with every indication of unalloyed pleasure, gravely thanking me for the delicious reward for their prowess and my heroic efforts on their behalf.

They were to follow the cart trail and turn west after passing Long Lake Creek. They couldn't go straight across, the way I intended to go, because of the loaded pack horses. I hoped to intersect the trail of our people again somewhere east of Island Lake. If for any reason the party had taken a different direction, I would return to meet them and guide them on the right road.

There was no difficulty in following the tracks of a whole troop of horses and cattle. Their first camp was at Mud Lake and I continued on the way. My companions would have to be blind not to be able to follow the various vehicles that carried the women and children; even the marks of the travois cut the stock tracks.

The road skirted the north of Island Lake through heavy timber. I was alert for any sign of scouts but I was caught unaware by Sam Bull, who stepped from behind a tree with his gun levelled. He recognized me at once and lowered his gun and I breathed freely once more. A young man like that might press the trigger too hard in his excitement and nervousness.

"Well, Sam, who is the man buried in that new grave?"

"It's a long story, Mr. Erasmus, and I do not know everything, but I do know that Big Bear sent his men to get the people to join the rebellion. Cardinal and three others went to Whitefish where the chief was holding a meeting in your store. The chief allowed Cardinal to speak. Some were for joining, others against. They were pretty well divided.

"They say the chief was sitting on the fence but Peter Shirt was very much opposed and spoke very strongly against them joining. Peter had gathered a good following, but Cardinal was gaining support; yet the chief did not interfere, and allowed Cardinal full liberty to speak as he wished. Suddenly Cardinal got mad and ordered Shirt to hand over the Hudson's Bay goods.

"Shirt promptly refused and defied any man to touch anything without his permission.

"Cardinal yelled out, 'I don't need your say so or any man's to take what I want,' and at the same time reached up to take something from the shelves.

"Cootsoo had been sitting at the door. He hadn't taken any part in the talks except to nod his head in approval of Shirt's words. He threw a blanket aside that covered a gun, deliberately aimed, and shot Cardinal through the heart.[11]

"Cardinal's partners were so surprised at watching their leader drop that they had no time to notice who had fired the shot. Cootsoo shifted his aim and told the others to drop their guns and walk out; he ordered them to get off the reserve if they didn't want to be killed. The chief was very angry with Cootsoo and drove him off the reserve. He ordered him not to show his face among the band again.

"Many of the people who had been inclined to agree with the dead man now changed their minds; they crowded around Shirt and wanted to know what they could do.

"'We will hitch up a cart and horse,' Shirt had told them. 'Fill the cart with provisions and anything for a present for Cardinal's relations. If they accept it, we may be able to save further deaths.' Peter Shirt gave a horse. Ben gave the cart, and all the others contributed something to fill the cart. No-one would risk delivering the cart but Shirt said he would take it and he did.

"All the people are camped at the Lone Pine Lake while the men cut roads further west. Shirt is the leader because when the chief drove Cootsoo away, the people were angry and would only listen to Shirt. When he delivered the cart and came back everybody was ready to move away. Shirt called some men to help dig a grave for Cardinal while the others gathered up the stock and started on the road to where they are camped now."

I went back to my companions and soon met them as they were only a couple of miles behind me. I was able to inform McLaughlin that his friend Yeoman was safe and in hiding in the bush with a friendly Indian. Shirt had sent him away as soon as Sam Jackson told him that Big Bear's agents had arrived at the south end of the reserve.

It was around eleven o'clock when we arrived at the camp, not however before we had been again stopped by two other scouts. Of course our first business was to obtain a meal. We had several offers but accepted where we thought they were closer to being ready. We three were seated on the ground, our dishes and food spread on a canvas in front of us. Young could not curb his appetite and started in to eat. I was not far behind but in looking up I noticed the minister's hestitation and was reminded of our neglect. I spoke to Young.

"I think this is one meal when we can dispense with our supplications for the Lord to provide our food. This table seems amply supplied."

Young, reminded of his obligations, merely looked up and grinned. It was too late now to observe the amenities; he had already made remarkable progress. The minister of course soon followed our example, and despite a poor start and with less indulgence in speed, nevertheless equalled Young's capacity. I will not report my own place in the contest, lest it reflect on the glory of my companions.

There were more than one hundred and fifty souls in the trek. After dinner I went to see the chief to ask his intentions regarding this migration. He replied rather impatiently, "Ask Shirt. He has taken charge of all the arrangements up to the present."

I was just a bit surprised at his tone, for I had a great deal of respect for the man. He had been most kind to my family over the years and was a frequent visitor to my home whenever I happened to be there. I always had considered that he and I were the best of friends, yet his abrupt answer was anything but friendly.

Remembering our trip to Regina in the summer of 1884 where we had succeeded in having an additional acreage set aside at Saddle Lake, I wondered whether his dissatisfaction that no papers were signed had begun to affect his loyalties. Up to that time he had received no official notification that the promise would be carried out, even though the land required had been already reserved from settlement.

Entering Peter Shirt's teepee, I asked him what were his intentions. "Yes," he replied, "you of all people should know what I intend to do. I am taking these people across country to Victoria."

"Indeed," I answered. "I surmised as much when I found all the people gone from their homes. You still persist in carrying out your dream. How many people know about this dream of yours?"

"The chief and three others. His councillors were becoming difficult. I had to tell them today as they were growing discontented and might have made trouble."

"Do you realize what they will do if it turns out that there are no soldiers at Victoria when you get there? Your dream will then have a bad ending for you."

He answered with a counter-question, "Is your white horse still alive? Will Cardinal rise from the grave now as he would have done had I not brought these people away? Do you think it would have ended with the gift of my horse and Ben's cart and the things our people gave to pacify his relations if they had all stayed home and waited to see what would happen?"

"No," he went on, "if I am wrong, I alone will suffer the consequences of my stubbornness and not a lot of harmless people."

"What about the chief? Has he no say in what you do with his band?"

"The chief lost control when he failed to stop Big Bear's men and allowed Cardinal a free hand to talk his tribe into rebellion. If he had ordered them away, the people would have carried out his orders and there were men enough to force them to go. When Cootsoo shot Cardinal, the people were frightened and did not know what to do. Then when the chief banished Cootsoo from the reserve, his friends were angry because he refused to give the man protection. I acted because no-one else knew what to do. I think I am right."

"Well, Peter, I agree with you completely. My own family are in your hands. I think you have acted well and wisely. I have brought ammunition and guns for your use. Carry on as you have been doing, but I would suggest that you move your camp across the lakes as soon as possible. You will have less distance to patrol and that will release more men to do your road cutting. I will escort Young to Lac La Biche and be back in a few days to join you."

Young called the people together for a talk and advised them to remain loyal to the government and they would be taken care of. "If you have any horned animals fit to beef, kill them when you need meat. I will take on the responsibility to see that you are paid for the animals you use for food."

One man got up and offered a steer. Others expressed willingness to help out with stock. I added the following to Young's speech that I interpreted for him: "Soon you will be in a good hunting area. Then you can save your cattle by killing wild game to care for meat needs. I have brought ammunition which Peter Shirt will distribute according to your needs. This will be my contribution to the welfare of the band and in appreciation for the protection of my family."

CHAPTER SIXTEEN

The End of the Open Prairie

W E WERE CLOSER to Lac La Biche at the Lone Pine camp than we would be by trailing back to the Lac La Biche pack trail twelve miles to the east, but Young insisted on going all the way back to the crossing at the Beaver. "The men that caused trouble at Whitefish may have gone to the Beaver Lake Indians, where I feel positive they will get help. I want to make certain that there is no-one ahead of us on that trail."

We had crossed the Big Beaver and were approaching the Little Beaver ford when we smelled smoke, though we had not seen any tracks ahead of us. We didn't take any chance but left our horses in the bush and approached cautiously on foot. Two men were seated at a campfire roasting meat. They were strangers to us and they were facing our way.

"Wait here," said Young, "while I go around and come at them from the back. They don't seem to be very alert. If they are peaceful travellers, they will not make any false move, but if they make a grab for their guns, I'll have the drop on them from behind."

Young came in sight from the opposite side of the small prairie and was slowly and quietly getting closer. When I thought he was close enough I stepped out of the brush into their view. They both made a grab for their guns but Young yelled behind them, "Hold everything or I'll shoot."

They probably didn't understand a word that Young said but at least they froze in their movements; then they sat up straight in a hurry and forgot their guns. There were two Hudson's Bay blankets hanging on willows to dry. They had a mess of bacon frying in a pan and two ducks roasting.

"How is everything with you men? I see you have two blankets from the Hudson's Bay stores, so I suppose you have been raiding the post. These blankets and bacon are some of the loot." I spoke to them in Cree. Young could understand some Cree but not enough to carry on a conversation.

Young kept his gun on the two Indians while I questioned them. "You'd better tell the truth," I told them. "The man who is holding a gun on you from behind is the man in charge of the Lac La Biche post. You know that you can be shot dead as you have stolen goods and are not on your reserve."

"All right," said one man. "Big Bear's men came to the reserve and forced the Beaver Lake Indians to join them. They all had guns and said they would shoot any man who didn't go with them. We made a feast for them that night they came and promised to go the next day. The chief sent word to Peachie Pruden and Pat Pruden that Big Bear's men were going to make a raid on the Hudson's Bay post the next day."

"Yes," the other man added, anxious I suppose to placate us as the other man was doing. "We sent a boy so that none of the men would be missed. They seemed to know and have the names of everyone on the reserve. They would have killed some of us if they had known we sent a messenger."

I replied, "I think you are right. We'll take your guns and leave them across the creek. If you are wise, you will go back to your reserve as quickly as you can and stay there. Big Bear's man was killed at Whitefish and the others driven away. You might have done the same and saved yourselves from trouble. Tell your friends that there are a lot of soldiers and Police on the way. They will shoot and kill any Indians not peacefully living on their own reserves."

"Where did your talkative friend get those new blankets?" asked Young.

"From your store. Where else would you suppose?"

"Remove their guns and fetch the horses while I continue to hold a gun on them," said Young. "I want these two blankets for evidence against the beggars."

I doubt if those chaps understood English but they sat like statues while I fetched the horses, took the blankets, tied them behind our saddles and picked up their guns. Under different circumstances I would have enjoyed the savoury roasted duck that might have been slightly overdone in the time it took me to question our suspects.

Four eyes glittered with anger when I picked up their guns and got on my saddle and prepared to ride away. In turn, I held my gun on them while Young walked out to get on his horse. I distinctly heard some Indian swear words when Young walked out to mount his horse. They thought that we would keep their guns and didn't believe I would leave them as I had promised. We were half way up the other side of the hill when I got off my horse, waved the empty guns, held them up so that they could see, then placed them against a willow clump, but not before I had removed the charges. I climbed my horse and rode out of sight where I jumped off and handed the lines to Young.

"What are you doing?" he asked.

"I intend to know just what our friends back there intend to do about those two blankets. Ride ahead a half mile, then hide the horses and wait for me."

I went back and took cover where I could watch our two Indians. They broke camp without finishing their tasty meal, caught their horses, and came after their guns. I was fully prepared for trouble but as soon as they had recovered their guns, they mounted their horses and took the east road. I followed behind to the top of the hill where I had a good view of their movements. They were riding at a good fast gallop towards the east, a direct route to their reserve.

When we reached the post, the place was a shambles. The raiders had broken into the store and scattered stuff around that they couldn't pack away. They had emptied flour on the floor and ground outside to get the sacks to pack away their stolen goods. They had made a good job of destroying anything they could not take away. Fortunately they had not destroyed the books and Young was pleased to find them intact.

The post manager was angry at the wanton waste but the thing that transformed him into a raging maniac was the sight of his little water spaniel that had been killed at his house gate, his entrails cut open and exposed as he lay on his back. Young was like a man possessed and it would have gone hard with any Indian who put in an appearance at that moment.

Everything at the store had been left in a terrible mess but strangely enough nothing had been disturbed at the house, except the dead dog that lay at the house gate. The vandals appeared to have respect for private property. The Hudson's Bay property was apparently their only objective in the raid. The promise of free booty was offered as an inducement to get the tribes to join the rebellion.

There was a big iron cauldron hanging on a tripod where

they had made tea and possible performed some war dances. I went over there in search of evidence as to the number of men taking part in the raid. I found a discarded half-gallon pot that some ambitious tea-drinker had used and found too heavy to pack away. There were considerable tea leaves still at the bottom.

I called Young over to investigate this startling piece of evidence. Perhaps it might sooth his ruffled temper. Such unrestrained anger was not good for a man's judgement. The moment he saw the tea leaves his anger evaporated into a high laugh. Now he was going to the other extreme. He laughed till the tears came to his eyes. Though I joined in laughing, I was somewhat worried that this sudden change might affect my friend's mental balance. The half-gallon measure was a child's chamber pot.

Finally Young regained his composure without any ill effect and said, "There is very little that we can do here now. We will go to the mission and inquire about my family."

We went to Umla's[1] store first, leaving our horses hidden in the bush. We approached the clearing on foot using the storehouse building to cover our presence. From there we watched for Umla to put in an appearance, which he soon did. Young stepped into the open and waved to him. He answered the signal, went back into the store, and came out a few minutes later with two bear robes in his arm and walked towards the storehouse where we were hidden.

I stepped out into the open as soon as he was near enough to talk to without speaking too loudly. He raised his right arm and made a motion with his hand towards the house. I knew then that the robes on his arm were an excuse to leave his visitors while he pretended to take them to the storeroom. I was about to go back into hiding when several men came out of his store. It was too late to hide from those twelve eyes so I motioned for Young to stay out of sight.

"There are a half dozen of the raiders at the store," whispered Umla. "I would not like you to be seen. I think I have them scared into submission but I'm not sure."

"It's too late to hide now," I replied. "They're already out and coming this way. We will run a bluff on them. You ask me questions about soldiers and the Police and what is going on about the Rebellion. We have just arrived from Edmonton and know that soldiers are already on the way."

I glanced back and saw that Young had not taken cover but stood a few feet away from the building. "Watch yourself, Young, and be ready to dive behind that building if they show any trouble!"

288

The six men came up to where I stood talking to Umla. Only two of them had flintlock guns against our two rifles and short guns. Umla spoke to me in Cree. "What news did you bring from Edmonton? I heard that you and Young just got back from there."

"There are soldiers on the way from Edmonton, and General Middleton is sending two armies into the trouble at Frog Lake. These armies are after Big Bear's skin and probably have his hide on a stretcher right now."

"How many men are on their way from Edmonton?" asked Umla.

"Oh, he must have a thousand soldiers, besides dozens of teamsters and scouts. Yes, and there is a troop of Police with the outfit and I think there must be a hundred or more of mounted men. Big Bear's man was killed at Whitefish and I expect that they will investigate that killing and be up here to look into the raiding of the Hudson's Bay store at Lac La Biche. The soldiers claim they are going to massacre every last Indian they find off his own reserve."

I hadn't noticed that Young had come up beside me but I saw an Indian lift his gun. I jumped across and knocked his gun aside, at the same time yelling in Cree, "You fool, do you want to die?" Young could have shot the man before he lifted his gun but when I jumped in his way, he merely shifted his aim to the other men.

"Peter, you are the fool to take such chances," said Young. "I could kill them all before they could raise a finger. I have five shots in this rifle and six in my short gun. If they want trouble, I'm willing to oblige."

"That would be murder, my hot-headed friend! Regardless of what they have done, the law will look after their crimes without any help from you. They only touched Company property and your hanged dog is replaceable."

"Take their guns then because I am not lifting my aim till they are disarmed."

The leader had released the gun to my twisting grasp when I jumped him. Now Umla stepped up to the other men and speaking in Cree said, "You had better give me your guns. I will keep them for you till these men are gone. You can have them back in a few days. Peter is wrong; the Company man can shoot you dead right here and nothing will be done to him, for you are all wearing clothes that you stole from the Company store."

They quietly yielded their arms: three tomahawks, two guns, and two wicked-looking knives.

"Now my good men," said Umla, "if you are smart you will go back to Beaver Lake Reserve and stay there. If you mind your own business and make no more trouble, I may be able to get you off with a small jail term."

"Yes," I added, speaking to the leader, "you're a lucky man in being still alive. Take Mr. Umla's advice and do as you're told. This man Young was very angry about his dog. Killing that little dog was a most cowardly and wicked thing that your raiding party did. No-one bothered his house and that is why I stopped him from trying to shoot. The gun that Young has could kill you before you could pull back the hammer of your flintlock. Better get going now as I might not be able to stop him next time."

The leader nodded to the others and they all followed after him, single file as is the custom of Indians on the warpath.

The bishop and a priest were all the people at the mission. The other occupants were in hiding on an island in La Biche lake. They were guarded by loyal Metis men whose wives and children were at the same place.

We had gone into Umla's store after the raiders had gone. Umla spoke rather sharply to the factor, "Now, Mr. Young, you have always been a welcome visitor to my place but after that miserable business outside, I think you would be wise to put considerable distance between you and those six men. They can easily obtain other guns and be back here tonight."

"I will not leave until I know where my family have gone. I'm not afraid of trouble."

"Yes, I know," said Umla. "Neither are you afraid of making trouble. Consider yourself lucky that Peter acted when he did. You should know better than to step up to men with your gun ready and aimed."

"I don't know what possessed you, Mr. Young," I added, "although I do know that you represent the Company in the eyes of those men. They had already ransacked the post. Your action in stepping up beside me with your gun aimed at the leader was stupid and entirely uncalled for. It triggered the man's immediate action. Umla and I had the matter well in hand. I do not intend to expose myself to another such foolish incident. I'm going back from here."

"Your family and Peachie Pruden's family have gone to Lac La Biche River where they have two canoes hidden," said Umla. "If you change for fresh horses in my corral out back, you can catch them before they reach the river. Peter, I wish you would reconsider your decision and go with him to fetch the horses back as I have no-one here that I can send."

Young was not feeling too happy over the situation, and resented the drubbing that we had both given him over his hot-headed action. Hudson's Bay factors were apt to consider themselves infallible. He might have been able to kill one man, but with odds of five, all with tomahawks and knives, he would have been dead before he could aim and pull the second trigger. I had watched too many skillful demonstrations with knife and axe to doubt the results of such a contest.

I went after our horses while Young went to see the Bishop. Turning our own horses into Umla's corral, I picked the best of the trader's ponies, shifted saddles, and changed that of the pack horse. I then led them over to the mission. Young was ready and I started out at a good fast pace. Umla had told me with a good deal of secretiveness where I could best pick up the trail of Pruden's party. Apparently he did not want Young to know exactly where to find them as there was some danger that the raiders had taken up Pruden's trail and perhaps killed them before we would reach them.

Those fears were soon dispelled when I found the tracks of the party where they had skirted around what was known later as Plamondon's Bay. I followed them for a mile and established the fact that there were no other tracks except those of the Pruden party.

We had covered about twenty miles when we came across a place where they had had a fire to cook a meal. Though they had packed water to put out the fire, there was still considerable heat underground. "Mr. Young, you can stop worrying about your family. They are just ahead of us. The fire is less than an hour old. You had better take the lead from here as you are well known in these parts. Peachie is sure to have a man working on his back track to be certain no-one is following. I don't propose to chance some trigger-happy fellow who may be inclined to use a bullet to do his talking before asking my name."

"Look here, Peter! Forget about that trigger-happy business. I know now I acted foolishly but I was nearly mad with anxiety for my family. The sight of those dog-butchers made me imagine that they had done that as a sign of what they would do to my family. Of course I will go ahead. You are right; Pruden certainly will have a man to challenge any stranger following their tracks."

We had not gone more than a mile when a man stepped out from behind a huge spruce. He had his gun centred on us as we were riding together, ready for a quick shot. Then he recognized Young, who rather shakily called him by name. The man sent us on ahead but still stayed behind. He was keeping at a distance of about two miles behind his people. He eyed me with curiosity and certainly evinced no friendliness. I was glad that I had set up Young for his target.

Young was an excellent companion and I felt rather guilty

for being so rough with him, but those were ticklish moments. If I hadn't acted fast there would have been some dead men back on our trail and a strong possibility that I might have been one, a prospect that I had no desire for without a very good reason. Young of course was overjoyed to meet up with his family and to find them in such good hands. He shed his former gloom in a twinkling and was again the good companion and friend that he had been for the three hundred and fifty mile return trip to Edmonton.

"Get off your high horse, Peter," he said. "Come meet my family and the rest of our people. They will get us something to eat before you start back. I will go on from here but I would be glad if you didn't mention that business at Umla's house."

"I've forgotten already, Mr. Young, if you have. Perhaps my own nerves were a bit strained."

They intended to go by canoe downriver to the Athabasca, thence to the landing, then overland to Edmonton. Travelling by horseback was a slow procedure and somewhat dangerous for the children as they only had a pack trail to follow.

Mr. Pruden had adopted an Indian device for carrying the small ones, with some innovations of his own invention — canvas sacks sewn together, similar to present-day baby rompers. These were hung in front of the mothers' saddles, two children to a horse. The bigger children rode behind the men. The party had been two days on the road and had travelled less than twenty-five miles.

The horse I rode was pretty tired, and Pruden said, "I'll lend you a horse if you are determined to start back tonight. My men will take all the horses back to the mission after we reach the river where our canoes are hidden."

Young went back with me till we passed the trail guard.

"Well, Peter, I guess this is goodbye. I left an order for your pay with the bishop. I think you will be satisfied. I don't intend to come back to these parts again if I can help it.[2] I will write a letter of recommendation to our next man at Lac La Biche if you care to carry on business at Whitefish when this trouble is over. Thanks a million for saving me from my anger." Smiling a kind of rueful smile, he added, "You are certainly a man of action which I doubly appreciate. I never killed a man in my life and I would hate to live with the thought that I had. Worse, my children might have been fatherless today but for your quick action."

Late that night I got back to Umla's house and stabled the horse without any thought that I might be watched. It was very dark and I was startled by a voice behind me, "Stand fast and give me your first name."

"Peter," I snapped out. I was getting tired of having guns poked at me.

"All right," the man ordered. "Walk straight ahead to the house. Knock three times on the door when you get there. You have the right word but the wrong horse. Umla will know if you're the right man."

For once I refused to pick up the argument and did exactly as I was told to do. Umla appeared at the door with the three knocks that must have shook the whole house. I noticed my knuckles were skinned the next morning. He had no light but there was no mistake about the gun that was pushed out ahead of him, almost within reach of my hands.

"Give your last name and the name of the man you were with today," the voice spoke out of the darkness.

"Damn it, man, I'm Peter Erasmus, the man was Young and you're Umla with the two bear skins."

The man spoke up behind me. "He's riding a different horse. I'll keep a gun on him while you get a light."

"Your confounded horse played out on me and Pruden loaned me a horse," I replied.

"All right, Adam. I guess you caught the right fish this time. You can go back on guard as soon as he reaches the light. Peter, you go ahead and push that door open straight ahead of you. There's a light in there but I advise you to go slow when you reach the light."

I was too tired to offer any objections. I recognized Umla's voice but just the same I was careful to do just as he wanted. I was boiling with anger inside but admired his caution.

"Go to that table, your supper is waiting. If you had spoken English instead of Cree all the time, you might have been eating sometime ago. There are lots of big men like you in this area but very few can talk English like you do."

He offered no apology but I suppose the well-supplied table and the kettle of tea kept warm by the fireplace served the same purpose. My ravenous appetite soon cooled my anger as I dug into the food with a vengeance. I noticed he eyed my short gun with a good deal of interest. What he didn't know was that I had never fired one of them in my life and later found out I couldn't come within two feet of a target when I did try it.

I think he figured he didn't have all the best cards. Many years afterward, when we were talking over old times, he told me he thought I was a very cool, brave man but when I told him what a poor shot I was with that short gun, he laughed uproariously and confessed to his own weakness at the time.

"Do you know that my own gun was shaking so badly that I probably would have missed you at point-blank range? Those six men came back a short time after you had gone and demanded their guns. I bluffed them till near sundown, thinking I would delay them until it was too late to find your tracks. I had reloaded the guns with wadding and no powder but hung them in plain sight. Three strangers came in to trade and that probably kept them from grabbing their guns and trying to shoot me. As soon as my new customers left the premises, I gave them the guns and told them to get out. I guess they went back to the reserve but I was taking no chances when you came along."

The next morning I called on the bishop as instructed by Young and found a pile of goods laid out for my wages. A whole web of canvas, a new suit of clothes, a web of print that must have been thirty or forty yards in the piece. Sugar, tea, and pemmican for the road. I wondered how I was going to pack all that stuff on my saddle horse.

"We will lend you a pack horse and you can send him back later," said the priest.

I was delighted, you'd better believe me. Now indeed I felt bad about speaking so harshly to Young. The man's generosity in the things given me were double the value of any service rendered.

I made inquiries about the general lie of the land that would take me straight to the Lone Pine. An Indian who was making a few purchases from Umla's store spoke up and said he knew the country and offered to show me the road. I thought it would save time if he would guide me. He had his own horse and we started as soon as I got my goods packed.

We crossed the Beaver River and camped about twelve miles south. I had never been in that area before but my guide appeared to know exactly where to find the best route. I was tired and slept like a log all night. My companion was up and had the fire going when I woke up.

"I will fetch the horses," he said, "while you're having your breakfast. I've already had mine."

The horses were not in sight but they were all hobbled and would not wander far. I had finished breakfast and was getting ready to pack when I noticed my rifle gone. He had left camp empty-handed as I had seen with my own eyes. Then I realized why it had taken so long for him to bring the horses. He had skipped out. The beggar had eaten a hearty breakfast at my expense and walked out bold as brass and I hadn't even suspicioned anything wrong.

Finding the horses about a mile from camp was a great relief. At least I would not have to pack my burdens. I was angry enough to take up his trail right there and then but I realized that I would probably have to trail him clear to Fort Garry. The rifle and ammunition was a loss but actually not a serious matter. If the man had taken a horse, then I would have been left stranded. I rode the horse back to camp and led the other, thankful that he had been satisfied with only the rifle. I made a thorough search of my things when I got back to camp but found not a thing missing except the rifle and shells. He hadn't even touched the food, other than what he ate at meals.

I had a laugh at the whole incident. I needed a guide about as much as a horse needs a fifth leg. Merely to save time I had lost a good rifle and had been taken in with the simplicity of a child. The beggar had gone to a great deal of trouble to cut pine boughs for a nice mattress for my undisturbed restful sleep, knowing that a comfortable bed would insure no interference with his plans of getting my rifle, which I had made certain was close to my hand in bed.

I was reminded of the time that Sam Jackson and I had made a trip to Smoking Lake and had stopped with two trappers. There I had expounded on the honesty of Indians of my experience and had been told flatly by one of the men in the camp that there were a few Indians in this country who could not be depended on in the best of times. I had been quite angry to find my friends thus malignly described. It was a good joke and a sound lesson for me in those troubled times, but you can believe me I never told that one for many a day after that year in 1885.

After the rebellion had become history — in fact the following year — I made some inquiries about my guide. I was told that he had joined Riel's men and been assigned a leading role in the sharp-shooters picked to defend the trenches at Batoche; he had become over-confident with his good rifle and exposed himself to the soldiers too openly, was badly wounded, and died from his wounds. Six months later, I had a visitor from that section of the country, a stranger who refused to give himself a name but handed me a canvas-wrapped parcel that I was not to open or mention to anyone until he was gone two days. "That parcel contains a dying man's wishes and I promised to give it into your hands." I knew at once that it was my rifle and that the half-breed stranger was one of the rebels, probably sought after by the authorities, but I never mentioned anything of my suspicions. I thanked the man for his trouble, and gave him a suitable present and enough food to carry him on his way for quite some time. In accepting the parcel I had become a party to the rebels, but I had to respect a dying man's wishes. I never used the rifle but kept it for many years as a grim reminder of troubled times.

Now that I was without a guide and had to depend on my own resources, I made my way without any trouble. Finding the crossing at the Beaver River gave me some delay but no real difficulty. I was forced to camp again but this time I made certain that my bed was not too comfortable, and got an early start just at break of day.

I had been away five days, and Peter Shirt had made a great deal more progress on his way than I expected. I caught up with his party around four o'clock that afternoon. I was stopped twice by scouts and recognized long before I spotted them. One young fellow grinned and remarked, "I'm surprised that Peter Erasmus, the great traveller, would expose his back for a muzzleloaded ball at ten yards." Paying no attention to his remark, I could have told him that no enemy would be following a wellmarked trail but would be scouting far off the road, merely touching the trail occasionally to establish its general direction. When I reached camp Peter Shirt told me, "We were about to set off to find you as you are two days overdue."

We exchanged information and I found everyone in camp well, and all in good spirits. I suggested some improvement in the scouting services and we had a laugh over the young man's boast about catching me unawares. Though I did not think there was much danger of being followed, his road scouts were pulled in and placed as camp guards while the hunters were advised to circle the back trail in their hunting for moose and deer, and to be on the watch for any sign of strangers in the locality.

I presumed it would be a tremendous task to cut a road through such thickly timbered country but many of the party were familiar with the terrain and mapped out their route to pick the easiest passages, using their natural sense of direction and uncanny skill at finding a trail in any direction they wished to go. This was accomplished with as little concern as if they were out on open prairie.

Chief Seenum had now assumed the reins of government of the tribe that he had abandoned to Peter at Whitefish after the shooting of Cardinal. Peter Shirt, with diplomacy that would have done credit to a Crown Prince, now consulted the chief on every phase of their present project. No detail of camp safety, or the provision of food by the hunters, or the matter of deciding the best route to their destination, the White Mud Creek north of Victoria, was undertaken without the advice and consultation of his leader. I was amazed at how this had been done but I considered the matter too delicate to make inquiry to satisfy my curiosity.

Four days later we were camped on the south side of the White Mud valley, which is about ten miles north of Victoria mission, perhaps a mile north of where the town of Smoky Lake is now situated.

The chief summoned Peter Shirt to his teepee and advised him that he wanted Peter Erasmus and himself to accompany him on a scouting trip. He made no mention of the purpose of the ride or the direction we would be going, but as soon as Peter told me I was certain of our direction. I was not too happy over the seemingly cordial relations that were apparent between the two men. I felt that the chief had the full intention of showing up Peter Shirt and his dreams as pure imagination, and thus regain some of his lost prestige with his tribe. Two of the chief's councillors were openly opposed to the way Peter Shirt had assumed leadership.

Reviewing the nature of the things on which Shirt's convictions were based, namely the recurrence of his dream and the dead white horse that we found on the very day we first learned of our trouble, there seemed to be evidence enough to convince any man. However, common sense refused to admit the probability of the last phase of Peter's dream being true. The time elapsed since leaving Whitefish Lake, almost two whole weeks, would make the meeting of the soldiers at Victoria an impossible occurrence. I had to admit that I was highly curious to see the sequel of this phenomenon, yet at the same time was worried over Peter's future with the tribe should this phase of the dream prove an illusion.

Calling Peter aside as we were preparing to leave, I asked, "What will you do, Peter, when we get to Victoria and there are no soldiers there?" He just looked at me with a quizzical look and surprise or rather disappointment that I should still doubt him after all the evidence that he and I were party to.

His reply was brief. "Father," he said, "Then you can watch me swallow my gun."

Three hours later Peter Shirt got off his horse and motioned for us to do the same. He had led us through a brushy approach to the face of the hills back of the settlement to an opening where we had a view of the valley below where the Hudson Bay's stockades and the mission building stood. There, pitched on the flats, were many tents, carts, horses, and wagons. There was much activity by the soldiers and a long string of horses tied to the one rope. Afterwards in the camp, I saw they were staked to iron pins that held the ropes in place. I watched the reaction of the chief as he silently studied the scene before him.

He turned to Peter and gripped his hand with a strong handshake. "Peter Shirt, you are a man of great vision. You've saved my people a great deal of grief and me from my own stubbornness. This I will never forget. You must become a member of my council."

"No! No!" replied Peter. "All I want is to be a member of your band and to live peacefully with your people. Even my father did not believe me. This very morning he doubted me. How then could you believe something that even I had doubts about sometimes?"

I felt humbled at Peter's unselfish words and following the chief's lead, I shook hands with him, "Peter, it was a kind providence that softened my heart to pick you up from a strange band and bring you up as my son. No father ever had a better son and I only hope that I can be as good a father as you are a son to me and to this man's tribe."

We went back to our horses hidden in the brush, but were challenged by a military scout before we reached the horses. He had probably followed our tracks and waited out our return. "We are friends," I said. "I have a chief and his lieutenants who wish to confer with your general."

"Very well," answered the scout. "I've taken your guns. They will be returned to you when the captain says so."

"Young fellow, do you think that we would have left our guns behind if we had been hostile? Don't be stupid; put them back on the horses from where you took them. If you're looking for glory and credit, you can ride behind us and shoot us the minute you think we are a danger to your whole army down there."

He very reluctantly replaced the guns. However, he held his gun at the ready till we had mounted and headed for the camp. He followed behind us, and thus we were escorted into the camp. Captain Oswald[3] met us at the entrance of the camp, and after a few questions took us to General Strange's tent, where he introduced the chief and his men as loyal Indians who had fled from their reserve after killing an enemy agent who had tried to intimidate the tribe. The general was most effusive in his praise of the chief's action in removing his Indians from trouble, thus saving the people from further killings.

Stirring up people to enemy action was a capital offense and the killing was perhaps justified, he said, but the army and the government took a dim view of private killings. However, he would take action to see that the man Cootsoo was officially exonerated from the crime. "Non-combatants, Sir, are strictly frowned upon in any killing not done by the proper authorities."

"I regret, Sir, that in this case there was hardly time to consult a law that has no representative nearer than Fort

Saskatchewan. The chief is making no apology for the action of a member of his tribe. He has already punished the man by driving him from the protection of his tribe and from that very fact almost lost control of his people."

"Certainly the act is justified but can hardly be approved in my capacity. The matter will be properly taken care of by official action later."

The chief was questioned about the number of people in his band, and about those who were absent with the party who had taken a different road and were possibly on their way to Victoria. These other members of the Seenum band had been advised by Peter Shirt to follow straight west from Goodfish Lake. His purpose in doing so was to prevent any clash of opinions with those who were related to the dead man and his sympathizers; of these there were less than one hundred souls.

"You will keep your band at its present camping grounds and draw on the post here for your supplies. Don't kill any more of your domestic stock. You will be paid for any that you have already killed for food supplies. We'll send a man out to your camp to check on your supplies and present cattle. You, Mr. Erasmus, can fetch your family here under the protection of the fort if you so desire. I think that it would be advisable to leave the Indian camp where it is. They'll be off the regular travelled routes and may be safer, in case of any general spreading of the rebellion."

The general wanted me to act as a scout for him but I informed him that I did not wish to leave my family any longer under the protection of other people. We intended to go to Edmonton where I had a daughter going to school. My oldest daughter, Eliza, was staying with Mrs. McDougall. However, I recommended Andrew Whitford, a much younger man, whom I knew would be glad of the employment and had no family responsibilities at that time. I sent word to Andrew and he was quite delighted to accept the general's offer. He was keen for the excitement of the fight that was in prospect.

I arranged for transportation by some people from Victoria who were going to Edmonton the next day. We went back to camp that afternoon. The chief called a meeting of his council in the evening and I was pleased to hear him give the others a true account of his trip to Victoria. He did not try to evade his own disbelief in Peter's dream, and gave the man full credit for the timely evacuation of his people from Whitefish Lake. Nor did he spare himself from blame in not immediately driving the troublemakers out of his reserve or for his mistake of allowing them to talk members of his tribe into revolt against the proper authorities. Peter Shirt was called in at this point and each man got to his feet and thanked Peter for his part in the matter of moving the tribe. One man offered to resign his office of councillor if Peter would consider taking his position.

Peter again refused and in his quiet way thanked them for their confidence and told them all he wanted was to live peaceably with the tribe as a common member, that he had no desire to assume the responsibilities of leadership, ending his reply by saying that two weeks in hot water was enough to last him a lifetime.

When we arrived in Edmonton, William Anderson, the Indian agent, informed me that officials of the department had instructed him to have me return to Victoria to help John A. Mitchell with the distribution of rations to the Whitefish Lake Indians. We moved back to Victoria and took up residence in a house I had hired built on land I chose in 1880, though I had not lived there, even for a day, up till then. I rode to work every day as it was only two and a half miles upriver.

The Beaver Lake Indians who had helped raid the Hudson's Bay post at Lac La Biche got off with a short period of detention. In fact, only a few were arrested out of the twenty who had been in on the destruction. I suspect that their friend Umla had interceded for them, or at least advised them to give themselves up to the Police, thus saving the others from being involved. Those few were the only ones the Police could get any evidence against.

The man Cootsoo was cleared by official investigation and the killing justified after hearing the evidence of those who were present at the shooting. Cootsoo never forgave the chief for refusing protection and for banishing him from the Whitefish Reserve where he then had his home. He had been forced to flee for his life with his family, and had abandoned his household effects and chattels, which were stripped and removed when the relations of Cardinal failed to catch up with him. It had been a close thing; only his skill as a woodsman in covering his tracks saved him.

Years afterwards we discussed those troubled times. We both agreed that his prompt action in stopping Cardinal from forcing a showdown was all that saved many from joining the rebellion. Likely many of them would have been killed. He had no regrets and lived to a ripe old age at Saddle Lake where he took up residence after hostilities were over.

Peter Shirt's dream has been told by others, but I feel compelled to relate the true facts from my personal knowledge of this quiet, honest, and unselfish young man who never during his whole life took any credit to himself for the praise

300

and official recognition that was accorded the chief for keeping the tribe loyal during those troubled times.

After the hostilities were over James Seenum received the name of Pakannuk meaning "hazel nut", because he was fond of the nuts that grew in abundance near his home at Whitefish Lake. The English, good at abbreviations, reduced this to Pakan. John A. Mitchell, who was a great friend of the chief, named the post office "Pakan", as he was its first postmaster; and the district had changed the name Victoria because the mail got mixed up with Victoria in British Columbia. Thus were the Whitefish Lake Indians honoured for their loyalty by having a place named for their chief.

My last buffalo hunt had been in the summer of 1876, the year the treaties were signed, when I had left to go to Carlton to interpret for Big Child and Star Blanket. True, I ate buffalo meat at Big Bear's camp in the Cypress Hills when I was sent there to help to persuade them to return to their reserves, but it tasted a great deal like beef — so much so that I didn't consider it polite to inquire too closely as to its source. It is just possible that the scarcity of buffalo at that time could have become blended with the cattle taste. It was variously rumoured at the time that ranchers were complaining to the government of cattle losses and that was the reason for having the Indians returned to their reserves.

The Rebellion of 1885 brought out many young easterners in the volunteer army who saw the country and the vast area of open farm land. Some of them stayed, and those who went back told of their experiences and fired the imagination of others who became prospects for the treeless prairie that was just waiting for the plough to turn it into fertile grain fields. Some big cattle and horse ranches were already established in their formative stages. Buffalo were no longer looked upon as a necessity of life as in previous years. Farming was only in its beginning, but already a flood of immigrants were pushing their way further into the western plains.

It is not the purpose of this story to record the entrance of so-called civilized living into these parts, but merely to record my experiences on the open uninhabited prairies. We have long passed the days when buffalo were the main source of our livelihood. Railways have replaced the Red River carts. Buffalo by the year of the Rebellion were practically non-existent. Wheat and beef were to reign supreme for many years in the future, so we leave the history of the settlements to other more able writers.

I have endeavoured to keep this story within the boundaries of the buffalo days and nights and to limit its scope to my experiences and impressions. If I have failed in rendering a true picture of those colourful times, it may be because truth can be less attractive than imaginary adventures and descriptions, couched in flowery language, of characters and things with which good writers delight their readers. If I have touched on any subject about which my readers disagree, I make no apology. These are my own experiences and are not tainted with imaginary fictions. These tales are true in so far as my knowledge and ability extend. I hope they may give the readers some interesting comparisons to present-day times and add a little pleasure and pride in the achievements of Alberta today.

A Note on Peter Erasmus's Family Background

P ETER ERASMUS WAS THE SON of another Peter Erasmus,[1] variously described as a Dane,[2] a Norwegian,[3] and a Swede,[4] who had left the service of the Hudson's Bay Company to settle at Red River. No record of his employment with the Company has been found in the Archives of the Company but the record of the baptism of two daughters in 1824 calls him a "Company Servant"[5] while the parish register at the time of his marriage in 1826 calls him a settler.[6] Details of his farm property are given in successive Red River censuses from 1827 onwards.[7]

Though no official record of the birth or baptism of Peter Erasmus, Junior, has come to light, a list compiled by him of family birth dates, kindly made available by Mr. Arnold Erasmus, confirms his statement in a letter to Dr. (Sir) James Hector[8] that he was born on June 27, 1833. The same list gives the date of birth of ten children including a mysterious William of whom no other mention has been found.[9]

Peter Junior's mother, Catherine or "Kitty", was of mixed blood,[10] a sister of Henry Budd,[11] the first native to be ordained in North America in the Anglican Church.[12] Mr. George Gooderham, in his sketch of Erasmus's life, states that she was a grand-daughter of Chief Factor William Hemmings Cook.[13] Cook in 1838 formally married one of Matthew Cocking's three daughters, thereby "bringing to a close," as a colleague remarked, a 37-year "courtship".[14] None of W.H. Cook's children who can be identified as Mrs. Cook's children seem to have been Catherine Erasmus's mother, in view of available information about their marriages.[15] Cook, however, seems to have had more than one wife according to the custom of the country. Miles MacDonnell[16] and the Rev. Charles Bourke,[17] when at York Factory in 1811 to 1812, both reported that he had three wives. Though the evidence is inconclusive, it seems probable that one of these other wives was another of Matthew Cocking's daughters. In any case there are strong indications that one of Cocking's daughters was Kitty Erasmus's grandmother.

Cocking named all his three daughters in the will in which he left them each an annuity of six pounds to be paid in goods to that value through the Hudson's Bay Company during their lives and their respective mothers' lives.[18] The eldest daughter, Ke-che-c[h]ow-e-com-e-coot, also known as Bets[e]y, became the wife of J.P. Holmes, of the Company's service.[19] Wash-e-soo E'Squaw seems to have been Kitty Erasmus's grandmother,[20] and Mith-coo-coo-man E'Squaw W.H. Cook's "partner" who eventually became his official wife.[21] The problem of identification is complicated by the fact that both Washe-e-soo E'Squaw and Mith-coo-coo-man E'Squaw were apparently known sometimes as Agathas (Aggathas/Agatha/Agathus) and sometimes as Mary. Though the register of marriages names Cook's formal wife Mary Cocking,[22] and he called her Mary in his will,[23] he had written in 1825 that this "partner", Agathas, had not received her annuity.[24] He thought that payments due to her had been given in mistake to Washehow Esqow. A box marked "Agathas" had been collected for Washu-ka (Washiha) Esquow by the Rev. John West, but debited to Cook's partner, "owing to the Gent[n] at the Factory not being able to identify the parties" and "the name of Agathas being an appelation suitable to any of the halfbreed Ladies".[25] It is not surprising that there was confusion. Writing on February 3, 1825, from Norway House to beg for clarification, Alex[r] Robertson mentioned Mrs. Holmes (Keye cowecum a coot), her sister, Washihoesquew, and Agatha (Mrs. Cook).[26] The annuity payments are recorded in the York Factory account books under the general heading "Aggathas, Washa-hoesquew, and Keeschicowceum a coot", which names are also used in some of the annual entries.[27] Annual entries between 1825 and 1828, however, give "Aggathas, Mrs. Cook, and Mrs. Holmes".[28] Charles Cook's baptismal record stated in

1823 that he was the son of W.H. Cook and "Agatha a halfbreed woman"[29]—but which Agathas was this?

Still further to confound confusion, on May 11, 1828, a halfbreed woman called Waso-eysquew was baptised as "Mary Budd" of the "Church Mission House".[30] The Winnipeg accounts have a note against the entry for one of [Cocking's] annuitants: "The Wom^a on Missionary Establishment".[31] Certainly yet another "Agathus" worked there. This was the mother of Henry Budd, a halfbreed (widow) woman speaking only the Indian language," who was employed to make clothes, wash, cook, etc. for the children at the mission.[32] Besides Henry Budd, one of these children was his sister Sally Budd. The name Budd, bestowed on Henry by the Rev. John West, in honour of his former Rector in England, was, seemingly, by extension applied to the entire family, including a brother, James, though it seems rather surprising that even the grandmother should be called Budd.[33] Another adult, "Indian Woman on the Church Mission Establishment Red River Settlement" was baptised in 1830, on June 3, under the name "Kitty" with nothing more.[34] Perhaps this was the Christianised name given to Agathus, the widow woman, Henry Budd's and Kitty Erasmus's mother, or perhaps this was Cocking's daughter and "Mary Budd" Henry's mother? That mother, whatever her Christian name, must have been the "granny" who young Peter reported, was in 1850 living with the Erasmus family.[35] The year before Henry Budd had taken her, as he wrote to his sister, Nancy, to Norway House on her way to Red River to live with their sister, Kitty.[36]

While, therefore, there are unresolved problems and uncertainties, the limited and by no means entirely clear information that has come to light suggests that Peter Erasmus was a descendant of two illustrious officers of the Hudson's Bay Company, both Englishmen; of a Scandinavian; and of an Indian great-grandmother (Ke-che-cho-wich),[37] and an Indian grandfather, a Muscaigoe Cree.[38]

NOTES

INTRODUCTION

1 Statement given to the editor on November 4, 1973. Mr. Thompson supplemented this information in conversation on that day and in a letter dated November 14, 1973.

2 For example: Evelyn Rowand, "The Rebellion at Lac La Biche", *Alberta Historical Review*", Vol. XXI, No. 3 (Summer, 1973) ; William B. Fraser, *Big Bear: Indian Patriot*, Calgary: Historical Society of Alberta, 1969; Irene M. Spry, *The Palliser Expedition*, Toronto: MacMillan, 1963; and Spry (ed.), *The Papers of the Palliser Expedition*, Toronto: The Champlain Society, 1968.

3 For the official report of the Palliser expedition and a discussion of other available sources concerning it, see Irene M. Spry (ed.), *The Papers of the Palliser Expedition*. For other sources, see the BIBLIOGRAPHY.

4 It is likely that Erasmus made this journey but at a later time and with other companions, perhaps Bill Cust and his associates, who were trading in the north in the 1870's, as witness the Hardisty Papers, Glenbow Archives, Lesser Slave Lake transcript. Here,

as elsewhere, though the order of events and specific protagonists in them may have become misty in an old man's memory, the substance of what happened seems to have remained in essence clear.

5 See "Indian Tribes and Vocabularies" in John Palliser, *The Journals, Detailed Reports, and Observations Relative to Explorations*, London: Eyres and Spottiswoode, 1863, p. 205; and Appendix III in Spry (ed), *The Papers of the Palliser Expedition*.

6 Provincial Archives of British Columbia, A/E/R731/C12/ Er12. Horatio Calder had gone to the "golden Mines," as Henry Budd wrote on August 10, 1849 (Provincial Archives of British Columbia, A/E/ R731/W921.91). Peter Erasmus's original letter has been transcribed as it stands.

7 Red River Census, 1832-49 Provincial Archives of Manitoba, and the Hudson's Bay Company Register B.

8 Peter Erasmus to Horatio Calder, August 11, 1851 (Provincial Archives of British Columbia, Wren Family Papers, A/E/R731/W921.91).

9 Henry Budd's Journal, June 27, 1851 (Church Missionary

Society, C1/0, Microfilm Reel A83, Public Archives of Canada) ; Rev. James Hunter's Journal, July 13, 1853 (Church Missionary Society, Microfilm Reel A91, Public Archives of Canada).

10 Provincial Archives of British Columbia, Charles Ross Collection, A/E/R731/C12/Er12. This letter is copied exactly as it is in the original.

11 Henry Budd's Journal, June 25, 1853. There are other approving reports in Budd's letters and Journal, such as: "Peter Erasmus is getting on steadily with the School, and the children get on very well with Him. . . . He is just now finishing a copy of the Cree Translations of the whole of the morning Service for Mr. Hunter." (Letter to Bishop Anderson, December 2, 1851) ; "The Day School continues to be regularly kept, and as regularly attended by the children. They are evidently improving much." (Journal, April 8, 1852). Church Missionary Society, C1/0, Microfilm Reel A-83 and C1/M5, Microfilm Reel A-79, Public Archives of Canada.

12 Henry Budd to the Secretary, Church Missionary Society, July 31, 1855; Journal, September 30, 1854; April 9, and May 19, 1855. Church Missionary Society, C1/0, Microfilm Reel A-83, Public Archives of Canada.

13 Henry Budd to Secretary, Church Missionary Society, July 31, 1855; and Bishop Anderson, to Secretary, Church Missionary Society,

n.d. but received July 30, 1855. Church Missionary Society, C1/0, Microfilm Reel A-83, Public Archives of Canada.

14 Erasmus had returned to Red River in 1855 and joined the Rev. Thomas Woolsey at Fort Pitt on September 5, 1856, so his time at the school was less than a year.

15 In the unedited typescript this Chief Factor is identified as Donald Smith, who was in Labrador at the time. It was probably Chief Factor John Swanston.

16 This is one of several scattered references to Peter Erasmus in Woolsey's Journal: September 5; October 5, 13, 17, 23; November 17, 1856; and July 14, September 3, November 15, 1857.

17 Spry (ed.), *The Papers of the Palliser Expedition*, p. 423.

18 *Ibid.*, p. 388.

19 *Ibid*, p. 423. Mitchell's letter is dated December 2 and 9, 1859.

20 The original spelling was "Colvile" after Andrew Colvile of the Hudson's Bay Company, but it was so often rendered "Colville" that this form has become the spelling accepted today.

21 The Commercial Bank failed in 1867, so either the name of the bank is confused with one of the other seventeen banks that failed in the course of the next twenty-five years, or what Erasmus lost was what he had made in his mining venture, rather than what he later saved from his government pay.

22 The Yukon Gold Rush was then under way.

23 This letter, from the Sir James Hector Papers, is published by kind permission of the Hocken Library, University of Otago, New Zealand.

24 Hector Papers, Correspondence, George Blenkinsop, October-December, 1859. Statement of wages paid to the expedition's men.

25 Mitchell Letters, December 2 and 8, 1859. Compare with Spry (ed.), *The Papers of the Palliser Expedition*, p. 473, footnote 1, which now requires revision.

26 No mining camp of this name has been identified, but Mr. Hugh Dempsey suggests that perhaps these were the diggings on the Pend d'Oreille River just north of the forty-ninth parallel, where miners were at work in 1859. Hector, however, says that when his men were paid off they went to the "Smillcomen" [Similkameen] Gold Mines." (*ibid*, p. 469).

27 *Ibid*, p. 370 and p. 379.

28 John McDougall, *Forest, Lake and Prairie: Twenty Years of Frontier Life in Western Canada*, Toronto: William Briggs, 1895; second edition The Ryerson Press, 1910, p. 141.

29 *Ibid*, p. 141, p. 155, and p. 197.

30 "Peter Erasmus . . . thanks your Lordship for the two books in Saulteaux language. . . . He can read them as well as Cree for he knows them both." Budd to Bishop Anderson, December 2, 1851, Church Missionary Society, C1/0, Microfilm Reel A-83, Public Archives of Canada; and John McDougall, *Saddle, Sled and Snowshoe: Pioneering in the Sixties*, Toronto: William Briggs, 1896; second edition, The Ryerson Press, p. 16. In addition, D. L. McRae states that he spoke Danish fluently (United Church of Canada Archives, Erasmus File, "An Indian Pensioner".)

31 George Gooderham, "Peter Erasmus, 1833-1931", typescript, Glenbow Archives, p. 7.

32 McDougall, *Saddle, Sled and Snowshoe: Pioneering in the Sixties*, p. 65.

33 *Ibid*, pp. 66-79, p. 190, and pp. 254-70.

34 The Hon. Alexander Morris, *The Treaties of Canada with the Indians of Manitoba and the North-West Territories*, Toronto: Belfords, Clarke, and Co., 1880, pp. 168-224 and pp. 351-67.

35 Compare p. 245 below and *ibid*, p. 184 and p. 208.

36 Hugh A. Dempsey, *Crowfoot*, Edmonton: Hurtig Publishers Ltd., 1972, pp. 8-9n.

37 Morris, *The Treaties of Canada with the Indians of Manitoba and the North-West Territories*, p. 196.

38 Canada, Department of Indian Affairs, *Annual Report* for 1884, p. xlvi.

39 Colin Waubageshig, (ed.), *The Only Good Indian*, Toronto: New Press, 1970, p. 55.

40 John McDougall, *Opening the Great West: Experiences of a Missionary in 1875-76*, Calgary: Glenbow-Alberta Institute, 1970; Erasmus, below, pp. 258-61; and Morris, *The Treaties of Canada with the Indians of Manitoba and the North-West Territories*, p. 192

and p. 360.

41 See below, Chapter XIV, but compare Morris's view of James McKay's intervention in *ibid*, p. 178, p. 185, and McKay's career see Allan R. Turner, "James McKay", DCB X; and Mary McCarthy Ferguson, "*The Honourable James McKay of Deer Lodge*, Winnipeg: private edition, 1972.

42 *Indian Treaties and Surrenders*, 1891, Vol. II, pp. 212-13. See also RG10, Vol. 3575, file 235, Public Archives of Canada.

43 Canada, Department of Indian Affairs, *Annual Report* for 1881, p. vii; and for 1882, p. xii and Part I, p. 49.

44 Hardisty Papers, Glenbow Archives.

45 Hudson's Bay Company Archives E.9/28, 29, and 30. These documents and others in its Archives have been used by kind permission of the Hudson's Bay Company. Among the losses that Erasmus sustained was the disappearance of the copy of the Palliser Report which Hector had sent him. Pearce Papers, University of Alberta Archives, Box 60, #364.

46 For another version of the dream and its sequel, see D. E. Cameron and A. H. Gibson, "The Dream of Peter Shirt", *Maclean's Magazine*, July 1, 1928.

47 Personal conversation with Mr. Pete Tompkins in September, 1964.

48 George Gooderham, "Peter Erasmus, 1833-1931", pp. 3-4.

49 Canada, *Indian Treaties and Surrenders*, Ottawa: The Queen's Printer, 1891, Vol. II, pp. 212-13. Erasmus had opened negotiations in 1884 for the surrender. See RG10, Vol. 3575, File No. 235, Public Archives of Canada.

50 D. E. Cameron and A. H. Gibson, "The Dream of Peter Shirt".

51 Reports of the Board of Education of the North-West Territories for 1888 and 1889, in the *Annual Reports* of the Department of the Interior, Sessional Papers (No. 15), 52 Vic., A. 1889: 58; and (No. 14), 53 Vic., A. 1890: 28. See also the Edmonton *Bulletin*, Sept. 10, 1887, which reports that Peter Erasmus had been engaged as a teacher at the Victoria Public School.

52 Sessional Papers of Canada (18), Pt. I: 52-53, 230; Sessional Papers (12), 1890: Pt. I: 74, 258.

53 Report for the year ended June 30, 1893, S.P. (14), 1894: 197. See also *Reports* for 1891: 238; and 1892: 302. In 1891 William Pearce met Peter Erasmus at Goodfish Lake. Writing that Erasmus was now a school teacher on the Indian reserve, he added that "he has deserved a better fate than he has met with." Pearce from Calgary, October 12, 1891. Pearce Papers, Box 60, #364.

54 *Report* for the year ended June 30, 1894, Sessional Papers (14), 1895: 174.

55 Frederick Zorhorst. *Report* for the year ended June 30, 1895, Sessional Papers (14) 1896: 302-03.

56 Edmonton *Bulletin*, December 2, 1882: "Peter Erasmus was married on 12th last [November 12] to Miss Mary Stanley of Whitefish Lake."

57 Rev. R. B. Steinhauer, Diary, Whitefish Lake: March 31, 1891: "About four o'clock in the afternoon the beloved wife of Mr. Peter Erasmus departed from this life. Left 3 children (all girls) to mourn her loss." Microfilm AB, Glenbow Archives.

58 Part II: 171.

59 *Report* of the Department of Indian Affairs for the year ended March 31, 1907, Part II: 172; 1908, Part I: 184, Part II: 161; 1909, Part II: 127.

60 Report for the year ended March 31, 1909, Part II: 124; 1910, Part II: 150; 1911, Part II: 146; 1912, Part II: 25.

61 George Gooderham, "Peter Erasmus, 1833-1931", p. 4.

62 Calgary *Nor'Wester*, July 1, 1884: Leader.

63 George Gooderham, "Peter Erasmus, 1833-1931", pp. 5-6. Another account of Erasmus's service on the Blackfoot Reserve says that he did work that would have taxed the strength of a man of forty. Typescript report of Erasmus's resignation, source unidentified, United Church of Canada Archives, Erasmus file.

64 Department of Indian Affairs, *Report* for the year ended March 31, 1913, S.P. (No. 27), 1914, Pt. II: 25.

65 George Gooderham, "Peter Erasmus, 1833-1931", p. 8; also *Scarlet and Gold*, eleventh annual issue, 1930; and Calgary *Herald*, May 30, 1931, which says he was "assistant interpreter at a salary of $200 a year at the time of his death."

66 United Church of Canada Archives, Typescript Account of Erasmus's resignation, Erasmus file: "Interpreter and Pioneer Leaves Gleichen; Peter Erasmus a Man of 79 Years Leaves the Blackfoot Agency to Go Homesteading."

67 Mr. Peter Shirt, son of Erasmus's adopted son, kindly identified the grave on October 5, 1973.

CHAPTER ONE
EARLY DAYS IN THE RED RIVER SETTLEMENT

1 In the end the government recognized the river-lot system of survey not only in the Red River Settlement but also on the Saskatchewan River. See R. G. Ironside and E. Tomasky, "Development of Victoria Settlement", *Alberta Historical Review*, Vol. XIX, No. 2 (Spring, 1971), pp. 20-29.

2 The whole question of the social and economic role of women in Indian society requires clarification. The fact that women did hard and exhausting work did not necessarily imply a menial status. Their work was essential to the survival of the band and their influence was in at least some cases very great.

3 The Rev. John West named Henry Budd after his former Rector, who contributed towards the boy's education. However, West himself is usually considered to have been the originator of the scheme for educating native boys, while the expenses of maintenance, clothing, and education were "defrayed through the kind assistance" of Benjamin Harrison, a director of the Hudson's Bay Company. See Katherine Pettipas, typescript biography of Henry Budd, 1974; also Report to the Hudson's Bay Company, December 3, 1823; and memorandum and accounts of the Church Missionary Establishment, Red River Settlement, Hudson's Bay, North America, from October 1, 1822, to May 31, 1823, Church Missionary Society, C.1/M1, Microfilm Reel A 77, Public Archives of Canada.

4 Charles Pratt.

5 No reference has been found to a teacher named Garrett; a Red River family named Garrioch numbered more than one teacher among its members, and perhaps it is one of these to whom Erasmus is referring.

6 Since he was born in 1833, Erasmus was 16 when his father died in the fall of 1849, but he seems (even though he did not remember it) to have worked on the farm for some time while his father was "unable to do anything" before his death, as his letter of August 10, 1852, indicates. See the INTRODUCTION for this letter.

7 The usual load over a portage was two "pieces" of 90 pounds each.

8 The Rev. James Evans had developed Cree Syllabics in 1840, but the Bible in Syllabics was not published until 1861.

CHAPTER TWO
OFF TO THE WEST

1 The original MS read "York Factory," but Norway House was by 1856 the great inland depot where boat brigades from York Factory, Red River, and the upper Saskatchewan connected with each other. To have gone to York Factory would have meant an unnecessary extra double trip that would have added more than a month to the time taken to travel from Red River to The Pas. See Irene Spry (ed.), *The Papers of the Palliser Expedition*, Toronto: The Champlain Society, 1968, p. 544.

2 The Rev. Henry Budd's biographers agree that he died in 1875. See Katherine Pettipas, typescript biography of Henry Budd, 1974, p. xl; also Rev. William Bertal Heeney, *Leaders of the Canadian Church*, Toronto: The Musson Book Co., 1920, pp. 63-85; and T. C. B. Boon, "Henry Budd: the First Native Indian Ordained in the Anglican Church on the North American Continent", *Canadian*

Churchman, Vol. LXXXIV, No. 10 (May 16, 1957). Perhaps Erasmus was thinking of his cousin, Henry Budd, Junior, who died within a year of his ordination.

3 This name has various other forms: Ballentine, Ballendine, Ballandine.

4 This account is puzzling, as the Rev. Thomas Woolsey's description of what must presumably have been the same episode was much less dramatic: "About four years ago, 18 Crees were murdered by a band of Sioux in this locality. The trees still bear the bullet marks." (Rev. Thomas Woolsey, typescript journal, Glenbow–Alberta Institute Archives, pp. 53-54.) Erasmus may well have been thinking of some other similar affair, such clashes being not uncommon.

CHAPTER THREE
FORT EDMONTON

1 Hector, on the other hand, remarked early in 1858 that the palisades of Fort Edmonton were "rather rotten." (Irene Spry [ed.], *The Papers of the Palliser Expedition*, Toronto: The Champlain Society, 1968, p. 201.)

2 The account given here seems to apply to the next year—Woolsey's diary records that he left Fort Edmonton on September 25 for Pigeon Lake to work among the Indians there.

3 Usually Father Lacombe was driven by a devoted and celebrated dog driver, Alexis Cardinal.

4 The Chief Factor in charge in 1856 was apparently William Sinclair II. Hardisty did not become a chief factor until 1872.

CHAPTER FOUR
THE PALLISER EXPEDITION

1 Hector was, of course, a Scot and not an Englishman.

2 Hector had arranged with the new chief factor, John Swanston, that the men should work their way down in the Company boats, but probably some of the men rode alongside the boat brigade, as was often done. See Irene Spry, (ed.), *The Papers of the Palliser Expedition*, Toronto: The Champlain Society, 1968, pp. 225-27, 232.

3 Hector, in fact, met the men at Fort Pitt and sent them off to the Eagle Hills to support themselves hunting buffalo until Palliser returned from the East. However, two of the men (one of whom was probably Erasmus) came to Fort Carlton to act as guides to the Eagle Hills where Palliser and the rest of the expedition later joined the Lac Ste. Anne men. *Ibid*, pp. 232-4.

4 Chief Trader Richard Hardi-

sty was then in charge at Carlton. C. F. Lawrence Clarke took command in 1872. See John McDougall, *Opening the Great West: Experiences of a Missionary in 1875-76*, Calgary: Glenbow–Alberta Institute, 1970, p. 53n.

5 This seems to be another time transposition. Vital[le] joined the expedition the following spring from Red River. See Spry, *The Papers of the Palliser Expedition*, p. 393.

6 At this time Palliser was 41, Bourgeau 45, and J. W. Sullivan 22 years of age. Captain Arthur Brisco and W. R. Mitchell did not join the party until the fall of 1858, when they were respectively 32 and 29 years of age.

7 This seems to be a reference to the next year's journey; in 1858 the expedition travelled pretty steadily until they reached "Slaughter Camp" not far from modern Irricana. There they paused to make pemmican for the trips through the mountains. It was in 1859 that they visited the Forks of the Red Deer and the South Saskatchewan rivers.

8 The original MS had "England," but Bourgeau came from the French Alps.

9 These reminiscences seem to have been transposed in Erasmus's memory from the following summer.

10 Erasmus was probably thinking of the trip made to Fort Benton by Brisco and Mitchell when the party broke up in 1859, as neither Palliser nor Hector went to Fort Benton while they were with the ex-

pedition. It seems likely that Erasmus was one of the two men Brisco and Mitchell took with them. They had intended to cross the mountains but changed their minds and headed down the Missouri when they heard that game was plentiful there. They sent the two men they had with them across the mountains with some horses to rejoin Palliser (see Mitchell Letters, December 2 and 9, 1859). Neither Erasmus nor Vital[le] is mentioned among the men who accompanied Palliser and Sullivan when they crossed the mountains, but the names of both appear in the list of wage payments made at Fort Colvile (see Hector Papers, Correspondence, George Blenkinsop, October-November, 1859; also Spry, *The Papers of the Palliser Expedition*, pp. 491-92.

11 The expedition did, indeed, see huge herds of buffalo, but in British territory.

12 The members of the expeditions certainly hoped that in British North America the "inevitable extermination" of the "wild Plains Indians" would "not be hastened, as on the Western frontiers of the United States, by ruthless warfare," but no statement by them about an American policy of extermination has come to light. See John Palliser, "Indian Tribes and Vocabularies", in *Journals, Detailed Reports, and Observations Relative to Exploration*, London: Eyre and Spottiswoode, 1863; also, Spry,

313

The Papers of the Palliser Expedition, Appendix III.

13 The dangers foreseen in 1858 and 1859 did not yet include the wholesale massacre of buffalo by hide hunters which in fact took place between 1867 and 1883.

CHAPTER FIVE
WITH DOCTOR HECTOR

1 A reference to one of James Sinclair's journeys has been omitted since it was not an account of a first-hand experience of Erasmus. It is, however, significant that Sinclair had tried to interest Peter Erasmus, Senior, "in joining the trek but he had refused and persuaded his friends to stay out of what he called a crazy and stupid move."

2 For the movements of the various parties, see Irene Spry (ed.), The Papers of the Palliser Expedition, Toronto: The Champlain Society, 1968, pp. 259-358 and 557-81. Palliser crossed the mountains through the North Kananaskis Pass, returning through the North Kootenay Pass and so to Edmonton.

3 Another version of this story says that Hector regained consciousness as the men were sadly burying him. Still unable to speak, he managed to wink and so saved himself from being buried alive!

4 See also Hector's account of this hungry journey and the eventual shooting of the moose, in Spry, The Papers of the Palliser Expedition, pp. 308-13.

5 Again, Hector's account differs in some respects. He says, for example, that it was Sutherland who climbed the glacier with him, while he did not reach the height of land from a headwater of the North Saskatchewan until the next year. Ibid, pp. 273, 319-38 and 447.

6 This is a vivid account of what happened later. Though the Sharps rifle was invented in 1850, the wholesale slaughter of buffalo by hide hunters did not begin until after the Civil War. See F. G. Roe, The North American Buffalo, Toronto: University of Toronto Press, 1951 and 1970, pp. 804-16.

7 Chief Factor William J. Christie, son of Governor Alexander Christie, at this time in charge at Fort Edmonton.

CHAPTER SIX
TO THE ATHABASCA
AND THE SOUTHERN PRAIRIES

1 There is a slight discrepancy here, Hector having in fact come back "just in time to join in the fun of Christmas Eve." (Irene Spry [ed.], The Papers of the Palliser Expedition,

Toronto: The Champlain Society, 1968, p. 360.)

2 Compare with the doctor's account of this journey in *Ibid*, pp. 361-369.

3 John Jeffrey, a botanist who had disappeared. See *Ibid*, p. 366.

4 He had, in fact, tramped much further than this. For his version of the journey, see *Ibid*, pp. 382-87.

5 Again, compare with Hector's account of the trip in *Ibid*, pp. 387-91.

6 This episode is not mentioned by either Palliser or Hector. It might well have happened on some other journey.

7 This name has many other variations, such as Cayen, Caen, or Cadieu. The Palliser expedition used "Old Paul" Cahen.

8 Though the expedition encountered an Englishman travelling with Indians further east, no account of an episode of precisely this character has been found.

9 In this and subsequent passages, two men seem to be confused: one (referred to here) was a Blackfoot chief, Pe-to-pe, the Perched Eagle, sometimes called Pentelope by Erasmus. The other, Felix Munroe (also Monroe, Monro, and Munro), the son of a Canadian, Hugh Munroe, and a Blackfoot woman, was an able and dependable interpreter. His brother, William, was also known as Piskan.

10 Compare Palliser for a somewhat different version of the race, in *Ibid*, p. 401.

11 Gull Lake is well to the west of the route from Edmonton to the Hand Hills. This was probably either Red Deer Lake or Buffalo Lake.

12 Erasmus perhaps put too much emphasis on Palliser's military experience, which was limited to intermittent service with the Waterford Artillery Militia. See *Ibid*, pp. xvi-xvii.

13 This passage seems to refer to the expedition's encounter with the Christian Stoneys in July, 1858. See *Ibid*, pp. 251-52.

14 The party in fact dispersed in early August, Palliser and Hector each to cross the mountains by a different route.

15 Erasmus refused to accompany Hector from the Cypress Hills to the mountains and through them by the Howse Pass to the Columbia. This was in August, 1859, but his memory has transposed the timing of this episode. The original MS states that the expedition afterwards returned to Fort Edmonton, but in fact neither Hector nor any of the other officers did so. After their separate mountain crossings they rejoined each other at Fort Colvile on the Columbia, and from there went back to England via the Pacific Coast. Erasmus probably saw Hector again at Fort Colvile in October, 1859.

16 The original MS renders this variously as "Calder" and "Callville." The fort at that time was spelled "Colvile", the spelling adopted here.

17 Palliser does not mention Vital[le] as being among his party crossing the mountains, but he does say that Vital[le]

took part in his later explorations to the west of the Columbia River north of Colvile. See *Ibid*, pp. 491-92.

CHAPTER SEVEN
GOLD

1 This was perhaps Baptiste An[n]as[s]e who is mentioned in the list of wages paid by the expedition at Fort Colvile. See Hector Papers, Correspondence, George Blenkinsop.

2 The original MS states that Erasmus went back to Edmonton before he went gold mining and that he met these two men there. His own letter to Hector, which is reproduced in the INTRODUCTION, as well as Christie's and Woolsey's contemporary letters, establish that he did not return to Edmonton before his mining venture. Where he met Whitford and An[n]as[s]e remains in doubt; it might have been at Fort Colvile itself, or perhaps somewhere between Fort Benton and Colvile.

3 This may have been Bill Cust, later a well-known trader in Edmonton who apparently had an interest in gold mining.

4 Fort Colvile was itself, of course, in American territory, but at a long distance from Fort Benton. The mining camp may have been north of the border but it has not been possible to find out where it was.

5 It was 900 miles from Fort Edmonton to Fort Garry, and another 500 miles or so from Fort Colvile to Edmonton. To catch the Saskatchewan boats Erasmus would first have had to make an arduous journey crossing the mountains and finding his way to Rocky Mountain House or Fort Edmonton.

CHAPTER EIGHT
TO SMOKING LAKE

1 This is perhaps a misspelling of "Pend d'Oreille". Miners were active in 1859 on this river in British territory just above its junction with the Columbia. See Irene Spry (ed.), *The Papers of the Palliser Expedition*, Toronto: The Champlain Society, 1968, p. 478.

2 This was Benjamin Sinclair, a "Swampy half-breed from the Hudson's Bay region. Big, strong, and honest, and a

mighty hunter." (John McDougall, *Forest, Lake and Prairie Twenty Years of Frontier Life in Western Canada*, Toronto: William Briggs, 1895, p. 152.

3 There are indications that "native antecedants" had at one time and in some cases been an obstacle to promotion in the Hudson's Bay Company, but they had not prevented a number of mixed-bloods from becoming high-

ranking officers in the Company—for example, William Sinclair II and William McKay. See Isaac Cowie *The Company of Adventurers*, Toronto: W. Briggs, 1913.

4 Erasmus never shaved—"not once in his whole life," as his grand-daughter Mrs. May stated in a recorded interview with his daughter Mrs. Williams. Provincial Museum and Archives of Alberta, Tape Recording 67.247.

5 If by the "young firebrand" is meant Louis Riel, there seems to be another discrepancy in date: Louis Riel came back from the East to Red River in 1868. See George F. G. Stanley, *Louis Riel*, Toronto: The Ryerson Press, 1963, p. 34.

6 The 1861 inscription seems to be out of place here, as it was presumably made when the building was finally completed the following year.

CHAPTER NINE
MISSION WORK

1 John McDougall's version is a little different: "We picked up Peter Erasmus, who was associated with the Rev. Henry Steinhauer, and was now freighting for the latter from Red River to White-fish Lake." This was apparently a day's journey before the party reached Fort Pitt. See John McDougall, *Forest, Lake and Prairie Twenty Years of Frontier Life in Western Canada*, Toronto: William Briggs, 1895, p. 141.

2 This is evidently the episode which John McDougall described in slightly different terms: ". . . I said to my nearest neighbour, 'Will you please pass the bread.' This produced a laugh all around the table, and an old gentleman said to me, 'Young man, you are out of the latitude of bread.'" (*Ibid*, p. 132.)

3 Now White-earth Creek.

4 The original in another passage that has been omitted states that the place was called Me-he-me-wush (Hairy Sack), so called because buffalo could always be found there in early summer, possibly shedding their winter coats on the hill or ridge that formed the background of a wide flat where the mission was built.

5 This statement apparently overlooks the house already built at Smoky Lake and the parsonage at Pigeon Lake.

6 The dates here are not entirely clear. According to John McDougall, the Rev. George McDougall brought his wife and family to Victoria (Pakan) in 1863, travelling up-river with the Hudson's Bay Company brigade of boats from Norway House (John McDougall, *Saddle, Sled and Snowshoe: Pioneering in the Sixties*, Toronto: William Briggs, 1896, pp. 60-63). He puts Woolsey's departure in the following summer (*Ibid*).

7 George Flett established the Hudson's Bay Company post at Victoria in 1864.

CHAPTER TEN
MARRIED LIFE

1 The rate of exchange was about $4.85 to one pound sterling. This meant that Mc-Dougall was asking Erasmus to accept a little more than £50 a year, the salary at which he had started with Woolsey nine years earlier.

2 This lovely site of Erasmus's first home can be seen from the little church which stands on the hill that overlooks Whitefish Lake.

3 It is uncertain on which trip Erasmus and Williams travelled together in the mountains. Williams was with the Palliser expedition in 1859 and his name appears in the list of wages at Colvile, but he is not mentioned by Hector as one of the men who accompanied him.

CHAPTER ELEVEN
FREE TRADING

1 Later, Erasmus seemed less impressed with the fertility of the soil. In 1884 he suggested that Seenum should apply for part of his reserve elsewhere, to adjoin the Saddle Lake Reserve where there was much good hay land and quite considerable good open farm land. The Whitefish–Goodfish Lake country was "practically all bush land." See below, p. 269.

2 Probably Cuthbert McGillis, an active free trader in the area. See Irene Spry (ed.), *The Papers of the Palliser Expedition*, Toronto: The Champlain Society, 1968, p. 191; and Hudson's Bay Archives, D.4/76 (b) (1857): fo.41.

3 This must have been either Colin or William Inkster. Colin attended the Collegiate School from 1855 to 1859,

while William entered the school in 1853.

4 This must have been in 1868 or 1869, when (in a passage in the original MS omitted by reason of reiteration) Erasmus reported that Murdoch Spence described the surveyors as "a stupid high-handed lot of conceited rascals who had less than an ounce of judgement or common sense among their whole crew."

5 Only one, Thomas Scott, was in fact executed.

6 Probably Beaverhill Lake, which was called Beaver Lake on some early maps, such as that of David Thompson.

7 Erasmus was involved in at least one election later on. See Calgary *Nor'Wester*, July 1, 1884, in Glenbow-Alberta Institute Archives.

CHAPTER TWELVE
SMALLPOX

1 At Fort Garry a Board of Health had been set up that was taking measures to prevent smallpox from being brought into the settlement. Special efforts were made to stop anyone from bringing in infected furs. See Archibald Papers, Provincial Archives of Manitoba.

2 For an account of this invasion from the south, see Paul F. Sharp, *Whoop-Up Country*, Minneapolis: University of Minnesota Press, 1955 and 1960.

3 On January 9, 1871, however, Erasmus was among the signatories of a petition asking for government action to solve the problems. See Archibald Papers, 169, Provincial Archives of Manitoba.

4 The reference is probably to Captain (later General Sir) William Butler, who was sent across the prairies in 1870 to study and report on the state of affairs in the North-West Territories. He visited Saddle Lake and Victoria. See William F. Butler, *The Great Lone Land*, London: Sampson Low, Marston, Low, and Searle, 1874.

5 This is the rendering also used by F. E. Mitchell in his booklet about Victoria, but McGillivray is a more common form.

CHAPTER THIRTEEN
THE LAST BIG BUFFALO HUNT

1 On December 10, 1873, an assembly of Métis living at St. Laurent established a Provisional Government. Gabriel Dumont was elected President, and laws and regulations were drawn up on the model of the discipline of the buffalo hunt. An attempt to enforce these regulations brought Commissioner French and fifty North-West Mounted Police to intervene, for fear of another Métis rising, but in the end Dumont was not arrested. Riel does not seem to have been involved. See George F. G. Stanley, *The Birth of Western Canada*, Toronto: University of Toronto Press, 1960, pp. 179-82.

2 Both names are rendered in a variety of forms: for example, Mist-ow-as-is and Ah-tuk-uk-koop.

3 One of these traders was another John McDougall. In J. G. MacGregor's book about him, *Edmonton Trader*, there are references to "Peter Erasmus, a famous half-breed, dignified and highly intelligent."

4 The Hon. Alexander Morris (1826-89) was Lieutenant-Governor of Manitoba and the North-West Territories from 1872 to 1877. He had served in Sir John A. Macdonald's cabinet as Minister of Inland Revenue, 1869-72, and later returned to Ontario, to serve

in the Provincial Legislature from 1878 to 1886.

The Hon. James McKay of Deer Lodge (1828-79) was a celebrated mixed-blood guide and hunter. He became President of the first Executive Council, Speaker of the first Legislative Council, and, later, Minister of Agriculture in Manitoba. He served on the Council of Assiniboia and the North-West Council, assisting in negotiating Treaties 1, 2, 3, 5, and 6.

The retired Inspecting Chief Factor, the Hon. William J. Christie (1824-1899), was a country-born son of Governor Alexander Christie. Educated in Aberdeen, he served the Hudson's Bay Company from 1843 to 1873, attaining the rank of Inspecting Chief Factor and Supervisor in 1872. For a time on the North-West Council he assisted in negotiating Treaty No. 4 as well as No. 6. He later retired to Brockville, Ontario.

A. G. Jackes, M.D., Secretary to the Commission, kept a narrative account of the proceedings. See The Hon. Alexander Morris, *The Treaties of Canada with the Indians of Manitoba and the North-West Territories*, Toronto: Belfords, Clarke, and Co., 1880, p. 180.

CHAPTER FOURTEEN

TREATY NO. SIX

1 No mention is made by Morris of McDougall at the Carlton House proceedings; nor is Chief Bearskin referred to, unless his name is among those given only in Cree. John McDougall says explicitly that he went to Fort Pitt but was not at the Carlton treaty-making. See John McDougall, *Opening the Great West: Experiences of a Missionary in 1875-76*, Calgary: Glenbow-Alberta Institute, 1970, p. 53.

2 There was one band of Chipewyan Indians in the region, but their chief, Kin-oo-say-oo (The Fish) signed for them at Fort Pitt. The opponents of the Treaty (from Morris's point of view the troublemakers) were the Saulteaux, also known as the Chippewas. Joseph Toma appears to have been the leader in question. (*Ibid*, pp. 184-85; 203; 214; 220-21; 233-34. See Morris, *The Treaties of Canada with the Indians of Manitoba and the North-West Territories*, Toronto: Belfords, Clarke and Co., 1880, pp. 94, 192, 359.

3 The reference is to the Cypress Hills Massacre of 1873. For an account of the abortive trials see John Peter Turner, *The North-West Mounted Police, 1873-1893*, two volumes, Ottawa: The King's Printer, 1950, 227-235; Dan Kennedy, *Recollections of an Assiniboine Chief*, Toronto: McClelland and Stewart, 1972, pp. 42-47; and a recent, very thorough study of the whole business, P. Goldring, "The Cypress Hills Massacre—a Retrospect",

Saskatchewan History, Vol. XXVI, No. 3 (Autumn, 1973), pp. 81-102. Despite Erasmus's evaluation of "the clear evidence of . . . guilt," to others the evidence seemed less clear. Turner comments: "Whether truthful or not, a mass of detail that was contradictory in the extreme was given." (Vol. 1, p. 230.) Goldring refers to the "extraordinary tangle of evidence." (p. 86.)

4 Jackes used almost the same words: "We want to think of our children; we do not want to be too greedy; when we commence to settle down on the reserves that we select, it is there we want your aid, when we cannot help ourselves and in case of troubles seen and unforeseen in the future." (Morris, *The Treaties of Canada with the Indians*, p. 211.)

5 Morris gives Sak-ah-moos and Soh-ah-moos. *Ibid.*, pp. 184-5 and 211.

6 Jackes reports him as saying: "My friends, I wish to make you a clear explanation of some things that it appears you do not understand. It has been said to you by your Governor that we did not come here to barter or trade with you for the land. You have made demands on the Governor, and from the way you have put them a white man would understand that you asked for daily provisions, also supplies for your hunt and for your pleasure excursions. Now my reasons for explaining to you are based on my past experience of treaties, for no sooner

will the Governor and Commissioners turn their backs on you than some of you will say this thing and that thing was promised and the promise not fulfilled; that you cannot rely on the Queen's representative, that even he will not tell the truth, whilst among yourselves are the falsifiers. Now before we rise from here it must be understood, and it must be in writing, all that you are promised by the Governor and Commissioners, and I hope you will not leave until you have thoroughly understood the meaning of every word that comes from us. We have not come here to deceive you, we have not come here to rob you, we have not come here to take away anything that belongs to you, and we are not here to make peace as we would to hostile Indians, because you are the children of the Great Queen as we are, and there has never been anything but peace between us. What you have not understood clearly we will do our utmost to make perfectly plain to you." (*Ibid*, pp. 211-12.)

7 Jackes delays The Badger's reply until after another interjection by the Governor, and then quotes him as saying: "I do not want you to feed me every day; you must not understand that from what I have said. When we commence to settle down on the ground to make there our own living, it is then we want your help, and that is the only way that I can see how the poor can get along." (*Ibid*, pp. 212-13.)

8 Morris noted that McKay was "speaking with effect in the Cree tongue." (*Ibid*, p. 185.)

9 GOVERNOR: "You will remember the promises which I have already made; I said you would get seed; you need not concern yourselves so much about what your grand-children are going to eat; your children will be taught, and then they will be as well able to take care of themselves as the whites around them."

MIS-TAH-WAH-SIS (one of the leading Chiefs): "It is well known that if we had plenty to live on from our gardens we would not still insist on getting more provision, but it is in case of any extremity, and from the ignorance of the Indian in commencing to settle that we thus speak; we are as yet in the dark; this is not a trivial matter for us." (*Ibid*, p. 213.)

10 Compare Jackes: "The things we have been talking about in our councils I believe are for our good. I think of the good Councillors of the Queen and of her Commissioners; I was told the Governor was a good man, and now that I see him I believe he is; in coming to see us, and what he has spoken, he has removed all obstacles and misunderstandings, and I hope he may remove them all. . . . We want food in the spring when we commence to farm; according as the Indian settles down on his reserves, and in proportion as he advances, his wants will increase." (*Ibid*, p. 213.)

11 Jackes has the name "Tee-tee-quay-say," and records his words: "Listen to me, my friends, all you who are sitting around here, and you will soon hear what the interpreter has to say for us." (*Ibid*, p. 214.)

12 Jackes's report of Morris's comment reads: "What I have offered does not take away your living, you will have it then as you have it now, and what I offer now is put on top of it." (*Ibid*, p. 211). The Indians were to have "the right to pursue their avocations of hunting and fishing throughout the tracts surrendered" but subject to "such regulations as may from time to time be made by her Government of her Dominion of Canada, and saving and excepting such tracts as may from time to time be required or taken up for settlement, mining, lumbering or other purposes by her said Government of the Dominion of Canada, or by any of the subjects thereof, duly authorized therefore, by the said Government." (*Ibid*, p. 353.) This was a very considerable qualification, in the actual text of the Treaty. The controversial "medicine chest" clause reads: "That a medicine chest shall be kept at the house of each Indian Agent for the use and benefit of the Indians, at the discretion of such Agent." (*Ibid*, p. 355.) The word "free" was not specifically included, although it is, perhaps, implied, and was apparently so understood.

The question of not being

compelled to go to war is not specifically mentioned in the Treaty and only very vaguely dealt with by the Governor in the negotiations: "With regard to war, they would not be asked to fight unless they desired to do so, but if the Queen did call on them to protect their wives and children, I believed they would not be backward." (See *Ibid*, p. 186, and Jackes's record (p. 218) in which Morris is reported as saying "I *think* the Queen would leave you to yourselves." (Italics added.)

13 Poundmaker had not concealed uneasiness about the terms of the Treaty, and his role in the Riel rising is far from clear. For an interesting view, see Norma Sluman, *Poundmaker*, Toronto: The Ryerson Press, 1967.

14 Subsequent events might well suggest that Poundmaker and The Badger perhaps had a shrewder understanding of the Treaty and its implications than those who accepted it.

15 This request does not appear in the record of the negotiations published by Morris.

16 The land allocation was in fact one square mile to each family of five and in proportion for larger or smaller families.

CHAPTER FIFTEEN
REBELLION

1 The report of Charlotte Erasmus's death in the Edmonton *Bulletin* for December 27, 1880, was even more tragic than that given here by her husband: "The wife of Peter Erasmus, interpreter at the Indian Agency here, was buried at Whitefish Lake on Saturday, the 11th inst. He did not reach home until the Thursday after."

2 The Hon. Edgar Dewdney was appointed Indian Commissioner for the North-West Territories in 1879 and continued to hold this position while Lieutenant - Governor f r o m 1881 to 1888. He was returned to the House of Commons in 1888 and became Minister of the Interior and Superintendent of Indian Affairs. On retiring in 1892 he became Lieutenant-Governor of British Columbia.

3 The *Report* of the Department of Indian Affairs for 1882 mentioned Crees who were induced to leave Fort Walsh in the early part of the season and come north. Besides reporting Erasmus's return on August 21, 1882, after persuading 3,000 Crees to return home, the Edmonton *Bulletin* stated in an editorial that he had been successful in inducing the Qu'Appelle and Fort Pitt Indians to return to their homes. (September 9 and October 21, 1882.)

4 Big Bear was the independent-minded Indian chief who held out against accepting a reserve and who was involved in the 1885 uprising. Fraser states that in 1881 "Big Bear was the undisputed leader of all the free Indians left on the North-

ern Plains." (William Fraser, *Big Bear: Indian Patriot*, Calgary: Historical Society of Alberta, 1969, p. 10). He came north but still resisted orders to take up a reserve.

5 The Edmonton *Bulletin* for September 9, 1882, reports that he got back on August 21, 1882.

6 The Hudson's Bay Company clerk Harrison Stevens Young.

7 The original MS has "Grandin", but it was Bishop Faraud who was then at Lac La Biche.

8 Inspector A. H. Griesbach had been a Chief Constable on the March West in 1874. He was promoted to Superintendent on September 15, 1885.

9 Major-General T. B. Strange arrived in Edmonton from Calgary on May 1, 1885, and left a couple of weeks later to rendezvous with General Middleton downriver.

10 Also spelled "James A. Yeomans", by Sam Bull (manuscript, Glenbow-Alberta Institute Archives); and "Youmans", according to the *Reports* of the Department of Indian Affairs, as well as Annie L. Gaetz, "Indian Uprising in Northern Alberta as Told to the Writer by the late James Youmans", *Farm and Ranch Review*, February, 1958.

11 Though Erasmus attributes this account to Sam Bull, Bull in his manuscript "100 Years at Whitefish Lake" calls Cootsoo (William Stamp) a murderer, and says that Erasmus (who was not present when the shooting took place) "made a false statement that the murdered man had been a rebel so the accused was released." Annie Gaetz's record of Youmans's story adds that Cootsoo was given a reward.

CHAPTER SIXTEEN
THE END OF THE OPEN PRAIRIE

1 Probably Alex Hamelin, an independent trader in the area. See Evelyn Rowand, "The Rebellion at Lac La Biche", *Alberta Historical Review*, Vol. XXI, No. 3 (Summer, 1973), pp. 1-9.

2 Young was still with the Company in the Edmonton district in 1887. See Hudson's Bay Archives D.24/19.

3 Presumably J. K. (Jamie) Oswald, who became second in command of Steele's Scouts. See Desmond Morton and Reginald H. Roy, *Telegrams of the North-West Campaign*, Toronto: The Champlain Society, 1972, pp. 7, 34, and 394.

A NOTE ON PETER ERASMUS'S
FAMILY BACKGROUND

1 There are many references to Peter Erasmus, Senior, in the Church Registers of Baptisms, Marriages, and Burials for Red River Settlement, while data about his family and

farm appear in successive Red River Census Returns.

2 Hudson's Bay Archives, E.5/2 and 3:fos.4d and 3d, Red River Settlement, Census Returns for 1828 and 1829 list Peter [E]Rasmus as from Denmark, as do subsequent returns to the last one in 1843 (E.5?4-11). One account of the life of Peter Erasmus, Junior, states that his father was taken to England as a boy by Nelson after the Battle of Copenhagen. UCCA, Erasmus file.

3 Hudson's Bay Archives, Red River Settlement, Registers of Marriages (E.4/1b:215d) and of Baptisms (E.4/1a:63d and 74d) give his origin as Norwegian.

4 Hudson's Bay Archives, Red River Settlement, Census Returns for January 31, 1827 (Hudson's Bay Archives, E.5/1:4d) give his place of origin as Sweden. The confusion is easy to understand in view of the close association and very recent separation of the Scandinavian countries.

5 The earliest known mention of Peter Erasmus, Senior, (in the records of the baptisms of his daughters Sophia and Catherine), describe him as a "Company Servant". Hudson's Bay Archives, Red River Settlement, Register of Baptisms, E.4/1a: fo.53, December 19, 1824.

6 Peter Erasmus is described as a "settler" in later records of baptisms of his wife (January 31, 1826, E.4/1a:fo.59) and his children, Henry (May 1, 1827, E.4/1a:63d) and Sally

(February 9, 1830, E.4/1a: 74d).

7 Hudson's Bay Archives, E.5/1-11.

8 Hocken Library, University of Otago, New Zealand, Sir James Hector Papers, II, Correspondence.

9 Peter Erasmus's list of family birth dates (made available by Mr. Arnold Erasmus) has "William Erasmus [born] February 7, 1862".

10 Hudson's Bay Archives, E.4/ 1b:215d, Register of Marriages, Red River Settlement, January 31, 1826, describes the older Peter Erasmus' wife as: "Half Breed of Red River".

11 Henry Budd writing to Nancy Calder, refers to "our sister Kitty" and gives news of the Erasmus family. August 11, 1849, PABC, Wren [Reine] Family Papers, A/E/R731/W 921.91.

12 T. C. B. Boon, Henry Budd: The First Native Indian Ordained in the Anglican Church on the North American Continent, Type script, PAM.

13 Glenbow-Alberta Institute, Peter Erasmus, 1833-1931:1.

14 Thomas Simpson, in a letter dated February 20, 1836 (Provincial Archives of British Columbia, A/E/R731/Si5), commented on Cook's "intention of bringing his 35 years' courtship to an early close." The marriage eventually took place on March 8, 1838 (Hudson's Bay Archives, E.4/ 1b: 254, Red River Settlement, Register of Marriages).

15 Hudson's Bay Archives, A.36/ 5: fos. 50-1, Will of William

325

Hemmings Cook and subsequent correspondence, and records of baptisms (E.4/1a and 2) and marriages in the Red River Settlement (Register of Marriages, E.4/1b and 2).

16 Miles MacDonnell to Selkirk, May 29, 1812: "The present chief of York has three wives by whom he has a numerous issue. One he has discarded for being old, the other two are younger and live with him at the Factory." Again, May 31, 1812: ". . . a chief who occupies himself the Mess room with a squaw occupying an apartment, on each side opening into it, . . ." (Hudson's Bay Archives, Copy Books, Letters Red River Settlement, Vol. I, Selkirk Transcripts: fos. 62-3 and 73). By September 10, 1815, Cook had 10 children, as is indicated in a petition signed by fathers in the service of the Company who were seeking an asylum for their children (E.8/5: fo. 128).

17 Public Archives of Canada, Selkirk Papers, MG 19/E1; Vol. 46, Rev. Charles Bourke's Journal: fos. 17868-9: "Governor Cook supports a Seraglio like the Grand Segnior. He maintains 3 wifes (sic) locked up; he keeps the keys himself . . .".

18 Matthew Cocking's Will (January 27, 1797) and codicil (August 22, 1798), Borthwick Institute, Prerogative Court Probate Records, April 1799.

19 Hudson's Bay Archives, York Factory, Servants' Ledgers,

Retired Servants, B.239/x/3: p. 405; York Factory, Correspondence Inward, 1808-1828, B.239/c/1: fo. 181, Alex Robertson from Norway House, February 3, 1825; Red River Settlement, Register of Baptisms, E.4/1a: fo. 27d; and Rich, E.E., ed., *Colin Robertson's Correspondence Book, September 1817 to September 1822* (London: Hudson's Bay Record Society, 1939): 220-1.

20 Henry Budd's mother worked at the Church Mission (George Harbidge, "Memorandums and Accounts of the Church Missionary Establishment, Red River Settlement, . . . from October 1, 1822 to May 31, 1823", and Harbidge to Secretary, Church Missionary Society, July 1, 1824, Church Missionary Society, C.1/M, Public Archives of Canada, Microfilm Reel A-77). One of [Cocking's] annuitants is described, in a note against the account, as "The Wom^a. on Missionary Establishment" (Hudson's Bay Archives, B.235 /d/18: fo.162, 1824-5), while the Rev. John West had collected the goods paid for by the annuity of one daughter who was neither Cook's eventual official wife, nor Mrs. Holmes, as Cook's letter to Robert Miles, May 25, 1825, and the York Factory and Winnipeg Account Books establish. Hudson's Bay Archives, B.239/c/1: fo. 201; B.239/d/124: fo.50; 129: fo.47; 130: fo 47d; 131: 48d; B.239/x/3: p.405; B.235/d/ 1: fo.63; 18: fos. 162 and 163; 19: fos. 4 and 5; 22: fo.

150, 23: fo. 250; 24: fos. 4 and 35; 25: Abstract of sales; 28: fos. 95, 152; 29: fo.180; 30: fos. 3 and 4; 31: fo.56; 34: fos. 3 and 4; 38: fos. 2 and 3; A.16/37: fo.110.

On May 11, 1828, "Wasoeysquew/alias Mary Budd" whose "abode" was the Church Mission House was baptised (St. John's Cathedral —Baptismal Register No. 1), and on June 3, 1830, "Kitty", "An Indian Woman on the Church Mission Establishment Red River Settlement" was also baptised (St. John's Cathedral—Baptismal Register No. 2). Together these scattered fragments of evidence suggest that Henry Budd's grandmother, (Cocking's Daughter) as well as his mother lived for a time at least at the Mission. Later on, Henry Budd's mother seems to have lived with her son at the Cumberland Mission (Pettipas, 1974: p.xx), but went back to Red River to live with Kitty Erasmus in 1849. Henry Budd to Nancy Calder, August 11, 1849, Provincial Archives of British Columbia, A/E/ R731/W 921.91.

21 She was also known as Agathas and later as Mary (E.4/ 1b: fo.254, and Cook to Miles, May 25, 1825, Hudson's Bay Archives, B.239/c/1: fo. 201) but was neither Wash-e-soo E'Squaw (alias Agathas), nor Ke-che-c[h]ow-e-com-e-coot, as Robertson's letter to Miles shows (B.239/c/1: fo. 181).

22 Hudson's Bay Archives, Red River Settlement, Register of Marriages, March 8, 1838,

E.4/1b: fo. 254.

23 Hudson's Bay Archives, A.36/ 5: fos. 50-51.

24 Hudson's Bay Archives, Cook to Miles, May 25, 1825, B.239/ c/1: fo. 201.

25 Ibid.

26 Hudson's Bay Archives, B.329/ c/1: fo. 181.

27 Hudson's Bay Archives, B.239/ x/3: p. 405. Another set of accounts (B.239/d/124: fo. 50) gives "Aggathas", Washoesquew," and "Wee mestu goos ishish".

28 Hudson's Bay Archives, B.239/ x/3: p. 405.

29 Hudson's Bay Archives, E.4/ 1a: fo. 46d.

30 St. John's Cathedral — Baptismal Register No. 1, "Wasoeysquew/ alias Mary Budd a Halfbreed Woman" whose "abode" was the "Church Mission House" was baptised by the Rev. William Cockran.

31 Hudson's Bay Archives, Winnipeg Account Book, B.235/d/ 18, 1824-5, Retired Servants' Accounts: fo. 162.

32 Church Missionary Society, C1/M1 (Public Archives of Canada, Microfilm Reel A-77), Item 15, George Harbidge, Schoolmaster, "Memorandums and Accounts of the Church Missionary Establishment", Red River Settlement, Hudson's Bay, North America, from October 1, 1822 to May 31, 1823; and item 23, George Harbidge to the Secretary, Church Missionary Society, July 1, 1824, also mentions her as the mother of Henry and Sally Budd.

33 Ibid. and Hudson's Bay Archives, Red River Settlement,

Register of Baptisms (E.4/1a: 43d, 69d) ; and Pettipas, 1974: xviii.

34 St. John's Cathedral — Baptismal Register No. 2.

35 Peter [E]Rasmus to his uncle [Horatio Nelson Calder], June 27, 1850, Provincial Archives of British Columbia, A/E/R731/C12/Er12.

36 Provincial Archives of British Columbia, A/E/R731/W921.91.

37 Matthew Cocking's Will, op. cit.

38 George Harbidge described Henry Budd as a Muskaigoe Half Breed, July 1, 1824, Church Missionary Society, C.1/M1, Public Archives of Canada, Microfilm Reel A-77.

BIBLIOGRAPHY

MANUSCRIPT SOURCES

Anderson, Right Rev. David, Bishop of Rupert's Land. Correspondence, Church Missionary Society, C.1/0, Microfilm Reels A83 and 84, PAC.

Archibald Papers, Provincial Archives of Manitoba.

Boon, T. C. B. "Henry Budd: The First Native Indian Ordained in the Anglican Church on the North American Continent", typescript, Public Archives of Manitoba, published in *Canadian Churchman*, Vol. LXXXIV, No. 10 (May 16, 1957).

Budd, Rev. Henry. Journal and Correspondence, Church Missionary Society, C.1/0, Microfilm Reels A/83 and 84, Public Archives of Canada.

—————. August 10, 1849, Wren Family Papers, A/E/R731/W921. 91, Provincial Archives of British Columbia.

Bull, Sam. "100 years at Whitefish Lake, 1855-1955", typescript reminiscences, Glenbow-Alberta Institute Archives.

Bundy, Freda Graham. "First Permanent White Settler of Alberta", *The Rocky Mountain Echo*, copied in Lethbridge *Herald*, April to November, 1958 (IV-XXIX), Glenbow-Alberta Institute Archives.

Canada Department of Indian Affairs, RG10, Vol. 3575, File 235; Vol. 3586, File 1195 [1175]; and Vol. 3632, File 6352, Public Archives of Canada.

Church Registers, Rupert's Land (Red River Settlement), Index and Microfilm, Public Archives of Manitoba; Hudson's Bay Company Archives, E.4/1a, 1 & 2.

Cocking, Matthew, Will, January 27, 1797, and codicil, August 22, 1798, Borthwick Institute, Prerogative Court Probate Records, April, 1799.

Cook, W. H. Will and correspondence, etc., Hudson's Bay Company Archives, A.36/5, fos. 50-51, 13-24, 26, 29, 30-31, 35, 55-58, 60-69, 70-73.

Denney, C. D., Genealogical Collection, Microfilm, Glenbow-Alberta Institute Archives.

Dion, Joseph Francois. "History of Cree Indians of Western Canada", xerox copy of a series of weekly newspaper articles in Bonnyville *Tribune*, April 4, 1958, to September 1, 1960. Glenbow-Alberta Institute Archives.

Fraser, Frances. "Peter Erasmus", Alberta Folklore and Local History, Collection, I, (10) Notebooks, Binder 4, Special Collections, University of Alberta Library.

Gladstone, W. S. "Life of an Old Timer", Alberta Folklore and Local History Collection, I (6), Special Collections, University of Alberta Library.

Gooderham, George. "Peter Erasmus, 1833-1931", typescript, Glenbow-Alberta Institute Archives.

Harbidge, George. Correspondence July 1, 1824, to Secretary, Church Missionary Society, C.1/M1, Microfilm Reel A-77, Public Archives of Canada; and Memorandums and Accounts of the Church Missionary Establishment, Red River Settlement . . . from October 1, 1822 to May 31, 1823.

Hardisty Papers, Glenbow-Alberta Institute Archives.

Hector, Sir James, Papers, Hocken Library, University of Otago, New Zealand.

Hudson's Bay Company Archives. Material from these archives have been used and published by the kind permission of the Company.
    Declarations and statements re losses caused by the North West Rebellion, E.9/28, 29, and 30.
    Officers' and Servants' Ledger—York, A.16/37.
    Officers' Wills. A.36/5, fos. 50-51.
    Red River Settlement—Registers of Baptisms, Marriages, and Burials, E.4/ 1a, 1b, and 2.
    Red River Settlement—Census Returns, E.5/1-11: 1827, 1828, 1829, 1830, 1831, 1833, 1835, 1838, 1840, and 1843.
    York Factory Account Books, B.239/d/124, 129, 130, 131.
    York Factory Servants' Ledgers, B.239/x/3.
    Winnipeg Account Books, B.235/d/1, 18, 19, 22, 23, 24, 25, 28, 29, 30, 31, 34, 38.

Hunter, Rev. James. Diary and Correspondence, Church Missionary Society, C.1/0, Microfilm Reels A-90 and 91, Public Archives of Canada.

Lowe, Susan. Dossier on Erasmus compiled for Fort Edmonton Park, Provincial Museum and Archives of Alberta.

Mitchell, W. R. Letters, in the possession of his son, Commander H. K. B. Mitchell, R. N. Retired, used by his kind permission.

Pearce, William. Papers, University Archives, University of Alberta.

Pettipas, Mrs. Katherine. Typescript biography of Henry Budd. Relevant excerpts kindly provided for use in this book.

Red River Census, 1832, 1833, 1838, 1840, 1843 and 1849, Provincial Archives of Manitoba.

Ross Collection, Provincial Archives of British Columbia. These and other documents in PABC have been used and published in part by kind permission of the Provincial Archivist.

St. John's College, Winnipeg. Papers, Archives of the Ecclesiastical Province of Rupert's Land, Provincial Archives of Manitoba. Cited orally by Mr. Tom Bredin.

Sandison, Alexander. Reminiscences of life in the "good old days", Schultz Collection, Box Ia, I, Miscellaneous Manuscripts, Public Archives of Manitoba.

Steinhauer, Rev. R. B. Diary, Microfilm AB, Glenbow-Alberta Institute Archives.

Williams, Mrs. C. M. Tape recording, Provincial Museum and Archives of Alberta, 67.247, October 12, 1967.

Woolsey, Rev. Thomas. Journal, typescript copy, Glenbow-Alberta Institute Archives.

Wren Family Papers, Provincial Archives of British Columbia.

NEWSPAPERS

The Albertan

Obituary, May 29, 1931.

Report of Memorial Service, June 1, 1931.

Calgary *Herald*

February 22, 1963, report of Henry Thompson's MS record of Erasmus's reminiscences, by Rev. Stuart Munro.

May 30, 1931, Report of death.

Calgary *Nor'Wester*

July 1, 1884

Edmonton *Bulletin*

December 27, 1880

February 14, 1881

September 9, 1882

October 21, 1882

December 2, 1882

February 17, 1883

April 25, 1885

May 15, 1885

May 28, 1887

September 10, 1887

June 22, 1889

August 7, 1926

Edmonton *Journal*

May 28, 1931 — Obituary

January 7, 1932 — Request of W. H. Day that grave should be marked.

July 13, 1957 — Resumé of life by "Old Timer".

June 18, 1962 — House moved to Pioneer Village.

February 8, 1963 — "Master Guide", by "Old Timer".

March 4, 1968 — Correction re Woolsey not living at Whitefish Lake.

February 12-14, 1968 — House moved to Fort Edmonton Park.

June 28, 1971 — Great-grandson's wedding.

PUBLISHED SOURCES

Allan, Iris. "The McDougalls: Pioneers of the Plains", *The Beaver*, Outfit 304 (Summer, 1973), pp. 14-19.

Bredin, Thomas F., "The Red River Academy", *The Beaver*, Outfit 303, 3(Winter, 1974), pp. 10-17.

Butler, Capt. W. F. *The Great Lone Land*, London: Sampson Low, Marston, Low, & Searle, 1874.

Cameron, D. E., and A. H. Gibson. "The Dream of Peter Shirt", *Maclean's Magazine*, July 1, 1928, pp. 16, 46-47, reprinted in *Scarlet and Gold*, 10th annual issue, 1929, pp. 86-89.

Canada, The Board of Education of the North-West Territories, *Reports* for 1888 and 1889, in *Annual Reports*, Department of the Interior, S.P. (No. 15) 1889, pp. 58-59; and S.P. (14) ; 1890, p. 28.

Canada, Department of Indian Affairs, *Annual Reports*, for the years 1879-1913, in *Sessional Papers of Canada*.

Canada, *Indian Treaties and Surrenders*, 3 vols., Ottawa: The Queen's Printer, 1891. Reproduced in Coles' Library, Vol. II.

Cowie, Isaac, *The Company of Adventurers*, Toronto, William Briggs, 1913.

Dempsey, Hugh A. *Crowfoot*, Edmonton: Hurtig Publishers Ltd., 1972.

Ferguson, Mary McCarthy. *The Honourable James McKay of Deer Lodge*, Winnipeg: private edition, 1972.

Fleming, Harvey (ed.). *Minutes of Council of the Northern Department of Rupert Land*, 1821-31, London, HBRS, 1940, pp. 432-33.

Fraser, William B. *Big Bear: Indian Patriot*, Calgary: Historical Society of Alberta, 1969. Reprinted in Swainson, Donald (ed.). *Historical Essays on the Prairie Provinces*, Toronto: McClelland and Stewart, Carleton Library No. 53, 1970.

Gaetz, Annie L. "Indian Uprising in Northern Alberta, as told to the writer by the late James Youmans", *Farm and Ranch Review*, February, 1958, from the Antoniuk Collection, used, together with other material from this collection, by the kindness of Mr. Antoniuk and Mr. and Mrs. Joe Bielish.

Goldring, P. "The Cypress Hills Massacre — a Century Retrospect", *Saskatchewan History*, Vol. XXVI, No. 3 (Autumn, 1973), pp. 81-102.

Healy, W. J. *Women of Red River*, Winnipeg: Russell Lang and Co., Ltd., 1923.

Heeney, Rev. William Bertal. *Leaders of the Canadian Church*, second series, Toronto: Musson Book Co., 1920.

Ironside, R. G., and E. Tomasky. "Development of Victoria Settlement", *Alberta Historical Review*, Vol. XIX, No. 2 (Spring, 1971), pp. 20-29.

Kennedy, Dan (Ochanghugake). *Recollections of an Assiniboine Chief*, Toronto: McClelland and Stewart, 1972.

McDougall, John. *George Millward McDougall, the Pioneer, Patriot and Missionary*, Toronto: William Briggs, 1888; second edition, 1902.

—————. *Forest, Lake and Prairie: Twenty Years of Frontier Life in Western Canada*, Toronto: William Briggs, 1895; reprint, The Ryerson Press, 1910.

—————. *Saddle, Sled and Snowshoe: Pioneering in the Sixties*, Toronto: William Briggs, 1896; reprint, The Ryerson Press, n.d.

—————. *Pathfinding on Plain and Prairie: Stirring Scenes of Life in the Canadian North-West*, Toronto: William Briggs, 1898. Reproduced in Coles' Canadiana Collection.

—————. *In the Days of the Red River Rebellion*, Toronto: William Briggs, 1903; republished, 1911.

—————. *On Western Trails in the Early Seventies: Frontier Life in the Canadian North-West*, Toronto: William Briggs, 1911.

—————. *Opening the Great West: Experiences of a Missionary in 1875-76*, Calgary: Glenbow-Alberta Institute, 1970. .

MacGregor, James C. *Edmonton Trader: The Story of John A. McDougall*, Toronto: McClelland and Stewart, 1963.

Martin, Archer. *The Hudson's Bay Company's Land Tenure and the Occupation of Assiniboinia by Lord Selkirk's Settlers, with a List of Grantees under the Earl and the Company*, London: William Clowes and Sons, 1898.

Mitchell, Frank E. *A History of Pioneering in the Pakan District* (place of publication not indicated; privately printed, n.d.). Made available by the kindness of Mr. and Mrs. Joe Bielish, Warspite, Alberta.

Moberly, Henry J., in collaboration with W. R. Cameron. *When Fur Was King*, Toronto: Dent, 1959.

Morris, The Hon. Alexander, P. C. *The Treaties of Canada with The Indians of Manitoba and the North-West Territories, including the Negotiations on which they were based, and other Information Relating Thereto*, Toronto: Belfords, Clarke and Co., 1880.

Morton, Desmond, and Reginald H. Roy. *Telegrams of the North-West Campaign*, Toronto: Champlain Society, 1972.

Morton, W. L. *Manitoba*, Toronto: University of Toronto Press, 1957.

Nelson, J. G. *The Last Refuge*, Montreal: Harvest House, 1973.

Neufeld, E. P. *The Financial System of Canada*, Toronto: Macmillan, 1972.

Oliver, E. H. *The Canadian North-West: its Early Development and Legislative Records*, 2 vols., Ottawa: Government Printing Bureau, 1914, Publication of the Canadian Archives, No. 9.

Palliser, John. *The Journals, Detailed Reports, and Observations Relative to the Exploration, by Captain Palliser, of that Portion of British North America, which, in latitude, lies between the British Boundary Line and the Height of Land or Watershed of the Northern or Frozen Ocean Respectively, and in Longitude, between the Western Shore of Lake Superior and the Pacific Ocean During the Years 1857, 1858, 1859 and 1860*, London: Eyre and Spottiswoode, Printers to the Queen's Most Excellent Majesty, 1863.

Pettipas, Katherine, *The Diary of the Reverend Henry Budd 1870-1875*, Winnipeg, Manitoba Record Society, 1974.

Roe, F. G. *The North American Buffalo*, Toronto: University of Toronto Press, 1951; second edition, 1970.

Rowand, Evelyn. "The Rebellion at Lac La Biche", *Alberta Historical Review*, Vol. XXI, No. 3 (Summer, 1973), pp. 1-9.

Sharp, Paul F. *Whoop-Up Country*, Minneapolis: University of Minnesota Press, 1955; republished, Helena, Montana: Historical Society of Montana, 1960.

Sibbald, Andrew. "West with the McDougalls", *Alberta Historical Review*, Vol. XIX, No. 1 (Winter, 1971), pp. 1-4.

Sluman, Norma. *Poundmaker*, Toronto: The Ryerson Press, 1967.

Spry, Irene M. *The Palliser Expedition*, Toronto: Macmillan, 1963; second edition (paper back), 1973.

——————(ed.). *The Papers of the Palliser Expedition*, Toronto: Champlain Society, 1968.

——————. "The Transition from a Nomadic to a Settled Economy in Western Canada, 1856-96", *Transactions* of The Royal Society of Canada, Vol. IV, Series IV: June 1968, Section II.

Stanley, G. F. G. *The Birth of Western Canada*, London: Longmans, Green and Co., Ltd., 1936; second edition, University of Toronto Press, 1960, 1963, reprinted in the U.S.A., 1966.

——————. *Louis Riel*, Toronto: The Ryerson Press, 1963.

Turner, Allan R. "James McKay", DCB, X.

Turner, John Peter. *The North-West Mounted Police, 1873-1893*, 2 vols., Ottawa: King's Printer, 1950.

MINI-BIOGRAPHIES OF PETER ERASMUS

Douglas, R. *Peter Erasmus, One of Minor Explorers.* Appears to be clipping, but no identification, nor date. Copies in Archives of the Canadian Rockies and the Special Collections, J. N. Wallace Papers, University of Alberta Library.

Fraser, Mrs. Frances. "Peter Erasmus", Alberta Folklore and Local History Collection, I Bound Volumes, (10) Notebooks, Binder No. 4, Special Collections, University of Alberta Library.

Gooderham, George. "Peter Erasmus, 1833-1931". Copy in Glenbow-Alberta Institute Archives and in editor's possession.

Lowe, Susan. Historical Outline of Erasmus's Life, prepared in connection with removal of his house to Fort Edmonton Park, Alberta Heritage Sites Service, Provincial Museum and Archives.

McRae, D. L. "An Alberta Pensioner", Erasmus, Peter (Mr.), file, United Church of Canada Archives.

Morrow, J. W. (of Medicine Hat), handwritten fragment concerning Peter Erasmus, Saskatchewan Archives, Regina, T/a/M834.

Nix, James Ernest. "Erasmus, Peter (1833-1931), Canadian Methodist lay assistant to Indian missionaries", St. Stephen's College Archives.

"Old Timer", "Master Guide", The Third Column, Edmonton *Journal*, July 13, 1857.

Saskatchewan Historical Society, compiler unknown, "Peter Erasmus. Guide, Interpreter, Translator and School Teacher." Saskatchewan Archives, Regina, File SHS 2D.

Scarlet and Gold, "Sole Survivor of Palliser Expedition is Pensioned by Alberta Government", Eleventh Annual Issue [1930].

United Church of Canada Archives, "Sketch", No author given, Erasmus, Peter (Mr.), file.

INDEX

Regina, Sask. 261, 269, 283
Richards, James 90, 91, 93, 94
Riel, Louis 183, 200, 275
Riel Rebellion 200, 215, 217, 254, 275 et seq.
Rocky Mountain House 38, 82, 172
Rolland 92
Royal Canadian Mounted Police see NWMP
Rundle, Rev. Robert 37, 108, 130

Sabbath, observance of 50, 66, 108
Saddle Lake 178, 200, 210, 232, 279
Saddle Lake Crossing 23-26, 35, 181, 182, 196, 208, 274
Saddle Lake Reserve 261, 269, 283, 300
St. Albert, Sask. 36, 40
Sakamoos 251
Saulteaux Indians 241
Sarcee Indians 104
Saskatchewan River 8, 9, 34, 40, 59, 65, 66, 72, 74, 82, 91, 130, 142
"Scottie" 2-3
Seenum, James 197, 203, 205, 209, 210, 212, 226, 227, 233, 239, 258, 262, 278
  grants land to P.E. 180-81, 185
  leads hunt 193, 195
  supervises camp election 202
  praises P.E. as interpreter 259
  requests better terms at Treaty 6 260
  negotiates extension of reserve 261, 269-70
  confusion over treaty terms 263-64
  relations with Peter Shirt 280-81, 283, 284, 296-300
  expels Cootsoo 282, 284
  renaming of Victoria 301
Selkirk, Lord 139
Settee, James 5
Sharps rifle 85, 135
Shirt, Peter 232-34, 268, 270-78, 281-84, 286-97, 300
Short (steersman) 8, 9
Sinclair (Factor) 145
Sinclair, Benjamin 37, 130, 181, 273-74, 280, 282
Sinclair, Thomas 200
Slave Lake Post 38
Smallpox 200, 204, 209-12, 227, 248
Smoky Lake 141, 145, 150-51, 158,
161, 163, 166, 169, 178, 185, 295
Snake Indians 104
Snyder (teacher) 197-98
Sparkling Eyes (Cree) 160-61
Spedden, Alta. 263
Spence, Murdoch 3-4, 5-6, 138-41, 159, 191, 215, 228-29
Spence, Mrs. Murdoch 4, 138
Stanley, Jacob 197
Star Blanket 229, 232, 241, 245-46, 249, 252, 254-59, 301
Stark (steersman) 19-21
Steinhauer, Arthur 197-98, 203
Steinhauer, Mrs. H.B. 174-76
Steinhauer, Rev. H.B. 28, 33, 34, 130, 157-61, 180, 181, 189-91, 197, 198, 210, 214, 226, 227, 230, 257, 265
  first meets P.E. 26
  buries dead Cree 28
  unpretentious mannerisms 33-34
  Indians question teaching 151-52
  learns of P.E.'s engagement 174
  officiates at P.E.'s wedding 175-76
  looks after Peter Shirt 233-34
  helps P.E. after wife's death 267
  death 273-74
Stony Indians 74, 78, 79, 80, 83, 84, 108, 109, 223
Strange, General T.B. 278-298
Sturgeon River 98
Sucker Creek 143
Sugden, Alta. 185
Sullivan, John William 69-105
Sutherland 74, 76, 78, 80, 84, 85
Swampy Cree 5, 10, 11, 56, 160, 241, 242
Sweet Grass 258-60

Teequaysay 253
Thompson family 223
Thompson, Henry T. 267
Thompson, Louis 265-67
Thompson River 82
Todd 126
Toma, Joseph 253
Treaty No. 6 236 et seq.
Turner (Métis) 182
Turner family 223

Umla see Hamelin (trader)
United States

342

343

Other Western Canadian Classics

Booze: When Whisky Ruled the West
  by James H. Gray

The Boy from Winnipeg
  by James H. Gray

Charcoal's World: The True Story of a
  Canadian Indian's Last Stand
  by Hugh A. Dempsey

Gully Farm: A Story of Homesteading on the Canadian Prairies
  by Mary Hiemstra

Men Against the Desert
  by James H. Gray

The Palliser Expedition: The Dramatic Story of Western
  Canadian Exploration, 1857–1860
  by Irene M. Spry

Peter Fidler: Canada's Forgotten Explorer, 1769–1822
  by J. G. MacGregor

Red Crow: Warrior Chief
  by Hugh A. Dempsey

Red Lights on the Prairies
  by James H. Gray

Where the Wagon Led
  by R.D. Symons